Madeleine Rosca's

Hollow Fields

VOLUME
3

COLORING BY
Honoel A. Ibardolaza

LETTERING BY
Nicky Lim

Seven Seas Entertainment

HOLLOW FIELDS (Color Edition) Volume 3

Seven Seas books may be purchased in bulk for promotional,
educational, or business use. Please contact your local
bookseller or the Macmillan Corporate and Premium Sales
Department at 1-800-221-7945, extension 5442, or by e-mail
at MacmillanSpecialMarkets@macmillan.com.

Follow Seven Seas Entertainment online at
sevenseasentertainment.com

COLORS
Honoel A. Ibardolaza

COVER ART
Niko Geyer

LETTERING AND COVER DESIGN
Nicky Lim

ASSISTANT EDITOR
Jenn Grunigen

PRODUCTION ASSISTANT
CK Russell

PRODUCTION MANAGER
Lissa Pattillo

EDITOR-IN-CHIEF
Adam Arnold

PUBLISHER
Jason DeAngelis

ISBN: 978-1-626929-64-7
Printed in Canada
First Printing: January 2019
10 9 8 7 6 5 4 3 2 1

~ENTR'ACTE~

Prelude to More Problems

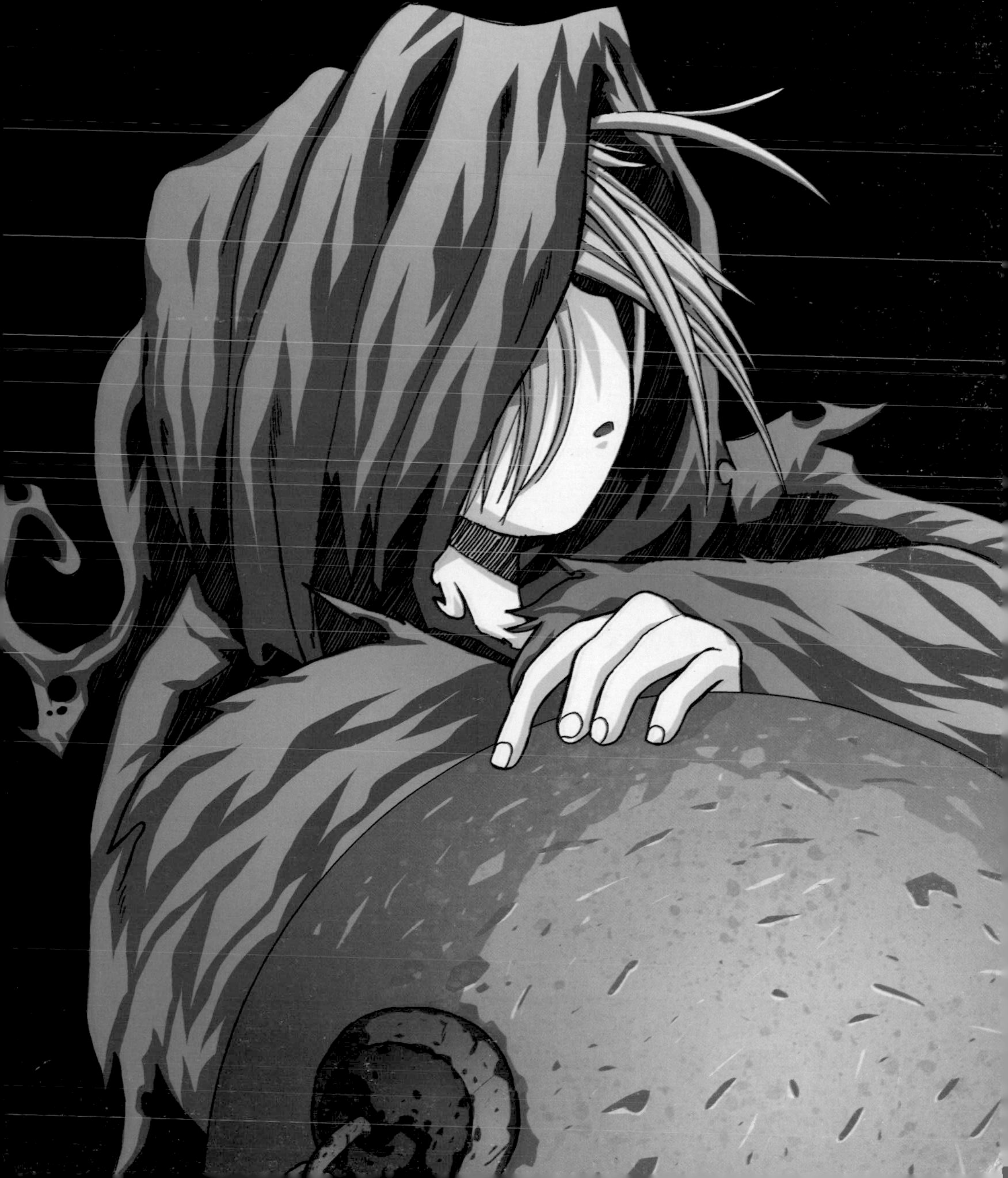

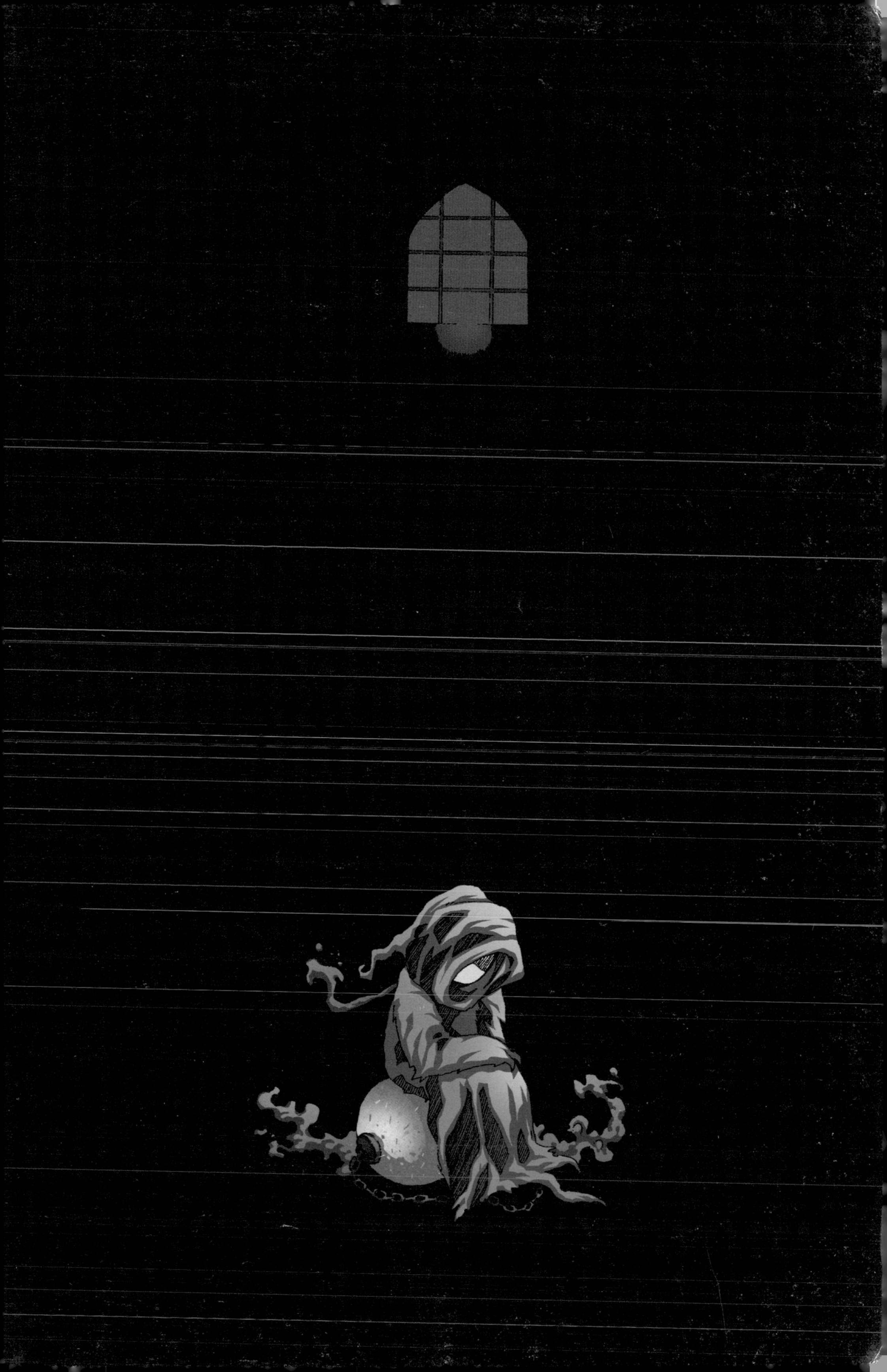

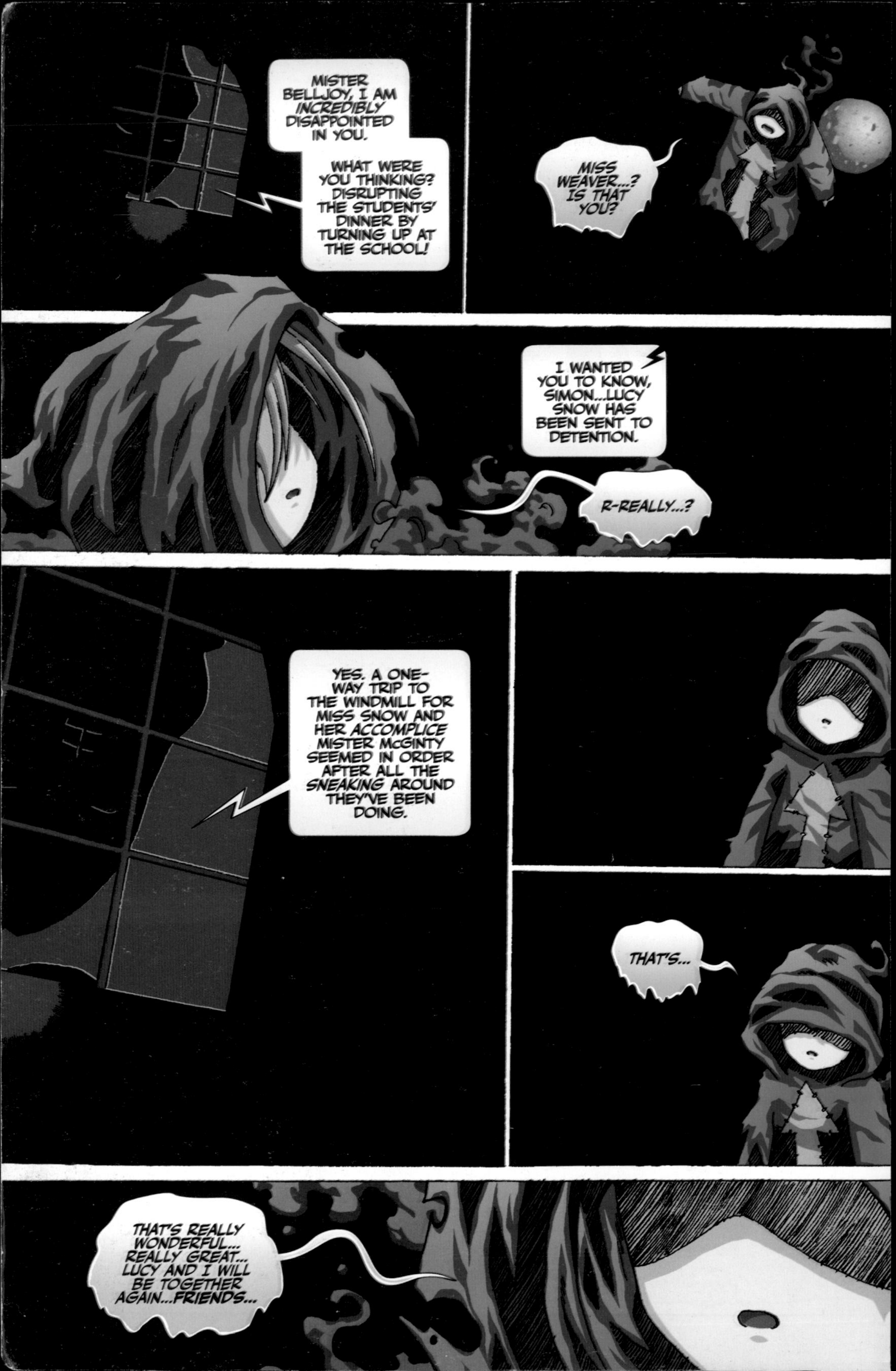
MISTER BELLJOY, I AM *INCREDIBLY* DISAPPOINTED IN YOU.
WHAT WERE YOU THINKING? DISRUPTING THE STUDENTS' DINNER BY TURNING UP AT THE SCHOOL!
MISS WEAVER...? IS THAT YOU?
I WANTED YOU TO KNOW, SIMON...LUCY SNOW HAS BEEN SENT TO DETENTION.
R-REALLY...?
YES. A ONE-WAY TRIP TO THE WINDMILL FOR MISS SNOW AND HER *ACCOMPLICE* MISTER McGINTY SEEMED IN ORDER AFTER ALL THE *SNEAKING* AROUND THEY'VE BEEN DOING.
THAT'S...
THAT'S REALLY WONDERFUL... REALLY GREAT... LUCY AND I WILL BE TOGETHER AGAIN...FRIENDS...

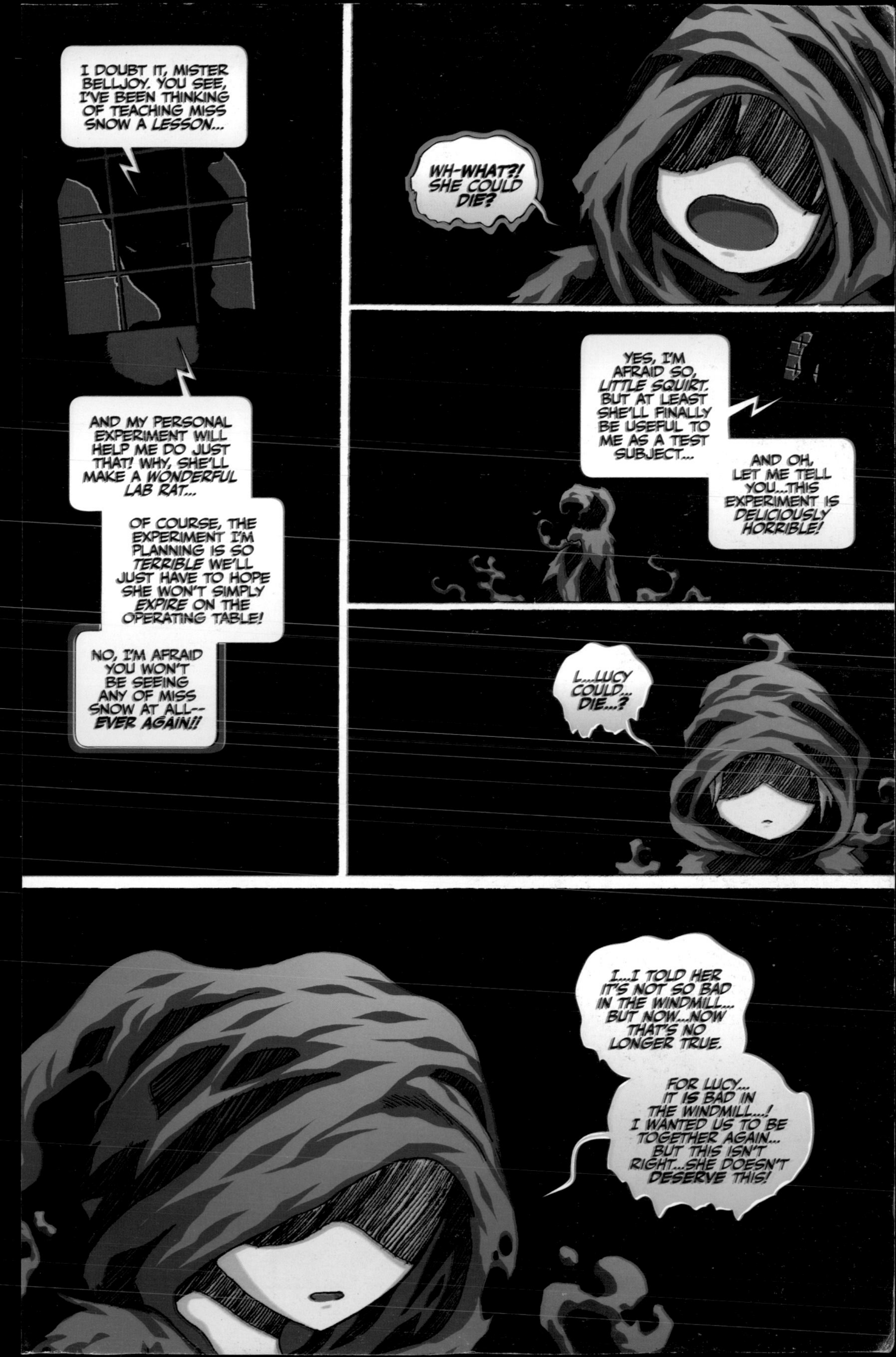
I DOUBT IT, MISTER BELLJOY. YOU SEE, I'VE BEEN THINKING OF TEACHING MISS SNOW A LESSON...
AND MY PERSONAL EXPERIMENT WILL HELP ME DO JUST THAT! WHY, SHE'LL MAKE A WONDERFUL LAB RAT...
OF COURSE, THE EXPERIMENT I'M PLANNING IS SO TERRIBLE WE'LL JUST HAVE TO HOPE SHE WON'T SIMPLY EXPIRE ON THE OPERATING TABLE!
NO, I'M AFRAID YOU WON'T BE SEEING ANY OF MISS SNOW AT ALL-- EVER AGAIN!!
WH-WHAT?! SHE COULD DIE?
YES, I'M AFRAID SO, LITTLE SQUIRT. BUT AT LEAST SHE'LL FINALLY BE USEFUL TO ME AS A TEST SUBJECT...
AND OH, LET ME TELL YOU...THIS EXPERIMENT IS DELICIOUSLY HORRIBLE!
L...LUCY COULD... DIE...?
I...I TOLD HER IT'S NOT SO BAD IN THE WINDMILL... BUT NOW...NOW THAT'S NO LONGER TRUE.
FOR LUCY... IT IS BAD IN THE WINDMILL...! I WANTED US TO BE TOGETHER AGAIN... BUT THIS ISN'T RIGHT...SHE DOESN'T DESERVE THIS!

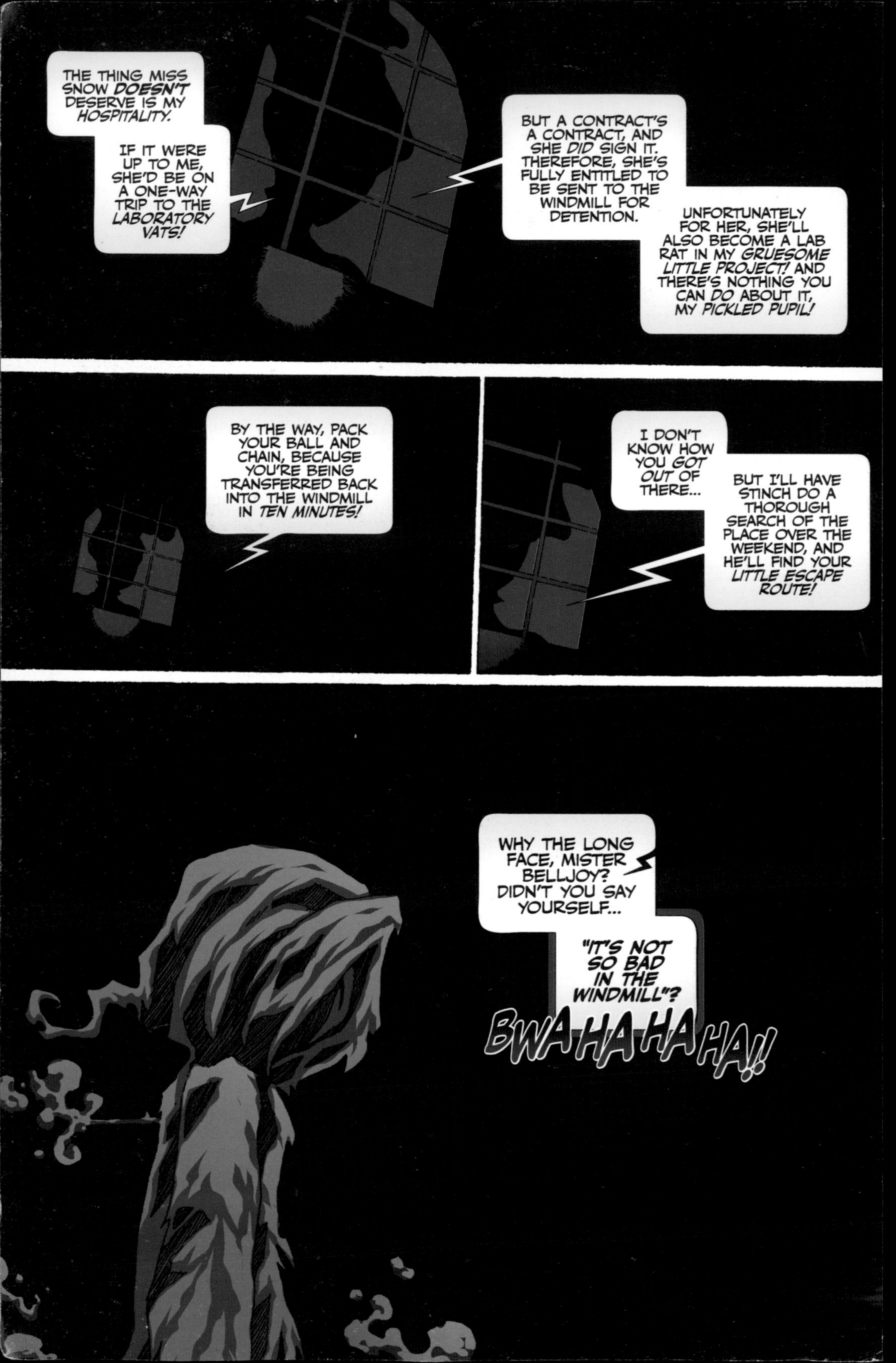
THE THING MISS SNOW DOESN'T DESERVE IS MY HOSPITALITY.
IF IT WERE UP TO ME, SHE'D BE ON A ONE-WAY TRIP TO THE LABORATORY VATS!
BUT A CONTRACT'S A CONTRACT, AND SHE DID SIGN IT. THEREFORE, SHE'S FULLY ENTITLED TO BE SENT TO THE WINDMILL FOR DETENTION.
UNFORTUNATELY FOR HER, SHE'LL ALSO BECOME A LAB RAT IN MY GRUESOME LITTLE PROJECT! AND THERE'S NOTHING YOU CAN DO ABOUT IT, MY PICKLED PUPIL!
BY THE WAY, PACK YOUR BALL AND CHAIN, BECAUSE YOU'RE BEING TRANSFERRED BACK INTO THE WINDMILL IN TEN MINUTES!
I DON'T KNOW HOW YOU GOT OUT OF THERE...
BUT I'LL HAVE STINCH DO A THOROUGH SEARCH OF THE PLACE OVER THE WEEKEND, AND HE'LL FIND YOUR LITTLE ESCAPE ROUTE!
WHY THE LONG FACE, MISTER BELLJOY? DIDN'T YOU SAY YOURSELF...
"IT'S NOT SO BAD IN THE WINDMILL"?
BWA HA HA HA!!

CHAPTER TEN

Past Travels, Future Encounters

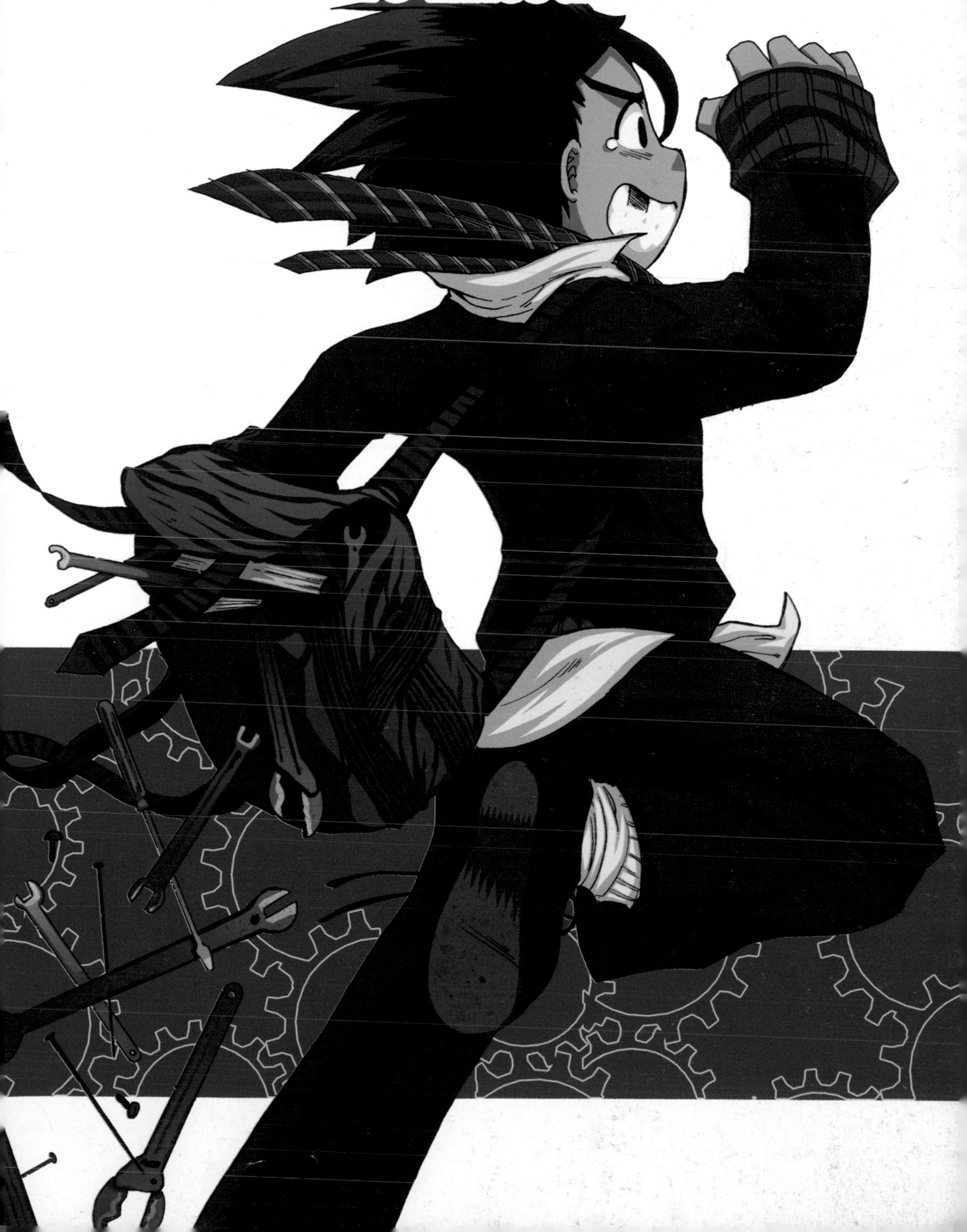

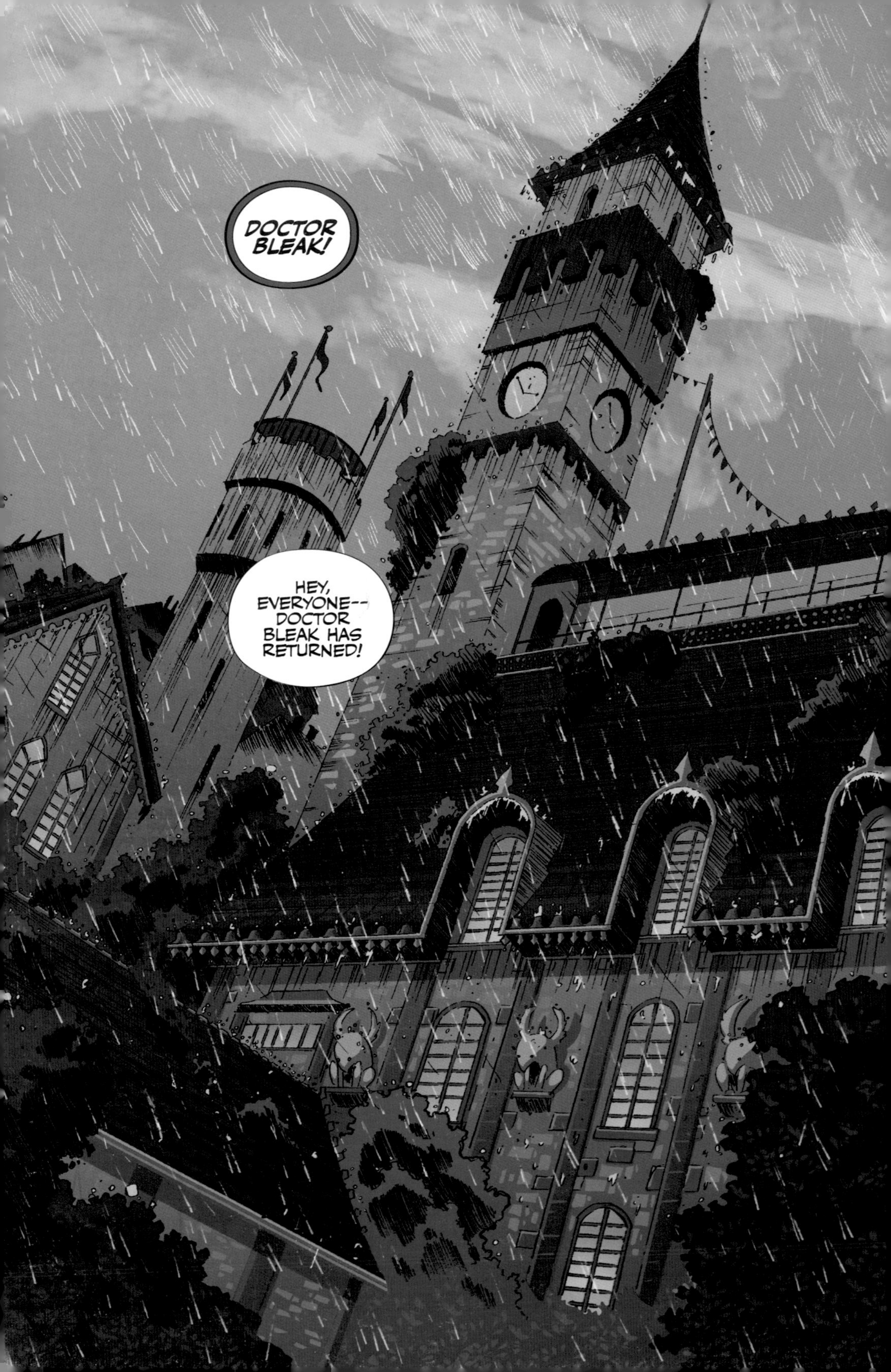
DOCTOR BLEAK!
HEY, EVERYONE-- DOCTOR BLEAK HAS RETURNED!

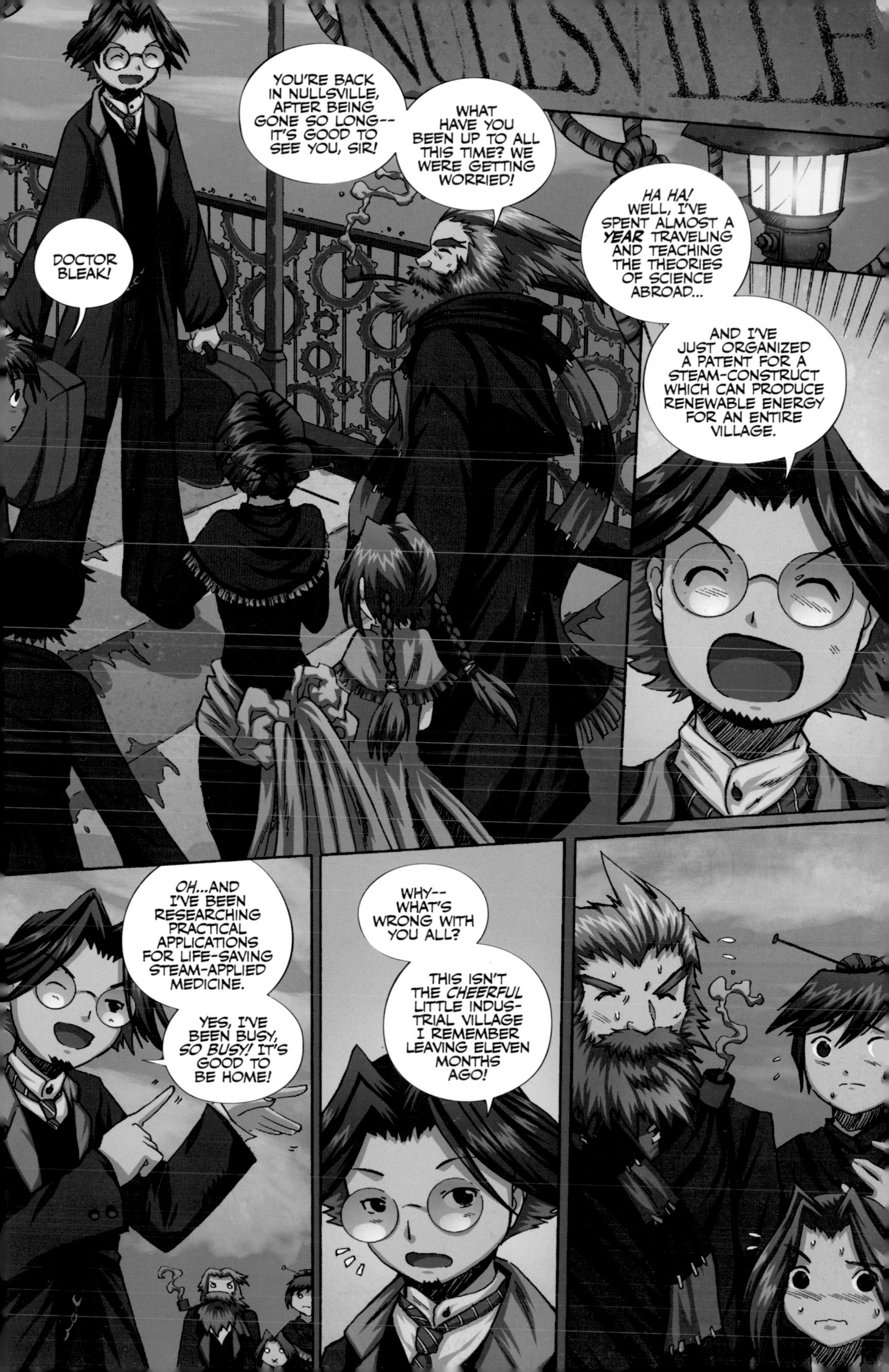
DOCTOR BLEAK!
YOU'RE BACK IN NULLSVILLE, AFTER BEING GONE SO LONG-- IT'S GOOD TO SEE YOU, SIR!
WHAT HAVE YOU BEEN UP TO ALL THIS TIME? WE WERE GETTING WORRIED!
HA HA! WELL, I'VE SPENT ALMOST A ***YEAR*** TRAVELING AND TEACHING THE THEORIES OF SCIENCE ABROAD...
AND I'VE JUST ORGANIZED A PATENT FOR A STEAM-CONSTRUCT WHICH CAN PRODUCE RENEWABLE ENERGY FOR AN ENTIRE VILLAGE.
OH...AND I'VE BEEN RESEARCHING PRACTICAL APPLICATIONS FOR LIFE-SAVING STEAM-APPLIED MEDICINE.
YES, I'VE BEEN BUSY, *SO BUSY!* IT'S GOOD TO BE HOME!
WHY-- WHAT'S WRONG WITH YOU ALL?
THIS ISN'T THE *CHEERFUL* LITTLE INDUSTRIAL VILLAGE I REMEMBER LEAVING ELEVEN MONTHS AGO!

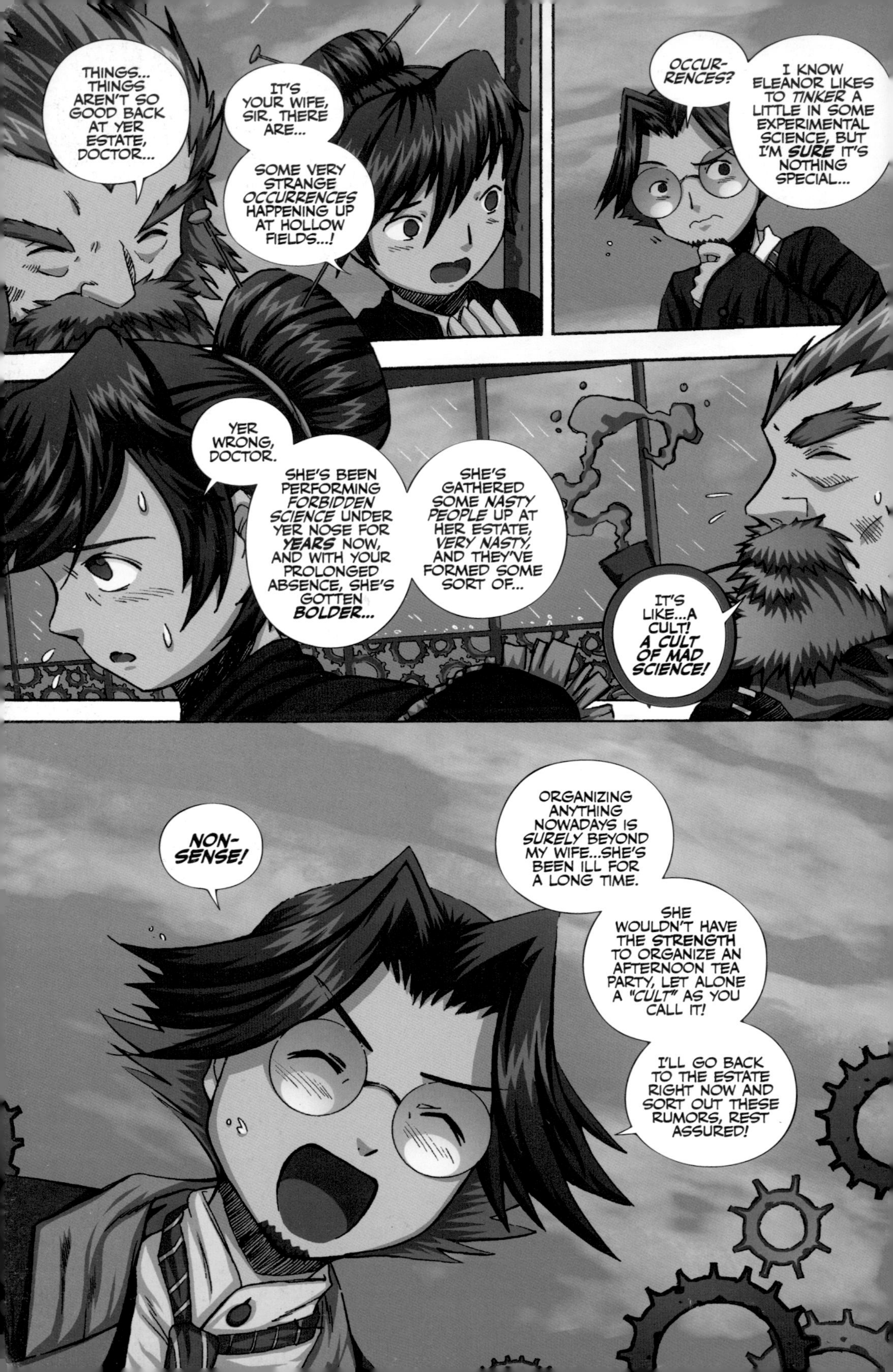
THINGS... THINGS AREN'T SO GOOD BACK AT YER ESTATE, DOCTOR...
IT'S YOUR WIFE, SIR. THERE ARE...
SOME VERY STRANGE *OCCURRENCES* HAPPENING UP AT HOLLOW FIELDS...!
OCCUR-RENCES?
I KNOW ELEANOR LIKES TO *TINKER* A LITTLE IN SOME EXPERIMENTAL SCIENCE, BUT I'M ***SURE*** IT'S NOTHING SPECIAL...
YER WRONG, DOCTOR.
SHE'S BEEN PERFORMING *FORBIDDEN SCIENCE* UNDER YER NOSE FOR ***YEARS*** NOW, AND WITH YOUR PROLONGED ABSENCE, SHE'S GOTTEN ***BOLDER...***
SHE'S GATHERED SOME *NASTY PEOPLE* UP AT HER ESTATE, *VERY NASTY,* AND THEY'VE FORMED SOME SORT OF...
IT'S LIKE...A CULT! ***A CULT OF MAD SCIENCE!***
NON-SENSE!
ORGANIZING ANYTHING NOWADAYS IS *SURELY* BEYOND MY WIFE...SHE'S BEEN ILL FOR A LONG TIME.
SHE WOULDN'T HAVE THE **STRENGTH** TO ORGANIZE AN AFTERNOON TEA PARTY, LET ALONE A *"CULT"* AS YOU CALL IT!
I'LL GO BACK TO THE ESTATE RIGHT NOW AND SORT OUT THESE RUMORS, REST ASSURED!

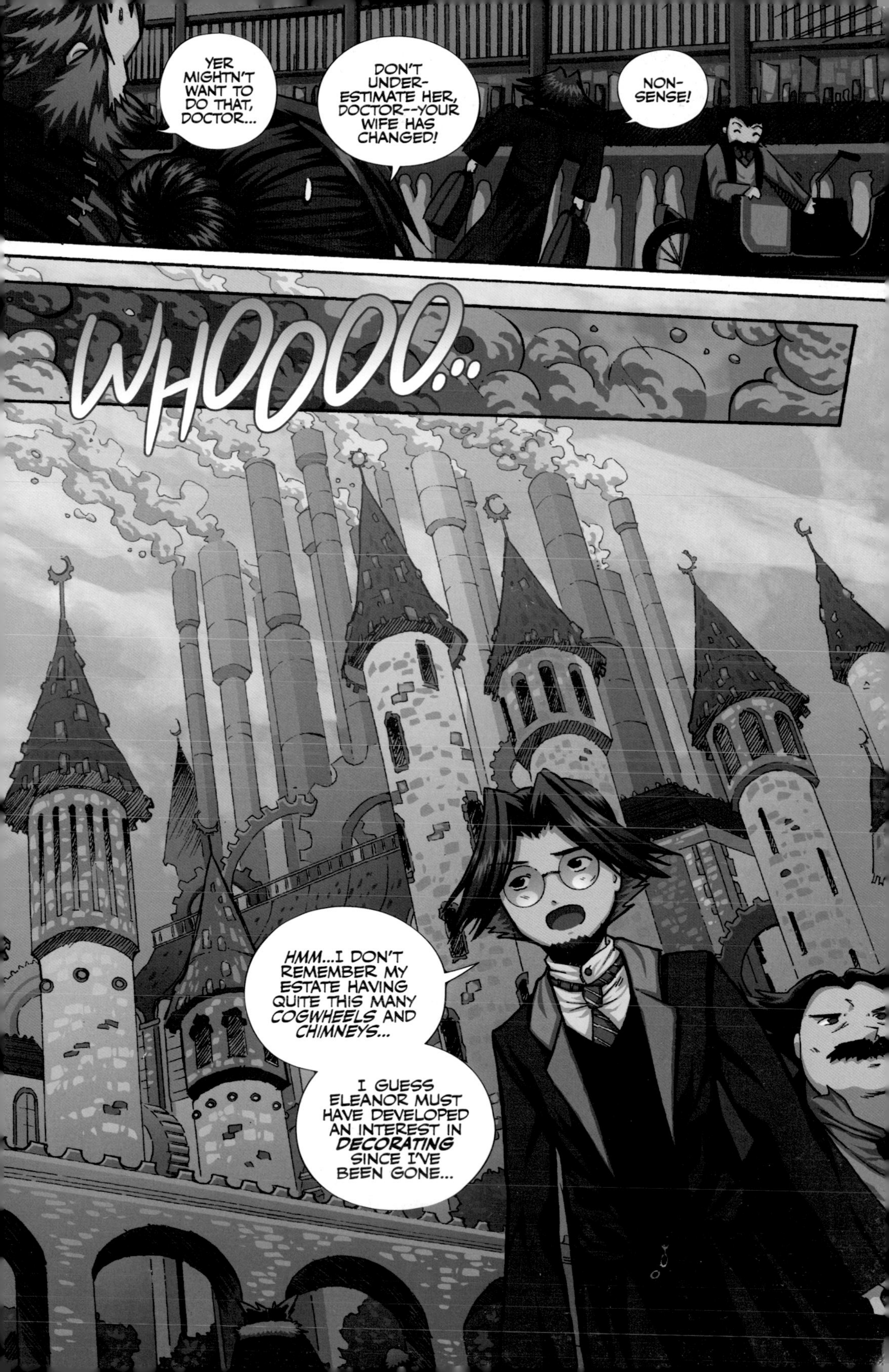
YER MIGHTN'T WANT TO DO THAT, DOCTOR...
DON'T UNDER-ESTIMATE HER, DOCTOR--YOUR WIFE HAS CHANGED!
NON-SENSE!
WHOOOO...
HMM...I DON'T REMEMBER MY ESTATE HAVING QUITE THIS MANY COGWHEELS AND CHIMNEYS...
I GUESS ELEANOR MUST HAVE DEVELOPED AN INTEREST IN DECORATING SINCE I'VE BEEN GONE...

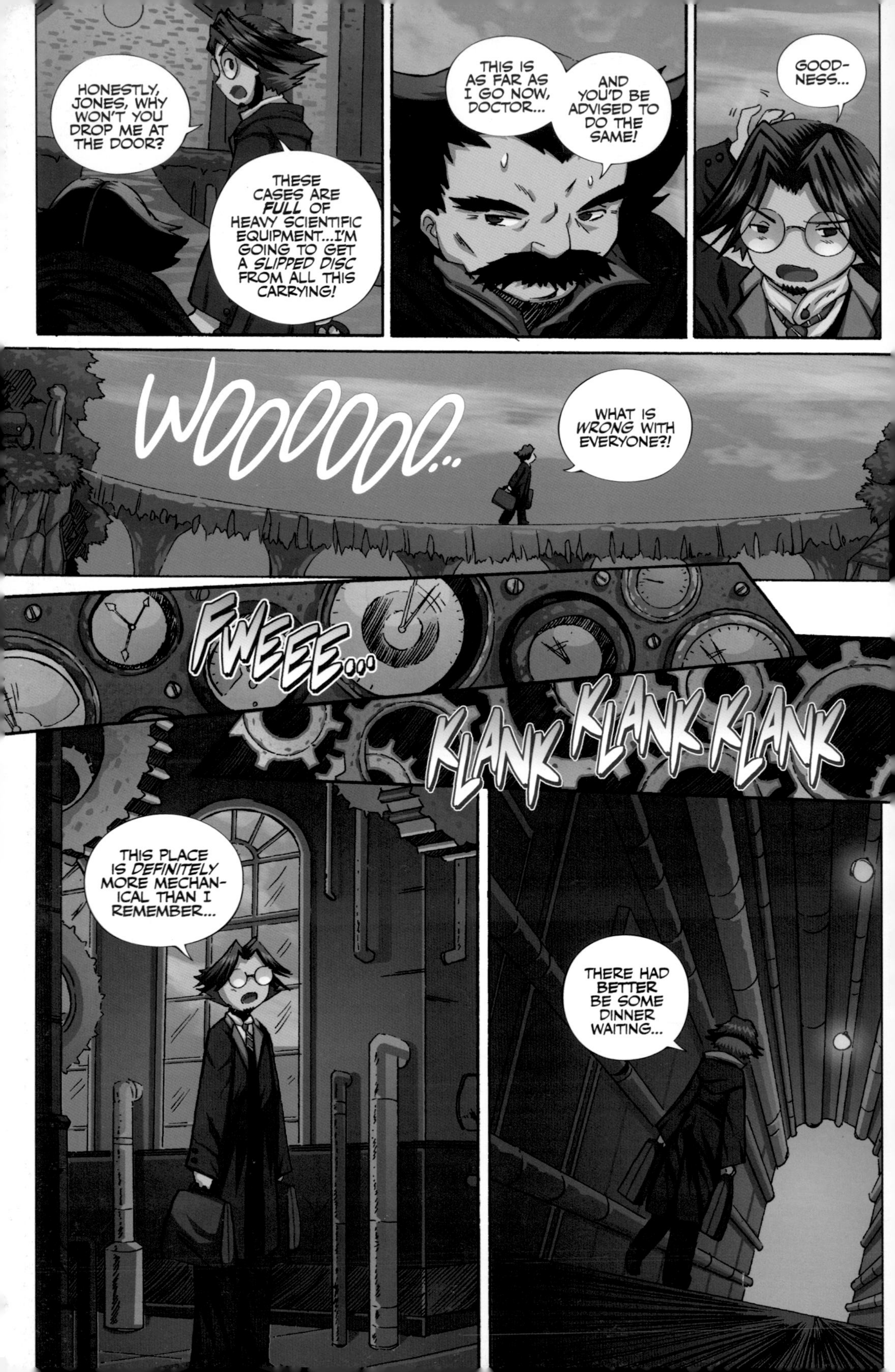
HONESTLY, JONES, WHY WON'T YOU DROP ME AT THE DOOR?
THESE CASES ARE *FULL* OF HEAVY SCIENTIFIC EQUIPMENT...I'M GOING TO GET A *SLIPPED DISC* FROM ALL THIS CARRYING!
THIS IS AS FAR AS I GO NOW, DOCTOR...
AND YOU'D BE ADVISED TO DO THE SAME!
GOOD-NESS...
WOOOOOO...
WHAT IS *WRONG* WITH EVERYONE?!
FWEEE...
KLANK KLANK KLANK
THIS PLACE IS *DEFINITELY* MORE MECHANICAL THAN I REMEMBER...
THERE HAD BETTER BE SOME DINNER WAITING...

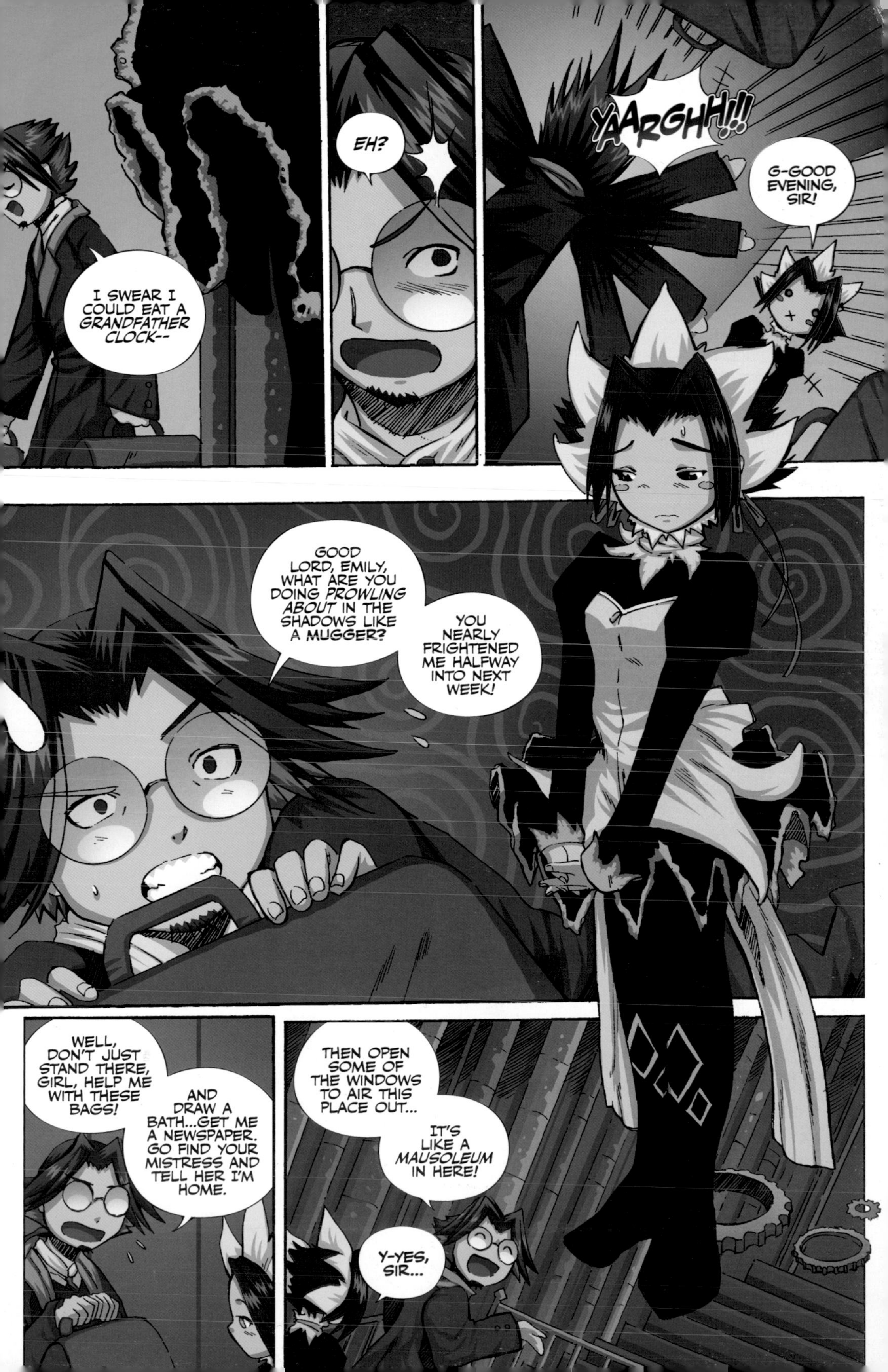
I SWEAR I COULD EAT A *GRANDFATHER CLOCK*--
EH?
YAARGHH!!!
G-GOOD EVENING, SIR!
GOOD LORD, EMILY, WHAT ARE YOU DOING *PROWLING ABOUT* IN THE SHADOWS LIKE A MUGGER?
YOU NEARLY FRIGHTENED ME HALFWAY INTO NEXT WEEK!
WELL, DON'T JUST STAND THERE, GIRL, HELP ME WITH THESE BAGS!
AND DRAW A BATH...GET ME A NEWSPAPER. GO FIND YOUR MISTRESS AND TELL HER I'M HOME.
THEN OPEN SOME OF THE WINDOWS TO AIR THIS PLACE OUT...
IT'S LIKE A *MAUSOLEUM* IN HERE!
Y-YES, SIR...

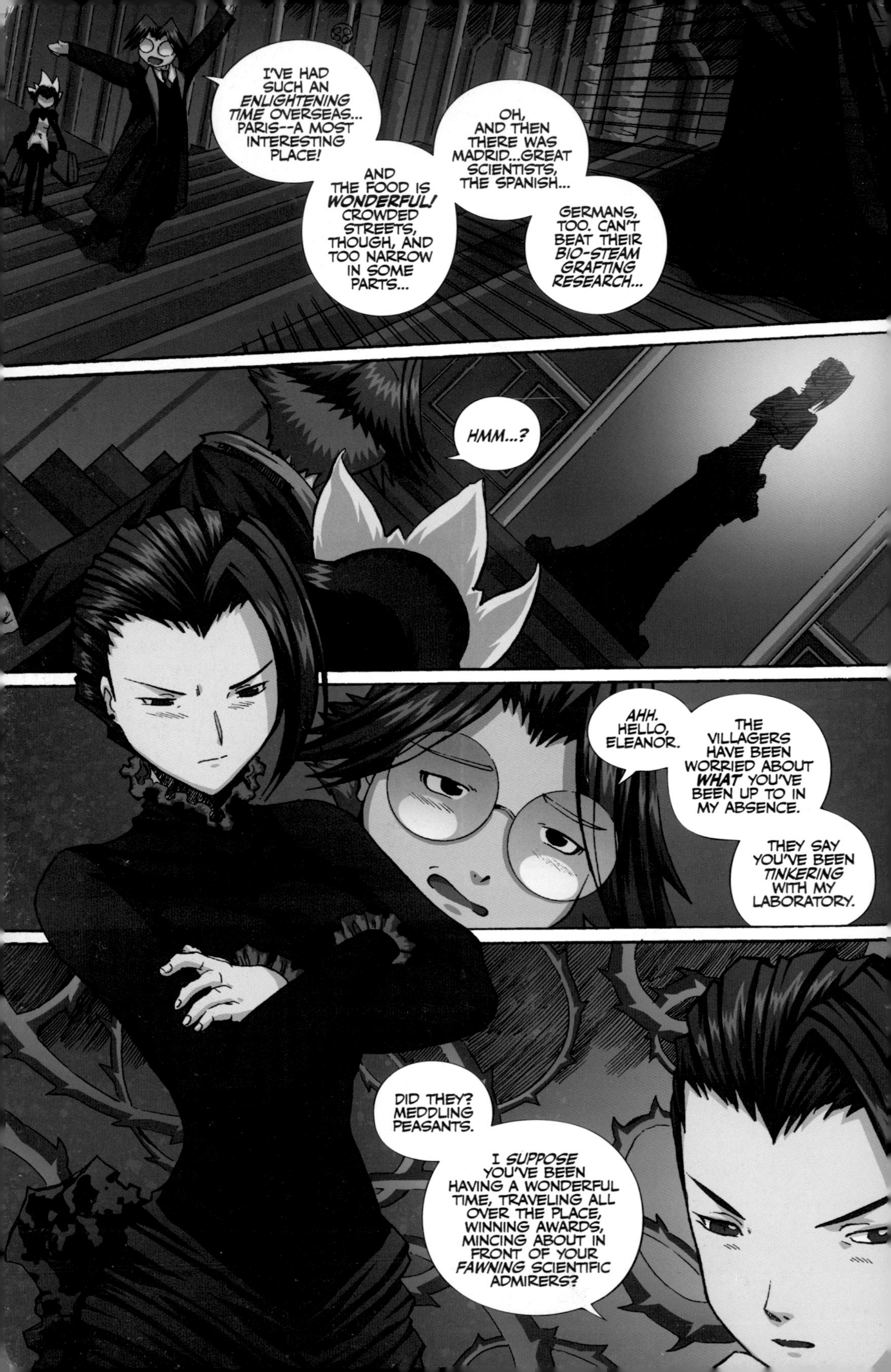
I'VE HAD SUCH AN *ENLIGHTENING TIME* OVERSEAS... PARIS--A MOST INTERESTING PLACE!
AND THE FOOD IS ***WONDERFUL!*** CROWDED STREETS, THOUGH, AND TOO NARROW IN SOME PARTS...
OH, AND THEN THERE WAS MADRID...GREAT SCIENTISTS, THE SPANISH...
GERMANS, TOO. CAN'T BEAT THEIR *BIO-STEAM GRAFTING RESEARCH*...
HMM...?
AHH. HELLO, ELEANOR.
THE VILLAGERS HAVE BEEN WORRIED ABOUT ***WHAT*** YOU'VE BEEN UP TO IN MY ABSENCE.
THEY SAY YOU'VE BEEN *TINKERING* WITH MY LABORATORY.
DID THEY? MEDDLING PEASANTS.
I *SUPPOSE* YOU'VE BEEN HAVING A WONDERFUL TIME, TRAVELING ALL OVER THE PLACE, WINNING AWARDS, MINCING ABOUT IN FRONT OF YOUR *FAWNING* SCIENTIFIC ADMIRERS?

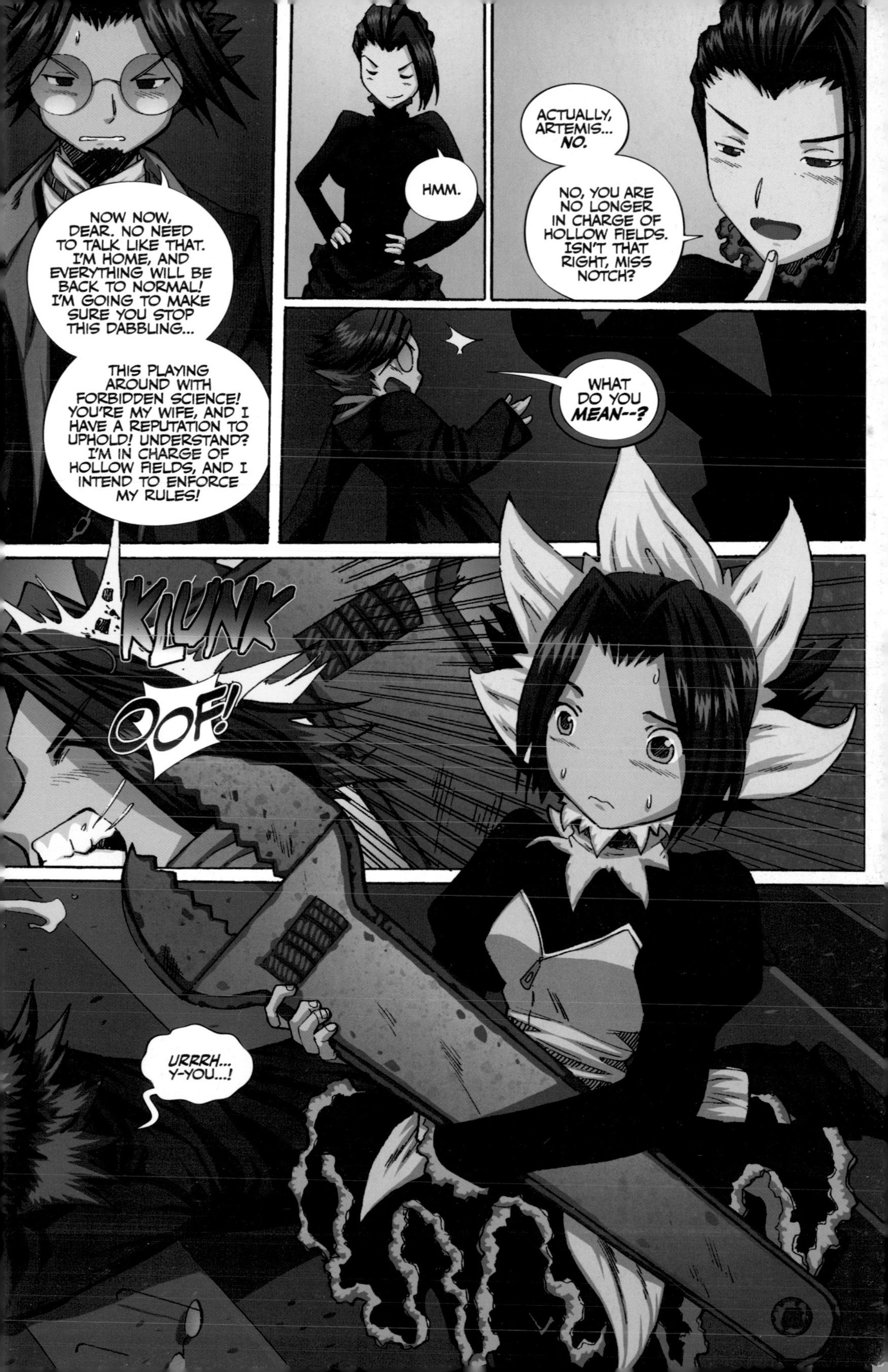
NOW NOW, DEAR. NO NEED TO TALK LIKE THAT. I'M HOME, AND EVERYTHING WILL BE BACK TO NORMAL! I'M GOING TO MAKE SURE YOU STOP THIS DABBLING...
THIS PLAYING AROUND WITH FORBIDDEN SCIENCE! YOU'RE MY WIFE, AND I HAVE A REPUTATION TO UPHOLD! UNDERSTAND? I'M IN CHARGE OF HOLLOW FIELDS, AND I INTEND TO ENFORCE MY RULES!
HMM.
ACTUALLY, ARTEMIS... **NO.**
NO, YOU ARE NO LONGER IN CHARGE OF HOLLOW FIELDS. ISN'T THAT RIGHT, MISS NOTCH?
WHAT DO YOU ***MEAN--?***
KLUNK
OOF!
URRRH... Y-YOU...!

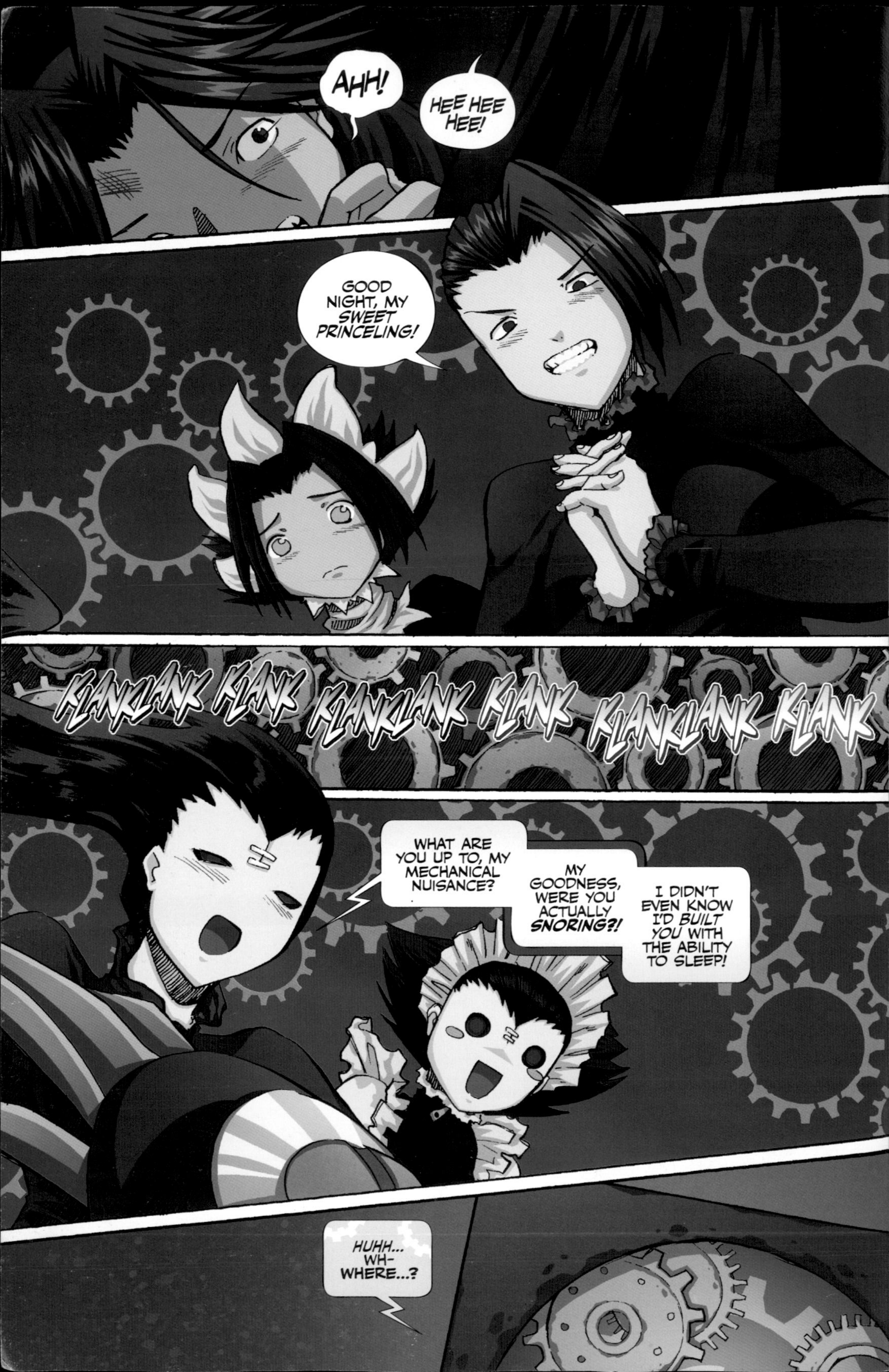
AHH!
HEE HEE HEE!
GOOD NIGHT, MY SWEET PRINCELING!
KLANKLANK KLANK KLANKLANK KLANK KLANKLANK KLANK
WHAT ARE YOU UP TO, MY MECHANICAL NUISANCE?
MY GOODNESS, WERE YOU ACTUALLY SNORING?!
I DIDN'T EVEN KNOW I'D BUILT YOU WITH THE ABILITY TO SLEEP!
HUHH... WH-WHERE...?

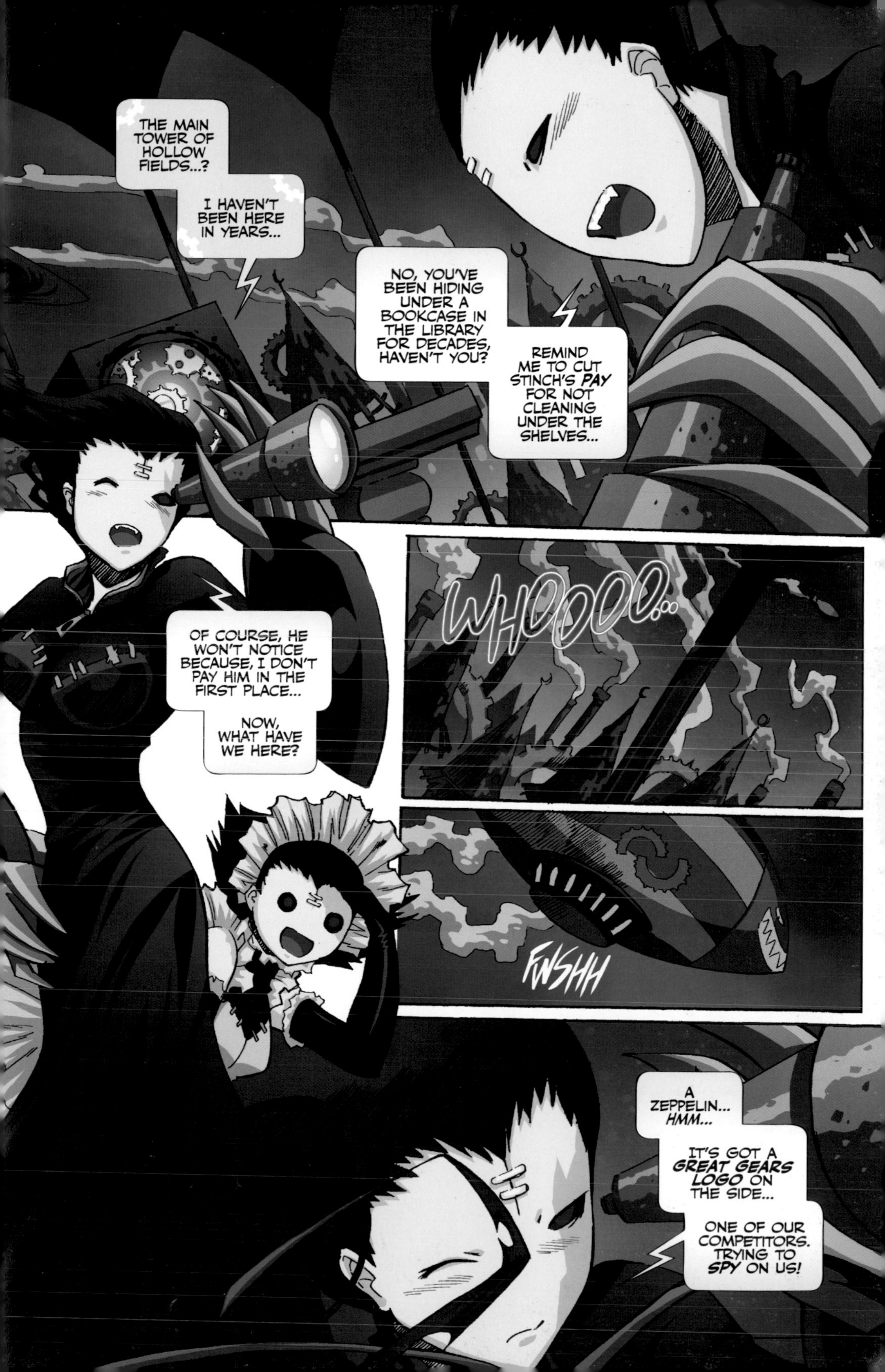
THE MAIN TOWER OF HOLLOW FIELDS...?
I HAVEN'T BEEN HERE IN YEARS...
NO, YOU'VE BEEN HIDING UNDER A BOOKCASE IN THE LIBRARY FOR DECADES, HAVEN'T YOU?
REMIND ME TO CUT STINCH'S *PAY* FOR NOT CLEANING UNDER THE SHELVES...
OF COURSE, HE WON'T NOTICE BECAUSE, I DON'T PAY HIM IN THE FIRST PLACE...
NOW, WHAT HAVE WE HERE?
WHOOOO...
FWSHH
A ZEPPELIN... *HMM*...
IT'S GOT A ***GREAT GEARS LOGO*** ON THE SIDE...
ONE OF OUR COMPETITORS. TRYING TO ***SPY*** ON US!

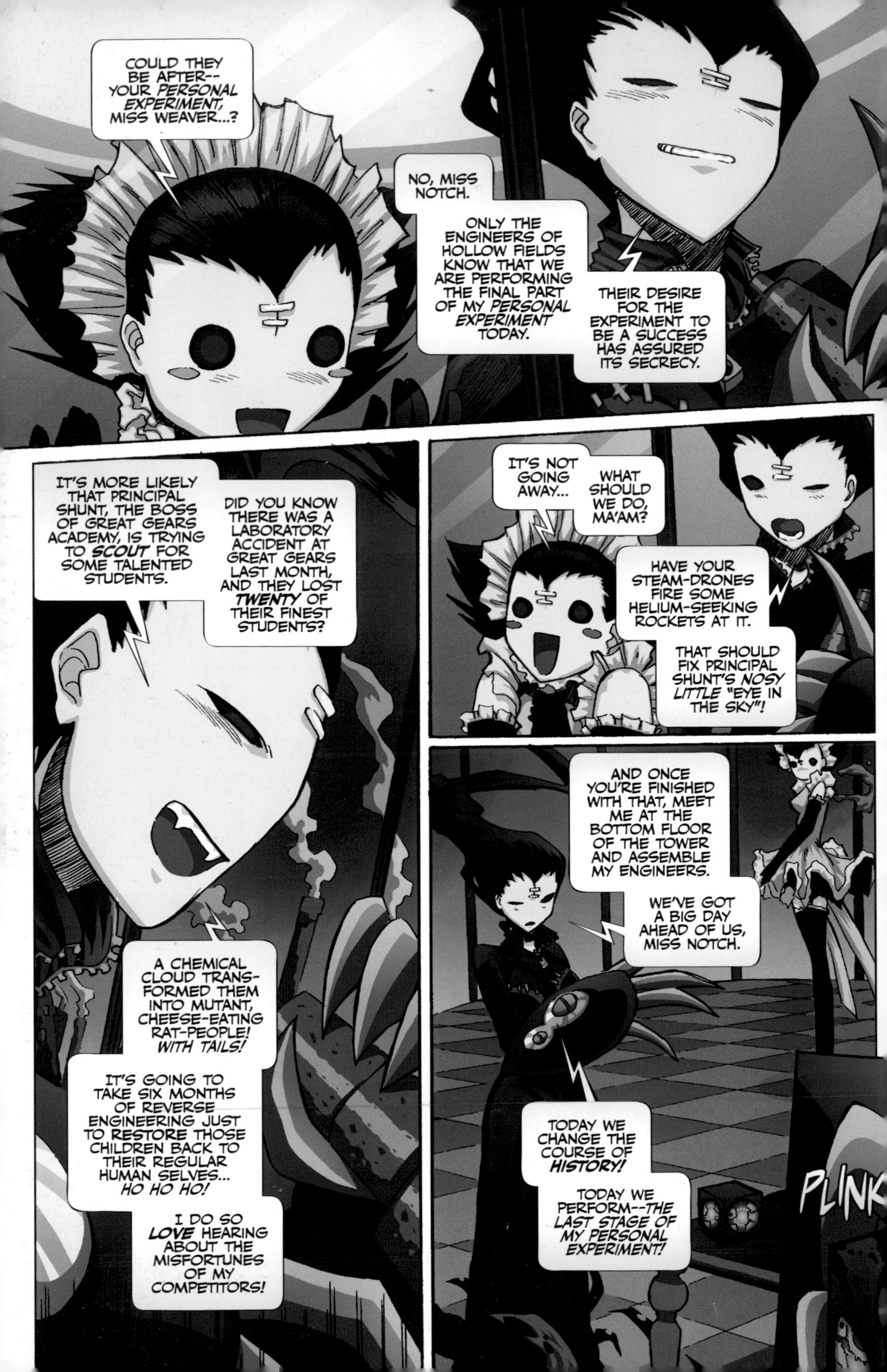

COULD THEY BE AFTER-- YOUR PERSONAL EXPERIMENT, MISS WEAVER...?
NO, MISS NOTCH.
ONLY THE ENGINEERS OF HOLLOW FIELDS KNOW THAT WE ARE PERFORMING THE FINAL PART OF MY PERSONAL EXPERIMENT TODAY.
THEIR DESIRE FOR THE EXPERIMENT TO BE A SUCCESS HAS ASSURED ITS SECRECY.
IT'S MORE LIKELY THAT PRINCIPAL SHUNT, THE BOSS OF GREAT GEARS ACADEMY, IS TRYING TO SCOUT FOR SOME TALENTED STUDENTS.
DID YOU KNOW THERE WAS A LABORATORY ACCIDENT AT GREAT GEARS LAST MONTH, AND THEY LOST TWENTY OF THEIR FINEST STUDENTS?
A CHEMICAL CLOUD TRANSFORMED THEM INTO MUTANT, CHEESE-EATING RAT-PEOPLE! WITH TAILS!
IT'S GOING TO TAKE SIX MONTHS OF REVERSE ENGINEERING JUST TO RESTORE THOSE CHILDREN BACK TO THEIR REGULAR HUMAN SELVES... HO HO HO!
I DO SO LOVE HEARING ABOUT THE MISFORTUNES OF MY COMPETITORS!
IT'S NOT GOING AWAY...
WHAT SHOULD WE DO, MA'AM?
HAVE YOUR STEAM-DRONES FIRE SOME HELIUM-SEEKING ROCKETS AT IT.
THAT SHOULD FIX PRINCIPAL SHUNT'S NOSY LITTLE "EYE IN THE SKY"!
AND ONCE YOU'RE FINISHED WITH THAT, MEET ME AT THE BOTTOM FLOOR OF THE TOWER AND ASSEMBLE MY ENGINEERS.
WE'VE GOT A BIG DAY AHEAD OF US, MISS NOTCH.
TODAY WE CHANGE THE COURSE OF HISTORY!
TODAY WE PERFORM--THE LAST STAGE OF MY PERSONAL EXPERIMENT!
PLINK

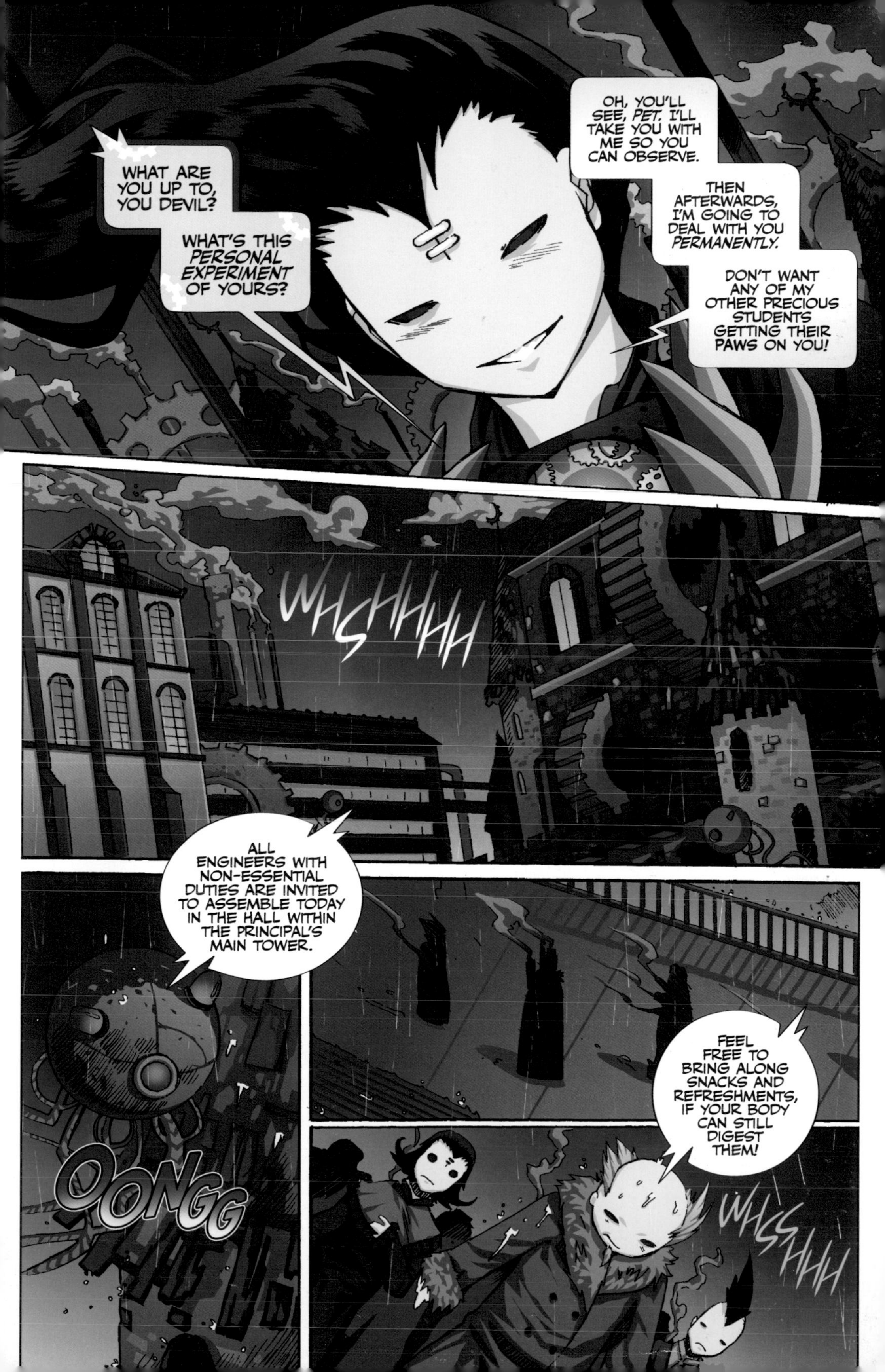
WHAT ARE YOU UP TO, YOU DEVIL?
WHAT'S THIS PERSONAL EXPERIMENT OF YOURS?
OH, YOU'LL SEE, PET. I'LL TAKE YOU WITH ME SO YOU CAN OBSERVE.
THEN AFTERWARDS, I'M GOING TO DEAL WITH YOU PERMANENTLY.
DON'T WANT ANY OF MY OTHER PRECIOUS STUDENTS GETTING THEIR PAWS ON YOU!
WHSHHHH
ALL ENGINEERS WITH NON-ESSENTIAL DUTIES ARE INVITED TO ASSEMBLE TODAY IN THE HALL WITHIN THE PRINCIPAL'S MAIN TOWER.
OONGG
FEEL FREE TO BRING ALONG SNACKS AND REFRESHMENTS, IF YOUR BODY CAN STILL DIGEST THEM!
WHSSHHH

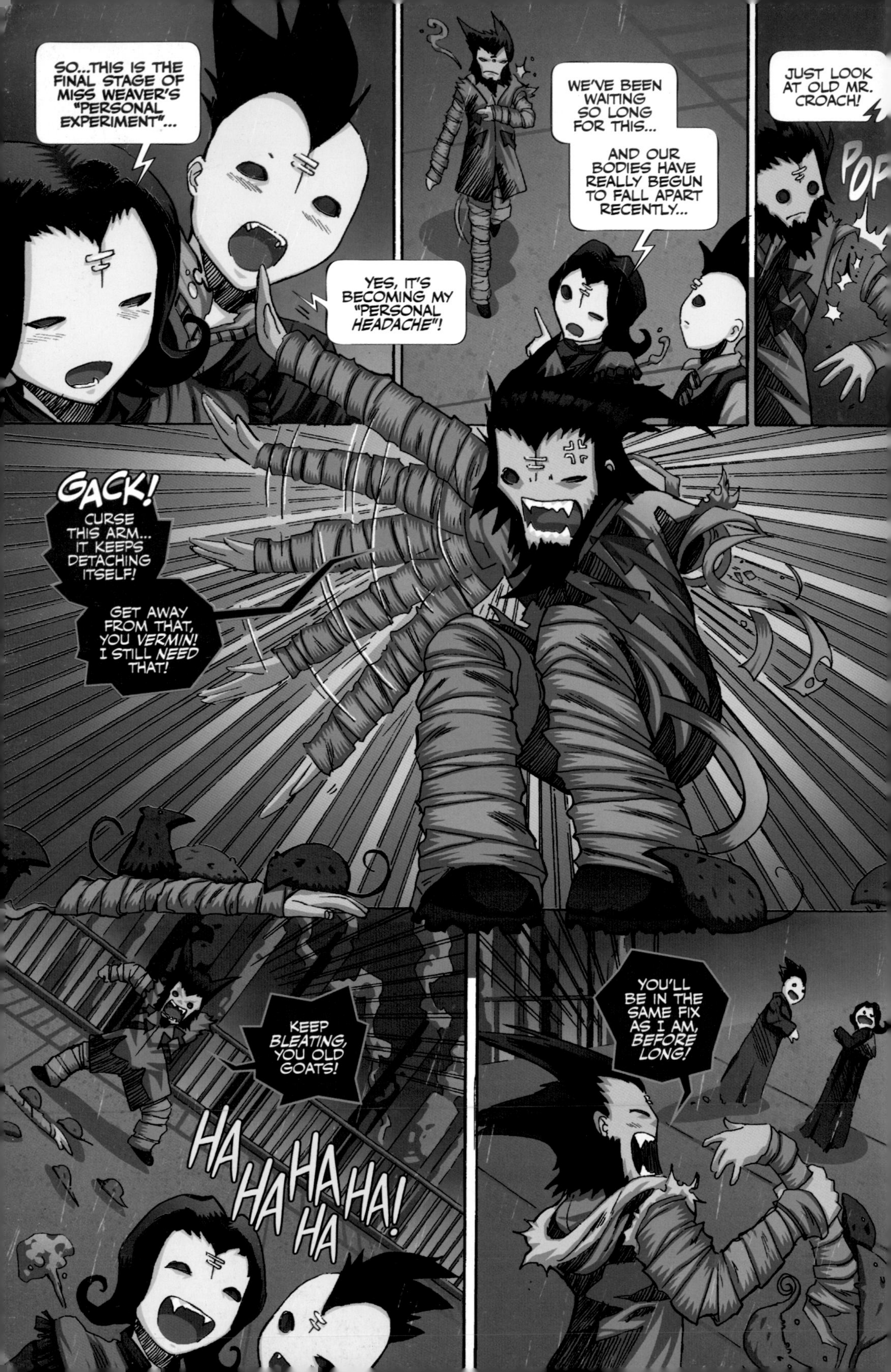

SO...THIS IS THE FINAL STAGE OF MISS WEAVER'S "PERSONAL EXPERIMENT"...
YES, IT'S BECOMING MY "PERSONAL HEADACHE"!
WE'VE BEEN WAITING SO LONG FOR THIS...
AND OUR BODIES HAVE REALLY BEGUN TO FALL APART RECENTLY...
JUST LOOK AT OLD MR. CROACH!
POP
GACK!
CURSE THIS ARM... IT KEEPS DETACHING ITSELF!
GET AWAY FROM THAT, YOU VERMIN! I STILL NEED THAT!
KEEP BLEATING, YOU OLD GOATS!
HA HA HA HA HA HA!
YOU'LL BE IN THE SAME FIX AS I AM, BEFORE LONG!

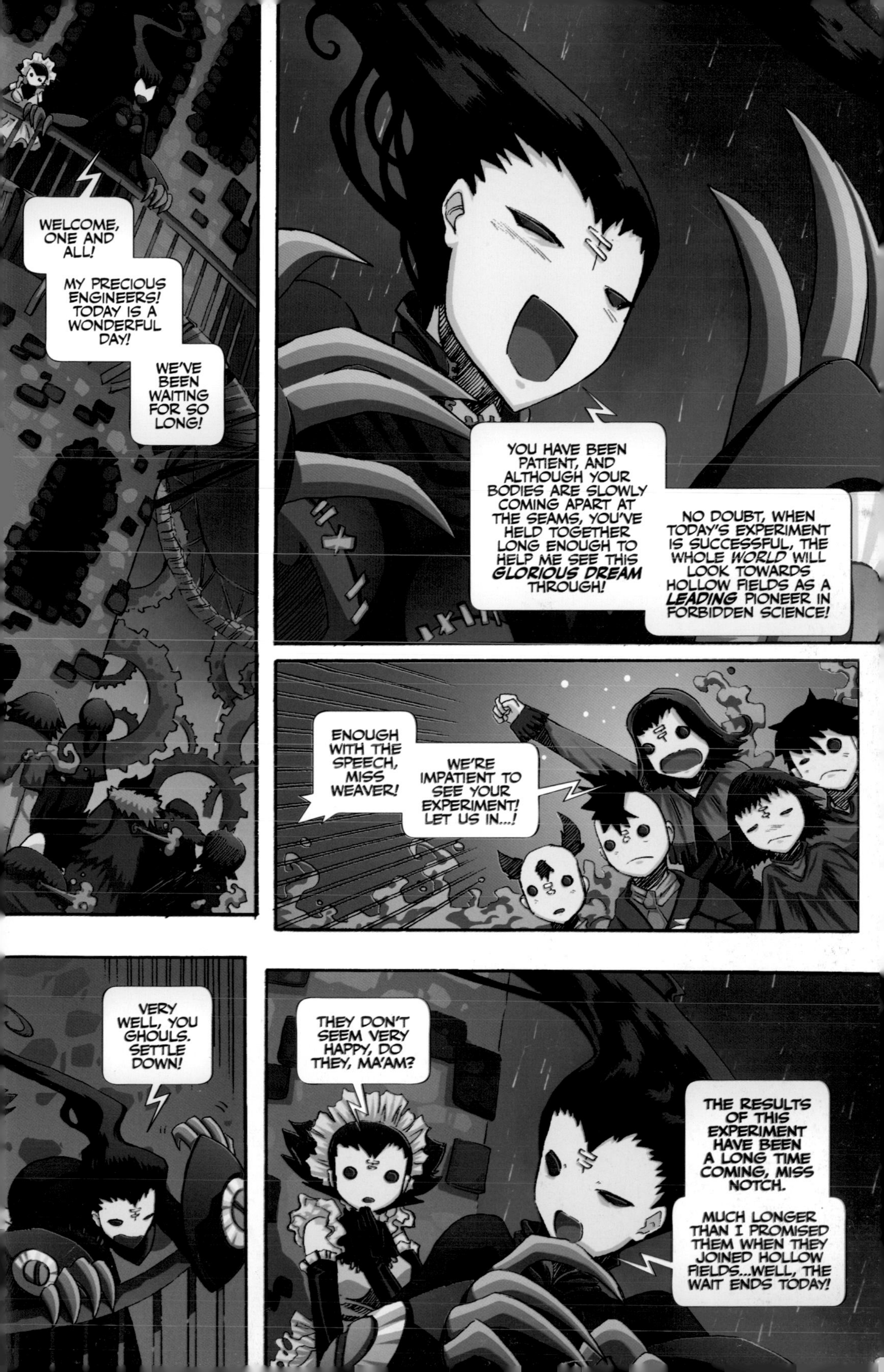
WELCOME, ONE AND ALL!
MY PRECIOUS ENGINEERS! TODAY IS A WONDERFUL DAY!
WE'VE BEEN WAITING FOR SO LONG!
YOU HAVE BEEN PATIENT, AND ALTHOUGH YOUR BODIES ARE SLOWLY COMING APART AT THE SEAMS, YOU'VE HELD TOGETHER LONG ENOUGH TO HELP ME SEE THIS ***GLORIOUS DREAM*** THROUGH!
NO DOUBT, WHEN TODAY'S EXPERIMENT IS SUCCESSFUL, THE WHOLE *WORLD* WILL LOOK TOWARDS HOLLOW FIELDS AS A ***LEADING*** PIONEER IN FORBIDDEN SCIENCE!
ENOUGH WITH THE SPEECH, MISS WEAVER!
WE'RE IMPATIENT TO SEE YOUR EXPERIMENT! LET US IN...!
VERY WELL, YOU GHOULS. SETTLE DOWN!
THEY DON'T SEEM VERY HAPPY, DO THEY, MA'AM?
THE RESULTS OF THIS EXPERIMENT HAVE BEEN A LONG TIME COMING, MISS NOTCH.
MUCH LONGER THAN I PROMISED THEM WHEN THEY JOINED HOLLOW FIELDS...WELL, THE WAIT ENDS TODAY!

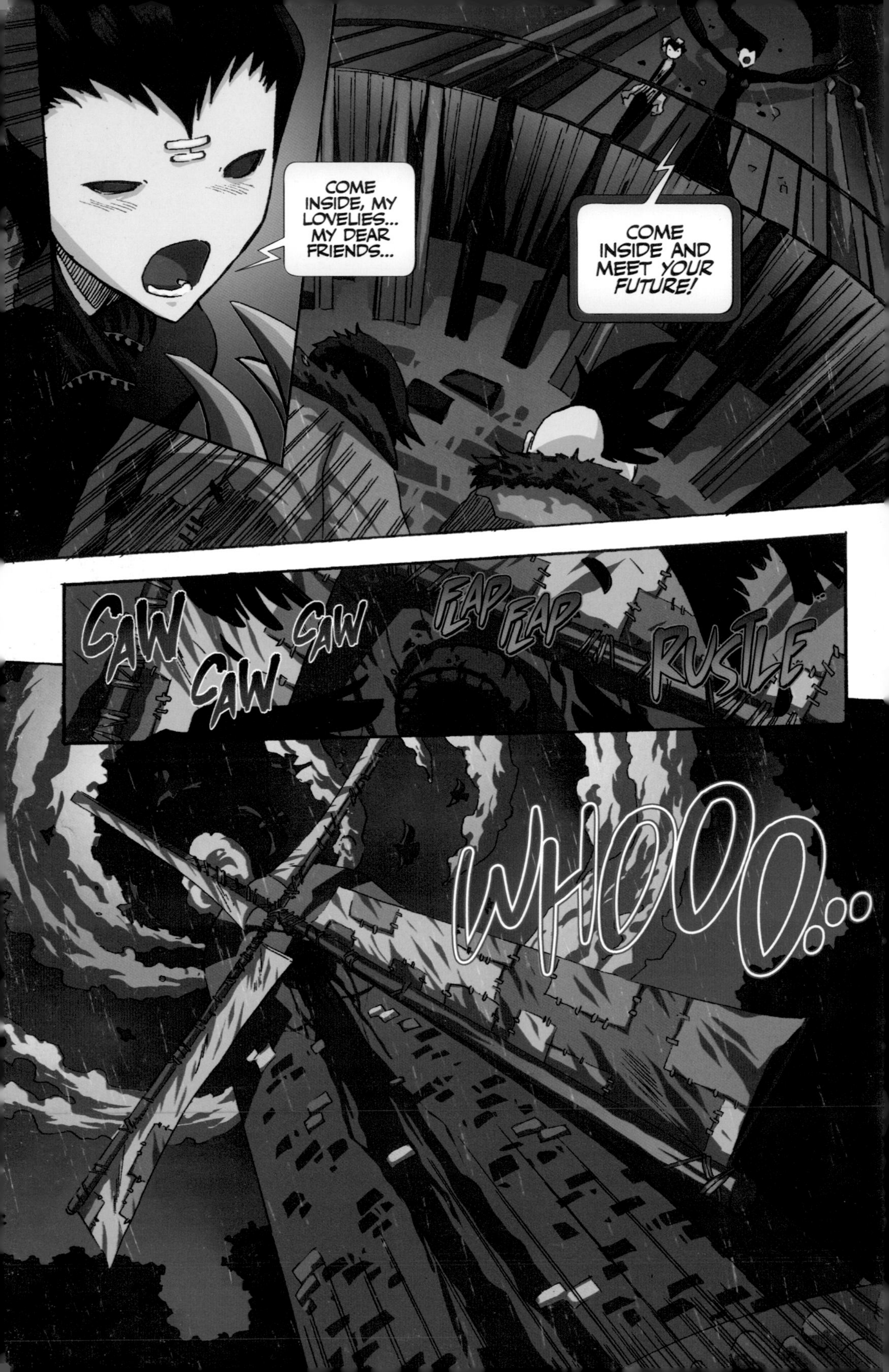
COME INSIDE, MY LOVELIES... MY DEAR FRIENDS...
COME INSIDE AND MEET YOUR FUTURE!
CAW CAW CAW
FLAP FLAP
RUSTLE
WHOOO...

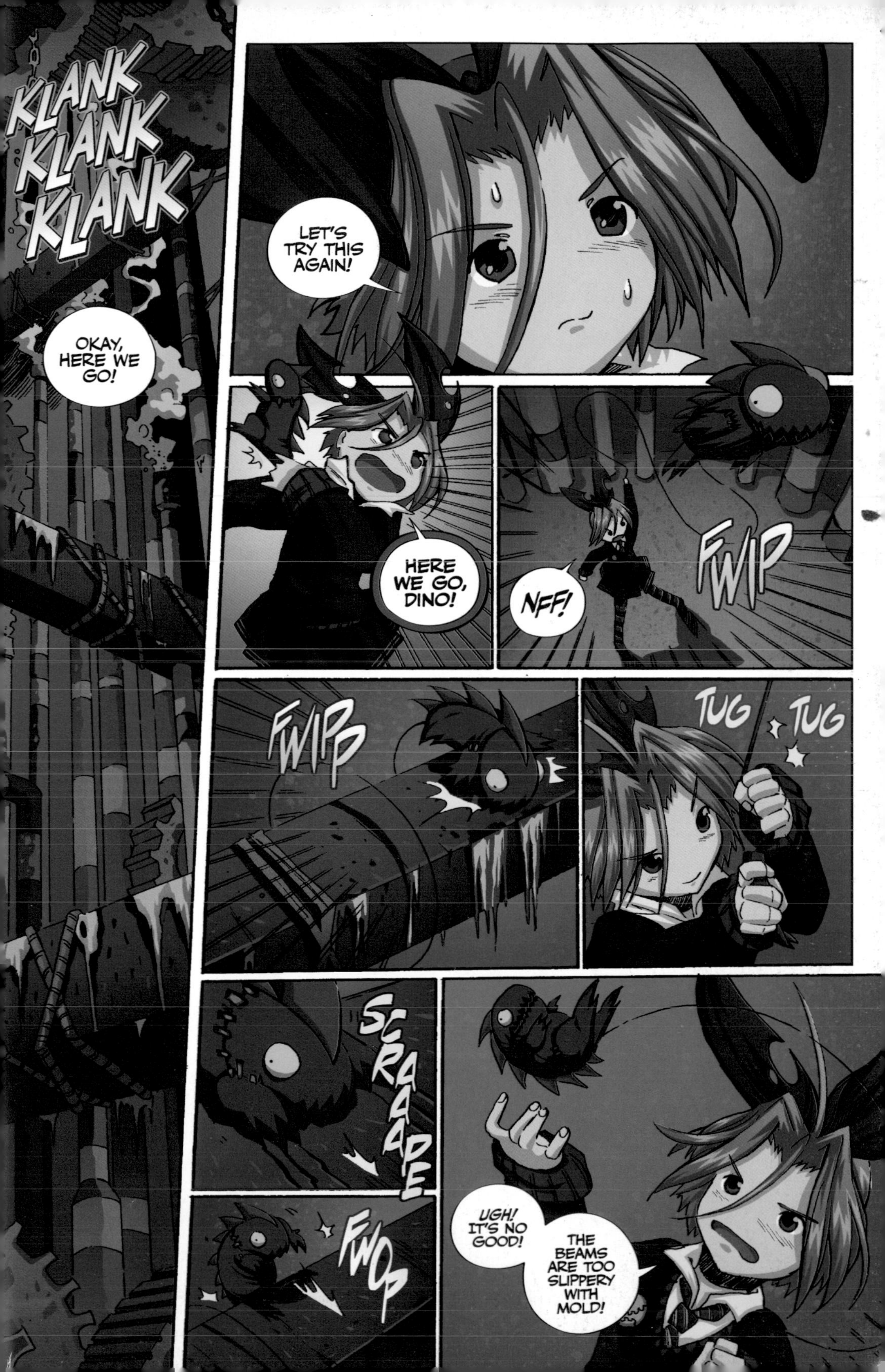
KLANK
KLANK
KLANK
OKAY, HERE WE GO!
LET'S TRY THIS AGAIN!
HERE WE GO, DINO!
NFF!
FWIP
FWIPP
TUG
TUG
SCRAAAPE
FWOP
UGH! IT'S NO GOOD!
THE BEAMS ARE TOO SLIPPERY WITH MOLD!

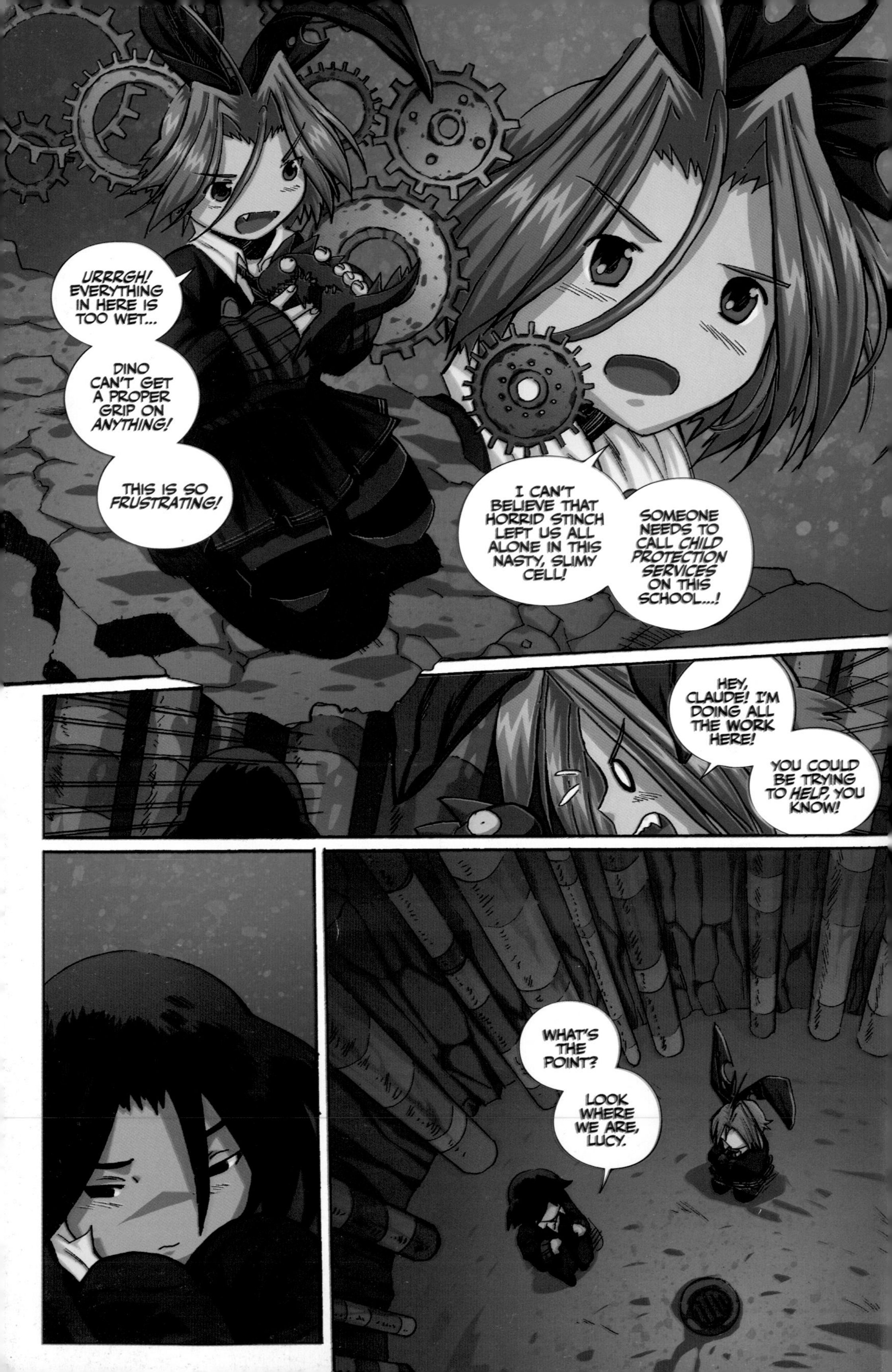
URRRGH! EVERYTHING IN HERE IS TOO WET...
DINO CAN'T GET A PROPER GRIP ON *ANYTHING!*
THIS IS SO *FRUSTRATING!*
I CAN'T BELIEVE THAT HORRID STINCH LEFT US ALL ALONE IN THIS NASTY, SLIMY CELL!
SOMEONE NEEDS TO CALL *CHILD PROTECTION SERVICES* ON THIS SCHOOL...!
HEY, CLAUDE! I'M DOING ALL THE WORK HERE!
YOU COULD BE TRYING TO *HELP*, YOU KNOW!
WHAT'S THE POINT?
LOOK WHERE WE ARE, LUCY.

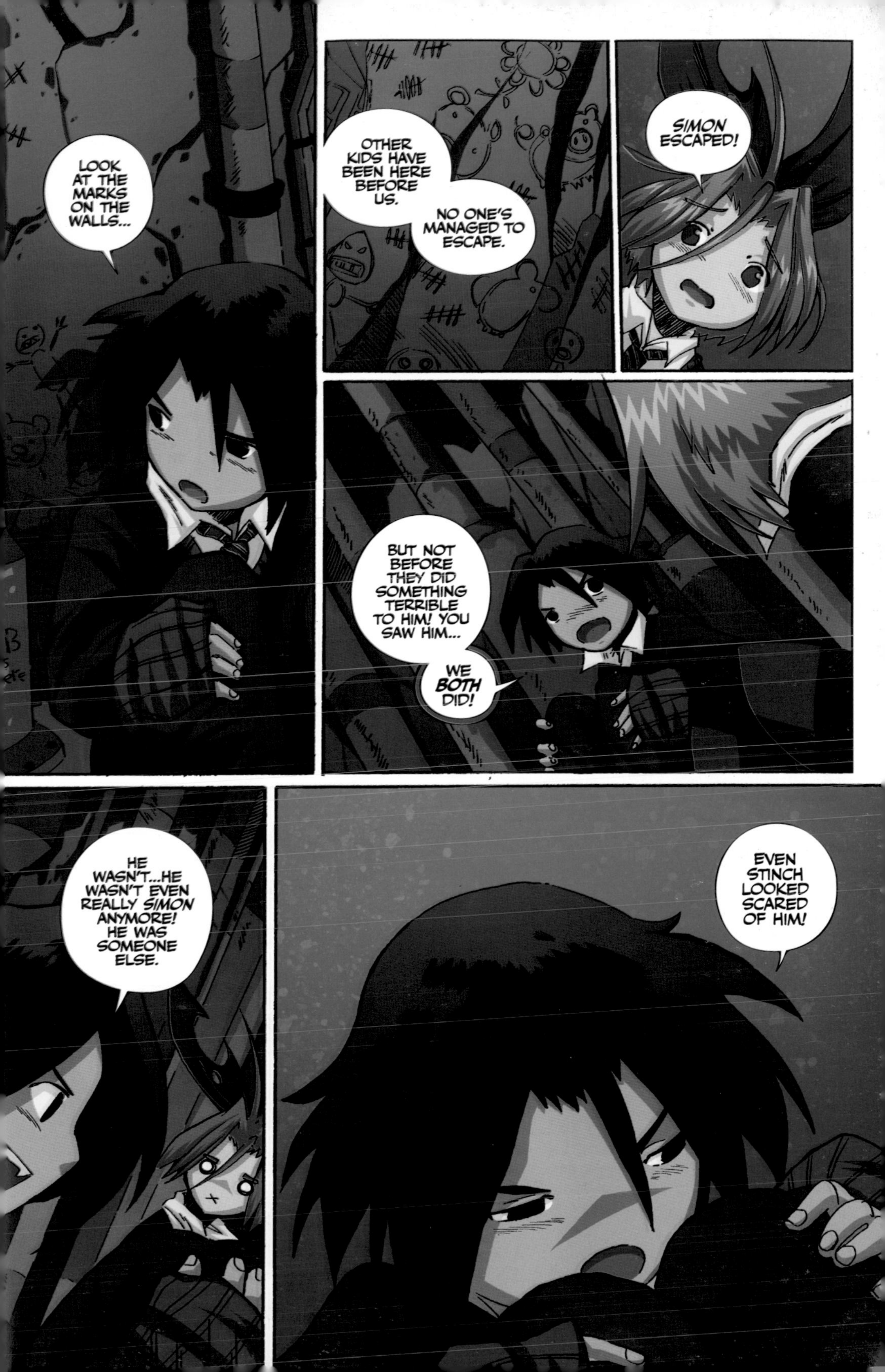
LOOK AT THE MARKS ON THE WALLS...
OTHER KIDS HAVE BEEN HERE BEFORE US.
NO ONE'S MANAGED TO ESCAPE.
SIMON ESCAPED!
BUT NOT BEFORE THEY DID SOMETHING TERRIBLE TO HIM! YOU SAW HIM...
WE BOTH DID!
HE WASN'T...HE WASN'T EVEN REALLY SIMON ANYMORE! HE WAS SOMEONE ELSE.
EVEN STINCH LOOKED SCARED OF HIM!

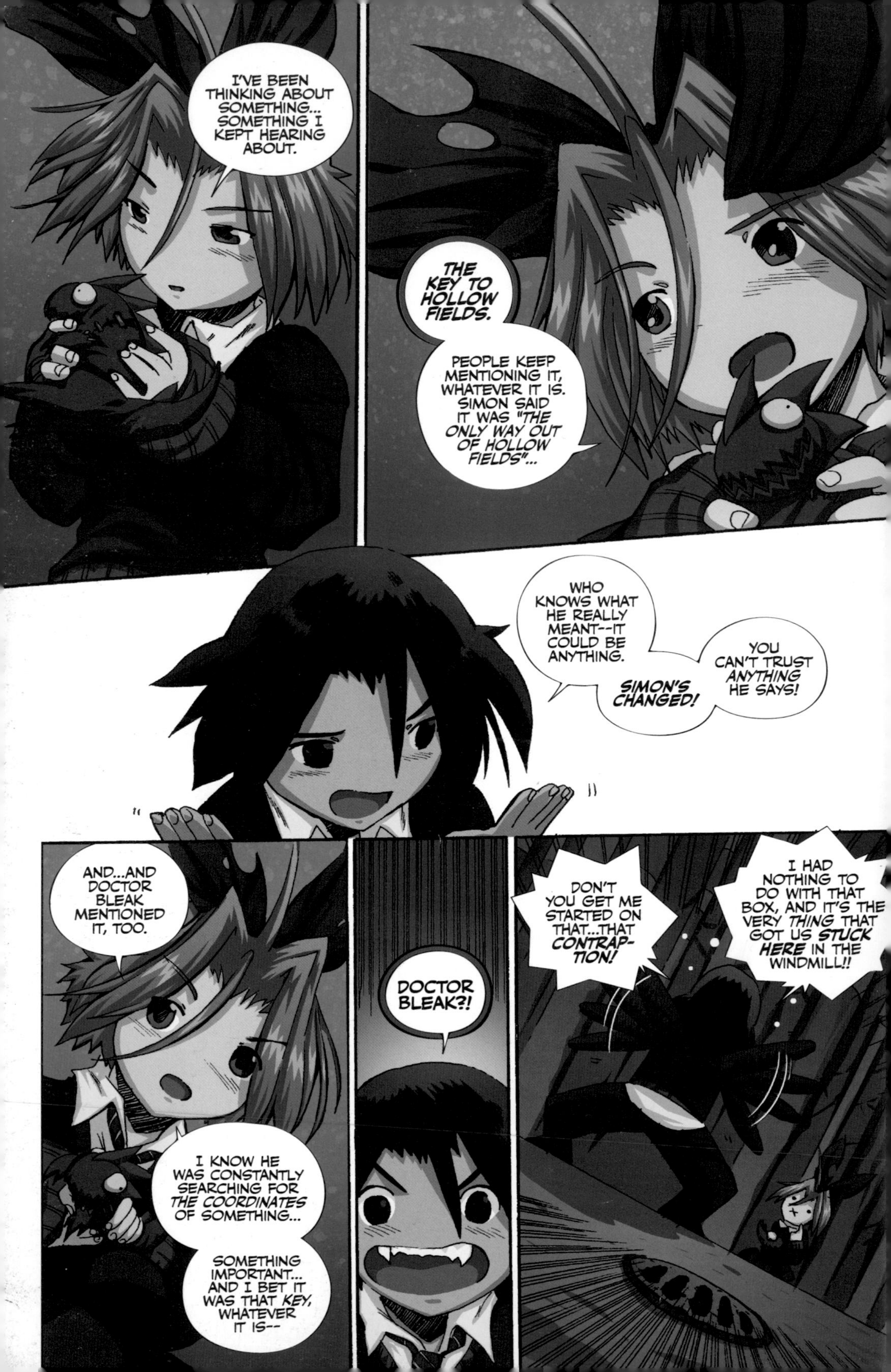

I'VE BEEN THINKING ABOUT SOMETHING... SOMETHING I KEPT HEARING ABOUT.
THE KEY TO HOLLOW FIELDS.
PEOPLE KEEP MENTIONING IT, WHATEVER IT IS. SIMON SAID IT WAS "THE ONLY WAY OUT OF HOLLOW FIELDS"...
WHO KNOWS WHAT HE REALLY MEANT--IT COULD BE ANYTHING.
SIMON'S CHANGED!
YOU CAN'T TRUST ANYTHING HE SAYS!
AND...AND DOCTOR BLEAK MENTIONED IT, TOO.
I KNOW HE WAS CONSTANTLY SEARCHING FOR THE COORDINATES OF SOMETHING...
SOMETHING IMPORTANT... AND I BET IT WAS THAT KEY, WHATEVER IT IS--
DOCTOR BLEAK?!
DON'T YOU GET ME STARTED ON THAT...THAT CONTRAPTION!
I HAD NOTHING TO DO WITH THAT BOX, AND IT'S THE VERY THING THAT GOT US STUCK HERE IN THE WINDMILL!!

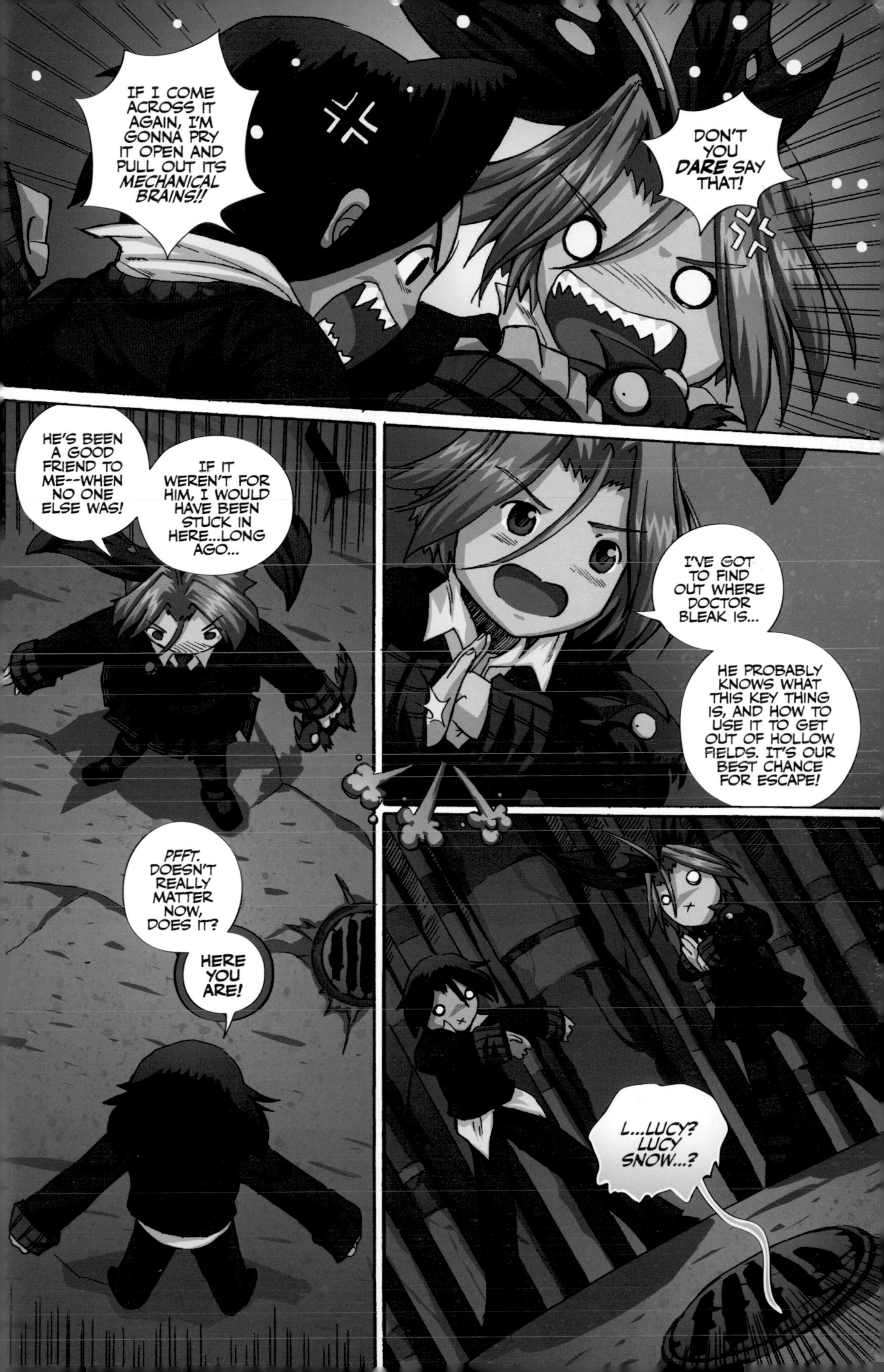
IF I COME ACROSS IT AGAIN, I'M GONNA PRY IT OPEN AND PULL OUT ITS *MECHANICAL BRAINS!!*
DON'T YOU ***DARE*** SAY THAT!
HE'S BEEN A GOOD FRIEND TO ME--WHEN NO ONE ELSE WAS!
IF IT WEREN'T FOR HIM, I WOULD HAVE BEEN STUCK IN HERE...LONG AGO...
I'VE GOT TO FIND OUT WHERE DOCTOR BLEAK IS...
HE PROBABLY KNOWS WHAT THIS KEY THING IS, AND HOW TO USE IT TO GET OUT OF HOLLOW FIELDS. IT'S OUR BEST CHANCE FOR ESCAPE!
PFFT. DOESN'T REALLY MATTER NOW, DOES IT?
HERE YOU ARE!
L...LUCY? LUCY SNOW...?

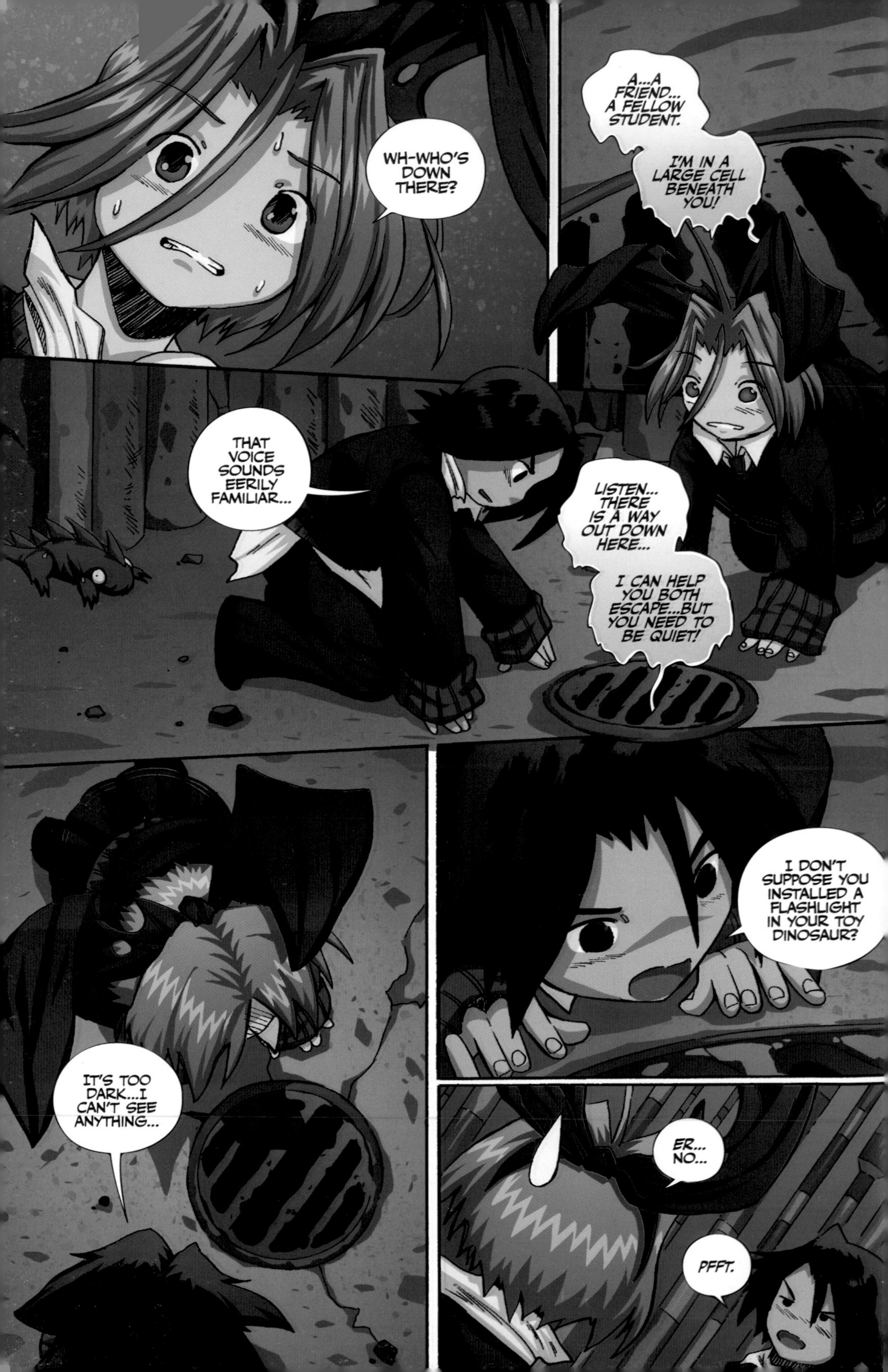
WH-WHO'S DOWN THERE?
A...A FRIEND... A FELLOW STUDENT.
I'M IN A LARGE CELL BENEATH YOU!
THAT VOICE SOUNDS EERILY FAMILIAR...
LISTEN... THERE IS A WAY OUT DOWN HERE...
I CAN HELP YOU BOTH ESCAPE...BUT YOU NEED TO BE QUIET!
IT'S TOO DARK...I CAN'T SEE ANYTHING...
I DON'T SUPPOSE YOU INSTALLED A FLASHLIGHT IN YOUR TOY DINOSAUR?
ER... NO...
PFFT.

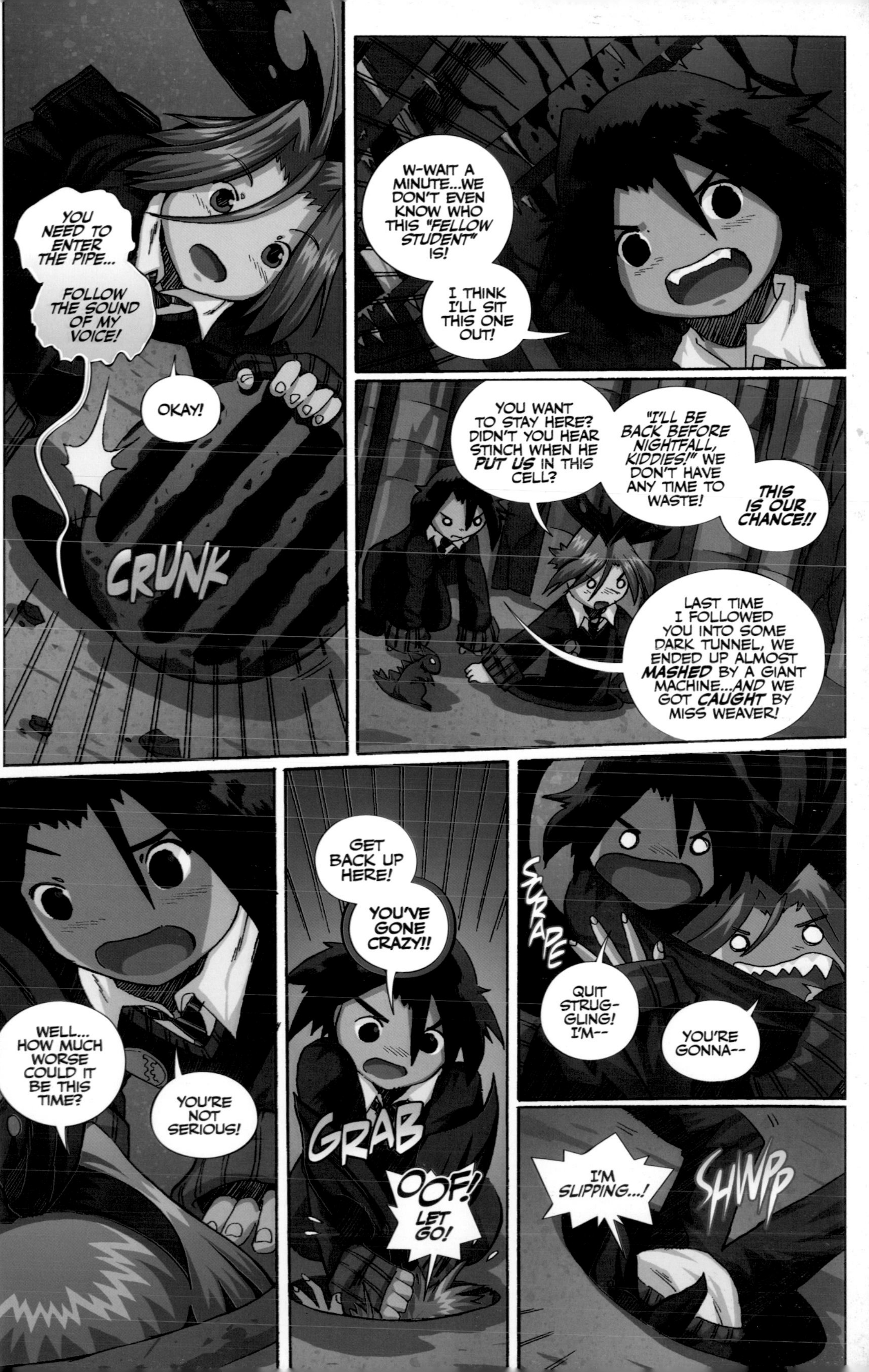
YOU NEED TO ENTER THE PIPE...
FOLLOW THE SOUND OF MY VOICE!
OKAY!
CRUNK
W-WAIT A MINUTE...WE DON'T EVEN KNOW WHO THIS "FELLOW STUDENT" IS!
I THINK I'LL SIT THIS ONE OUT!
YOU WANT TO STAY HERE? DIDN'T YOU HEAR STINCH WHEN HE PUT US IN THIS CELL?
"I'LL BE BACK BEFORE NIGHTFALL, KIDDIES!" WE DON'T HAVE ANY TIME TO WASTE!
THIS IS OUR CHANCE!!
LAST TIME I FOLLOWED YOU INTO SOME DARK TUNNEL, WE ENDED UP ALMOST MASHED BY A GIANT MACHINE...AND WE GOT CAUGHT BY MISS WEAVER!
WELL... HOW MUCH WORSE COULD IT BE THIS TIME?
YOU'RE NOT SERIOUS!
GET BACK UP HERE!
YOU'VE GONE CRAZY!!
GRAB
OOF! LET GO!
SCRAPE
QUIT STRUG-GLING! I'M--
YOU'RE GONNA--
I'M SLIPPING...!
SHWPP

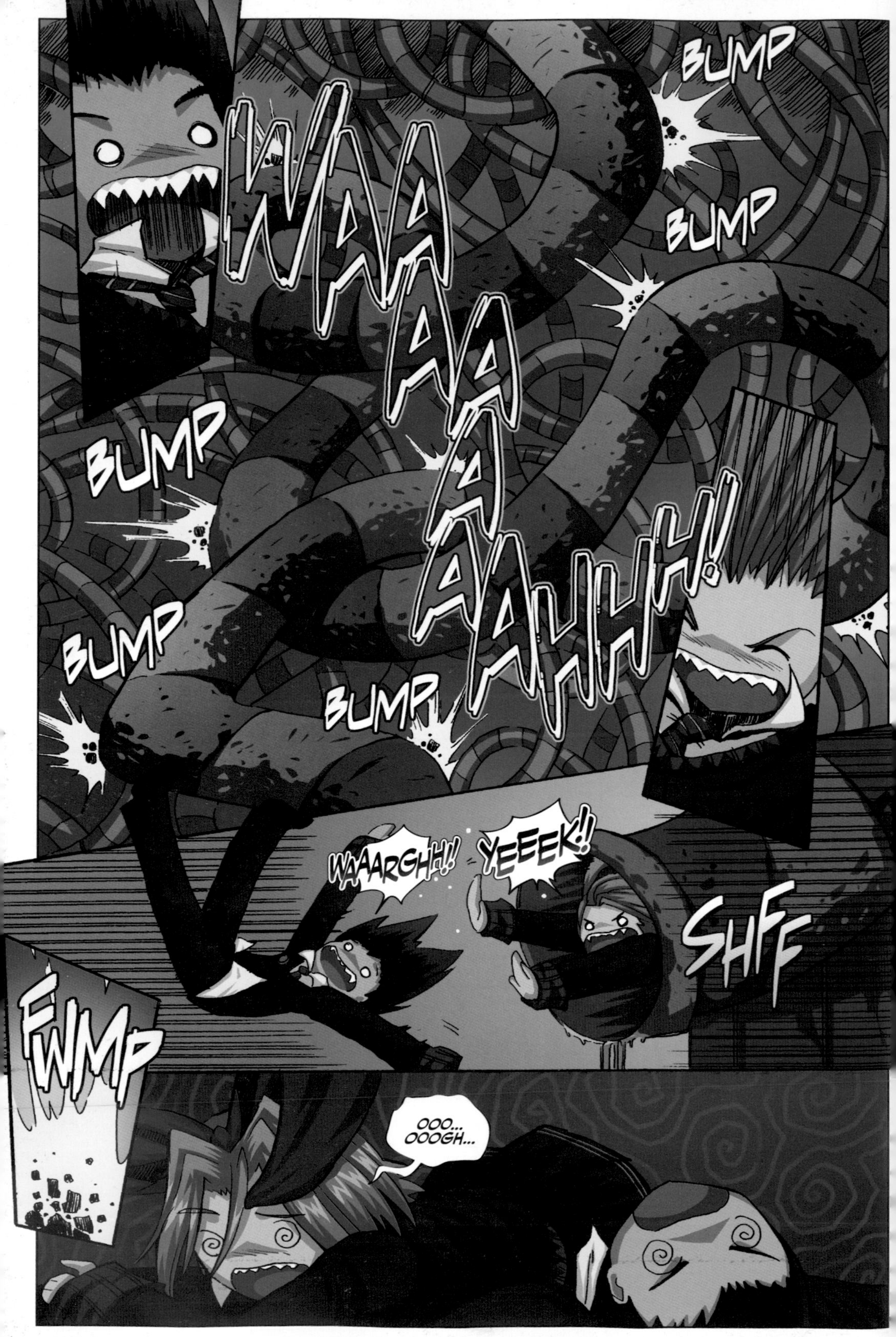
WAAAAAAAAAAHHH!
BUMP
BUMP
BUMP
BUMP
BUMP
WAAARGHH!!
YEEEK!!
SHFF
FWMP
OOO...
OOOGH...

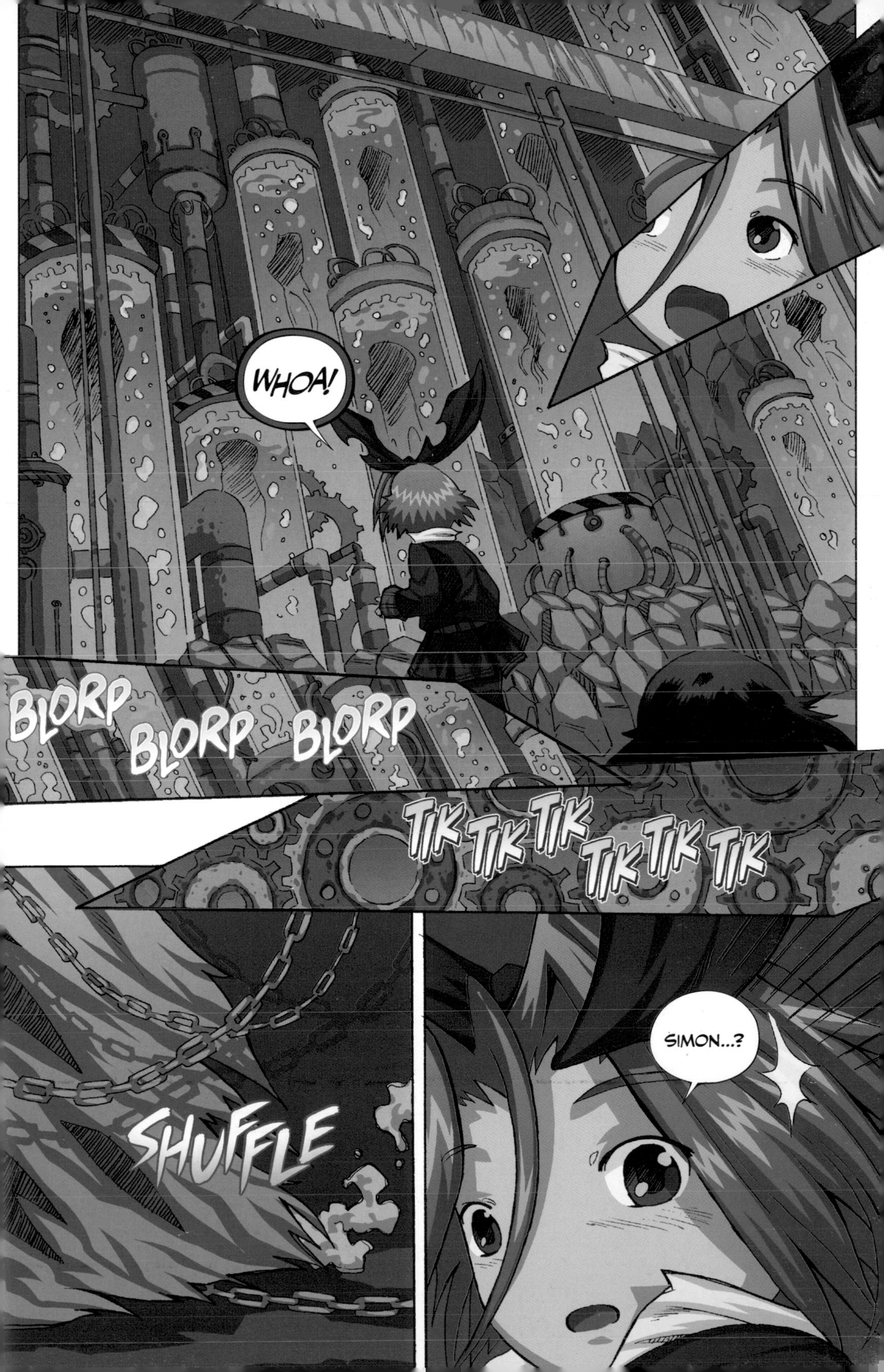
WHOA!
BLORP BLORP BLORP
TIK TIK TIK TIK TIK TIK
SHUFFLE
SIMON...?

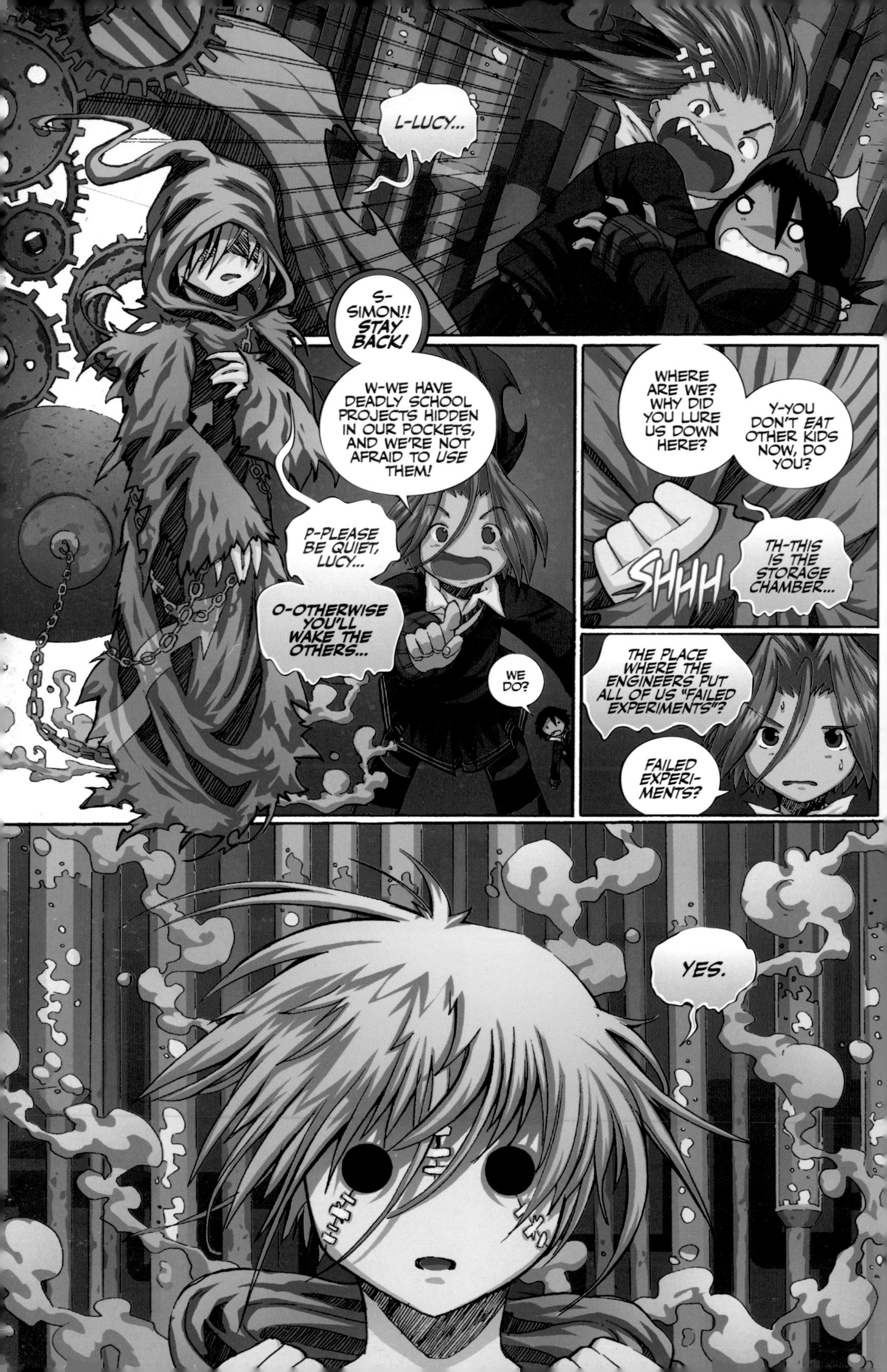
L-LUCY...
S-SIMON!! STAY BACK!
W-WE HAVE DEADLY SCHOOL PROJECTS HIDDEN IN OUR POCKETS, AND WE'RE NOT AFRAID TO USE THEM!
P-PLEASE BE QUIET, LUCY...
O-OTHERWISE YOU'LL WAKE THE OTHERS...
WE DO?
WHERE ARE WE? WHY DID YOU LURE US DOWN HERE?
Y-YOU DON'T EAT OTHER KIDS NOW, DO YOU?
SHHH
TH-THIS IS THE STORAGE CHAMBER...
THE PLACE WHERE THE ENGINEERS PUT ALL OF US "FAILED EXPERIMENTS"?
FAILED EXPERI-MENTS?
YES.

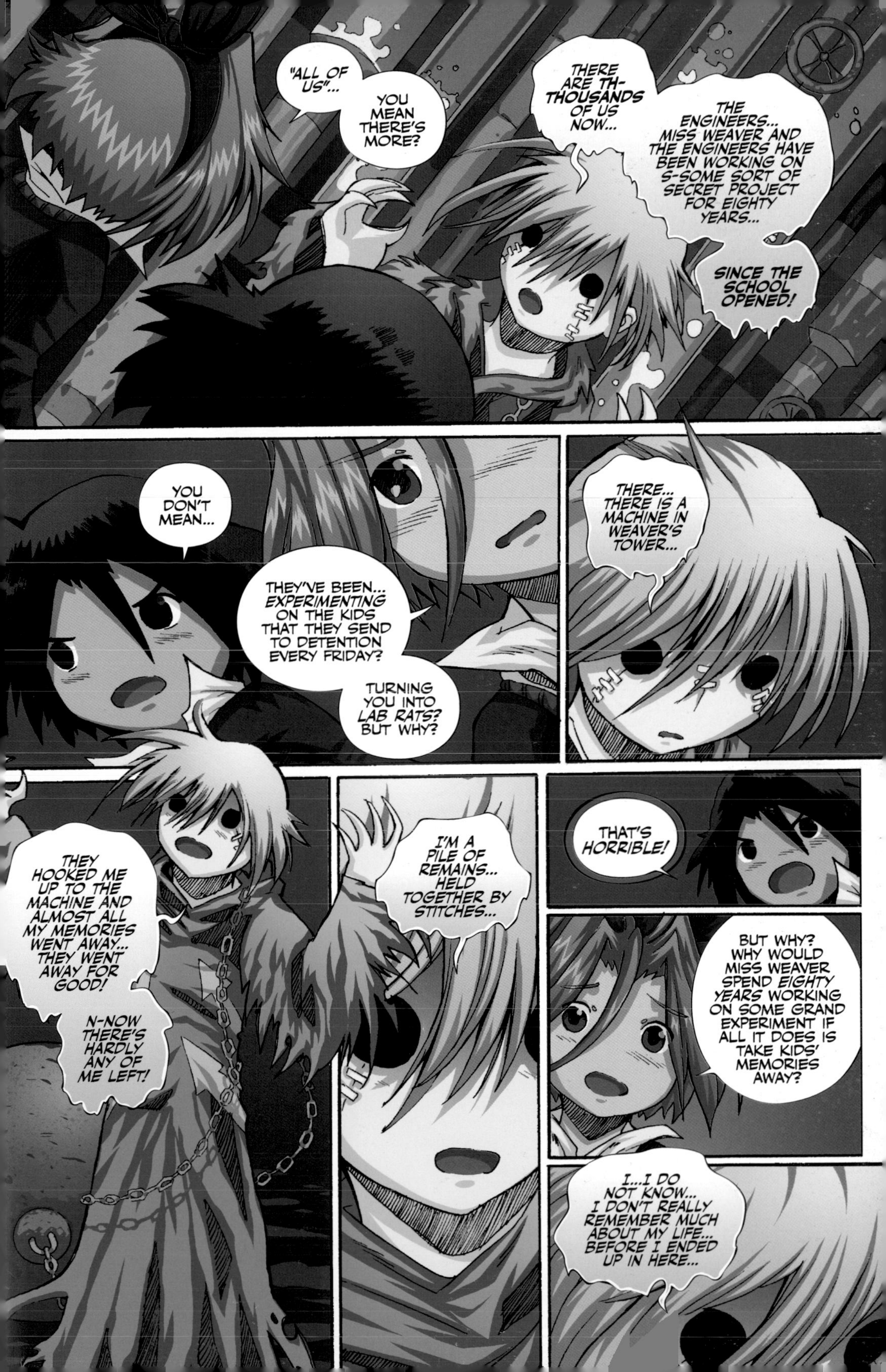
"ALL OF US"...
YOU MEAN THERE'S MORE?
THERE ARE TH-THOUSANDS OF US NOW...
THE ENGINEERS... MISS WEAVER AND THE ENGINEERS HAVE BEEN WORKING ON S-SOME SORT OF SECRET PROJECT FOR EIGHTY YEARS...
SINCE THE SCHOOL OPENED!
YOU DON'T MEAN...
THEY'VE BEEN... EXPERIMENTING ON THE KIDS THAT THEY SEND TO DETENTION EVERY FRIDAY?
TURNING YOU INTO LAB RATS? BUT WHY?
THERE... THERE IS A MACHINE IN WEAVER'S TOWER...
THEY HOOKED ME UP TO THE MACHINE AND ALMOST ALL MY MEMORIES WENT AWAY... THEY WENT AWAY FOR GOOD!
N-NOW THERE'S HARDLY ANY OF ME LEFT!
I'M A PILE OF REMAINS... HELD TOGETHER BY STITCHES...
THAT'S HORRIBLE!
BUT WHY? WHY WOULD MISS WEAVER SPEND EIGHTY YEARS WORKING ON SOME GRAND EXPERIMENT IF ALL IT DOES IS TAKE KIDS' MEMORIES AWAY?
I...I DO NOT KNOW... I DON'T REALLY REMEMBER MUCH ABOUT MY LIFE... BEFORE I ENDED UP IN HERE...

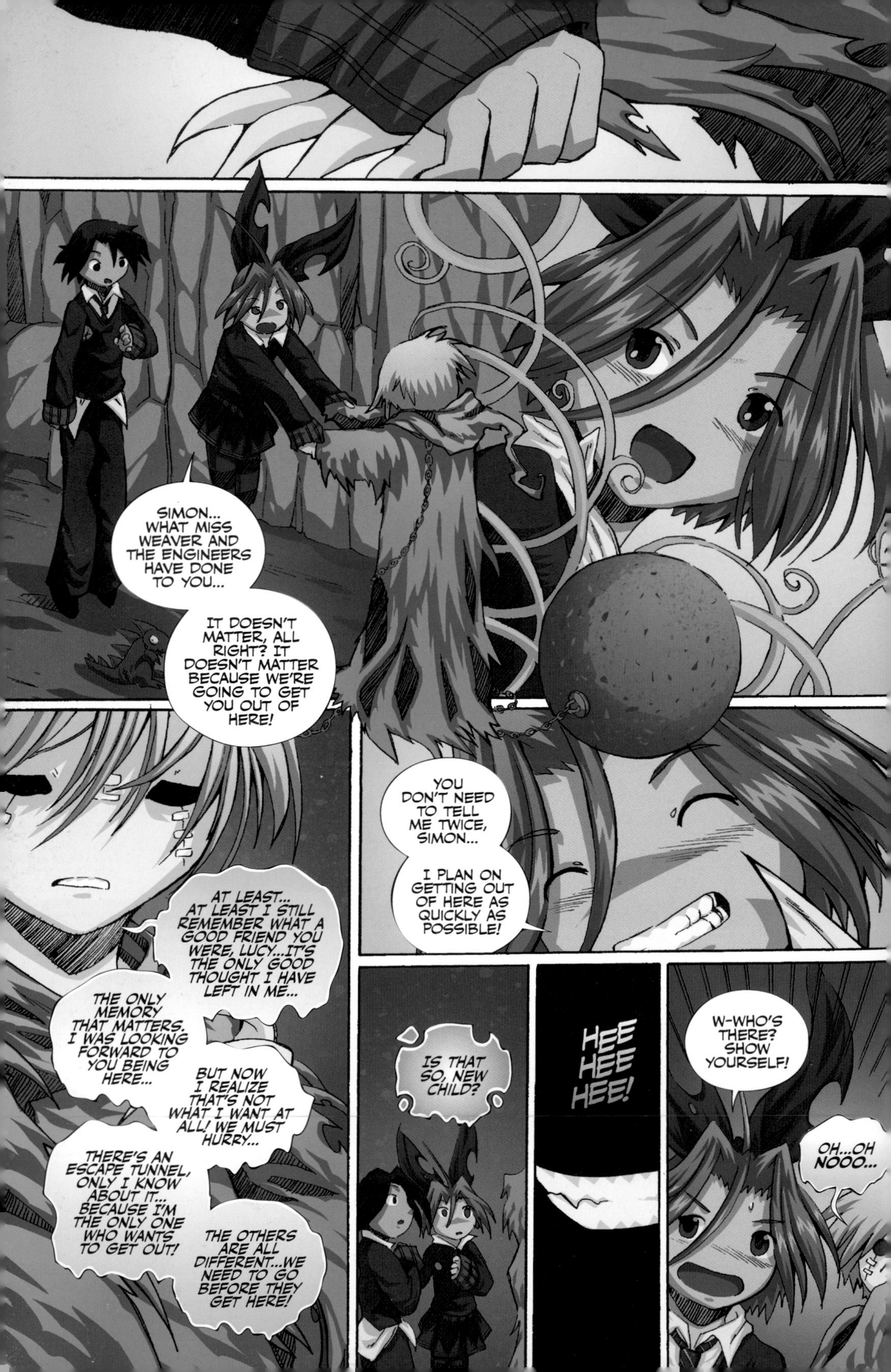
SIMON... WHAT MISS WEAVER AND THE ENGINEERS HAVE DONE TO YOU...
IT DOESN'T MATTER, ALL RIGHT? IT DOESN'T MATTER BECAUSE WE'RE GOING TO GET YOU OUT OF HERE!
AT LEAST... AT LEAST I STILL REMEMBER WHAT A GOOD FRIEND YOU WERE, LUCY...IT'S THE ONLY GOOD THOUGHT I HAVE LEFT IN ME...
THE ONLY MEMORY THAT MATTERS. I WAS LOOKING FORWARD TO YOU BEING HERE...
BUT NOW I REALIZE THAT'S NOT WHAT I WANT AT ALL! WE MUST HURRY...
THERE'S AN ESCAPE TUNNEL, ONLY I KNOW ABOUT IT... BECAUSE I'M THE ONLY ONE WHO WANTS TO GET OUT!
THE OTHERS ARE ALL DIFFERENT...WE NEED TO GO BEFORE THEY GET HERE!
YOU DON'T NEED TO TELL ME TWICE, SIMON...
I PLAN ON GETTING OUT OF HERE AS QUICKLY AS POSSIBLE!
IS THAT SO, NEW CHILD?
HEE HEE HEE!
W-WHO'S THERE? SHOW YOURSELF!
OH...OH NOOO...

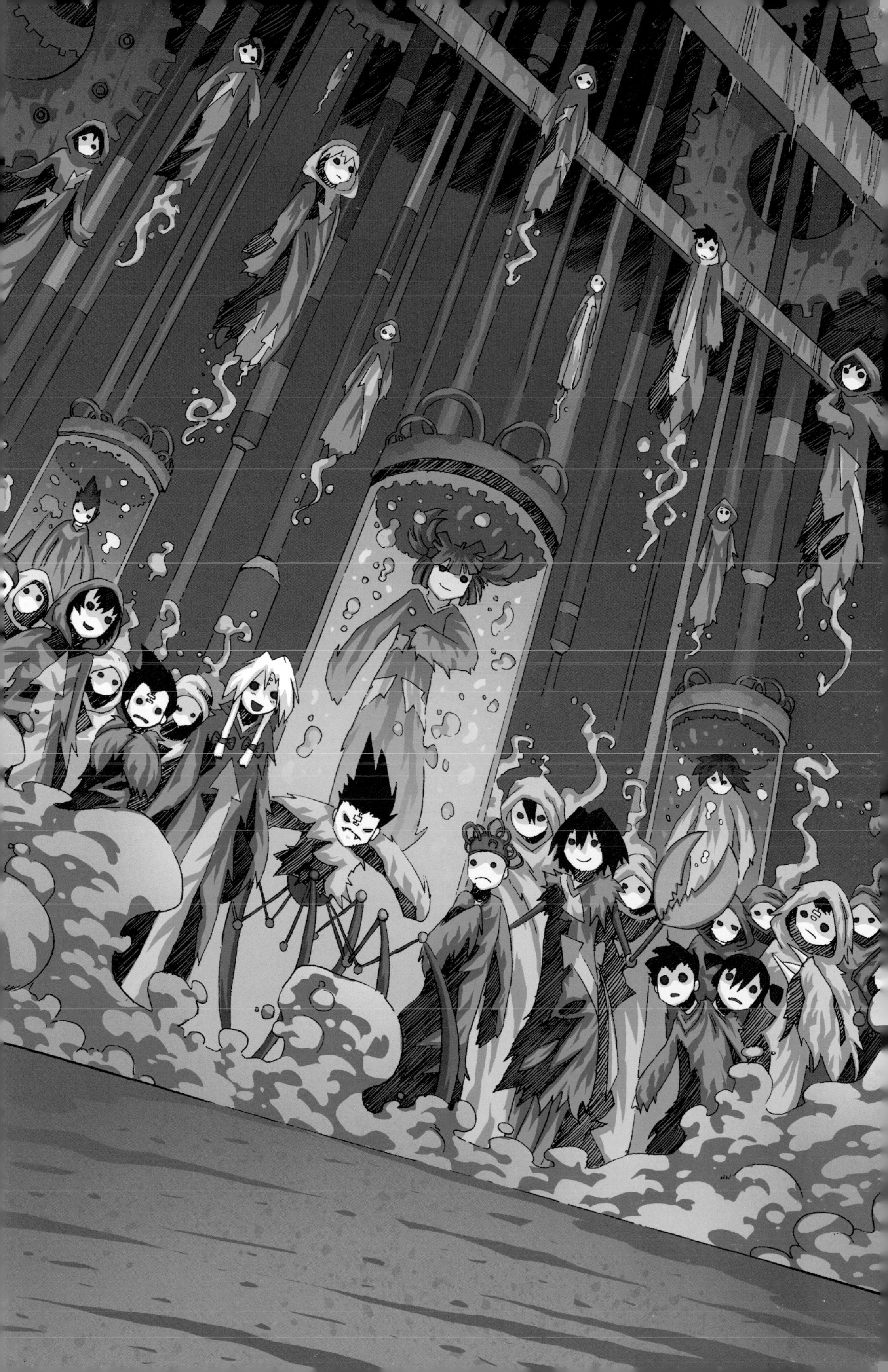

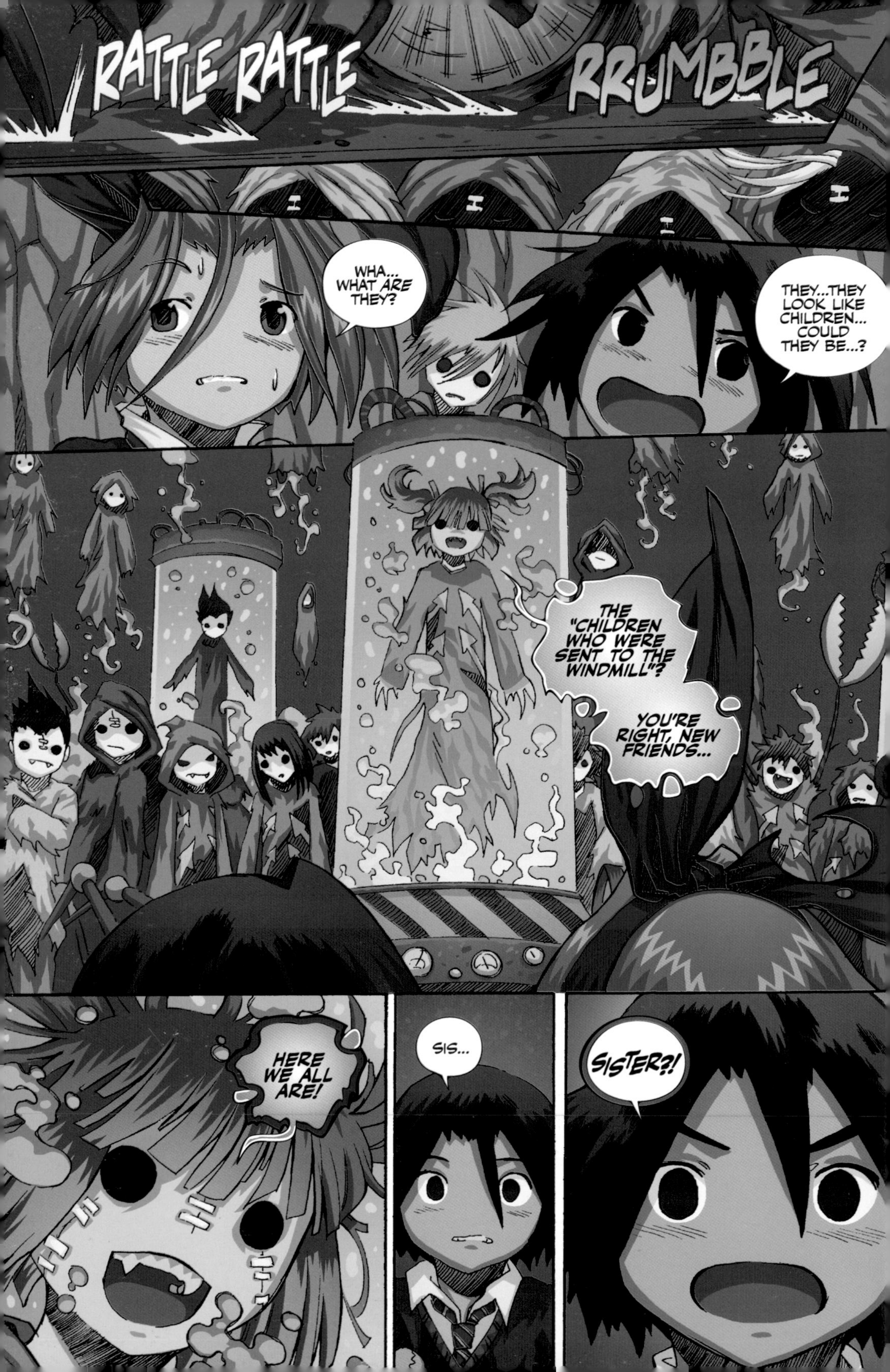
RATTLE RATTLE
RRUMBBLE
WHA... WHAT ARE THEY?
THEY...THEY LOOK LIKE CHILDREN... COULD THEY BE...?
THE "CHILDREN WHO WERE SENT TO THE WINDMILL"?
YOU'RE RIGHT, NEW FRIENDS...
HERE WE ALL ARE!
SIS...
SISTER?!

CHAPTER ELEVEN

Miss Weaver's Personal Experiment

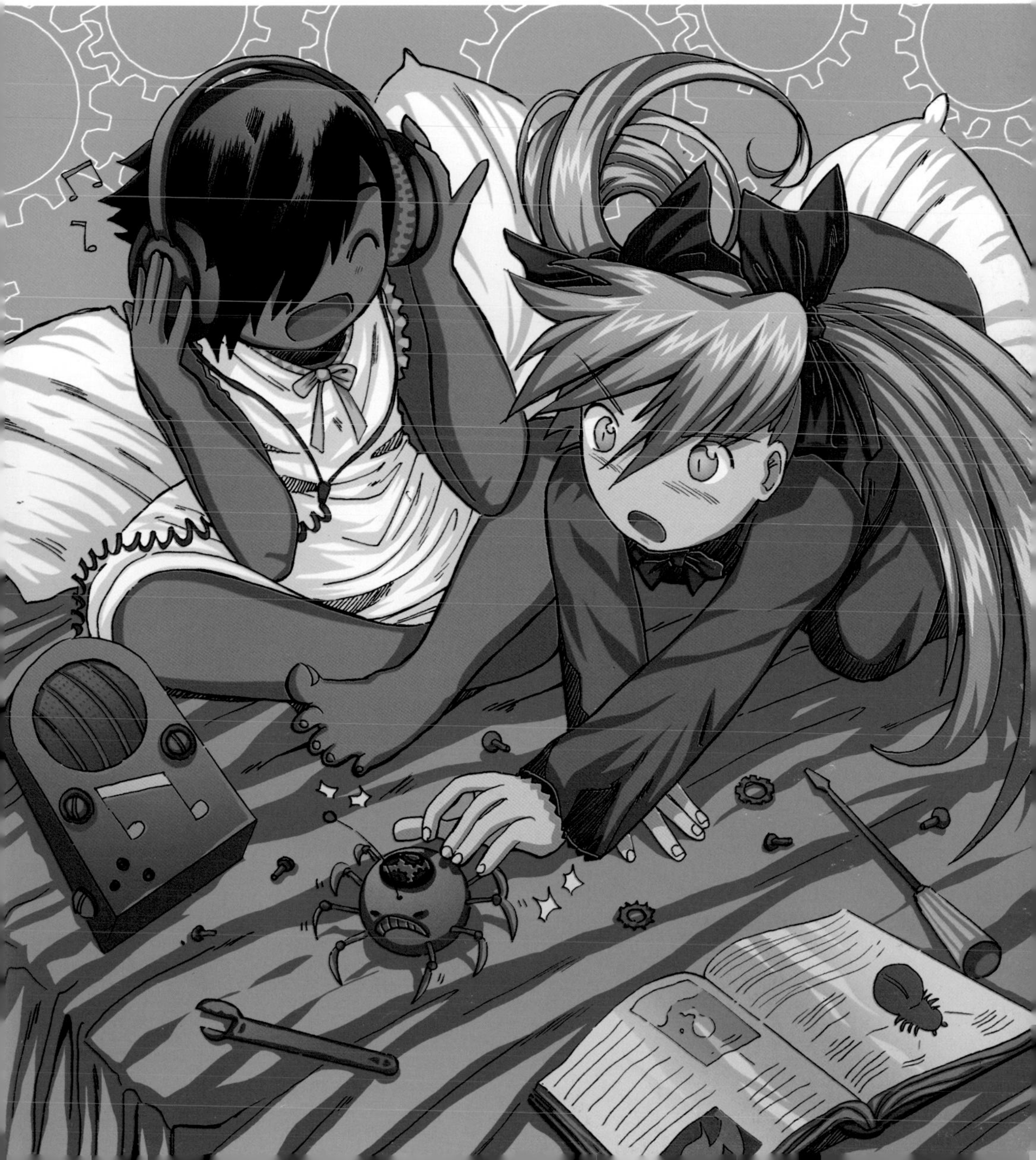

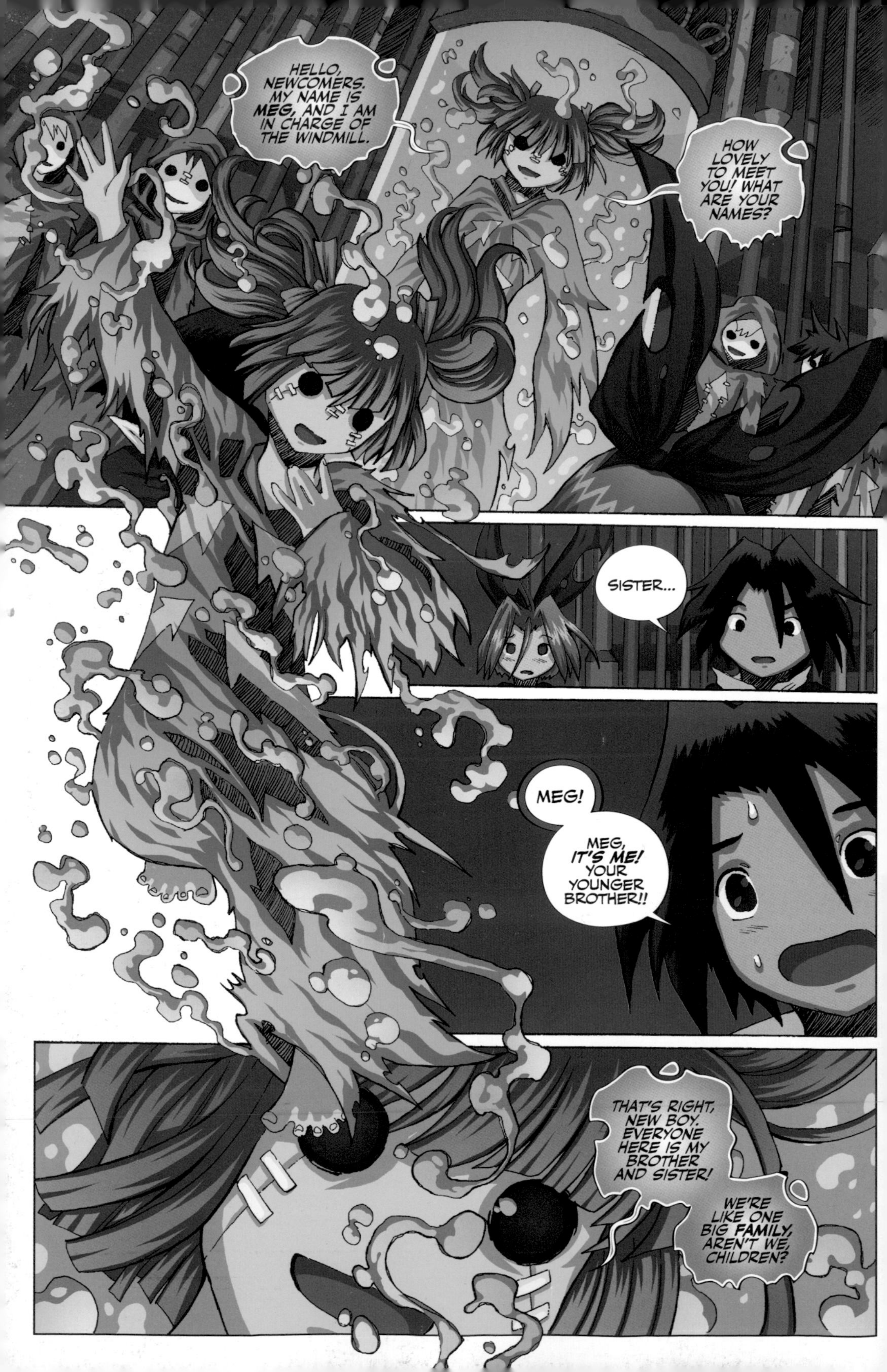
HELLO, NEWCOMERS. MY NAME IS MEG, AND I AM IN CHARGE OF THE WINDMILL.
HOW LOVELY TO MEET YOU! WHAT ARE YOUR NAMES?
SISTER...
MEG!
MEG, IT'S ME! YOUR YOUNGER BROTHER!!
THAT'S RIGHT, NEW BOY. EVERYONE HERE IS MY BROTHER AND SISTER!
WE'RE LIKE ONE BIG FAMILY, AREN'T WE, CHILDREN?

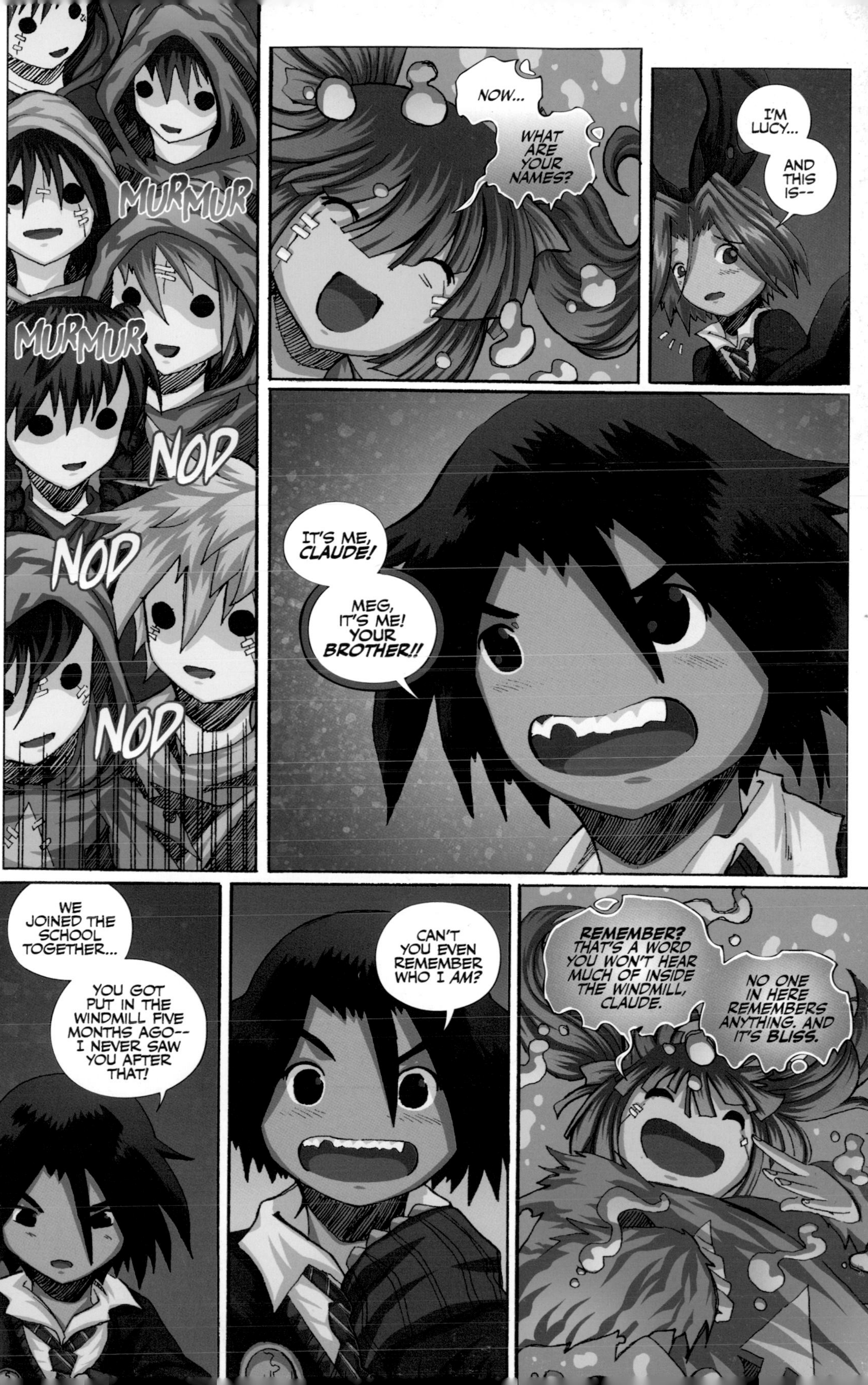
MURMUR
MURMUR
NOD
NOD
NOD
NOW...
WHAT ARE YOUR NAMES?
I'M LUCY...
AND THIS IS--
IT'S ME, CLAUDE!
MEG, IT'S ME! YOUR BROTHER!!
WE JOINED THE SCHOOL TOGETHER...
YOU GOT PUT IN THE WINDMILL FIVE MONTHS AGO-- I NEVER SAW YOU AFTER THAT!
CAN'T YOU EVEN REMEMBER WHO I AM?
REMEMBER? THAT'S A WORD YOU WON'T HEAR MUCH OF INSIDE THE WINDMILL, CLAUDE.
NO ONE IN HERE REMEMBERS ANYTHING. AND IT'S BLISS.

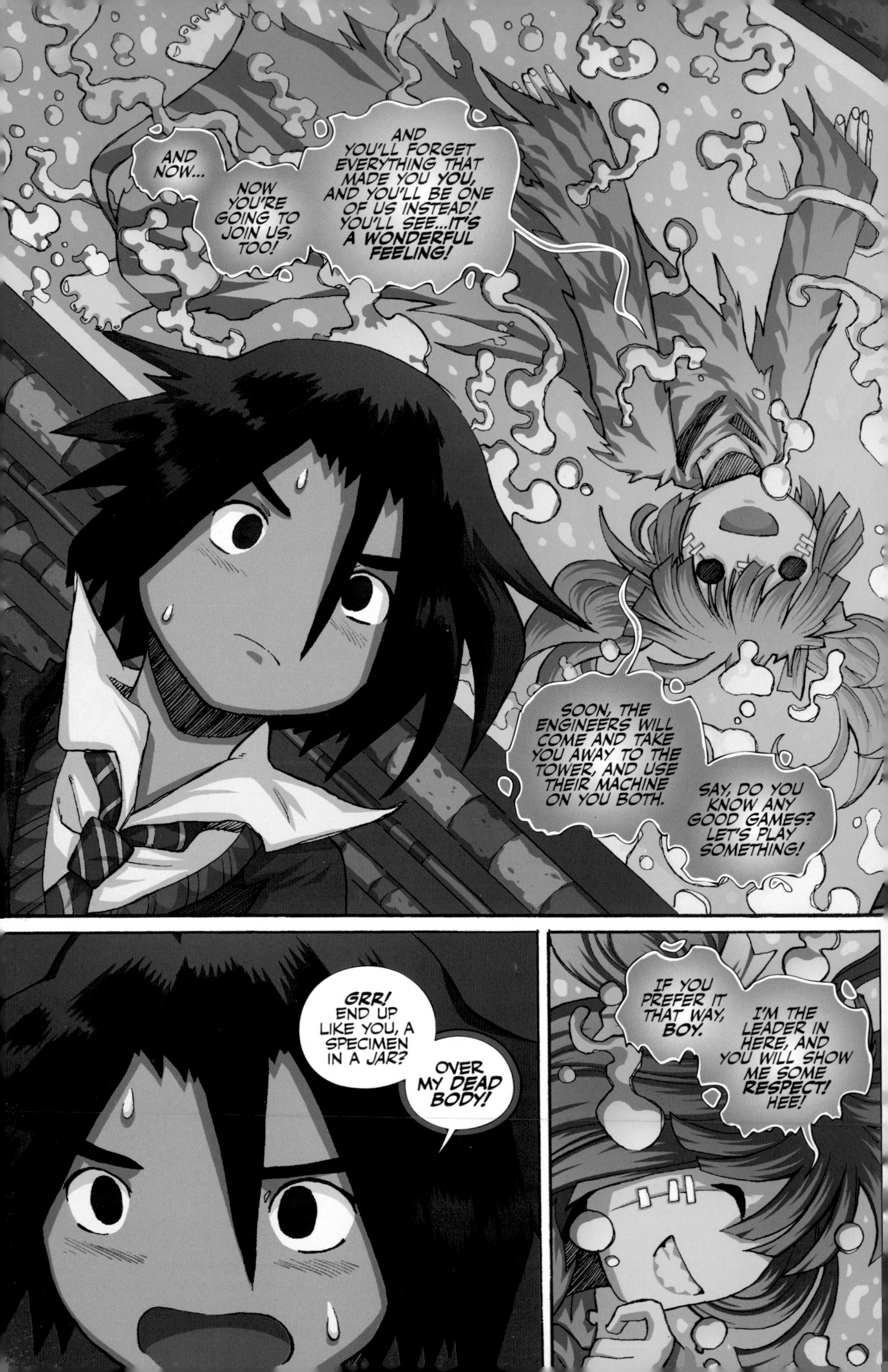
AND NOW...
NOW YOU'RE GOING TO JOIN US, TOO!
AND YOU'LL FORGET EVERYTHING THAT MADE YOU YOU, AND YOU'LL BE ONE OF US INSTEAD! YOU'LL SEE...IT'S A WONDERFUL FEELING!
SOON, THE ENGINEERS WILL COME AND TAKE YOU AWAY TO THE TOWER, AND USE THEIR MACHINE ON YOU BOTH.
SAY, DO YOU KNOW ANY GOOD GAMES? LET'S PLAY SOMETHING!
GRR! END UP LIKE YOU, A SPECIMEN IN A JAR?
OVER MY DEAD BODY!
IF YOU PREFER IT THAT WAY, BOY.
I'M THE LEADER IN HERE, AND YOU WILL SHOW ME SOME RESPECT! HEE!

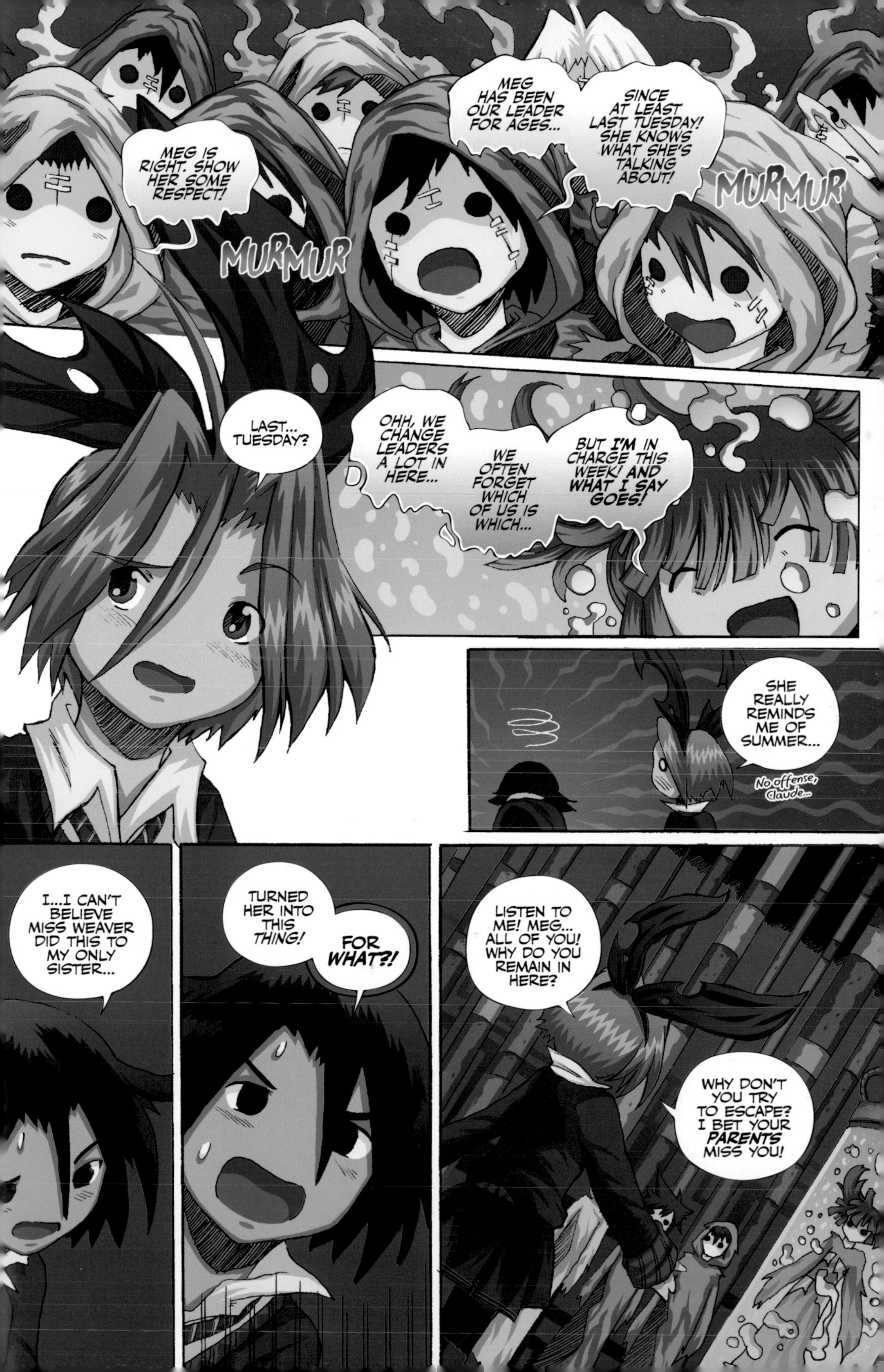

MEG IS RIGHT. SHOW HER SOME RESPECT!
MURMUR
MEG HAS BEEN OUR LEADER FOR AGES...
SINCE AT LEAST LAST TUESDAY! SHE KNOWS WHAT SHE'S TALKING ABOUT!
MURMUR
LAST... TUESDAY?
OHH, WE CHANGE LEADERS A LOT IN HERE...
WE OFTEN FORGET WHICH OF US IS WHICH...
BUT **I'M** IN CHARGE THIS WEEK! **AND WHAT I SAY GOES!**
SHE REALLY REMINDS ME OF SUMMER...
No offense, Claude...
I...I CAN'T BELIEVE MISS WEAVER DID THIS TO MY ONLY SISTER...
TURNED HER INTO THIS *THING!*
FOR *WHAT?!*
LISTEN TO ME! MEG... ALL OF YOU! WHY DO YOU REMAIN IN HERE?
WHY DON'T YOU TRY TO ESCAPE? I BET YOUR ***PARENTS*** MISS YOU!

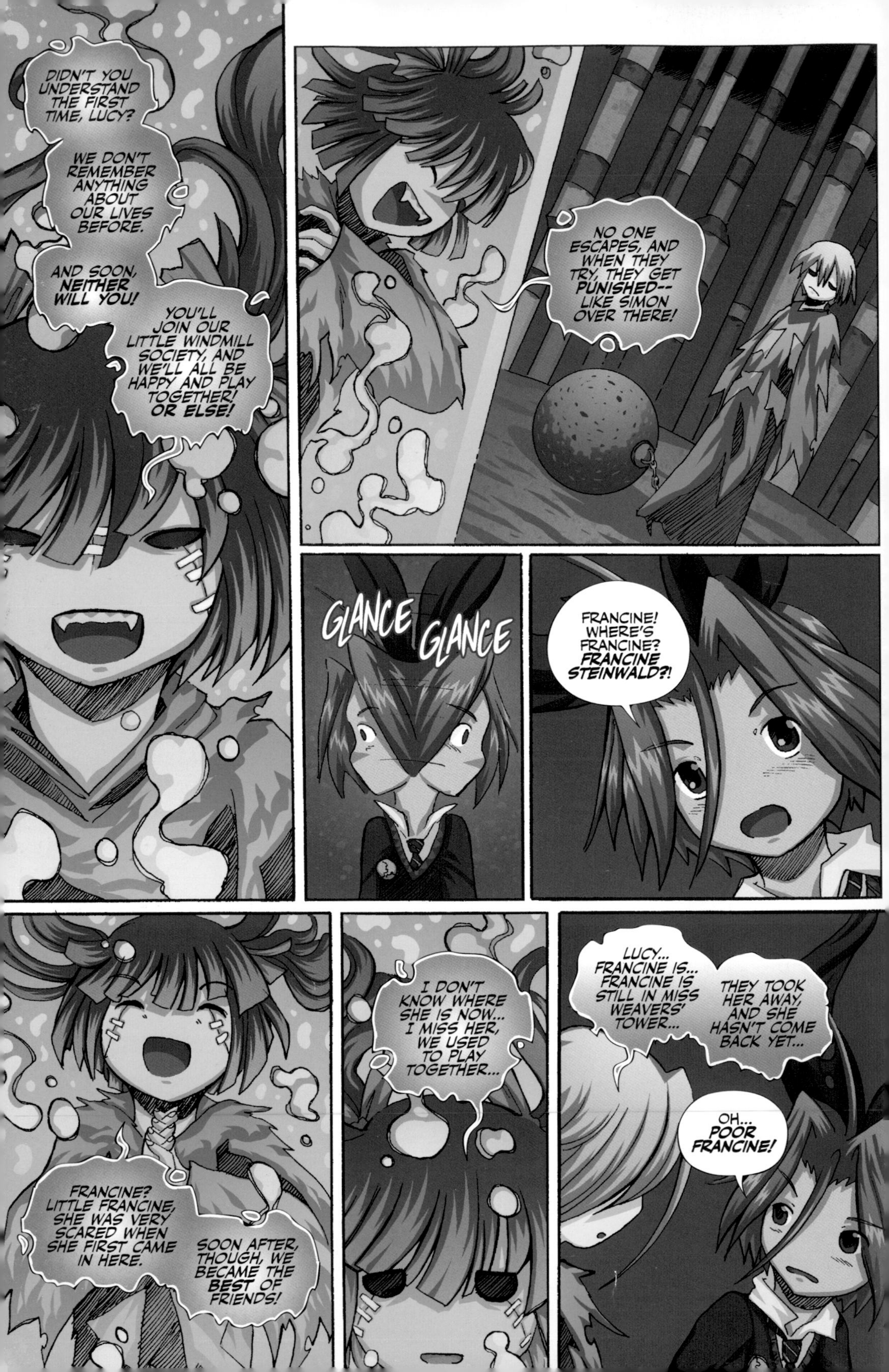
DIDN'T YOU UNDERSTAND THE FIRST TIME, LUCY?
WE DON'T REMEMBER ANYTHING ABOUT OUR LIVES BEFORE.
AND SOON, **NEITHER WILL YOU!**
YOU'LL JOIN OUR LITTLE WINDMILL SOCIETY, AND WE'LL ALL BE HAPPY AND PLAY TOGETHER! **OR ELSE!**
NO ONE ESCAPES, AND WHEN THEY TRY, THEY GET **PUNISHED**-- LIKE SIMON OVER THERE!
GLANCE GLANCE
FRANCINE! WHERE'S FRANCINE? **FRANCINE STEINWALD?!**
FRANCINE? LITTLE FRANCINE, SHE WAS VERY SCARED WHEN SHE FIRST CAME IN HERE.
SOON AFTER, THOUGH, WE BECAME THE **BEST** OF FRIENDS!
I DON'T KNOW WHERE SHE IS NOW... I MISS HER, WE USED TO PLAY TOGETHER...
LUCY... FRANCINE IS... FRANCINE IS STILL IN MISS WEAVERS' TOWER...
THEY TOOK HER AWAY, AND SHE HASN'T COME BACK YET...
OH... **POOR FRANCINE!**

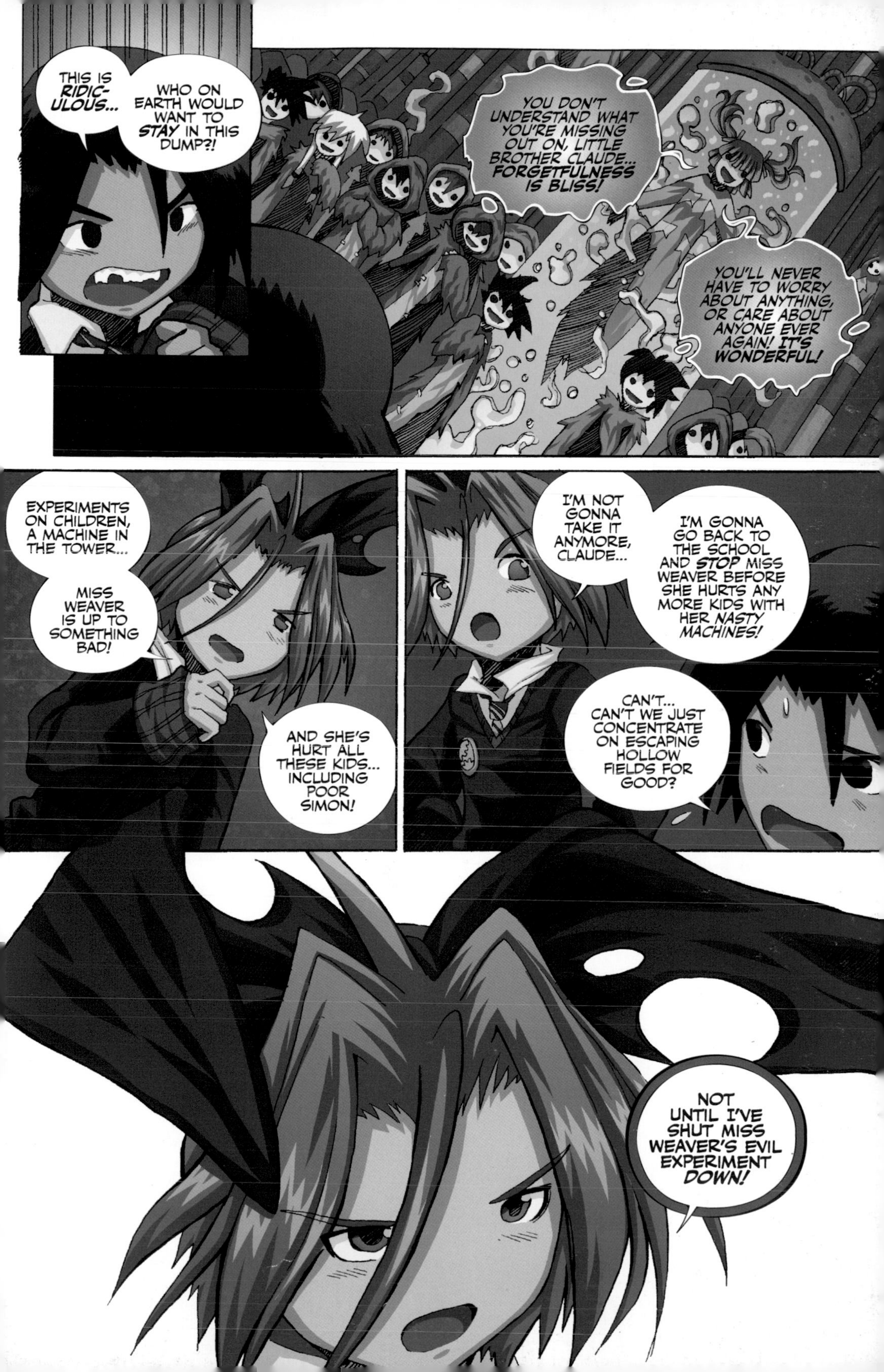
THIS IS RIDIC-ULOUS...
WHO ON EARTH WOULD WANT TO STAY IN THIS DUMP?!
YOU DON'T UNDERSTAND WHAT YOU'RE MISSING OUT ON, LITTLE BROTHER CLAUDE... FORGETFULNESS IS BLISS!
YOU'LL NEVER HAVE TO WORRY ABOUT ANYTHING, OR CARE ABOUT ANYONE EVER AGAIN! IT'S WONDERFUL!
EXPERIMENTS ON CHILDREN, A MACHINE IN THE TOWER...
MISS WEAVER IS UP TO SOMETHING BAD!
AND SHE'S HURT ALL THESE KIDS... INCLUDING POOR SIMON!
I'M NOT GONNA TAKE IT ANYMORE, CLAUDE...
I'M GONNA GO BACK TO THE SCHOOL AND STOP MISS WEAVER BEFORE SHE HURTS ANY MORE KIDS WITH HER NASTY MACHINES!
CAN'T... CAN'T WE JUST CONCENTRATE ON ESCAPING HOLLOW FIELDS FOR GOOD?
NOT UNTIL I'VE SHUT MISS WEAVER'S EVIL EXPERIMENT DOWN!

SIMON... BEFORE, WHEN WE MET INSIDE THE SCHOOL...

YOU MENTIONED SOMETHING ABOUT A KEY--

SIMON!

ERK!

DID YOU TELL THIS GIRL ABOUT THE KEY TO HOLLOW FIELDS?

YOU'VE BEEN A BAD BOY...YES YOU HAVE, SIMON!

THE KEY IS A SECRET... A BIG, BIG SECRET!

EVEN YOU SHOULDN'T KNOW ABOUT IT, SIMON...

YOU'VE BEEN EAVESDROPPING ON THE ENGINEERS WHEN THEY VISIT OUR WINDMILL, YES YOU HAVE!

YOU'RE IN EXTRA BIG TROUBLE NOW, SIMON!

MEG... PLEASE...

DO YOU KNOW MORE ABOUT THIS KEY? WHERE CAN WE FIND IT?

IF IT'S REALLY POWERFUL ENOUGH TO STOP MISS WEAVER SOMEHOW... I'M GOING TO NEED IT...

"STOP MISS WEAVER"?

WHY, MISS WEAVER'S EXPERIMENTS PROVIDE US WITH A NEW BROTHER OR SISTER EVERY WEEK!

WHY WOULD WE WANT TO DO THAT?

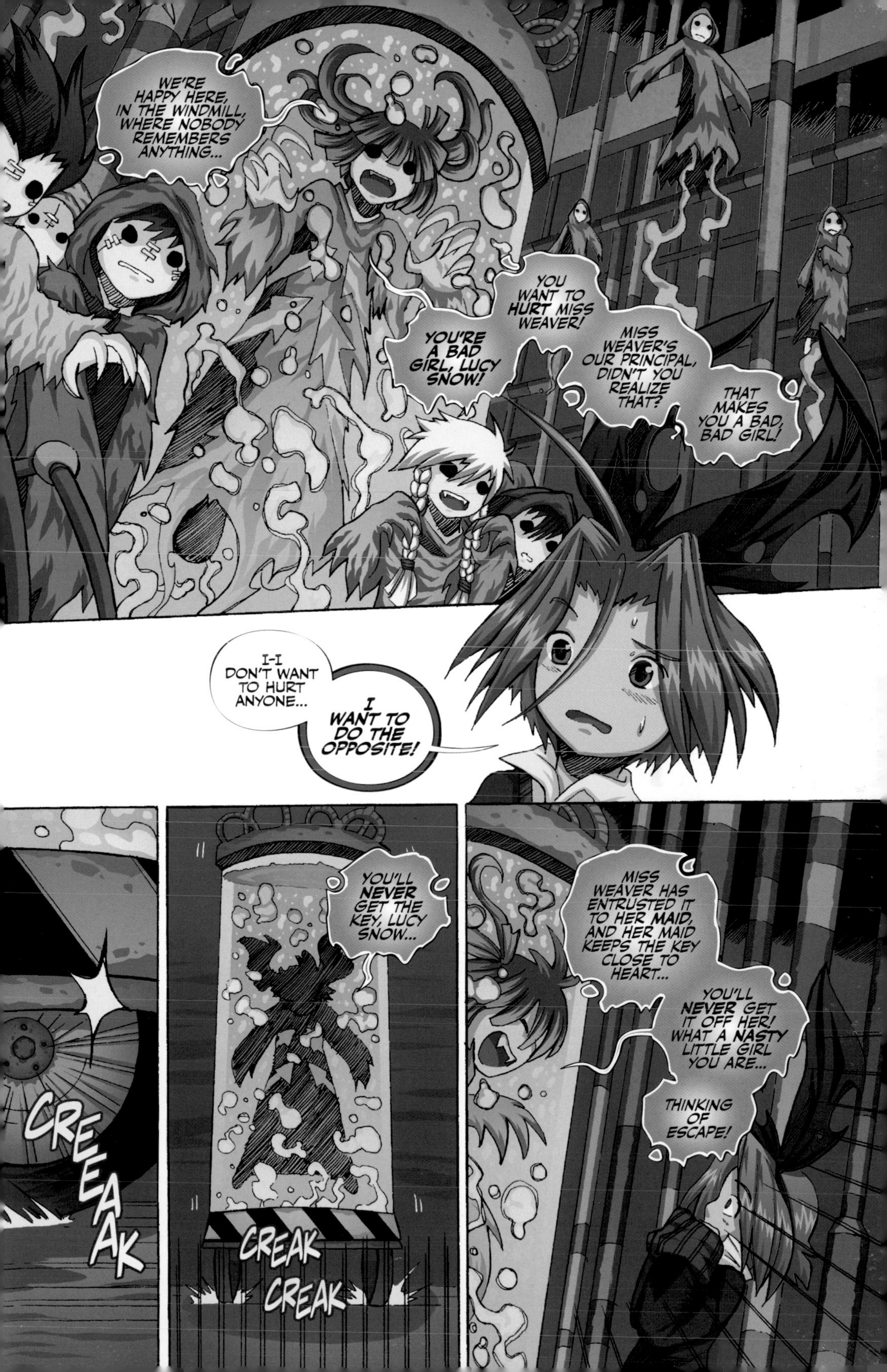
WE'RE HAPPY HERE, IN THE WINDMILL, WHERE NOBODY REMEMBERS ANYTHING...
YOU'RE A BAD GIRL, LUCY SNOW!
YOU WANT TO HURT MISS WEAVER!
MISS WEAVER'S OUR PRINCIPAL, DIDN'T YOU REALIZE THAT?
THAT MAKES YOU A BAD, BAD GIRL!
I-I DON'T WANT TO HURT ANYONE...
I WANT TO DO THE OPPOSITE!
CREEAAK
YOU'LL NEVER GET THE KEY, LUCY SNOW...
CREAK
CREAK
MISS WEAVER HAS ENTRUSTED IT TO HER MAID, AND HER MAID KEEPS THE KEY CLOSE TO HEART...
YOU'LL NEVER GET IT OFF HER! WHAT A NASTY LITTLE GIRL YOU ARE...
THINKING OF ESCAPE!

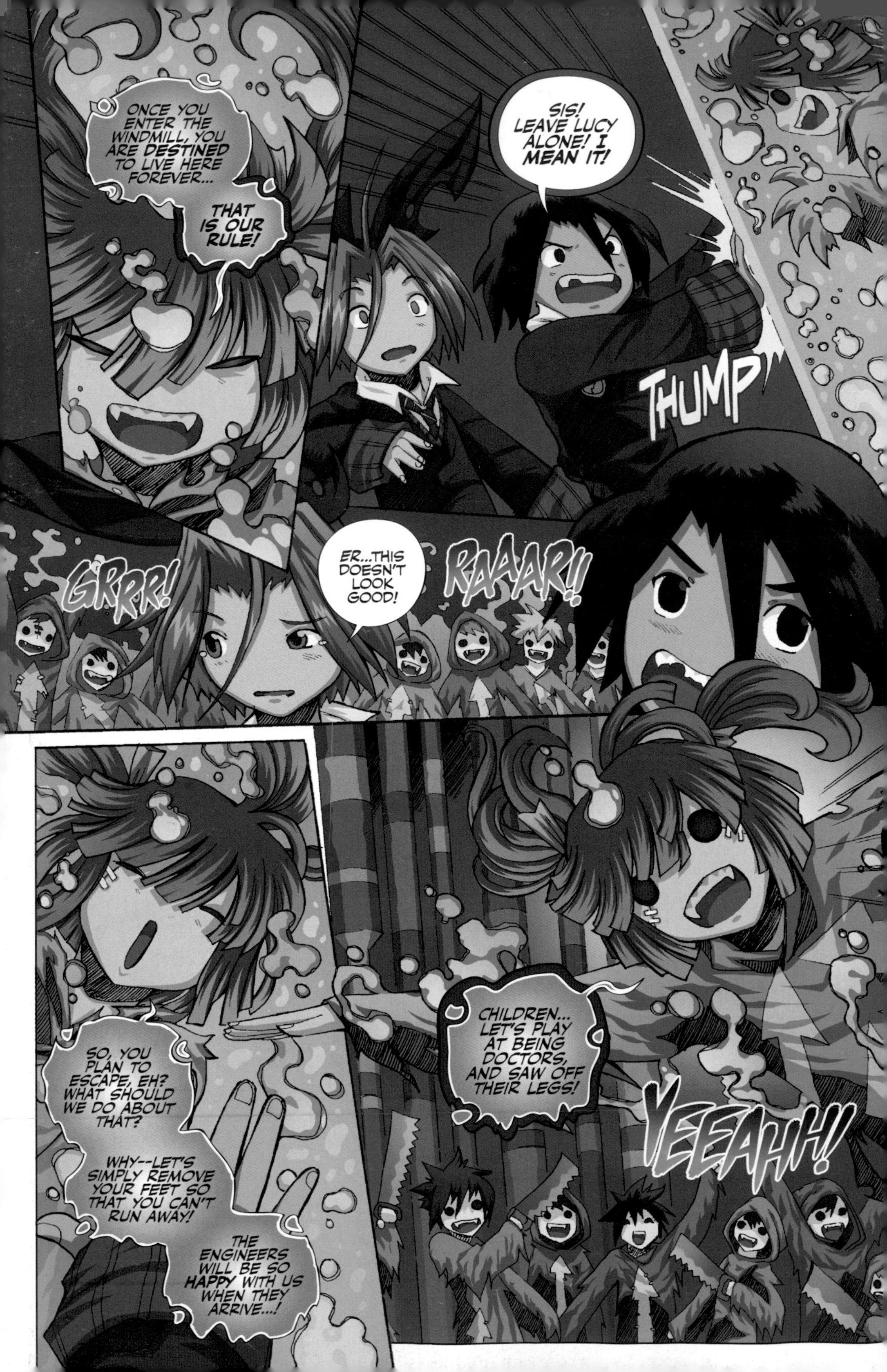
ONCE YOU ENTER THE WINDMILL, YOU ARE DESTINED TO LIVE HERE FOREVER...
THAT IS OUR RULE!
SIS! LEAVE LUCY ALONE! I MEAN IT!
THUMP
GRRR!
ER...THIS DOESN'T LOOK GOOD!
RAAAR!!
SO, YOU PLAN TO ESCAPE, EH? WHAT SHOULD WE DO ABOUT THAT?
WHY--LET'S SIMPLY REMOVE YOUR FEET SO THAT YOU CAN'T RUN AWAY!
THE ENGINEERS WILL BE SO HAPPY WITH US WHEN THEY ARRIVE...!
CHILDREN... LET'S PLAY AT BEING DOCTORS, AND SAW OFF THEIR LEGS!
YEEAHH!

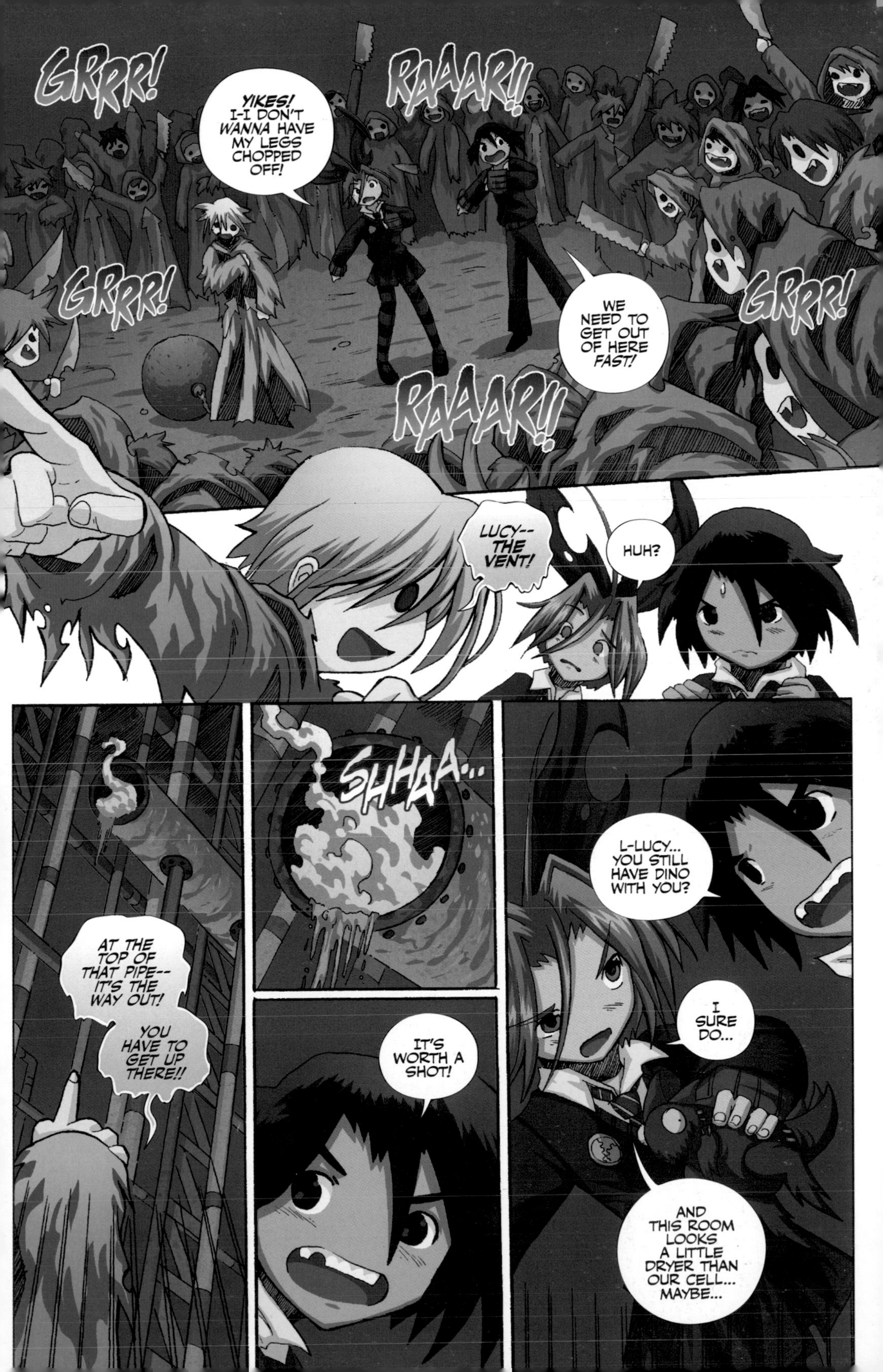
GRRR!
YIKES! I-I DON'T WANNA HAVE MY LEGS CHOPPED OFF!
RAAAR!!
GRRR!
WE NEED TO GET OUT OF HERE FAST!
GRRR!
RAAAR!!
LUCY-- THE VENT!
HUH?
AT THE TOP OF THAT PIPE-- IT'S THE WAY OUT!
YOU HAVE TO GET UP THERE!!
SHHAA...
IT'S WORTH A SHOT!
L-LUCY... YOU STILL HAVE DINO WITH YOU?
I SURE DO...
AND THIS ROOM LOOKS A LITTLE DRYER THAN OUR CELL... MAYBE...

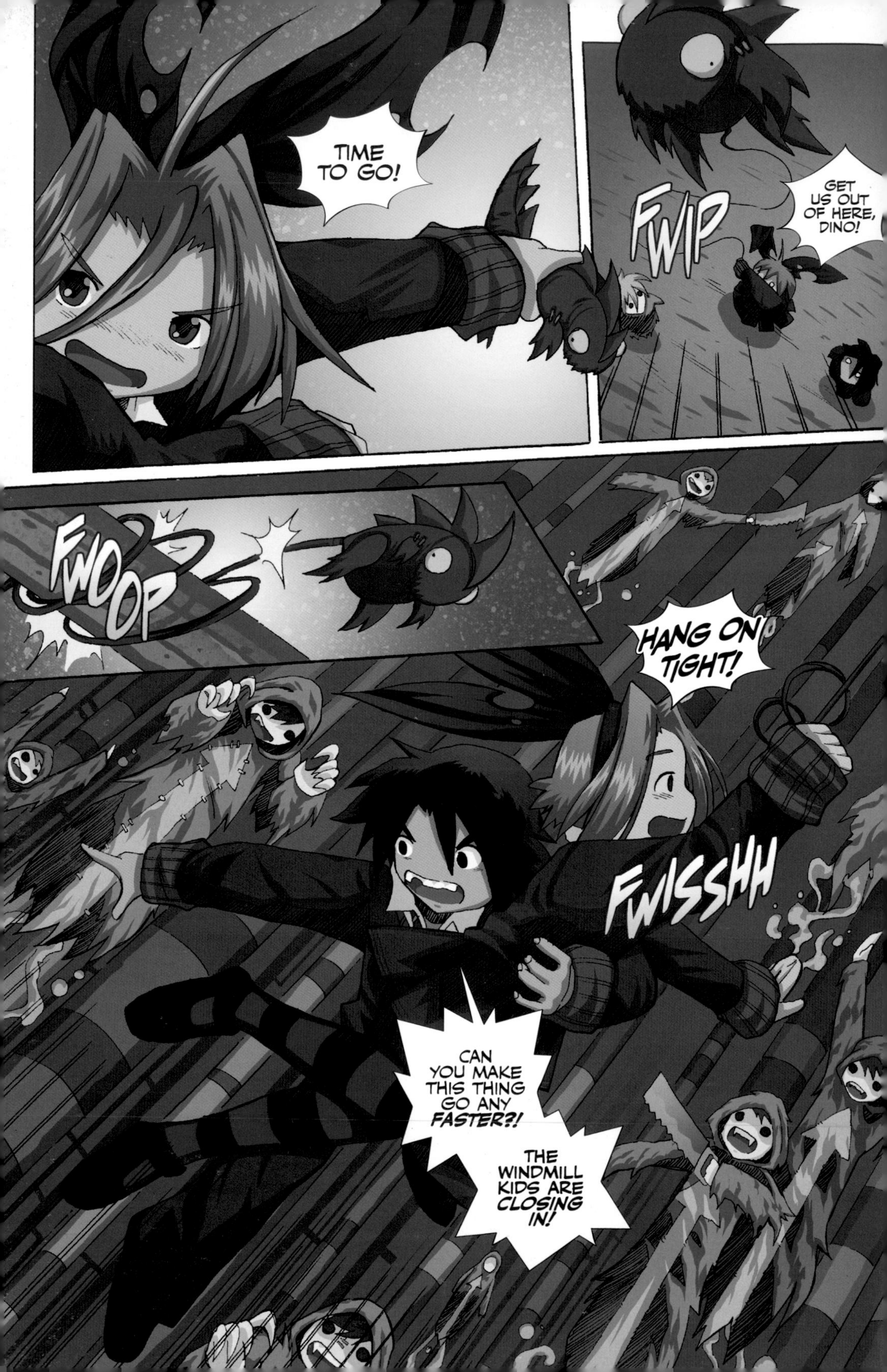
TIME TO GO!
FWIP
GET US OUT OF HERE, DINO!
FWOOP
HANG ON TIGHT!
FWISSHH
CAN YOU MAKE THIS THING GO ANY FASTER?!
THE WINDMILL KIDS ARE CLOSING IN!

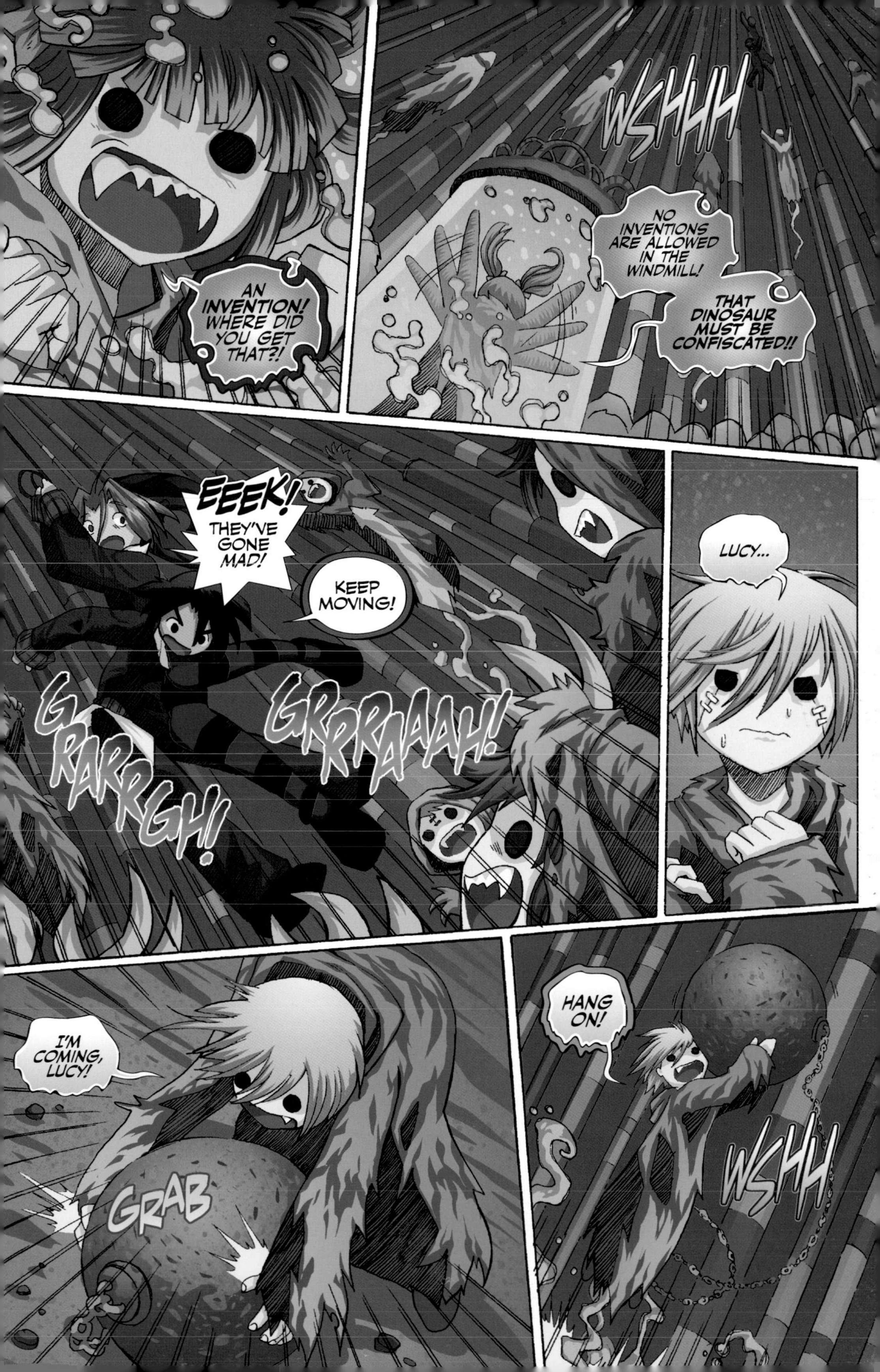
AN INVENTION! WHERE DID YOU GET THAT?!
WSHHH
NO INVENTIONS ARE ALLOWED IN THE WINDMILL!
THAT DINOSAUR MUST BE CONFISCATED!!
EEEK! THEY'VE GONE MAD!
KEEP MOVING!
GRARRRGH!
GRRRAAAAH!
LUCY...
I'M COMING, LUCY!
GRAB
HANG ON!
WSHH

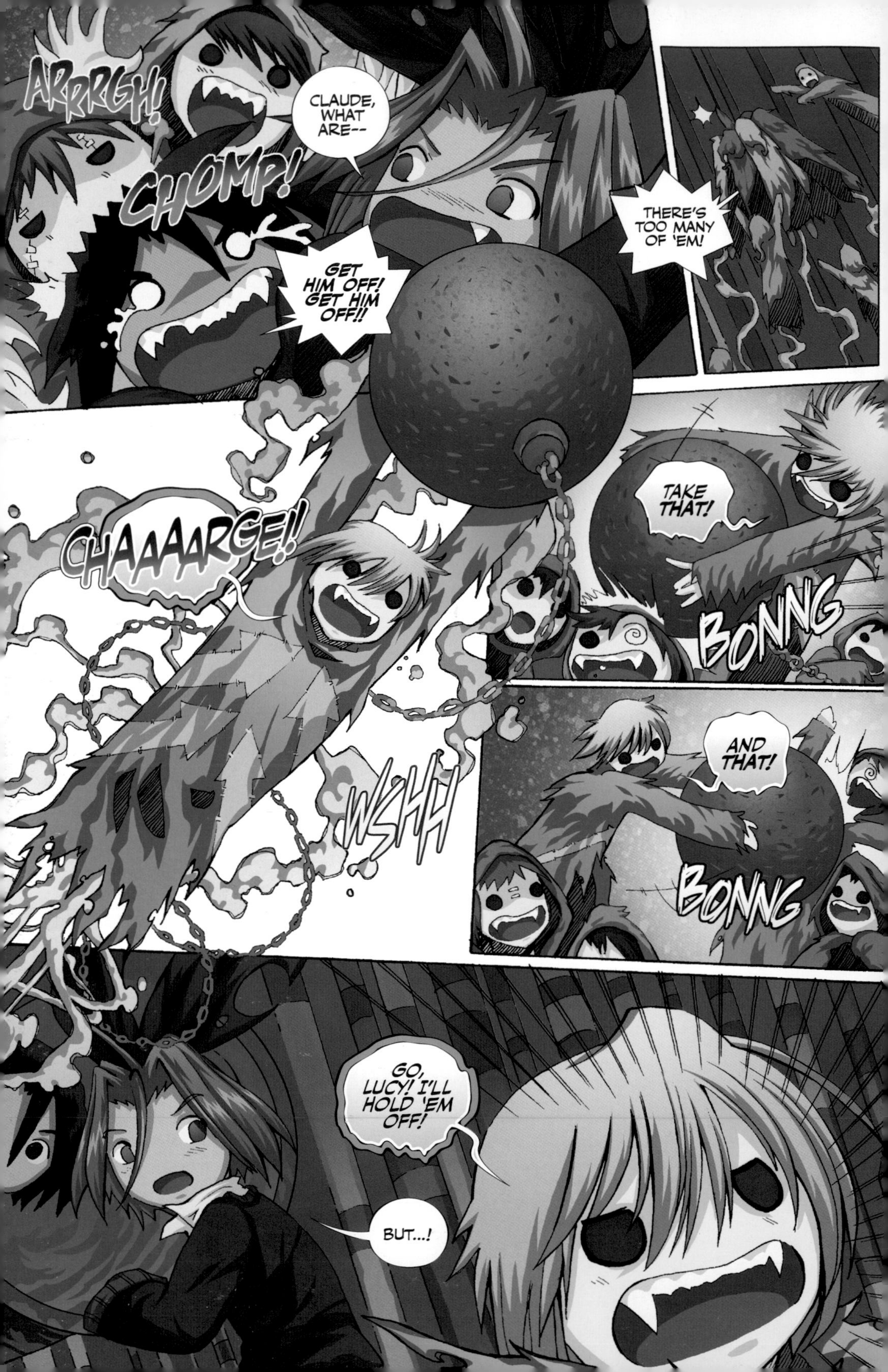
ARRRGH!
CLAUDE, WHAT ARE--
CHOMP!
GET HIM OFF! GET HIM OFF!!
THERE'S TOO MANY OF 'EM!
CHAAAARGE!!
WSHH
TAKE THAT!
BONNG
AND THAT!
BONNG
GO, LUCY! I'LL HOLD 'EM OFF!
BUT...!

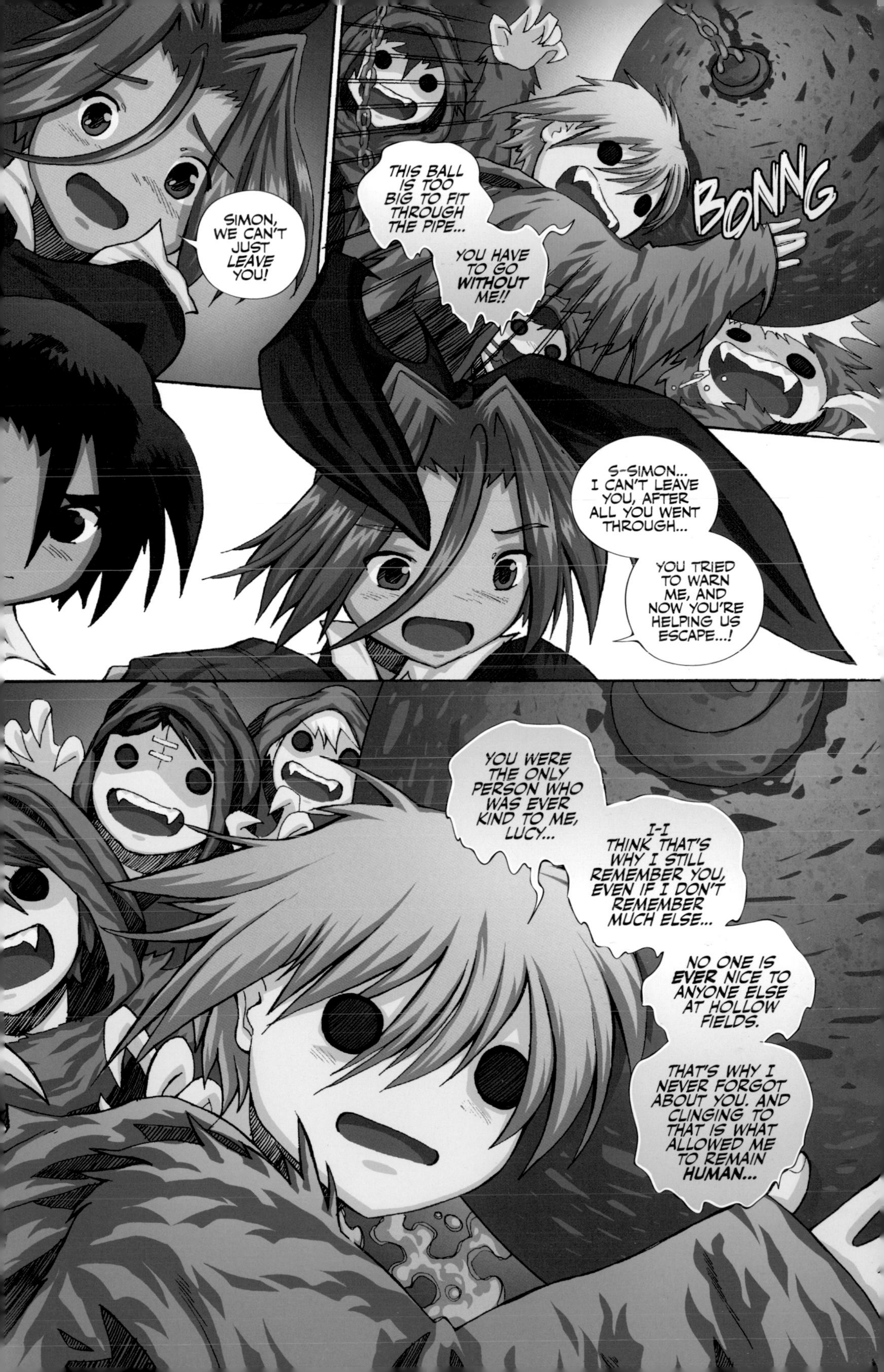
SIMON, WE CAN'T JUST LEAVE YOU!
THIS BALL IS TOO BIG TO FIT THROUGH THE PIPE...
YOU HAVE TO GO WITHOUT ME!!
BONNG
S-SIMON... I CAN'T LEAVE YOU, AFTER ALL YOU WENT THROUGH...
YOU TRIED TO WARN ME, AND NOW YOU'RE HELPING US ESCAPE...!
YOU WERE THE ONLY PERSON WHO WAS EVER KIND TO ME, LUCY...
I-I THINK THAT'S WHY I STILL REMEMBER YOU, EVEN IF I DON'T REMEMBER MUCH ELSE...
NO ONE IS EVER NICE TO ANYONE ELSE AT HOLLOW FIELDS.
THAT'S WHY I NEVER FORGOT ABOUT YOU. AND CLINGING TO THAT IS WHAT ALLOWED ME TO REMAIN HUMAN...

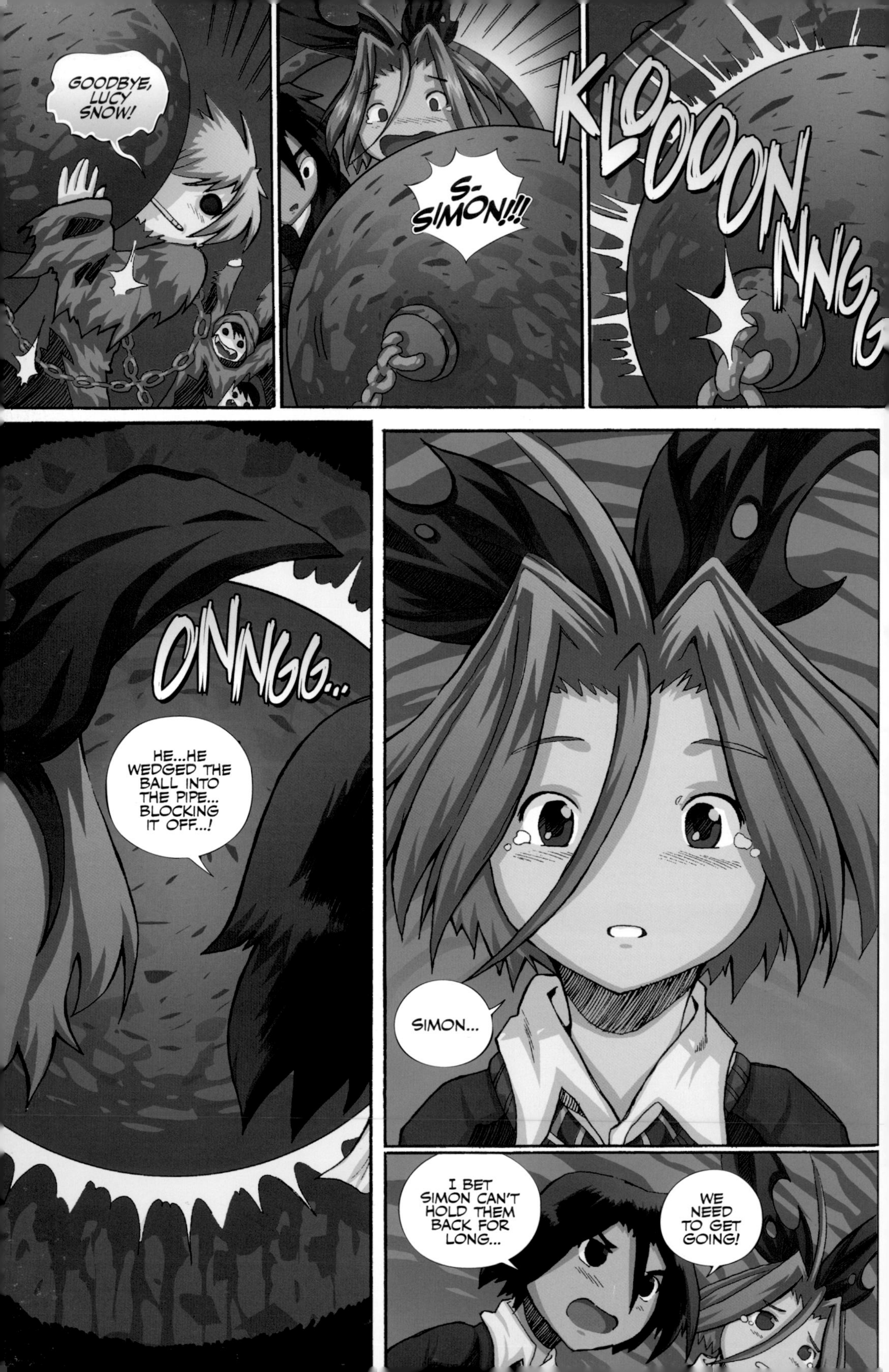
GOODBYE, LUCY SNOW!
S-SIMON!!!
KLOOOOONNNGG
ONNGG...
HE...HE WEDGED THE BALL INTO THE PIPE... BLOCKING IT OFF...!
SIMON...
I BET SIMON CAN'T HOLD THEM BACK FOR LONG...
WE NEED TO GET GOING!

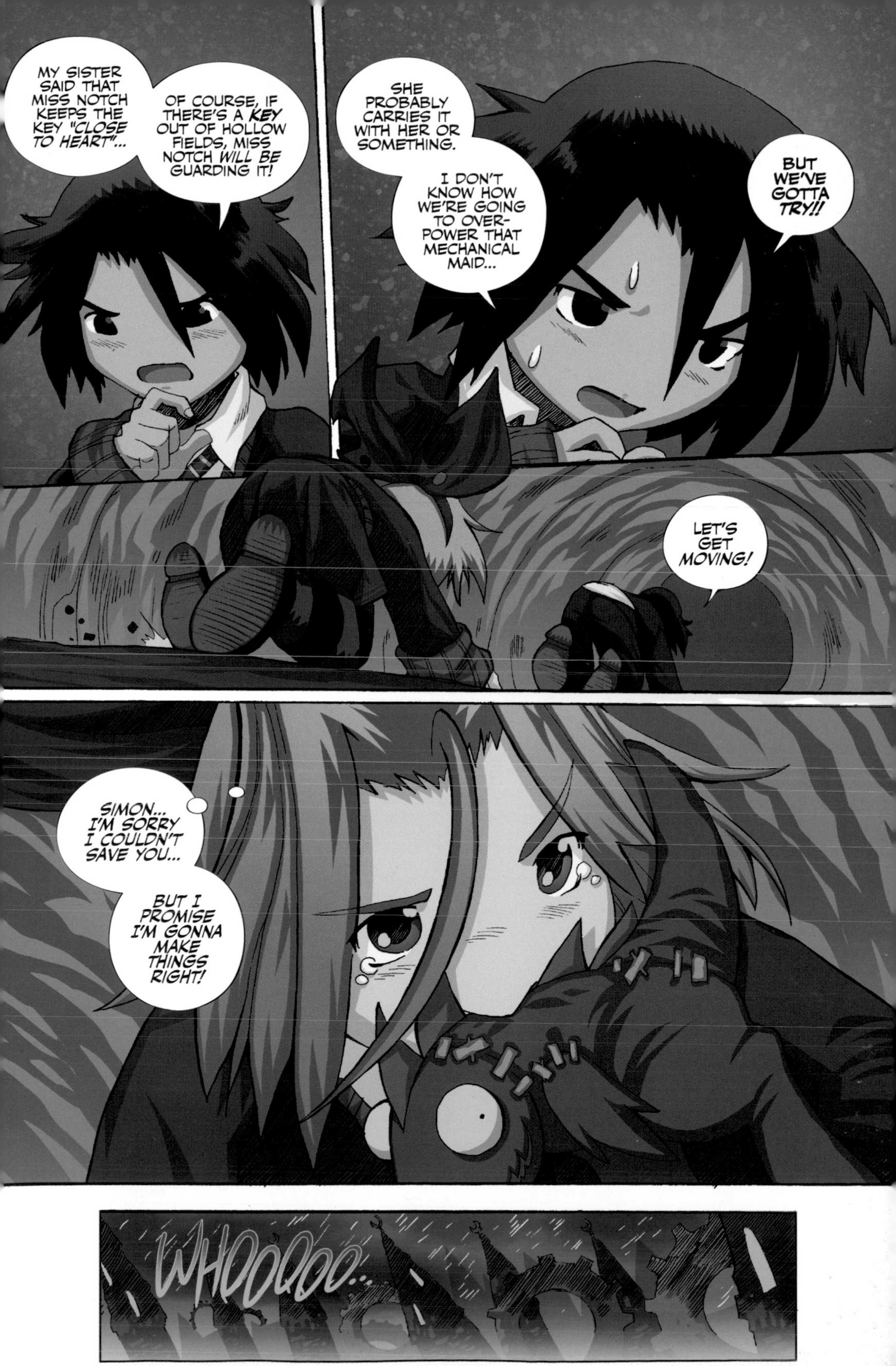
MY SISTER SAID THAT MISS NOTCH KEEPS THE KEY "CLOSE TO HEART"...
OF COURSE, IF THERE'S A KEY OUT OF HOLLOW FIELDS, MISS NOTCH WILL BE GUARDING IT!
SHE PROBABLY CARRIES IT WITH HER OR SOMETHING.
I DON'T KNOW HOW WE'RE GOING TO OVER-POWER THAT MECHANICAL MAID...
BUT WE'VE GOTTA TRY!!
LET'S GET MOVING!
SIMON... I'M SORRY I COULDN'T SAVE YOU...
BUT I PROMISE I'M GONNA MAKE THINGS RIGHT!
WHOOOOO...

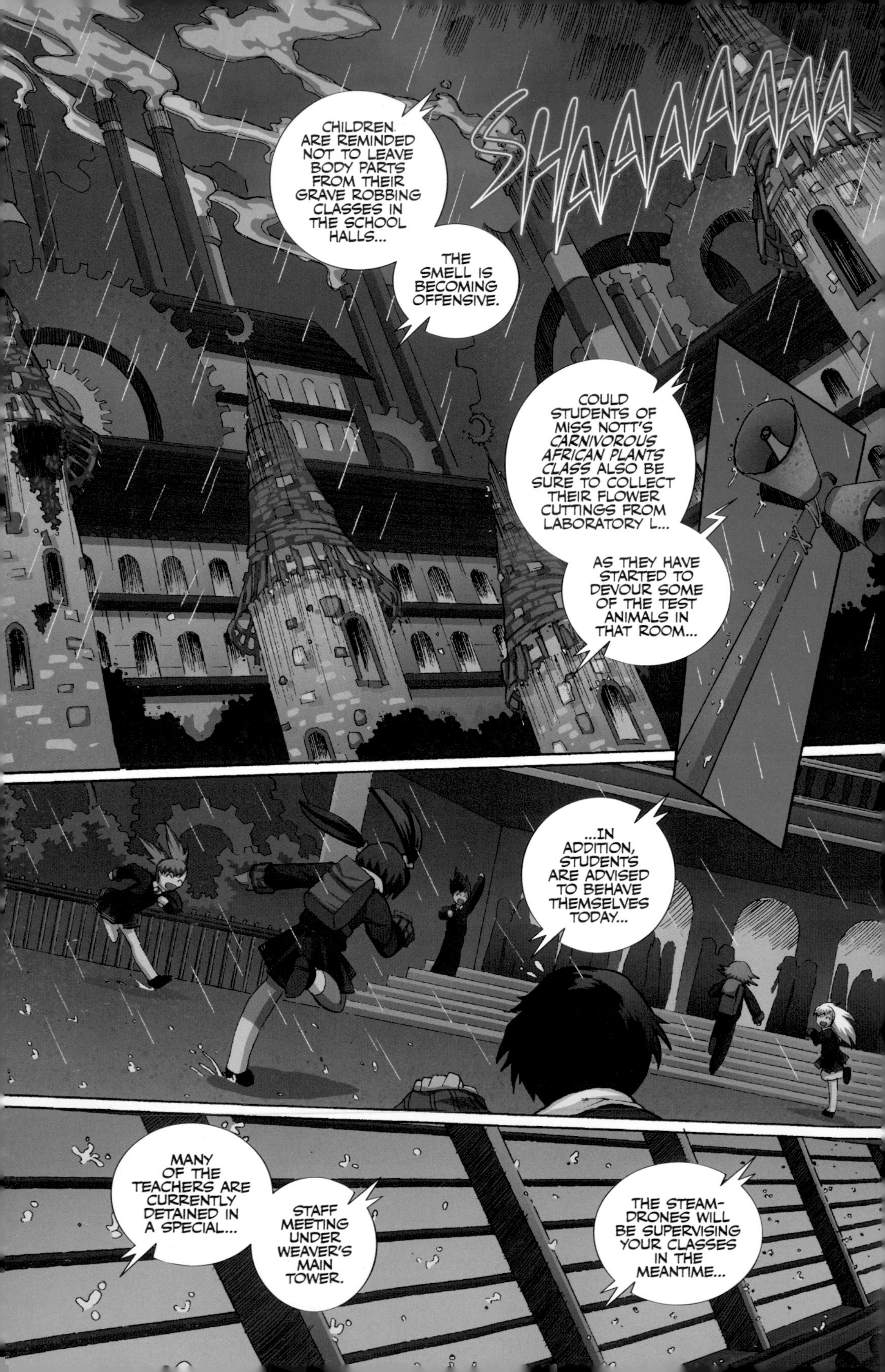
CHILDREN ARE REMINDED NOT TO LEAVE BODY PARTS FROM THEIR GRAVE ROBBING CLASSES IN THE SCHOOL HALLS...
THE SMELL IS BECOMING OFFENSIVE.
SHAAAAAAAA
COULD STUDENTS OF MISS NOTT'S *CARNIVOROUS AFRICAN PLANTS CLASS* ALSO BE SURE TO COLLECT THEIR FLOWER CUTTINGS FROM LABORATORY L...
AS THEY HAVE STARTED TO DEVOUR SOME OF THE TEST ANIMALS IN THAT ROOM...
...IN ADDITION, STUDENTS ARE ADVISED TO BEHAVE THEMSELVES TODAY...
MANY OF THE TEACHERS ARE CURRENTLY DETAINED IN A SPECIAL...
STAFF MEETING UNDER WEAVER'S MAIN TOWER.
THE STEAM-DRONES WILL BE SUPERVISING YOUR CLASSES IN THE MEANTIME...

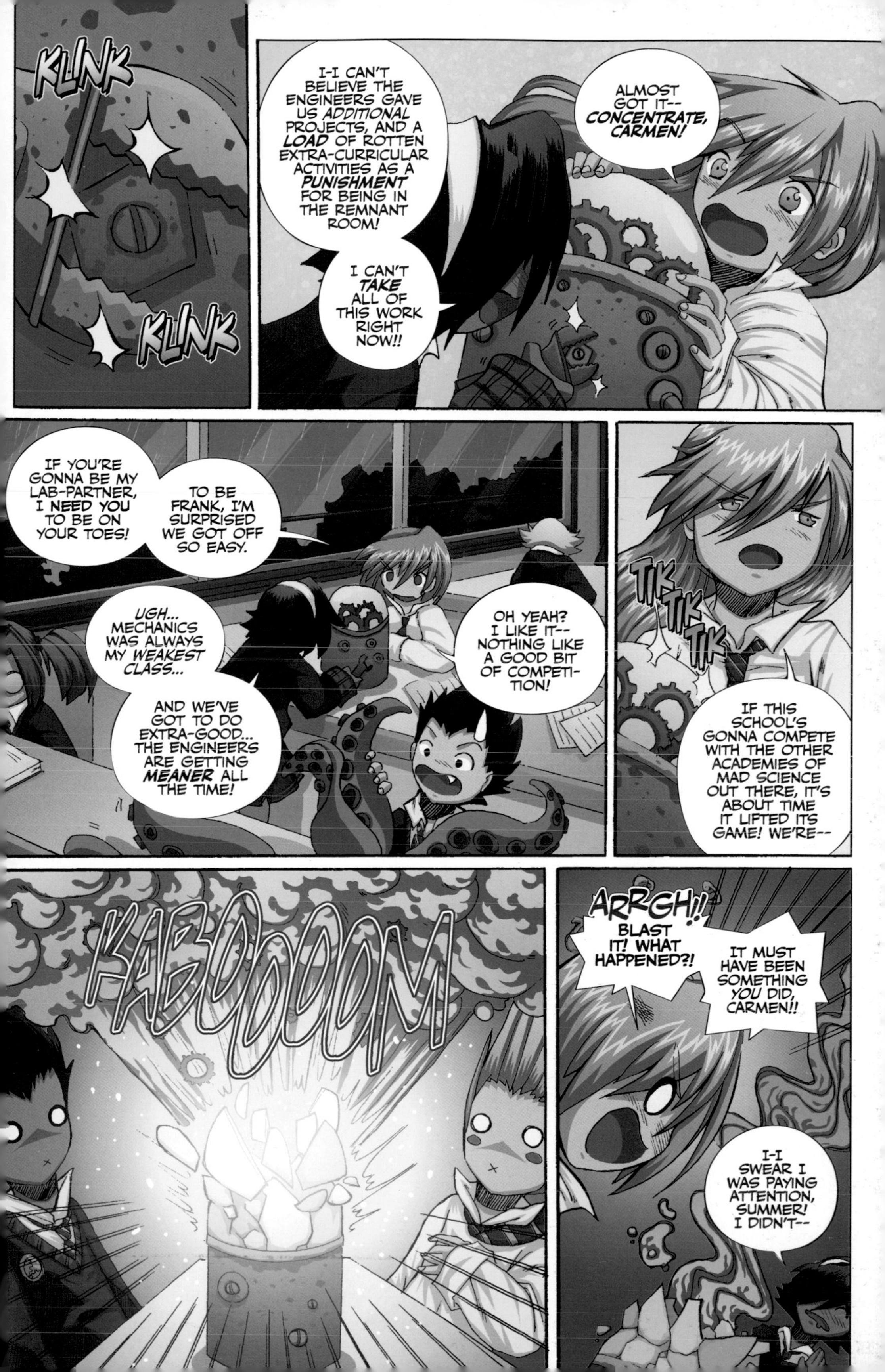
KLINK
KLINK
I-I CAN'T BELIEVE THE ENGINEERS GAVE US ADDITIONAL PROJECTS, AND A LOAD OF ROTTEN EXTRA-CURRICULAR ACTIVITIES AS A PUNISHMENT FOR BEING IN THE REMNANT ROOM!
I CAN'T TAKE ALL OF THIS WORK RIGHT NOW!!
ALMOST GOT IT-- CONCENTRATE, CARMEN!
IF YOU'RE GONNA BE MY LAB-PARTNER, I NEED YOU TO BE ON YOUR TOES!
TO BE FRANK, I'M SURPRISED WE GOT OFF SO EASY.
UGH... MECHANICS WAS ALWAYS MY WEAKEST CLASS...
AND WE'VE GOT TO DO EXTRA-GOOD... THE ENGINEERS ARE GETTING MEANER ALL THE TIME!
OH YEAH? I LIKE IT-- NOTHING LIKE A GOOD BIT OF COMPETI-TION!
TIK TIK TIK
IF THIS SCHOOL'S GONNA COMPETE WITH THE OTHER ACADEMIES OF MAD SCIENCE OUT THERE, IT'S ABOUT TIME IT LIFTED ITS GAME! WE'RE--
KABOOOOOM
ARRGH!! BLAST IT! WHAT HAPPENED?!
IT MUST HAVE BEEN SOMETHING YOU DID, CARMEN!!
I-I SWEAR I WAS PAYING ATTENTION, SUMMER! I DIDN'T--

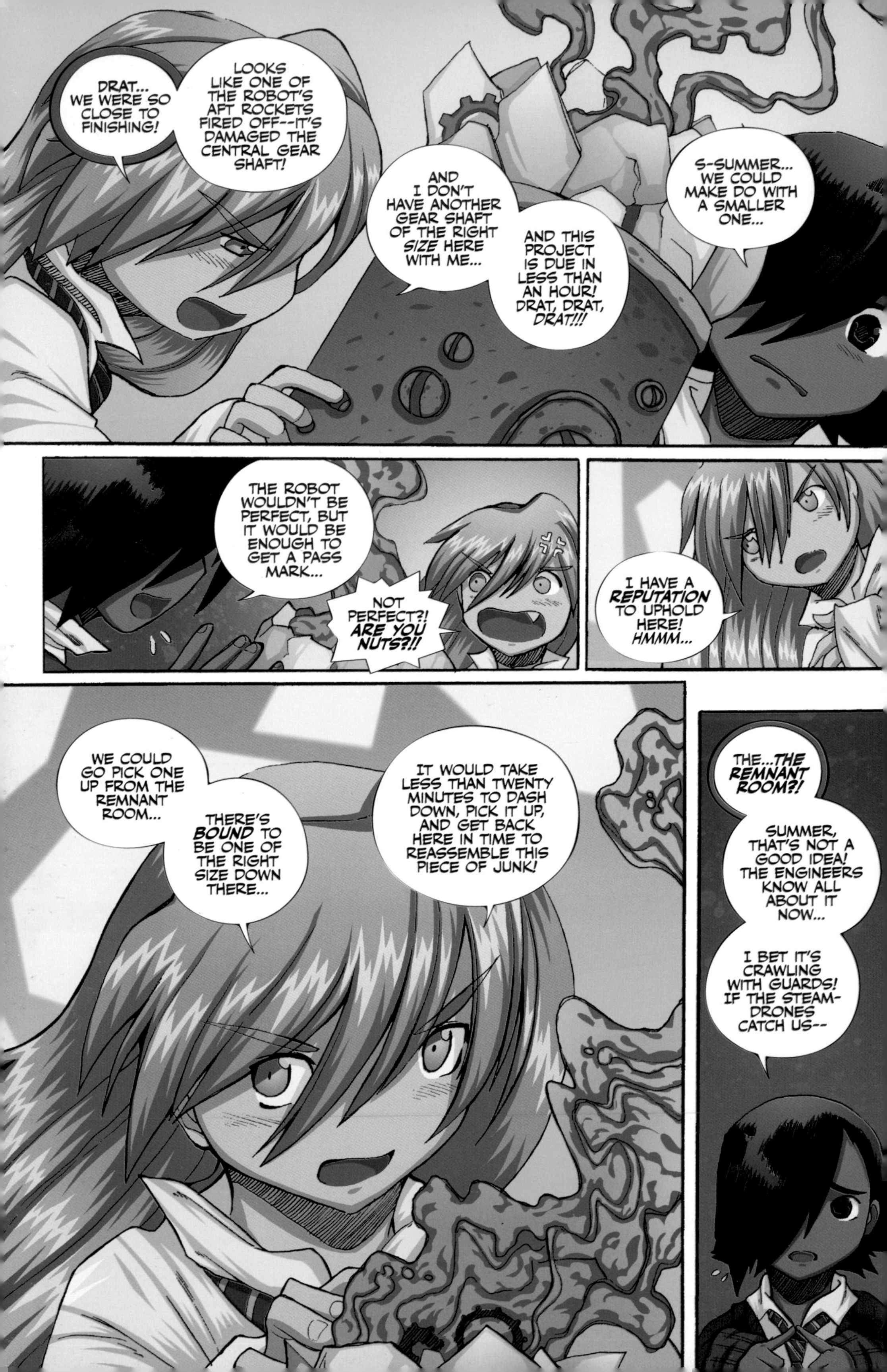
DRAT... WE WERE SO CLOSE TO FINISHING!
LOOKS LIKE ONE OF THE ROBOT'S AFT ROCKETS FIRED OFF--IT'S DAMAGED THE CENTRAL GEAR SHAFT!
AND I DON'T HAVE ANOTHER GEAR SHAFT OF THE RIGHT *SIZE* HERE WITH ME...
AND THIS PROJECT IS DUE IN LESS THAN AN HOUR! DRAT, DRAT, *DRAT!!!*
S-SUMMER... WE COULD MAKE DO WITH A SMALLER ONE...
THE ROBOT WOULDN'T BE PERFECT, BUT IT WOULD BE ENOUGH TO GET A PASS MARK...
NOT PERFECT?! ***ARE YOU NUTS?!!***
I HAVE A ***REPUTATION*** TO UPHOLD HERE! *HMMM...*
WE COULD GO PICK ONE UP FROM THE REMNANT ROOM...
THERE'S ***BOUND*** TO BE ONE OF THE RIGHT SIZE DOWN THERE...
IT WOULD TAKE LESS THAN TWENTY MINUTES TO DASH DOWN, PICK IT UP, AND GET BACK HERE IN TIME TO REASSEMBLE THIS PIECE OF JUNK!
THE...***THE REMNANT ROOM?!***
SUMMER, THAT'S NOT A GOOD IDEA! THE ENGINEERS KNOW ALL ABOUT IT NOW...
I BET IT'S CRAWLING WITH GUARDS! IF THE STEAM-DRONES CATCH US--

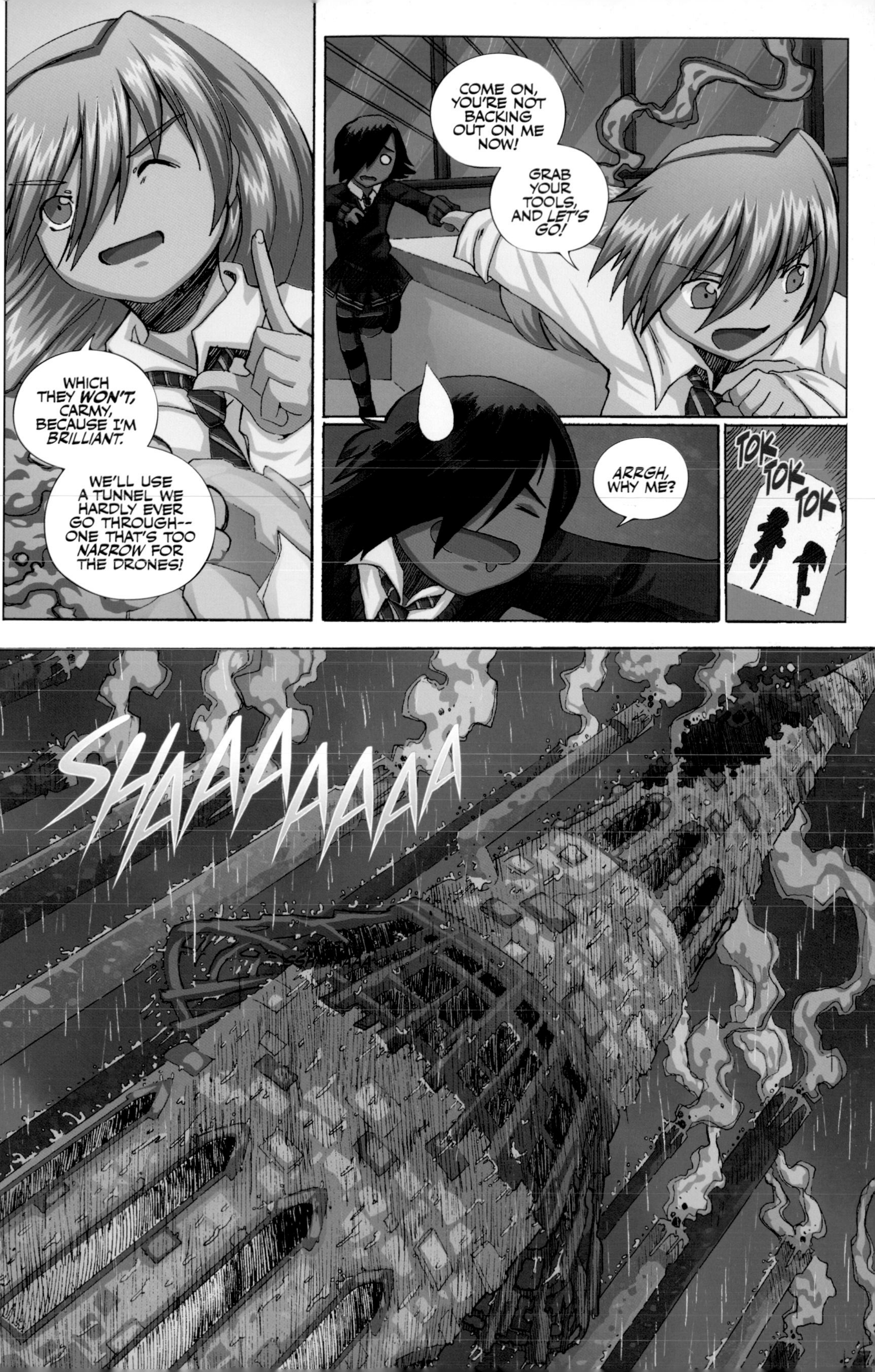
WHICH THEY *WON'T*, CARMY, BECAUSE I'M *BRILLIANT*.
WE'LL USE A TUNNEL WE HARDLY EVER GO THROUGH-- ONE THAT'S TOO *NARROW* FOR THE DRONES!
COME ON, YOU'RE NOT BACKING OUT ON ME NOW!
GRAB YOUR TOOLS, AND *LET'S GO!*
ARRGH, WHY ME?
TOK TOK TOK
SHAAAAAAA

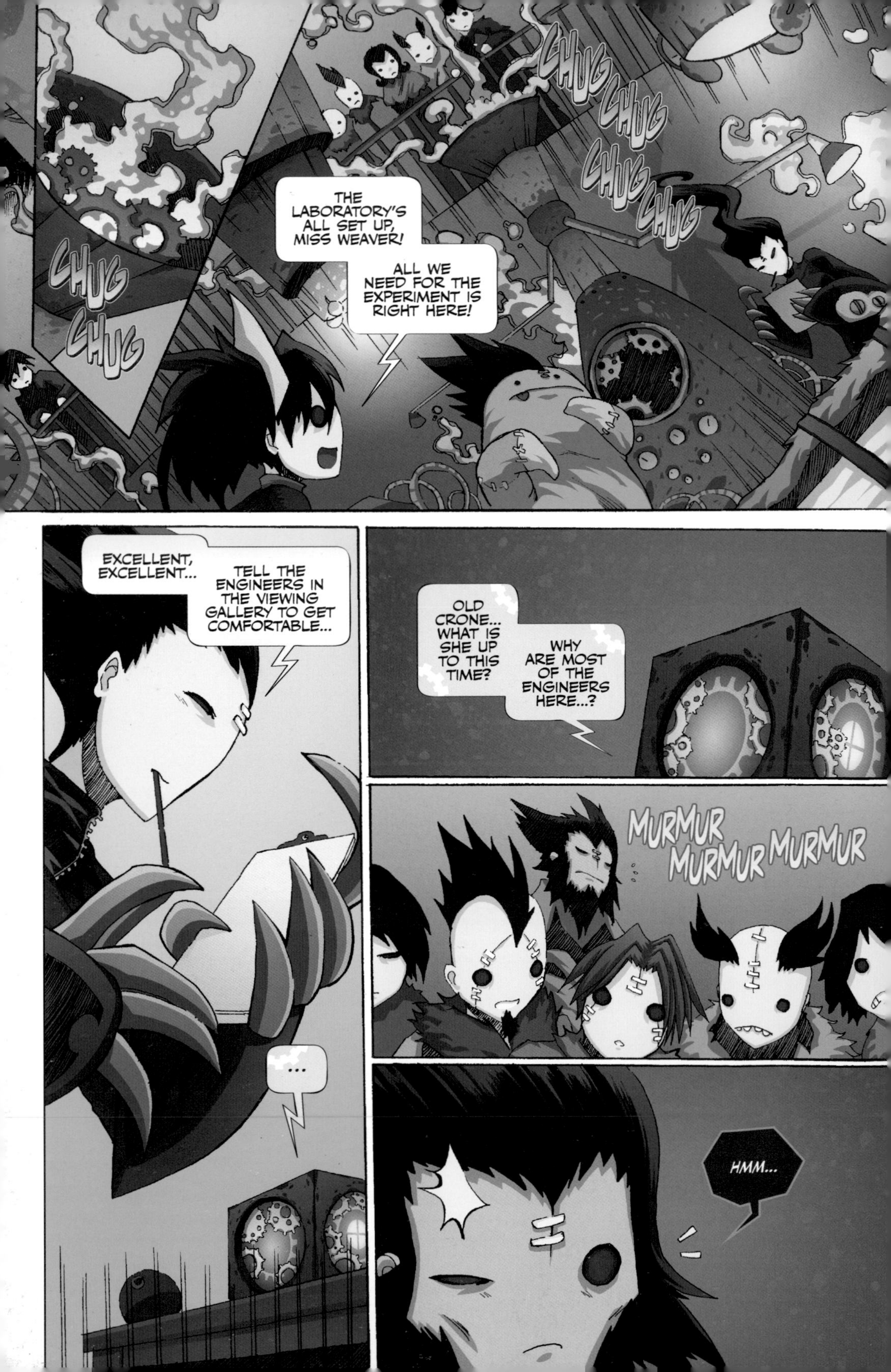
CHUG CHUG CHUG CHUG
THE LABORATORY'S ALL SET UP, MISS WEAVER!
ALL WE NEED FOR THE EXPERIMENT IS RIGHT HERE!
CHUG CHUG
EXCELLENT, EXCELLENT...
TELL THE ENGINEERS IN THE VIEWING GALLERY TO GET COMFORTABLE...
...
OLD CRONE... WHAT IS SHE UP TO THIS TIME?
WHY ARE MOST OF THE ENGINEERS HERE...?
MURMUR MURMUR MURMUR
HMM...

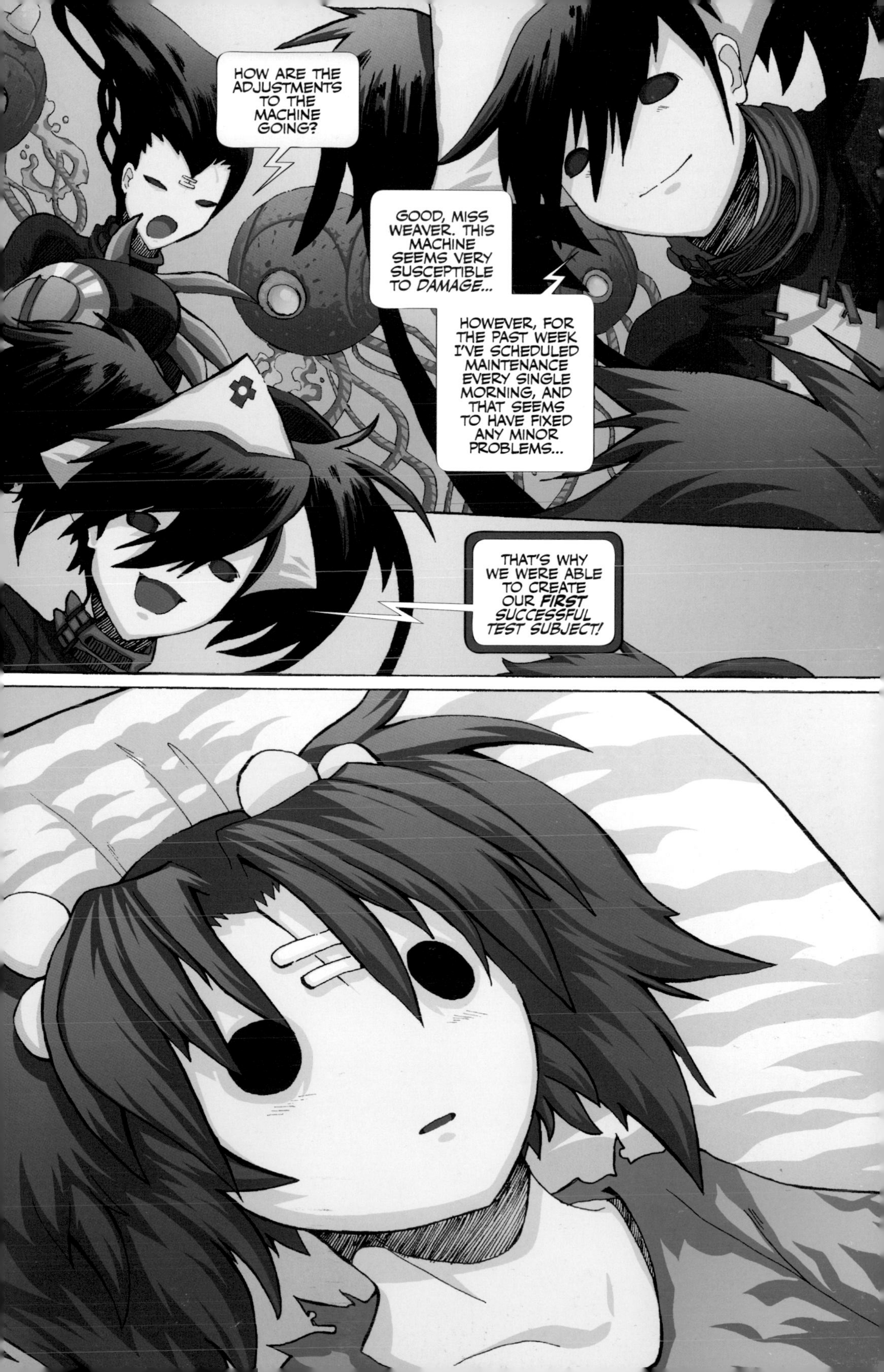
HOW ARE THE ADJUSTMENTS TO THE MACHINE GOING?
GOOD, MISS WEAVER. THIS MACHINE SEEMS VERY SUSCEPTIBLE TO *DAMAGE*...
HOWEVER, FOR THE PAST WEEK I'VE SCHEDULED MAINTENANCE EVERY SINGLE MORNING, AND THAT SEEMS TO HAVE FIXED ANY MINOR PROBLEMS...
THAT'S WHY WE WERE ABLE TO CREATE OUR ***FIRST*** *SUCCESSFUL TEST SUBJECT!*

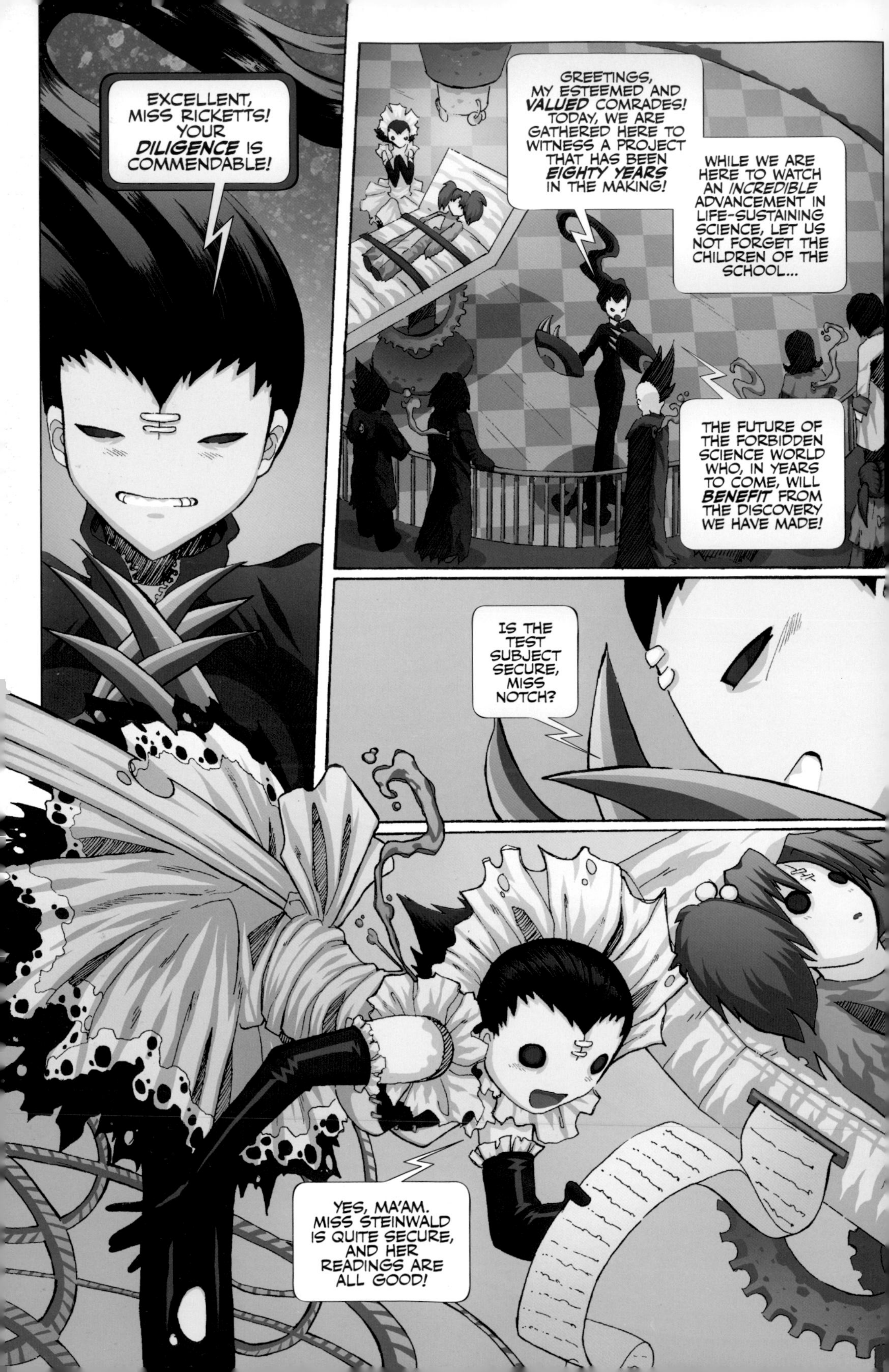

EXCELLENT, MISS RICKETTS! YOUR DILIGENCE IS COMMENDABLE!
GREETINGS, MY ESTEEMED AND VALUED COMRADES! TODAY, WE ARE GATHERED HERE TO WITNESS A PROJECT THAT HAS BEEN EIGHTY YEARS IN THE MAKING!
WHILE WE ARE HERE TO WATCH AN INCREDIBLE ADVANCEMENT IN LIFE-SUSTAINING SCIENCE, LET US NOT FORGET THE CHILDREN OF THE SCHOOL...
THE FUTURE OF THE FORBIDDEN SCIENCE WORLD WHO, IN YEARS TO COME, WILL BENEFIT FROM THE DISCOVERY WE HAVE MADE!
IS THE TEST SUBJECT SECURE, MISS NOTCH?
YES, MA'AM. MISS STEINWALD IS QUITE SECURE, AND HER READINGS ARE ALL GOOD!

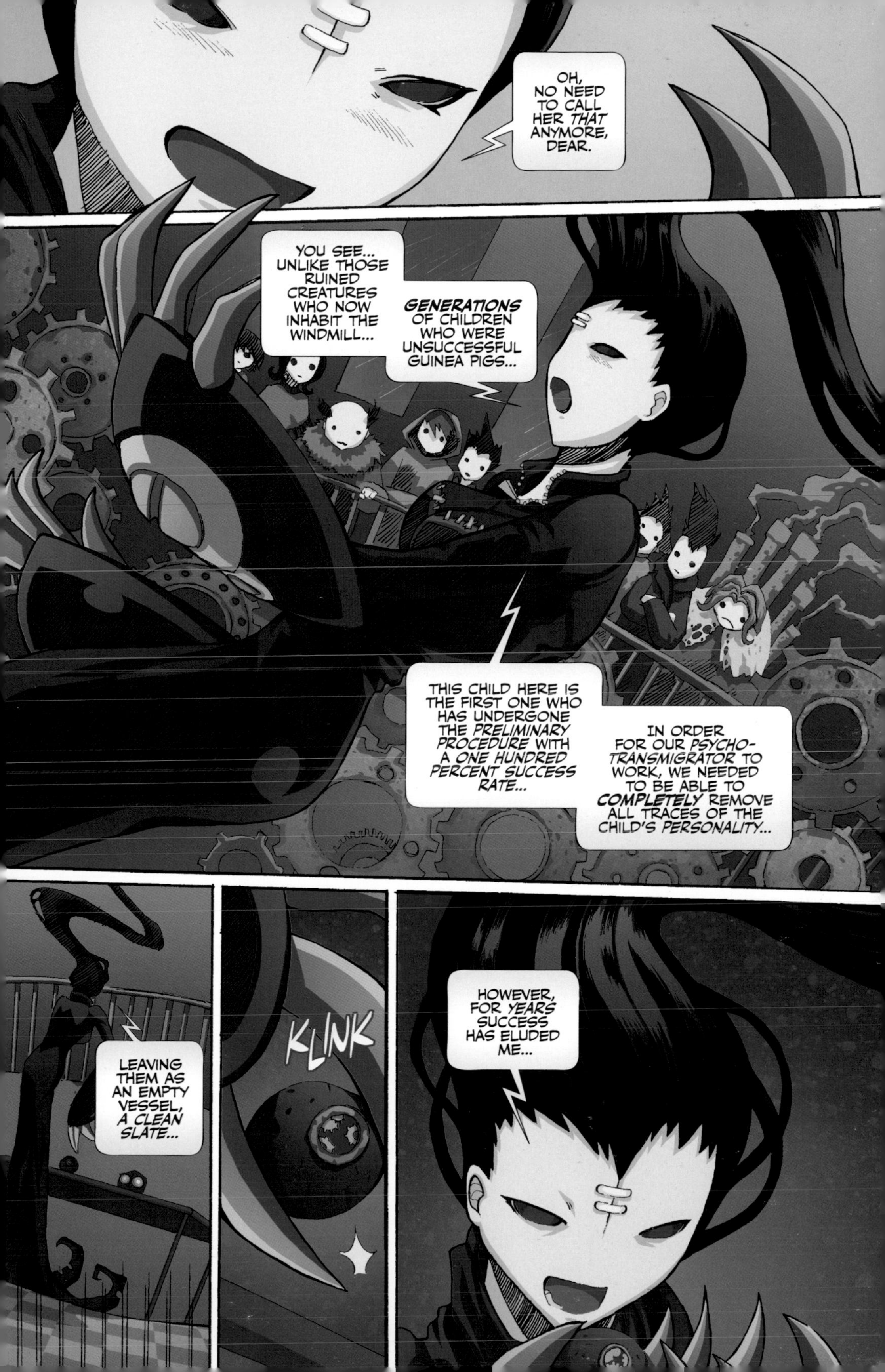
OH, NO NEED TO CALL HER *THAT* ANYMORE, DEAR.
YOU SEE... UNLIKE THOSE RUINED CREATURES WHO NOW INHABIT THE WINDMILL...
GENERATIONS OF CHILDREN WHO WERE UNSUCCESSFUL GUINEA PIGS...
THIS CHILD HERE IS THE FIRST ONE WHO HAS UNDERGONE THE *PRELIMINARY PROCEDURE* WITH A *ONE HUNDRED PERCENT SUCCESS RATE*...
IN ORDER FOR OUR *PSYCHO-TRANSMIGRATOR* TO WORK, WE NEEDED TO BE ABLE TO ***COMPLETELY*** REMOVE ALL TRACES OF THE CHILD'S *PERSONALITY*...
LEAVING THEM AS AN EMPTY VESSEL, *A CLEAN SLATE*...
KLINK
HOWEVER, FOR *YEARS* SUCCESS HAS ELUDED ME...

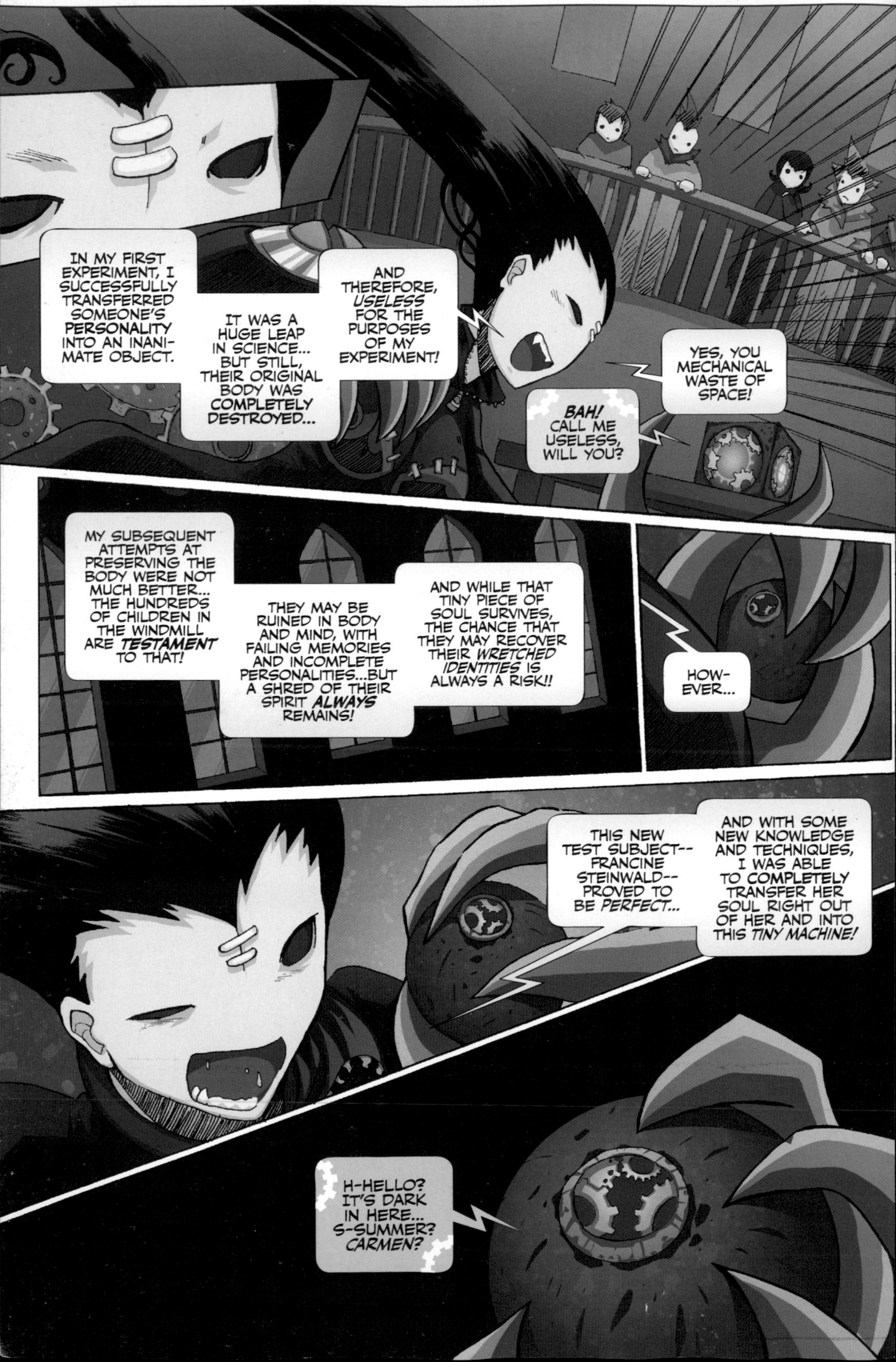
IN MY FIRST EXPERIMENT, I SUCCESSFULLY TRANSFERRED SOMEONE'S PERSONALITY INTO AN INANI-MATE OBJECT.
IT WAS A HUGE LEAP IN SCIENCE... BUT STILL, THEIR ORIGINAL BODY WAS COMPLETELY DESTROYED...
AND THEREFORE, USELESS FOR THE PURPOSES OF MY EXPERIMENT!
BAH! CALL ME USELESS, WILL YOU?
YES, YOU MECHANICAL WASTE OF SPACE!
MY SUBSEQUENT ATTEMPTS AT PRESERVING THE BODY WERE NOT MUCH BETTER... THE HUNDREDS OF CHILDREN IN THE WINDMILL ARE TESTAMENT TO THAT!
THEY MAY BE RUINED IN BODY AND MIND, WITH FAILING MEMORIES AND INCOMPLETE PERSONALITIES...BUT A SHRED OF THEIR SPIRIT ALWAYS REMAINS!
AND WHILE THAT TINY PIECE OF SOUL SURVIVES, THE CHANCE THAT THEY MAY RECOVER THEIR WRETCHED IDENTITIES IS ALWAYS A RISK!!
HOW-EVER...
THIS NEW TEST SUBJECT-- FRANCINE STEINWALD-- PROVED TO BE PERFECT...
AND WITH SOME NEW KNOWLEDGE AND TECHNIQUES, I WAS ABLE TO COMPLETELY TRANSFER HER SOUL RIGHT OUT OF HER AND INTO THIS TINY MACHINE!
H-HELLO? IT'S DARK IN HERE... S-SUMMER? CARMEN?

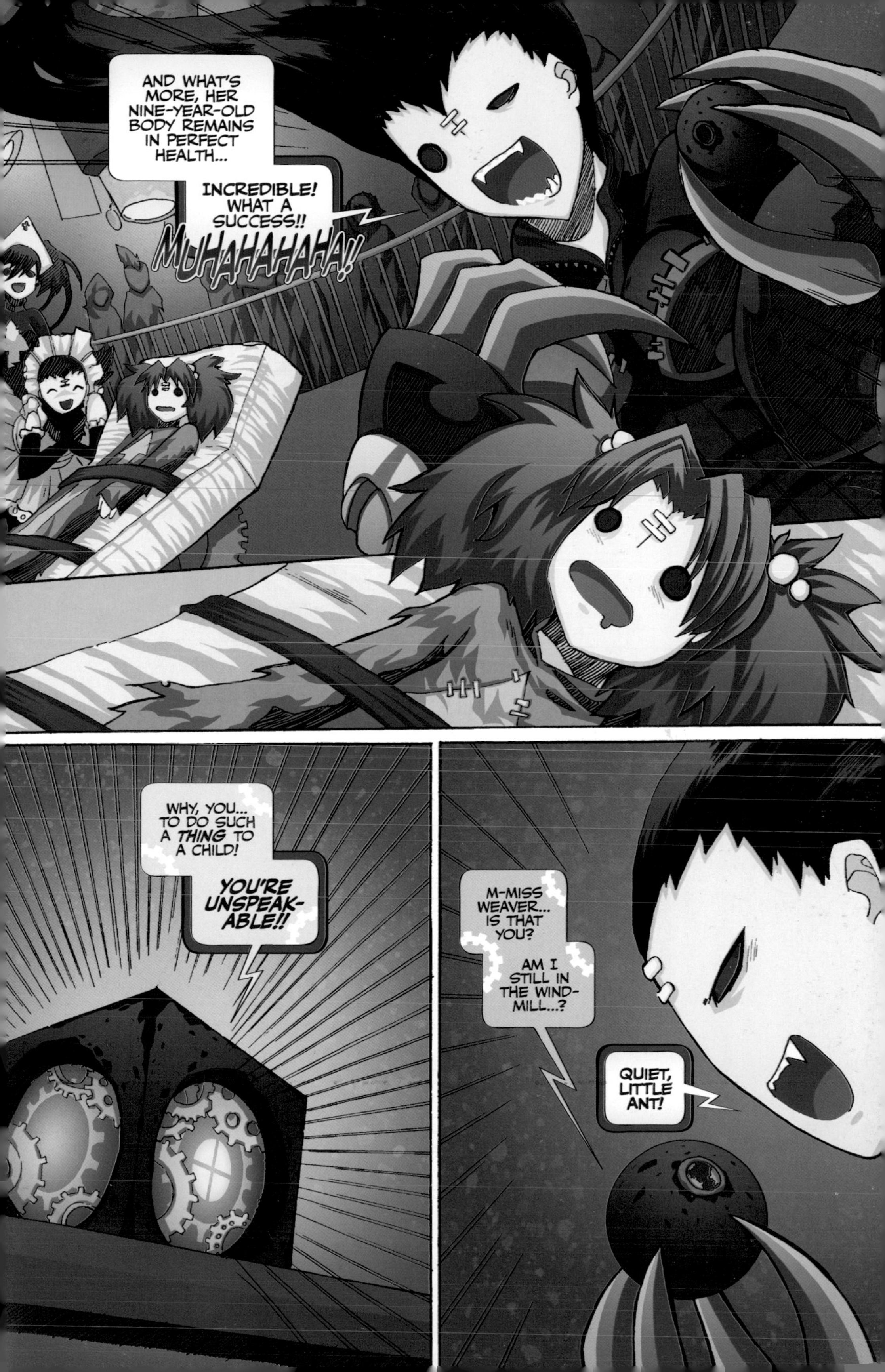
AND WHAT'S MORE, HER NINE-YEAR-OLD BODY REMAINS IN PERFECT HEALTH...
INCREDIBLE! WHAT A SUCCESS!!
MUHAHAHAHA!!
WHY, YOU... TO DO SUCH A THING TO A CHILD!
YOU'RE UNSPEAK-ABLE!!
M-MISS WEAVER... IS THAT YOU?
AM I STILL IN THE WIND-MILL...?
QUIET, LITTLE ANT!

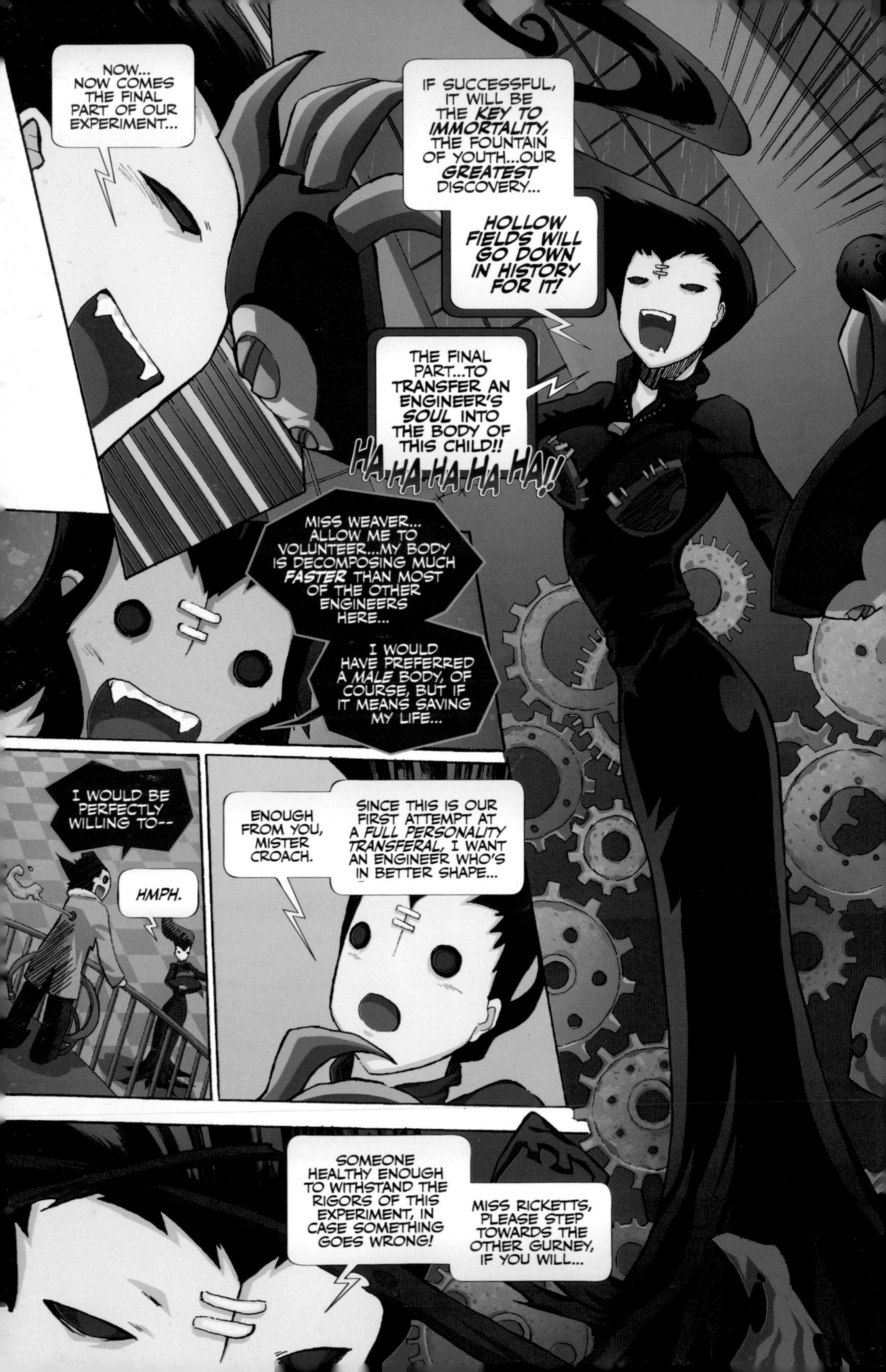
NOW... NOW COMES THE FINAL PART OF OUR EXPERIMENT...
IF SUCCESSFUL, IT WILL BE THE *KEY TO IMMORTALITY,* THE FOUNTAIN OF YOUTH...OUR *GREATEST* DISCOVERY...
HOLLOW FIELDS WILL GO DOWN IN HISTORY FOR IT!
THE FINAL PART...TO TRANSFER AN ENGINEER'S *SOUL* INTO THE BODY OF THIS CHILD!!
HA HA HA HA HA!!
MISS WEAVER... ALLOW ME TO VOLUNTEER...MY BODY IS DECOMPOSING MUCH *FASTER* THAN MOST OF THE OTHER ENGINEERS HERE...
I WOULD HAVE PREFERRED A *MALE* BODY, OF COURSE, BUT IF IT MEANS SAVING MY LIFE...
I WOULD BE PERFECTLY WILLING TO--
HMPH.
ENOUGH FROM YOU, MISTER CROACH.
SINCE THIS IS OUR FIRST ATTEMPT AT A *FULL PERSONALITY TRANSFERAL,* I WANT AN ENGINEER WHO'S IN BETTER SHAPE...
SOMEONE HEALTHY ENOUGH TO WITHSTAND THE RIGORS OF THIS EXPERIMENT, IN CASE SOMETHING GOES WRONG!
MISS RICKETTS, PLEASE STEP TOWARDS THE OTHER GURNEY, IF YOU WILL...

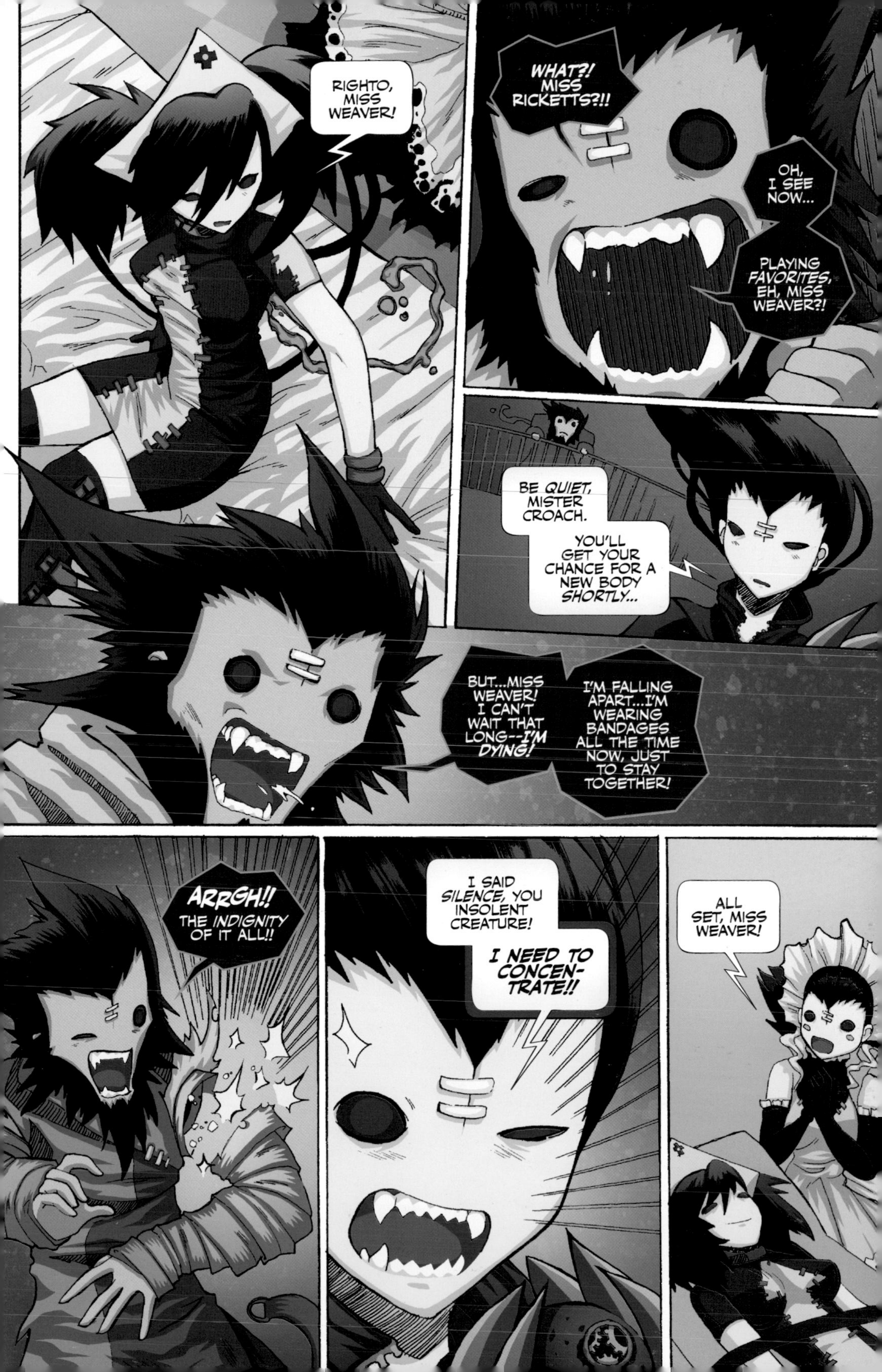

RIGHTO, MISS WEAVER!
WHAT?! MISS RICKETTS?!!
OH, I SEE NOW...
PLAYING FAVORITES, EH, MISS WEAVER?!
BE QUIET, MISTER CROACH.
YOU'LL GET YOUR CHANCE FOR A NEW BODY SHORTLY...
BUT...MISS WEAVER! I CAN'T WAIT THAT LONG--I'M DYING!
I'M FALLING APART...I'M WEARING BANDAGES ALL THE TIME NOW, JUST TO STAY TOGETHER!
ARRGH!! THE INDIGNITY OF IT ALL!!
I SAID SILENCE, YOU INSOLENT CREATURE!
I NEED TO CONCEN-TRATE!!
ALL SET, MISS WEAVER!

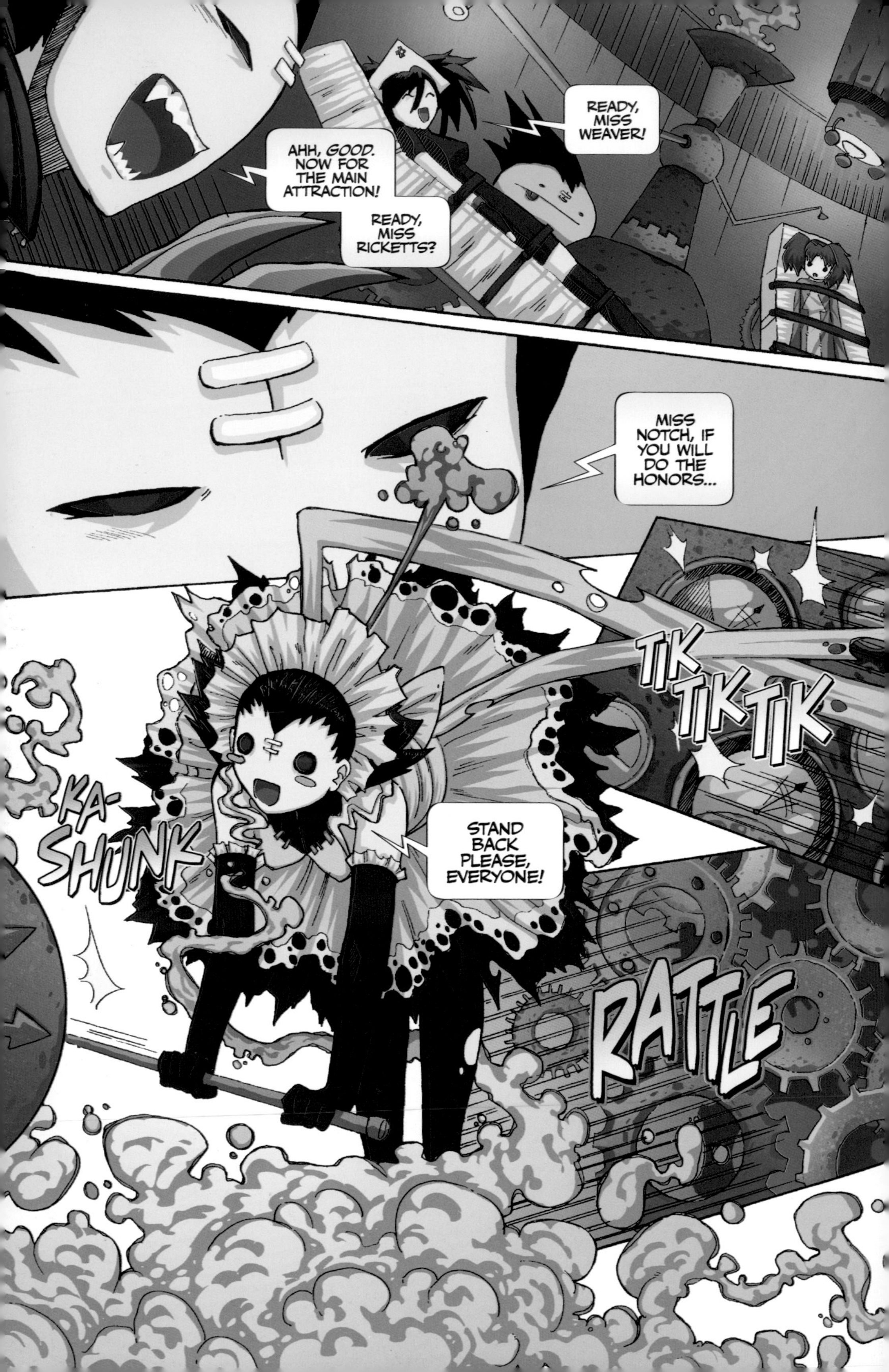
AHH, *GOOD.* NOW FOR THE MAIN ATTRACTION!
READY, MISS RICKETTS?
READY, MISS WEAVER!
MISS NOTCH, IF YOU WILL DO THE HONORS...
KA-SHUNK
TIK TIKTIK
STAND BACK PLEASE, EVERYONE!
RATTLE

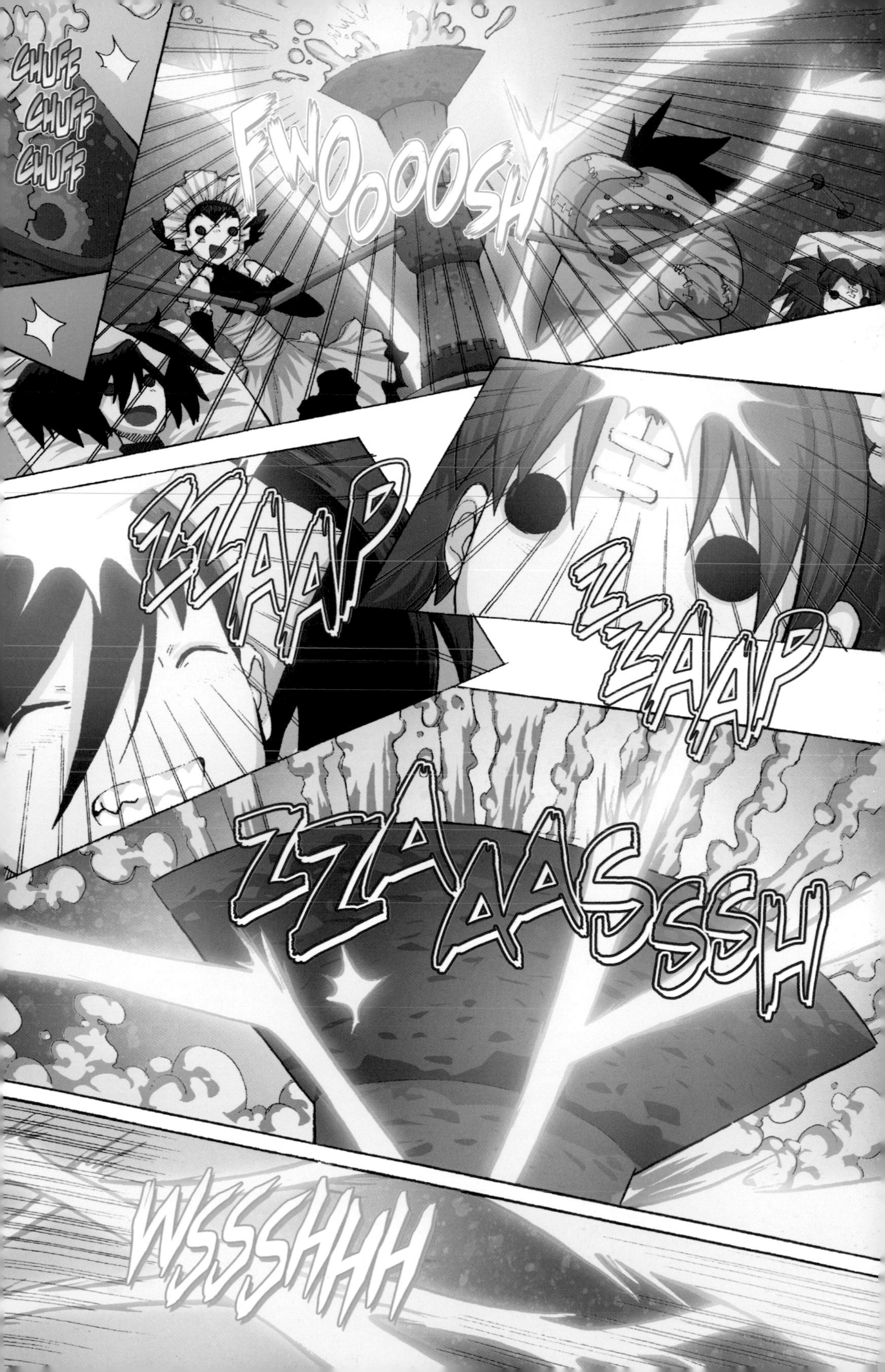
CHUFF
CHUFF
CHUFF
FWOOOOOSH
ZZAAP
ZZAAP
ZZAAASSSH
WSSSHHH

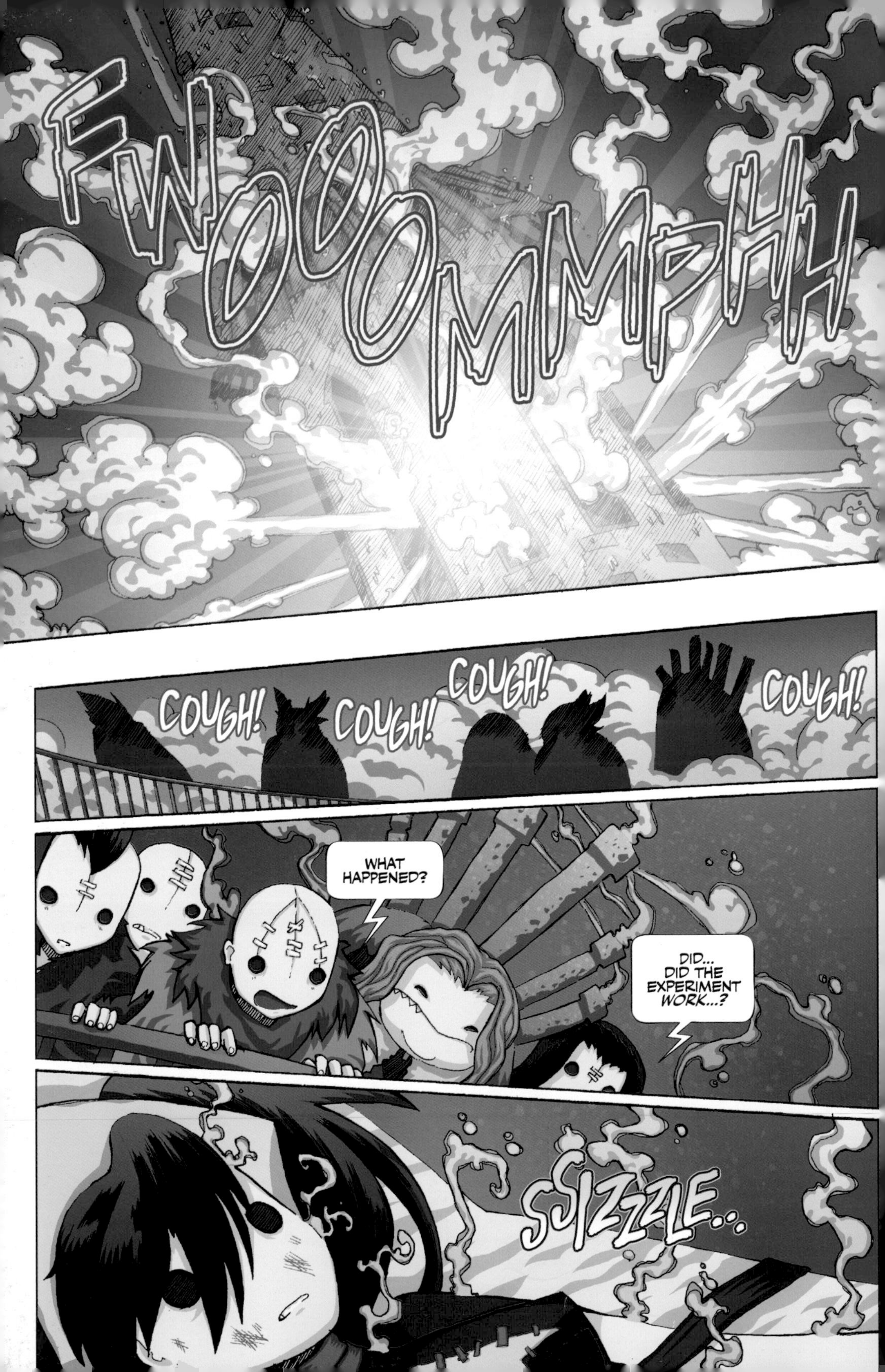
FWOOOMMPHH
COUGH!
COUGH!
COUGH!
COUGH!
WHAT HAPPENED?
DID... DID THE EXPERIMENT WORK...?
SSIZZZLE...

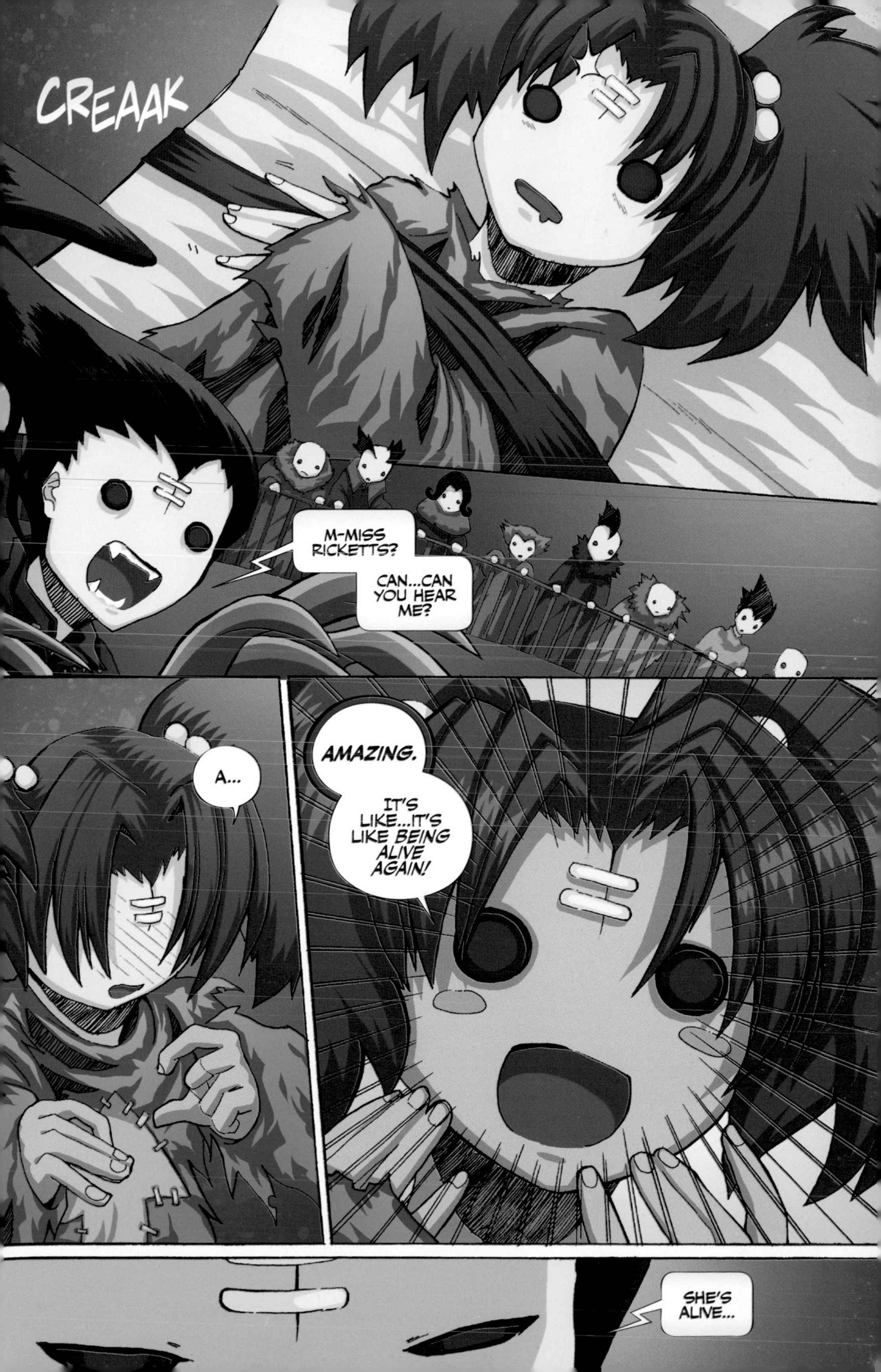
CREAAK
M-MISS RICKETTS?
CAN...CAN YOU HEAR ME?
A...
AMAZING.
IT'S LIKE...IT'S LIKE BEING ALIVE AGAIN!
SHE'S ALIVE...

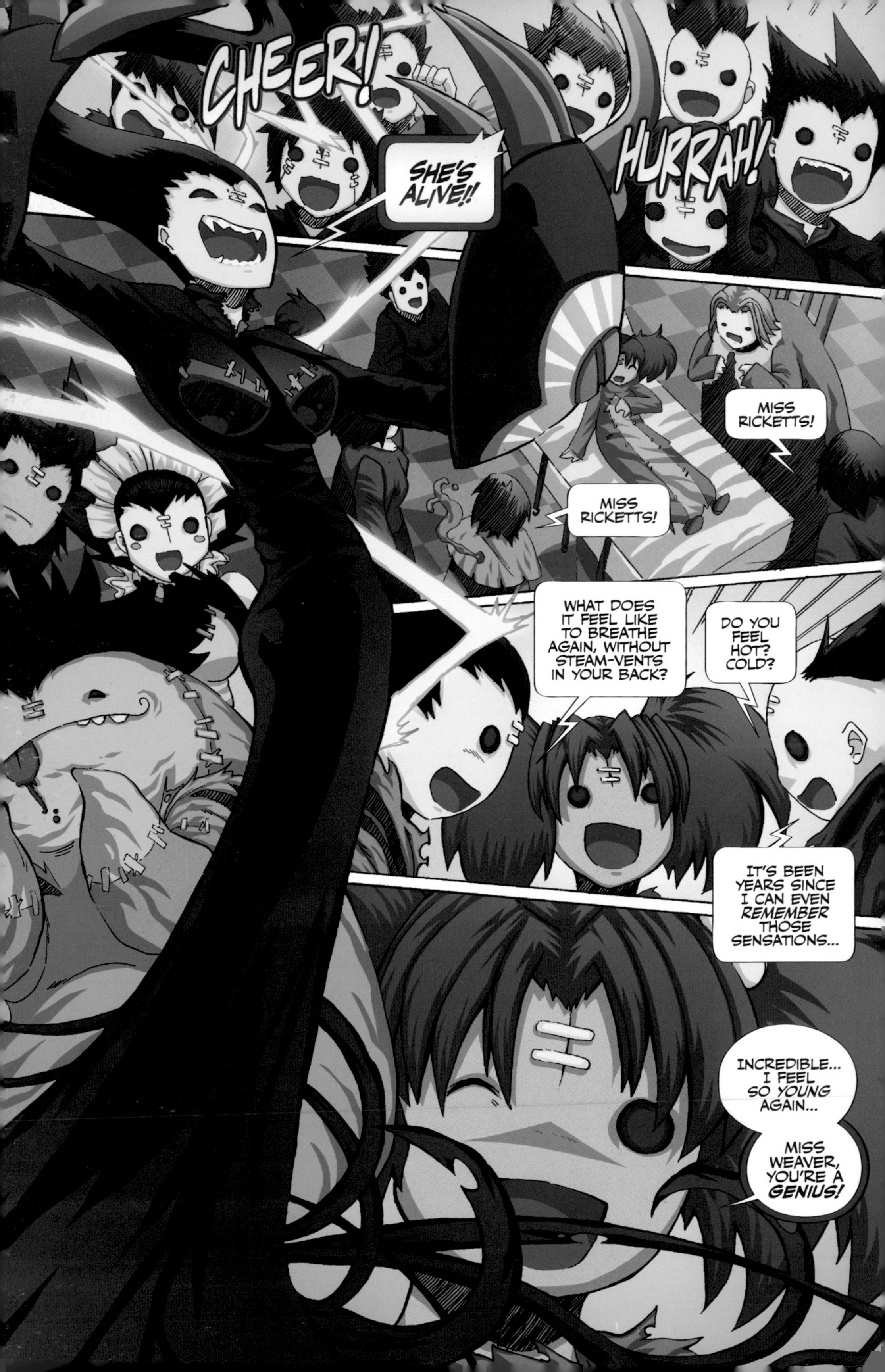
CHEER!
SHE'S ALIVE!!
HURRAH!
MISS RICKETTS!
MISS RICKETTS!
WHAT DOES IT FEEL LIKE TO BREATHE AGAIN, WITHOUT STEAM-VENTS IN YOUR BACK?
DO YOU FEEL HOT? COLD?
IT'S BEEN YEARS SINCE I CAN EVEN *REMEMBER* THOSE SENSATIONS...
INCREDIBLE... I FEEL SO *YOUNG* AGAIN...
MISS WEAVER, YOU'RE A ***GENIUS!***

ARCHIE, YOU REALLY HAVEN'T BEEN TAKING CARE OF YOURSELF, HAVE YOU?

JUST LOOK AT THE *STATE* OF YOU!

LISTEN... THERE ARE TWO FRESH CHILDREN IN THE WINDMILL RIGHT NOW...

WHY DON'T YOU GET OVER THERE WITH STINCH AND RETRIEVE THEM?

WE HAD BETTER GET YOU INTO *McGINTY'S* BODY BEFORE YOUR LIMBS DISMANTLE THEMSELVES COMPLETELY!

WHAT ARE... WHAT ARE YOU GOING TO DO WITH LUCY?

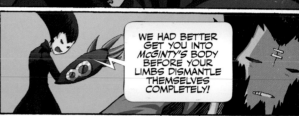

WELL, I WOULD HAVE THOUGHT THAT WOULD BE OBVIOUS, DOCTOR BLEAK.

I HAVE SPENT THE LONGEST TIME IN THIS SHAMBLING MECHANICAL FORM...

NO ONE NEEDS A NEW BODY MORE THAN I DO! *HEE HEE!*

YOU *MONSTER!*

YOU'LL *NEVER* GET AWAY WITH THIS!

WRONG! WITH THE SECRET TO IMMORTALITY *CRACKED...*

THE REPUTATION OF HOLLOW FIELDS WILL BE FAR GREATER THAN THAT OF ANY FORBIDDEN SCIENCE SCHOOL IN THE *WORLD!*

HA HA HA!!

ER... MISS WEAVER...

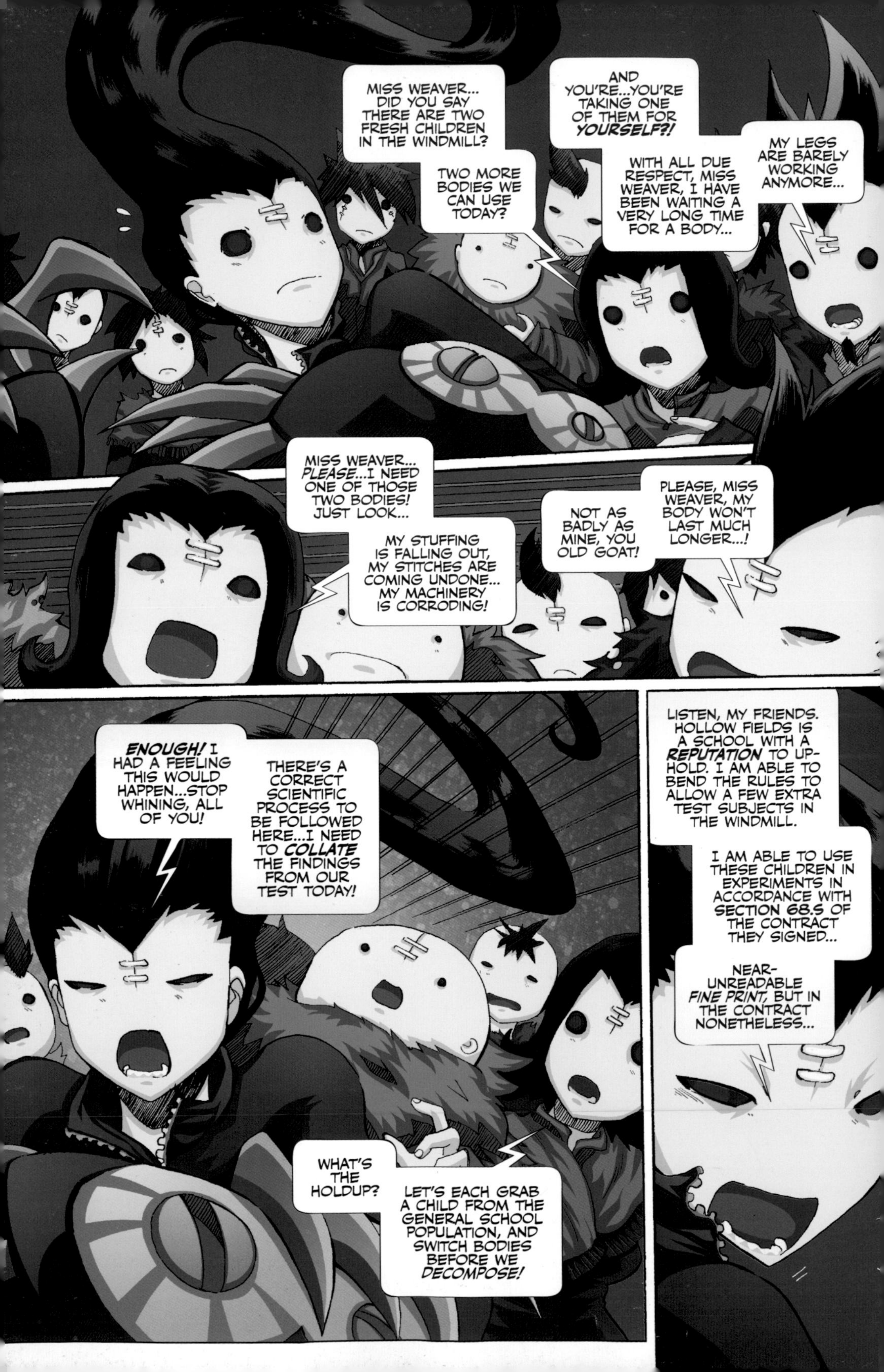
MISS WEAVER... DID YOU SAY THERE ARE TWO FRESH CHILDREN IN THE WINDMILL?
TWO MORE BODIES WE CAN USE TODAY?
AND YOU'RE...YOU'RE TAKING ONE OF THEM FOR *YOURSELF?!*
WITH ALL DUE RESPECT, MISS WEAVER, I HAVE BEEN WAITING A VERY LONG TIME FOR A BODY...
MY LEGS ARE BARELY WORKING ANYMORE...
MISS WEAVER... *PLEASE*...I NEED ONE OF THOSE TWO BODIES! JUST LOOK...
MY STUFFING IS FALLING OUT, MY STITCHES ARE COMING UNDONE... MY MACHINERY IS CORRODING!
NOT AS BADLY AS MINE, YOU OLD GOAT!
PLEASE, MISS WEAVER, MY BODY WON'T LAST MUCH LONGER...!
ENOUGH! I HAD A FEELING THIS WOULD HAPPEN...STOP WHINING, ALL OF YOU!
THERE'S A CORRECT SCIENTIFIC PROCESS TO BE FOLLOWED HERE...I NEED TO ***COLLATE*** THE FINDINGS FROM OUR TEST TODAY!
WHAT'S THE HOLDUP?
LET'S EACH GRAB A CHILD FROM THE GENERAL SCHOOL POPULATION, AND SWITCH BODIES BEFORE WE *DECOMPOSE!*
LISTEN, MY FRIENDS. HOLLOW FIELDS IS A SCHOOL WITH A ***REPUTATION*** TO UPHOLD. I AM ABLE TO BEND THE RULES TO ALLOW A FEW EXTRA TEST SUBJECTS IN THE WINDMILL.
I AM ABLE TO USE THESE CHILDREN IN EXPERIMENTS IN ACCORDANCE WITH **SECTION 68.S** OF THE CONTRACT THEY SIGNED...
NEAR-UNREADABLE *FINE PRINT,* BUT IN THE CONTRACT NONETHELESS...

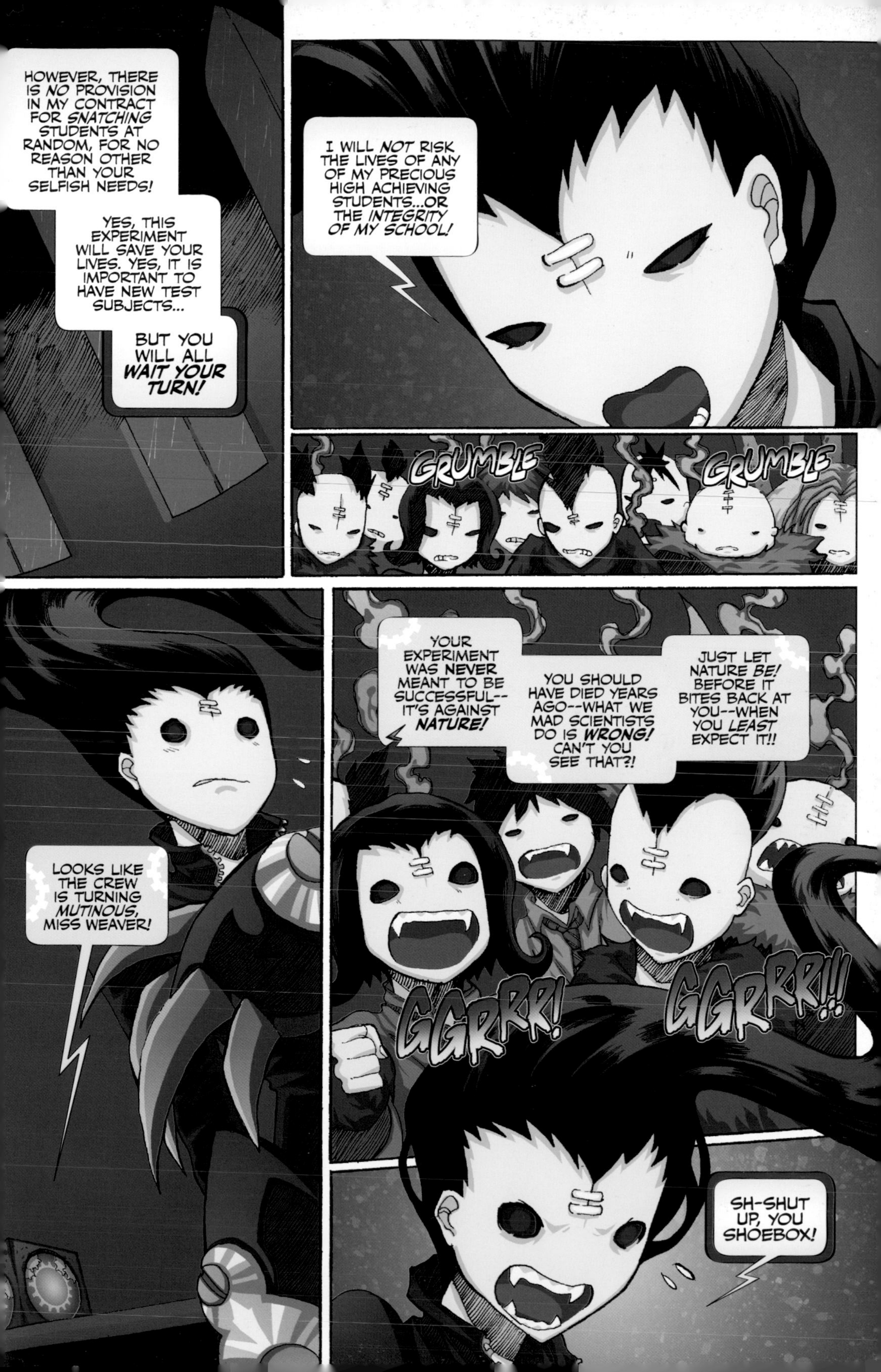
HOWEVER, THERE IS NO PROVISION IN MY CONTRACT FOR SNATCHING STUDENTS AT RANDOM, FOR NO REASON OTHER THAN YOUR SELFISH NEEDS!
YES, THIS EXPERIMENT WILL SAVE YOUR LIVES. YES, IT IS IMPORTANT TO HAVE NEW TEST SUBJECTS...
BUT YOU WILL ALL WAIT YOUR TURN!
I WILL NOT RISK THE LIVES OF ANY OF MY PRECIOUS HIGH ACHIEVING STUDENTS...OR THE INTEGRITY OF MY SCHOOL!
GRUMBLE
GRUMBLE
LOOKS LIKE THE CREW IS TURNING MUTINOUS, MISS WEAVER!
YOUR EXPERIMENT WAS NEVER MEANT TO BE SUCCESSFUL-- IT'S AGAINST NATURE!
YOU SHOULD HAVE DIED YEARS AGO--WHAT WE MAD SCIENTISTS DO IS WRONG! CAN'T YOU SEE THAT?!
JUST LET NATURE BE! BEFORE IT BITES BACK AT YOU--WHEN YOU LEAST EXPECT IT!!
GGRRR!
GGRRR!!
SH-SHUT UP, YOU SHOEBOX!

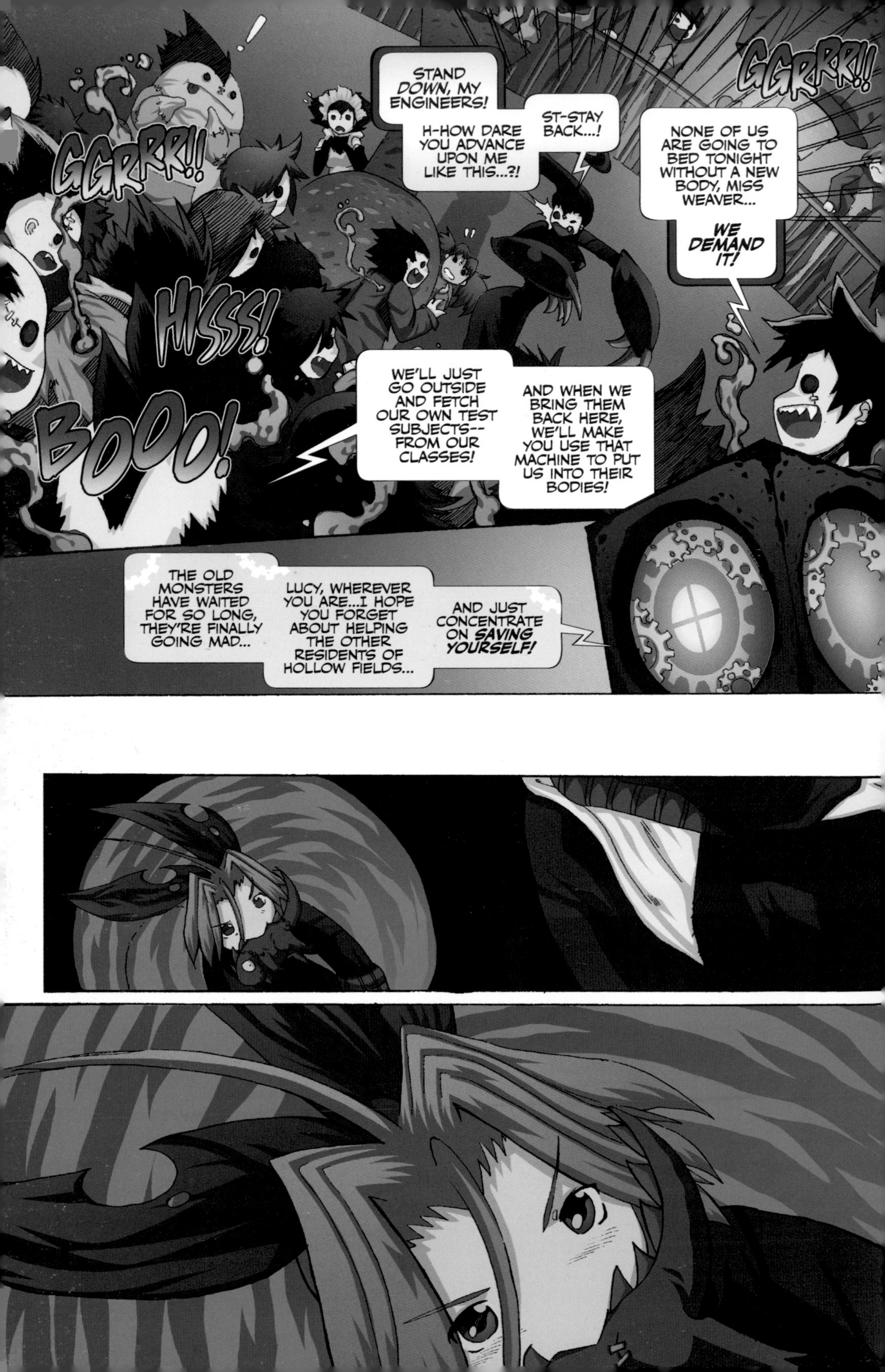
GGRRR!!
STAND DOWN, MY ENGINEERS!
H-HOW DARE YOU ADVANCE UPON ME LIKE THIS...?!
ST-STAY BACK...!
GGRRR!!
NONE OF US ARE GOING TO BED TONIGHT WITHOUT A NEW BODY, MISS WEAVER...
WE DEMAND IT!
HISSS!
BOOO!
WE'LL JUST GO OUTSIDE AND FETCH OUR OWN TEST SUBJECTS-- FROM OUR CLASSES!
AND WHEN WE BRING THEM BACK HERE, WE'LL MAKE YOU USE THAT MACHINE TO PUT US INTO THEIR BODIES!
THE OLD MONSTERS HAVE WAITED FOR SO LONG, THEY'RE FINALLY GOING MAD...
LUCY, WHEREVER YOU ARE...I HOPE YOU FORGET ABOUT HELPING THE OTHER RESIDENTS OF HOLLOW FIELDS...
AND JUST CONCENTRATE ON SAVING YOURSELF!

CHAPTER TWELVE

Croach's Revenge

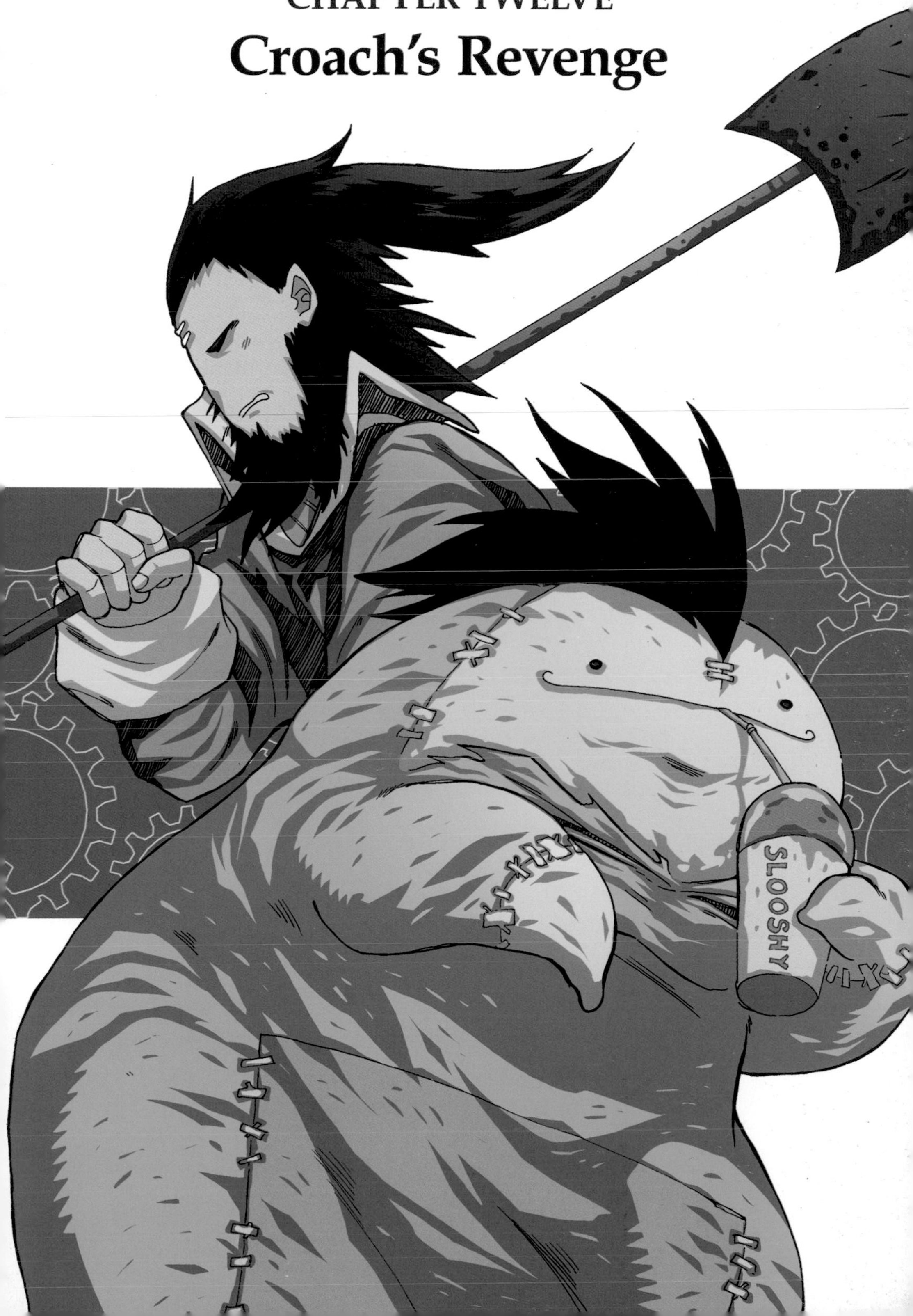
SLOOSHY

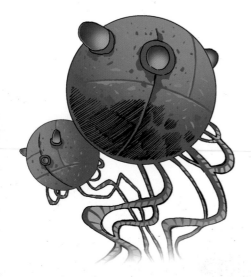

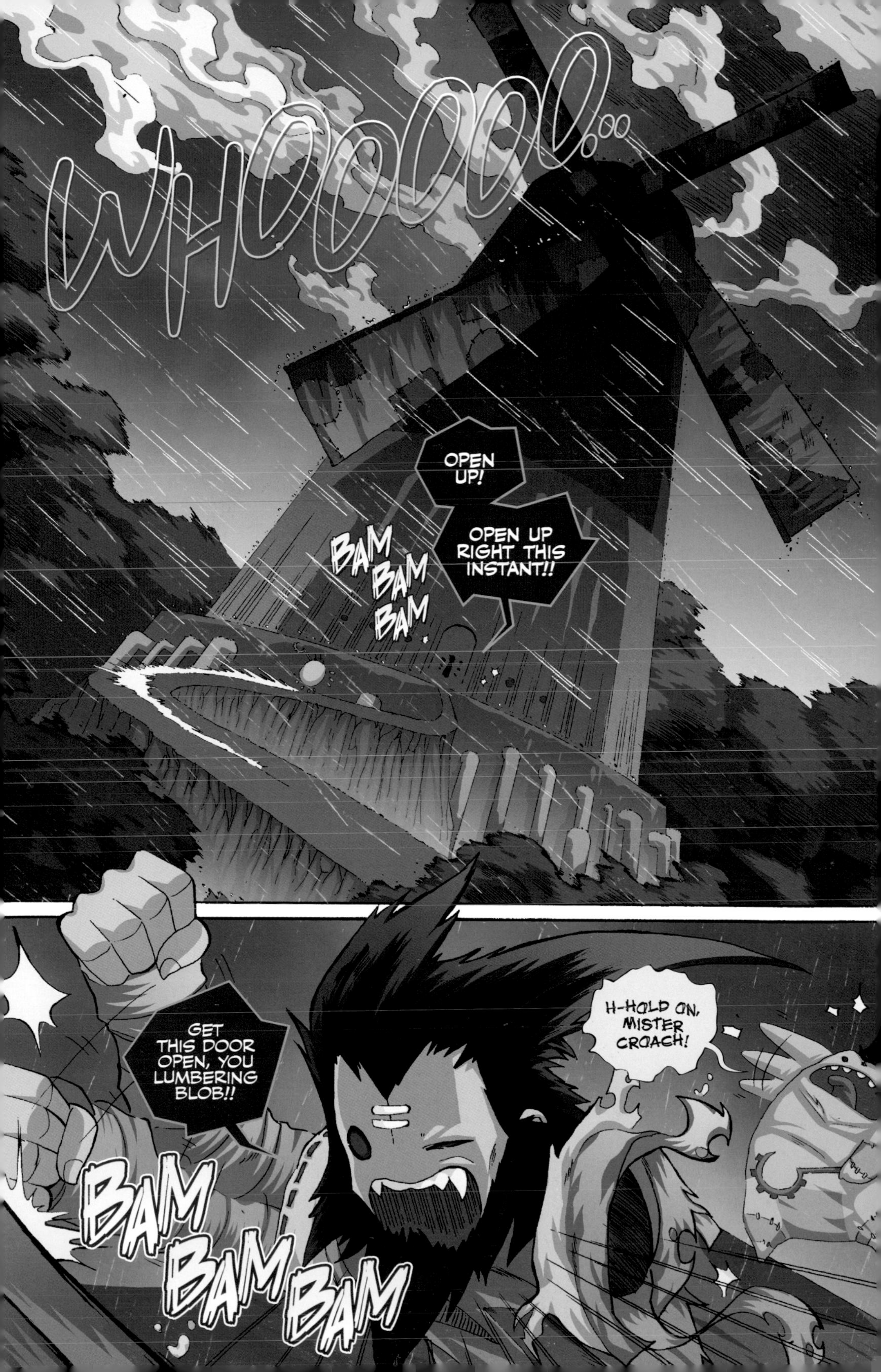
WHOOOOOO...
OPEN UP!
BAM BAM BAM
OPEN UP RIGHT THIS INSTANT!!
GET THIS DOOR OPEN, YOU LUMBERING BLOB!!
H-HOLD ON, MISTER CROACH!
BAM BAM BAM

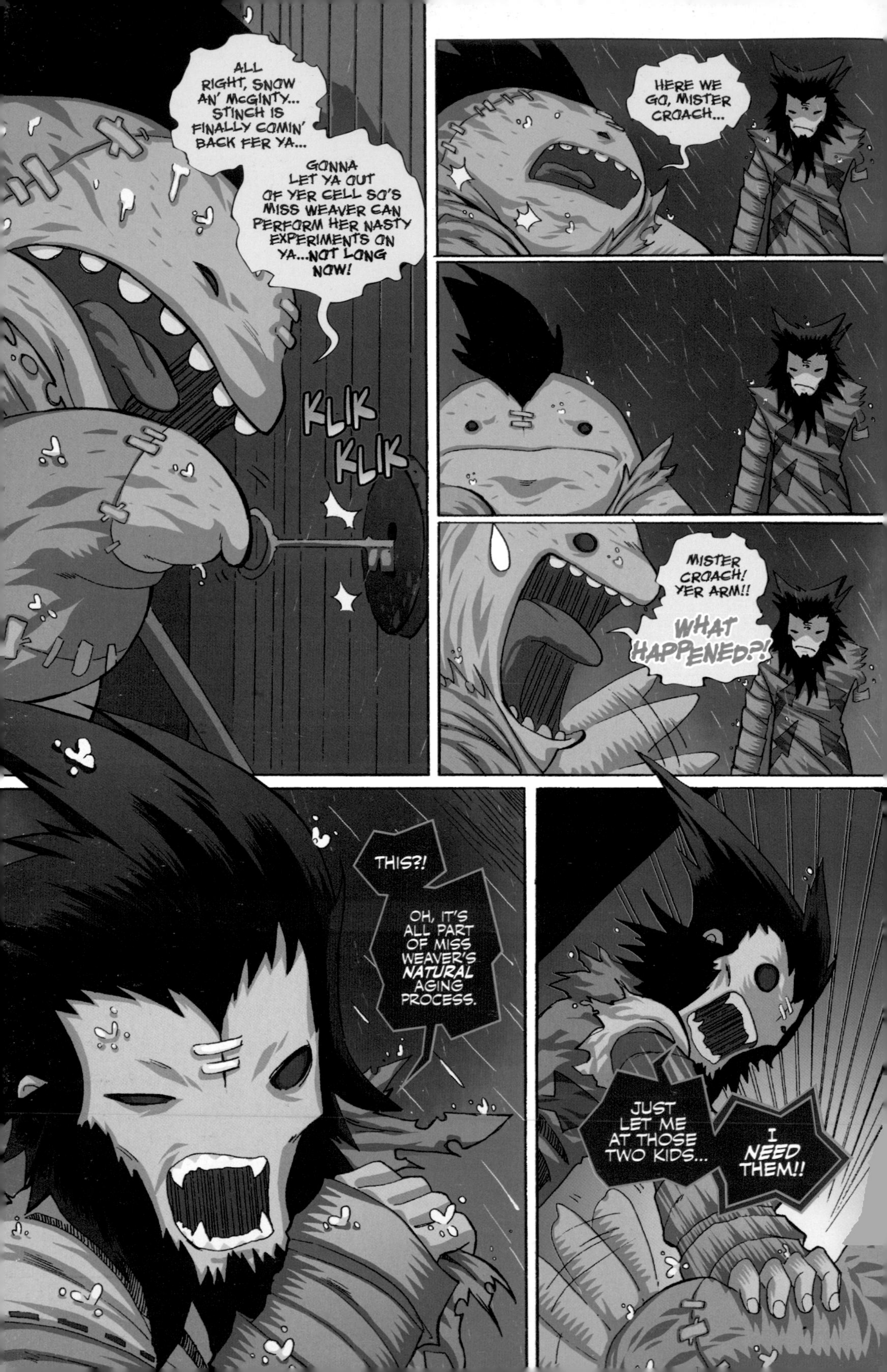

ALL RIGHT, SNOW AN' McGINTY... STINCH IS FINALLY COMIN' BACK FER YA...
GONNA LET YA OUT OF YER CELL SO'S MISS WEAVER CAN PERFORM HER NASTY EXPERIMENTS ON YA...NOT LONG NOW!
KLIK KLIK
HERE WE GO, MISTER CROACH...
MISTER CROACH! YER ARM!!
WHAT HAPPENED?!
THIS?!
OH, IT'S ALL PART OF MISS WEAVER'S NATURAL AGING PROCESS.
JUST LET ME AT THOSE TWO KIDS...
I NEED THEM!!

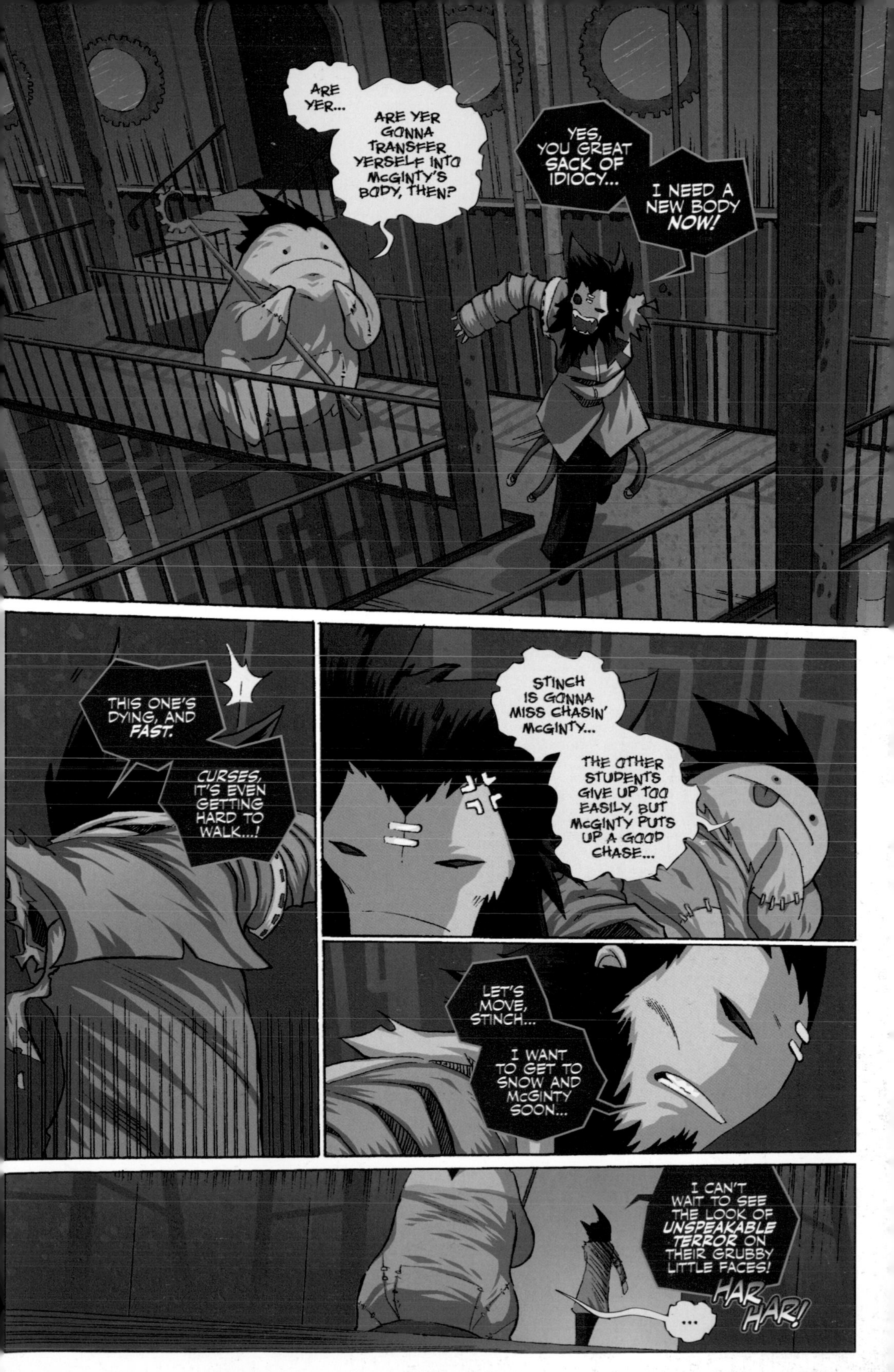

ARE YER...
ARE YER GONNA TRANSFER YERSELF INTO McGINTY'S BODY, THEN?
YES, YOU GREAT SACK OF IDIOCY...
I NEED A NEW BODY *NOW!*
THIS ONE'S DYING, AND *FAST.*
!
CURSES, IT'S EVEN GETTING HARD TO WALK...!
STINCH IS GONNA MISS CHASIN' McGINTY...
THE OTHER STUDENTS GIVE UP TOO EASILY, BUT McGINTY PUTS UP A GOOD CHASE...
LET'S MOVE, STINCH...
I WANT TO GET TO SNOW AND McGINTY SOON...
I CAN'T WAIT TO SEE THE LOOK OF ***UNSPEAKABLE TERROR*** ON THEIR GRUBBY LITTLE FACES!
HAR HAR!
...

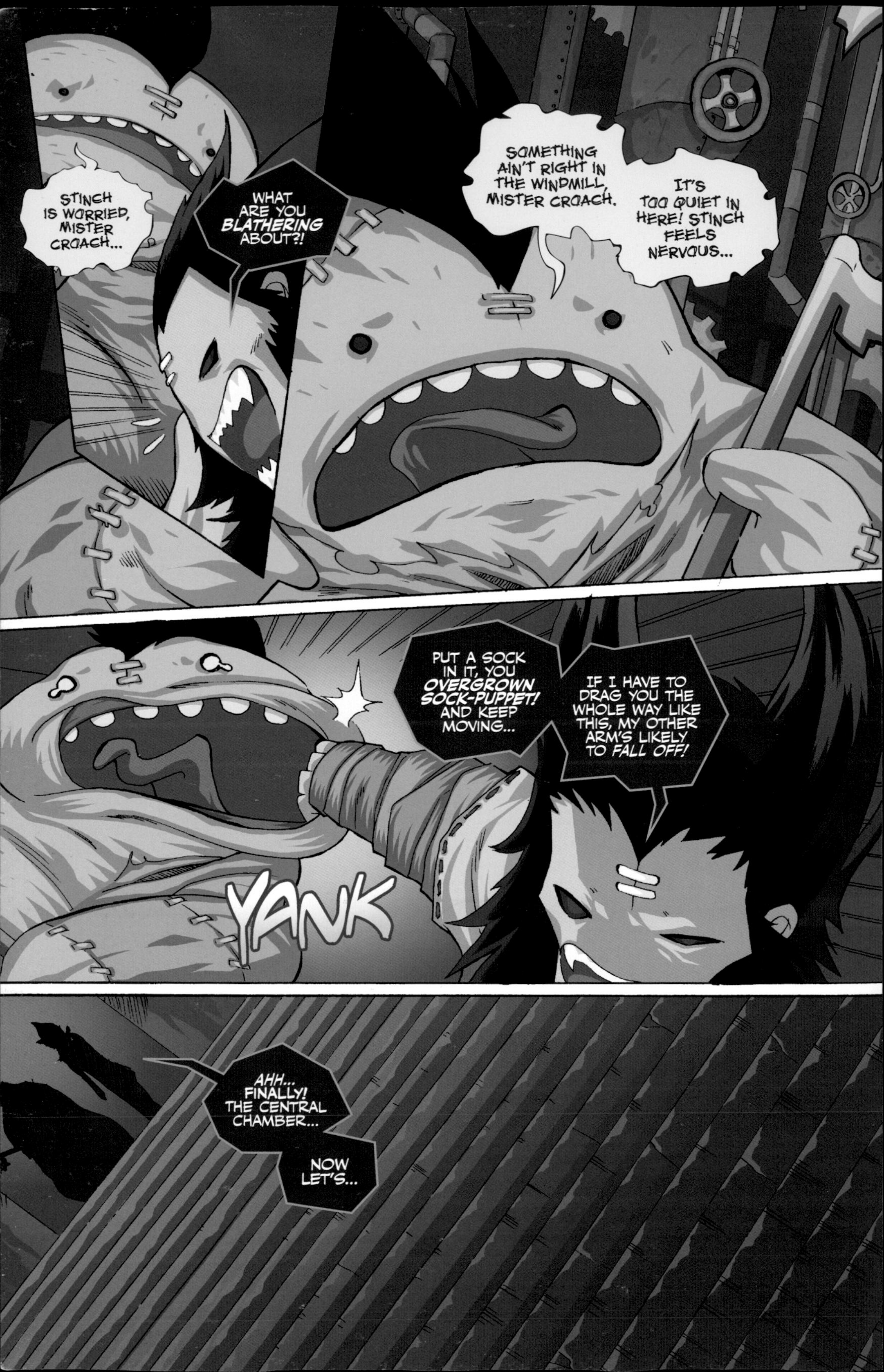
STINCH IS WORRIED, MISTER CROACH...
WHAT ARE YOU BLATHERING ABOUT?!
SOMETHING AIN'T RIGHT IN THE WINDMILL, MISTER CROACH.
IT'S TOO QUIET IN HERE! STINCH FEELS NERVOUS...
PUT A SOCK IN IT, YOU OVERGROWN SOCK-PUPPET! AND KEEP MOVING...
IF I HAVE TO DRAG YOU THE WHOLE WAY LIKE THIS, MY OTHER ARM'S LIKELY TO FALL OFF!
YANK
AHH... FINALLY! THE CENTRAL CHAMBER...
NOW LET'S...

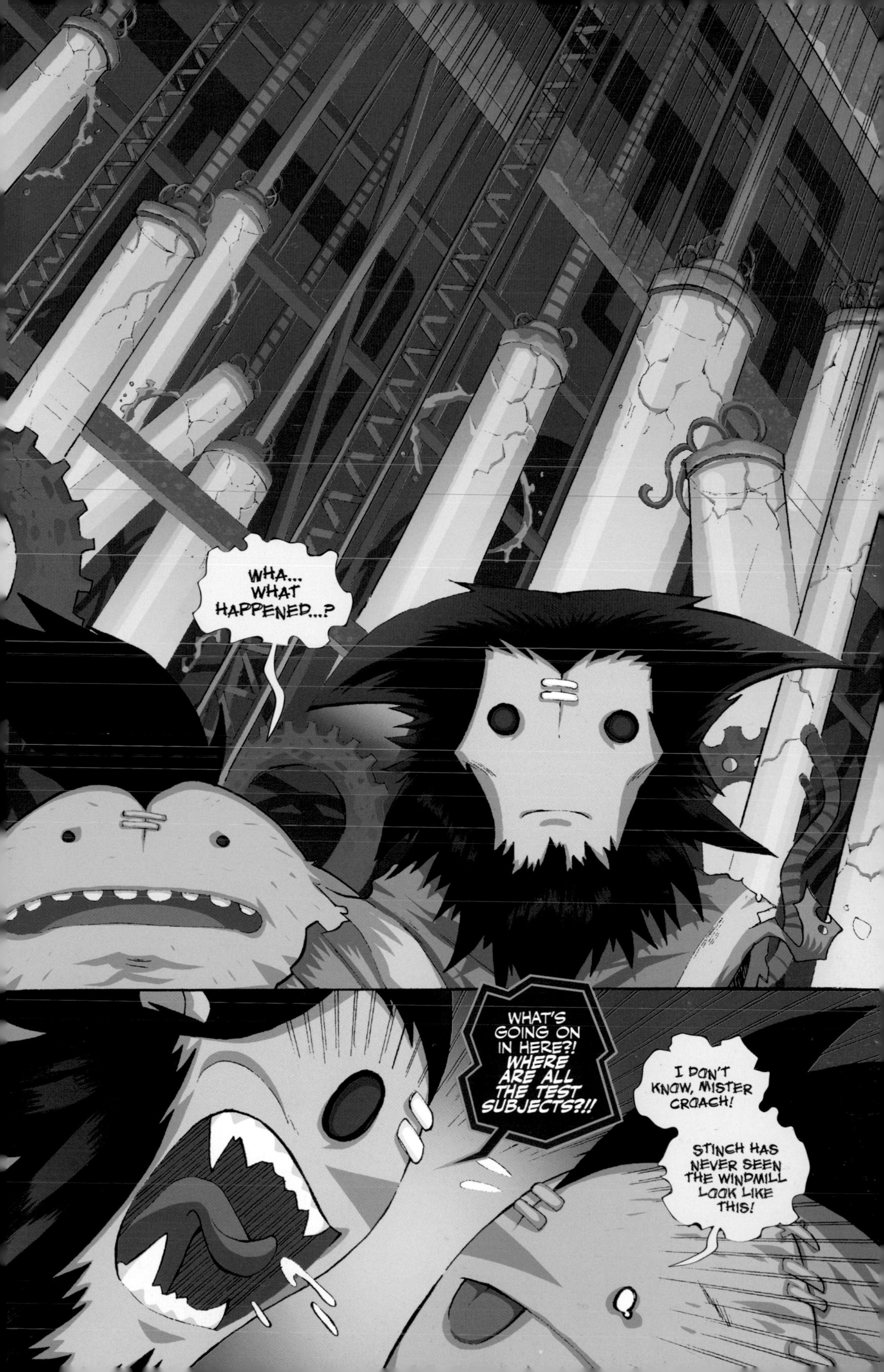
WHA... WHAT HAPPENED...?
WHAT'S GOING ON IN HERE?! WHERE ARE ALL THE TEST SUBJECTS?!!
I DON'T KNOW, MISTER CROACH!
STINCH HAS NEVER SEEN THE WINDMILL LOOK LIKE THIS!

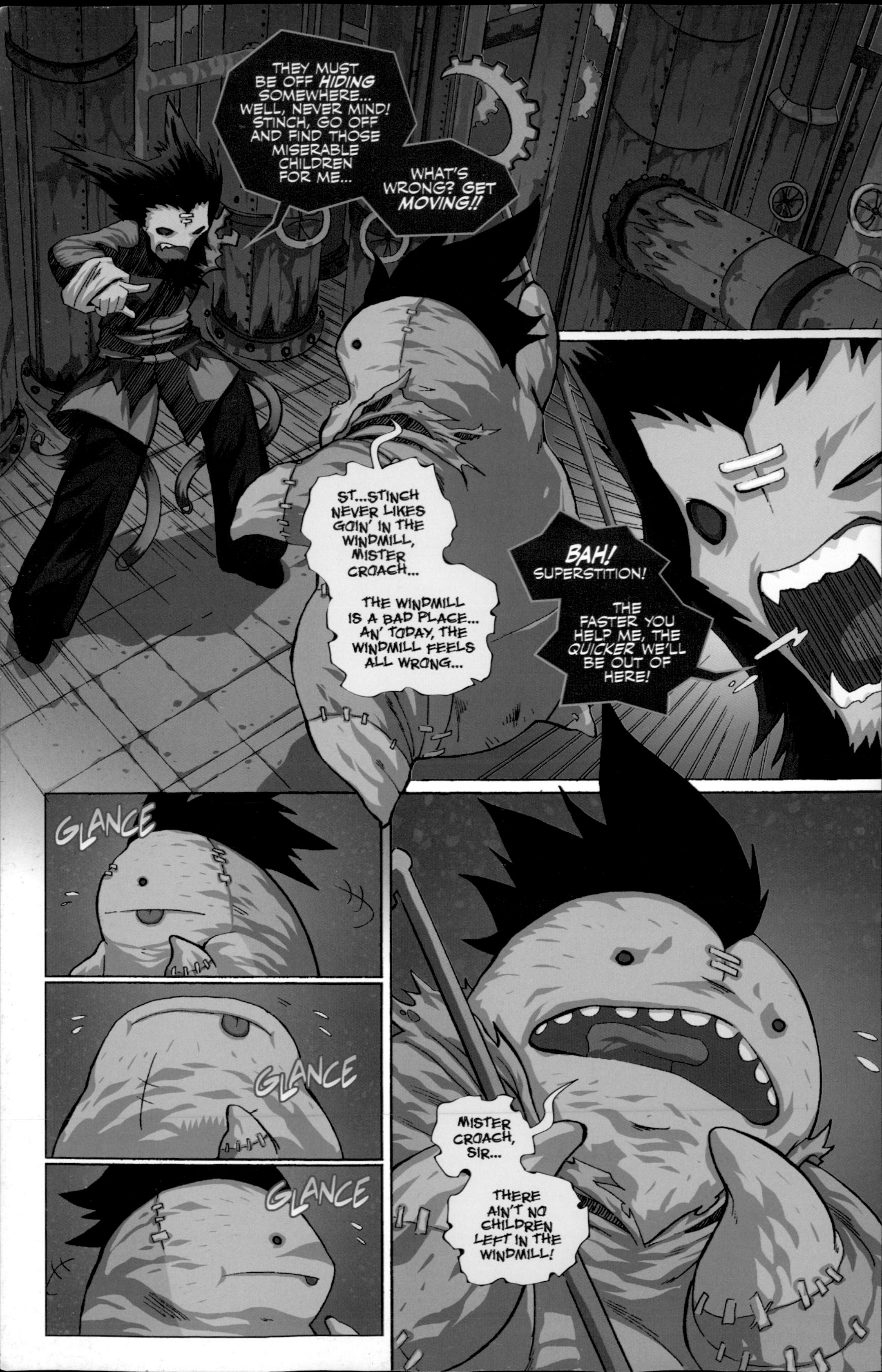
THEY MUST BE OFF *HIDING* SOMEWHERE... WELL, NEVER MIND! STINCH, GO OFF AND FIND THOSE MISERABLE CHILDREN FOR ME...
WHAT'S WRONG? GET *MOVING!!*
ST...STINCH NEVER LIKES GOIN' IN THE WINDMILL, MISTER CROACH...
THE WINDMILL IS A BAD PLACE... AN' TODAY, THE WINDMILL FEELS ALL WRONG...
BAH! SUPERSTITION!
THE FASTER YOU HELP ME, THE *QUICKER* WE'LL BE OUT OF HERE!
GLANCE
GLANCE
GLANCE
MISTER CROACH, SIR...
THERE AIN'T NO CHILDREN LEFT IN THE WINDMILL!

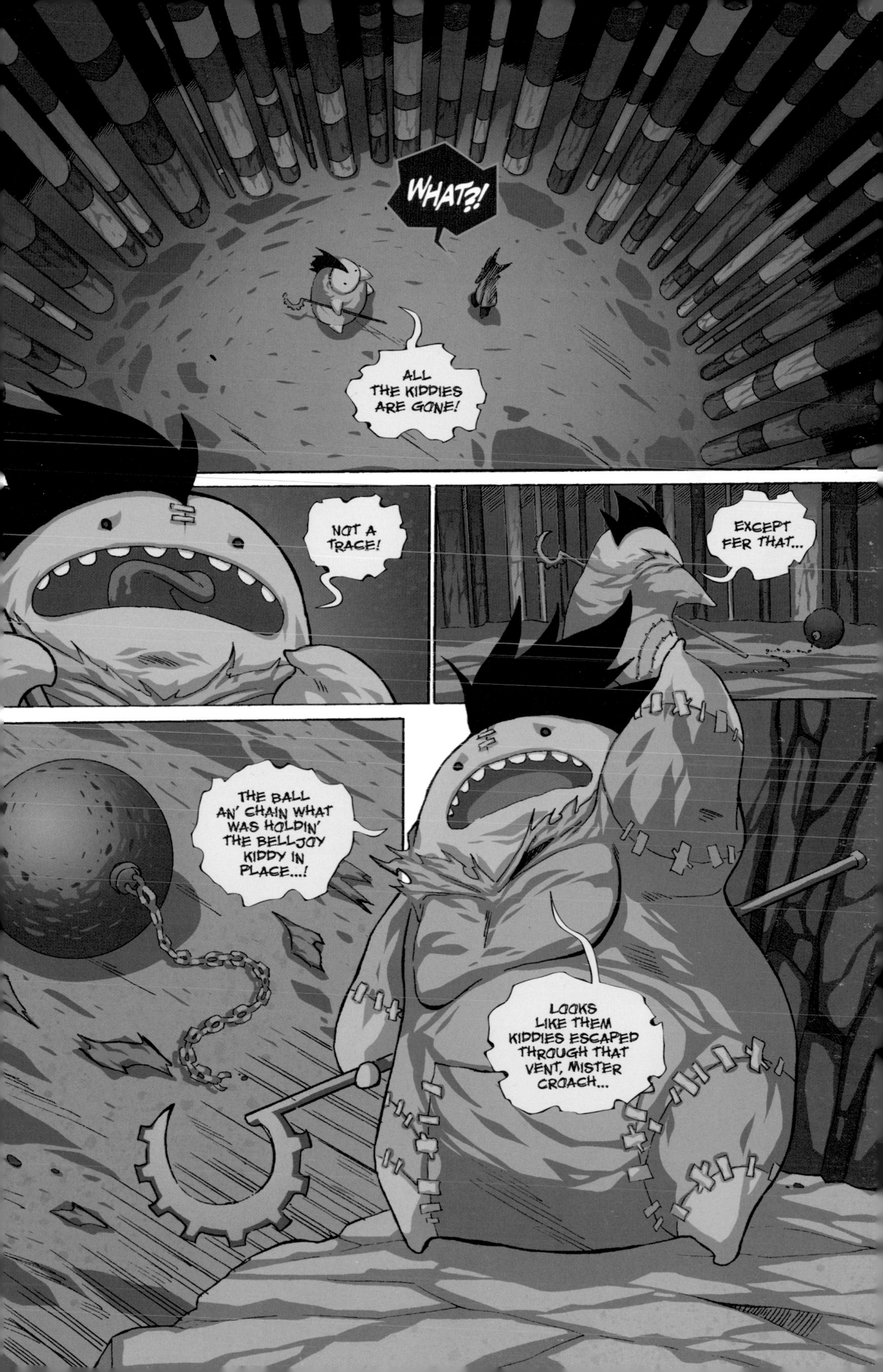
WHAT?!
ALL THE KIDDIES ARE GONE!
NOT A TRACE!
EXCEPT FER THAT...
THE BALL AN' CHAIN WHAT WAS HOLDIN' THE BELLJOY KIDDY IN PLACE...!
LOOKS LIKE THEM KIDDIES ESCAPED THROUGH THAT VENT, MISTER CROACH...

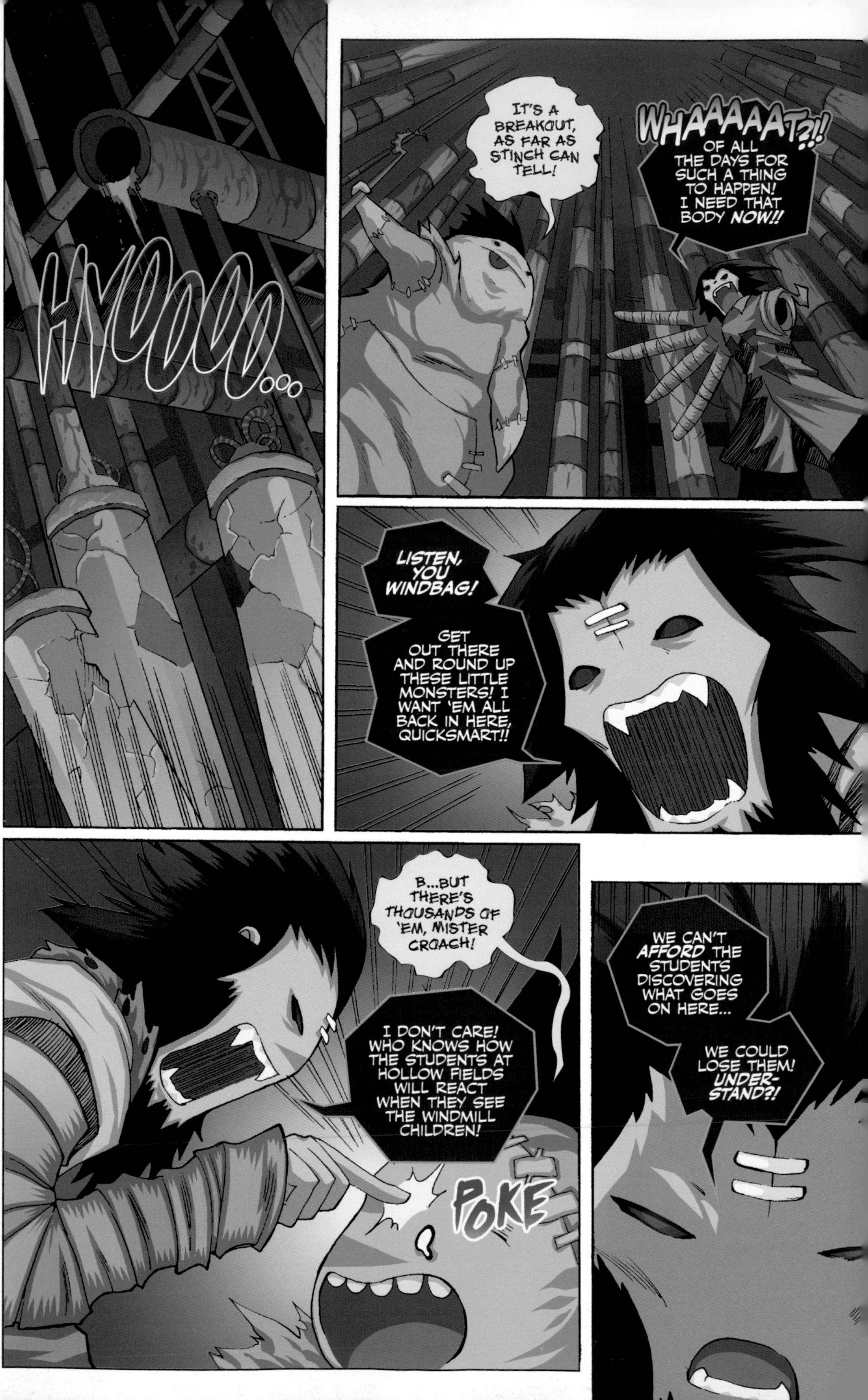
HYOOOO...ooo
IT'S A BREAKOUT, AS FAR AS STINCH CAN TELL!
WHAAAAAT?!!
OF ALL THE DAYS FOR SUCH A THING TO HAPPEN! I NEED THAT BODY NOW!!
LISTEN, YOU WINDBAG!
GET OUT THERE AND ROUND UP THESE LITTLE MONSTERS! I WANT 'EM ALL BACK IN HERE, QUICKSMART!!
B...BUT THERE'S THOUSANDS OF 'EM, MISTER CROACH!
I DON'T CARE! WHO KNOWS HOW THE STUDENTS AT HOLLOW FIELDS WILL REACT WHEN THEY SEE THE WINDMILL CHILDREN!
POKE
WE CAN'T AFFORD THE STUDENTS DISCOVERING WHAT GOES ON HERE...
WE COULD LOSE THEM! UNDER-STAND?!

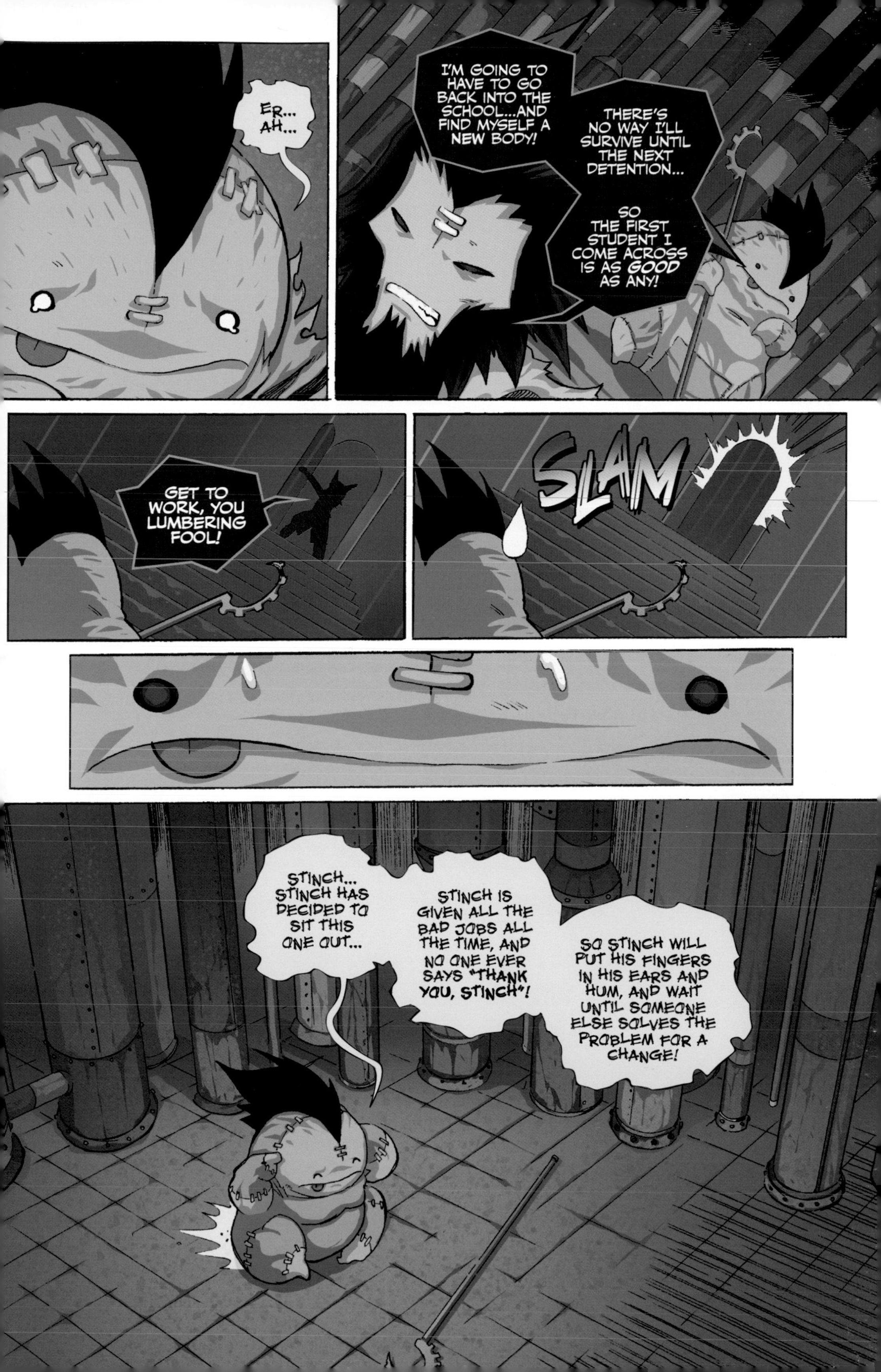
ER... AH...
I'M GOING TO HAVE TO GO BACK INTO THE SCHOOL...AND FIND MYSELF A NEW BODY!
THERE'S NO WAY I'LL SURVIVE UNTIL THE NEXT DETENTION...
SO THE FIRST STUDENT I COME ACROSS IS AS GOOD AS ANY!
GET TO WORK, YOU LUMBERING FOOL!
SLAM
STINCH... STINCH HAS DECIDED TO SIT THIS ONE OUT...
STINCH IS GIVEN ALL THE BAD JOBS ALL THE TIME, AND NO ONE EVER SAYS "THANK YOU, STINCH"!
SO STINCH WILL PUT HIS FINGERS IN HIS EARS AND HUM, AND WAIT UNTIL SOMEONE ELSE SOLVES THE PROBLEM FOR A CHANGE!

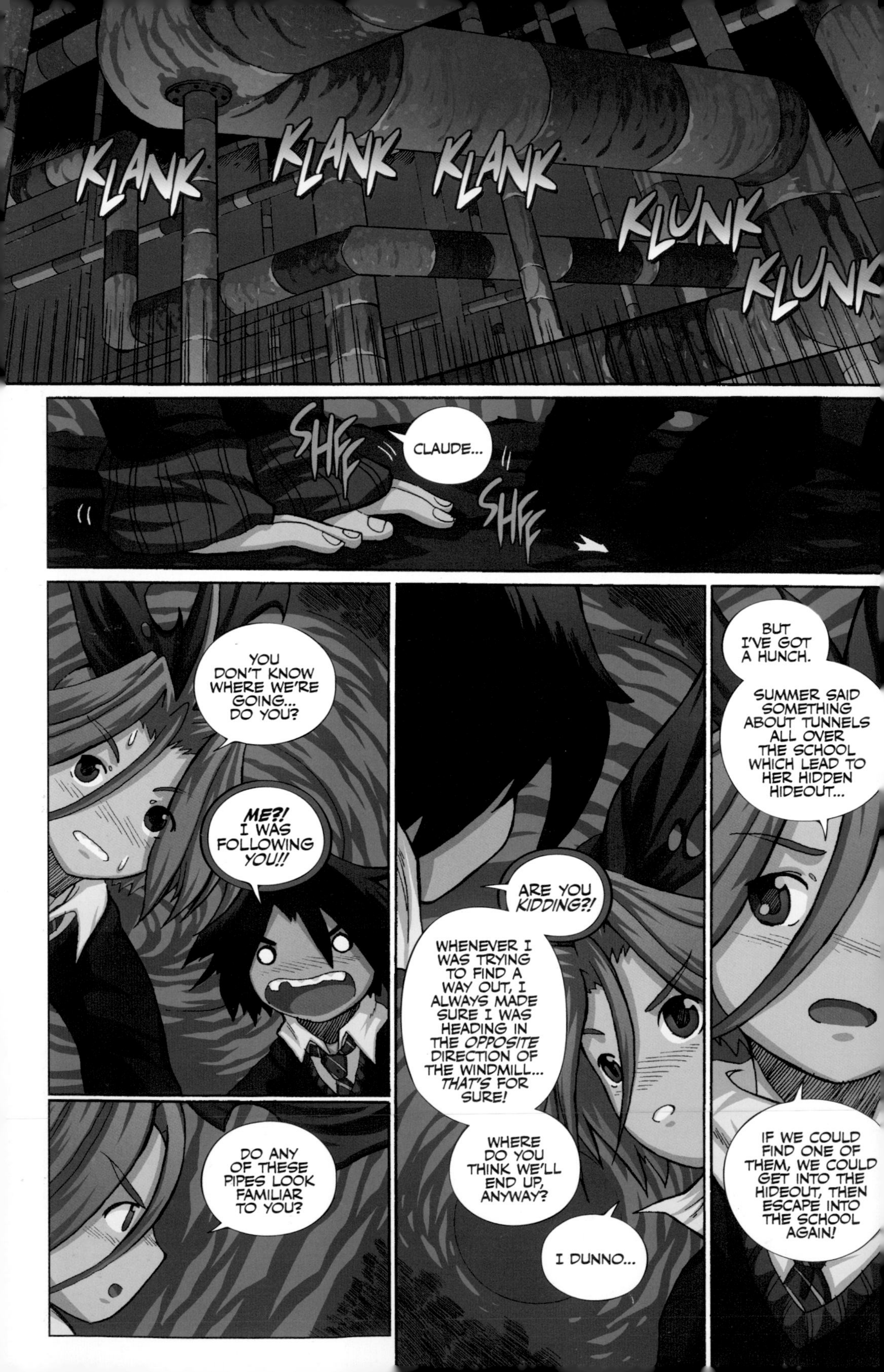
KLANK
KLANK
KLANK
KLUNK
KLUNK
SHFF
CLAUDE...
SHFF
YOU DON'T KNOW WHERE WE'RE GOING... DO YOU?
ME?! I WAS FOLLOWING *YOU!!*
DO ANY OF THESE PIPES LOOK FAMILIAR TO YOU?
ARE YOU *KIDDING?!*
WHENEVER I WAS TRYING TO FIND A WAY OUT, I ALWAYS MADE SURE I WAS HEADING IN THE *OPPOSITE* DIRECTION OF THE WINDMILL... *THAT'S* FOR SURE!
WHERE DO YOU THINK WE'LL END UP, ANYWAY?
I DUNNO...
BUT I'VE GOT A HUNCH.
SUMMER SAID SOMETHING ABOUT TUNNELS ALL OVER THE SCHOOL WHICH LEAD TO HER HIDDEN HIDEOUT...
IF WE COULD FIND ONE OF THEM, WE COULD GET INTO THE HIDEOUT, THEN ESCAPE INTO THE SCHOOL AGAIN!

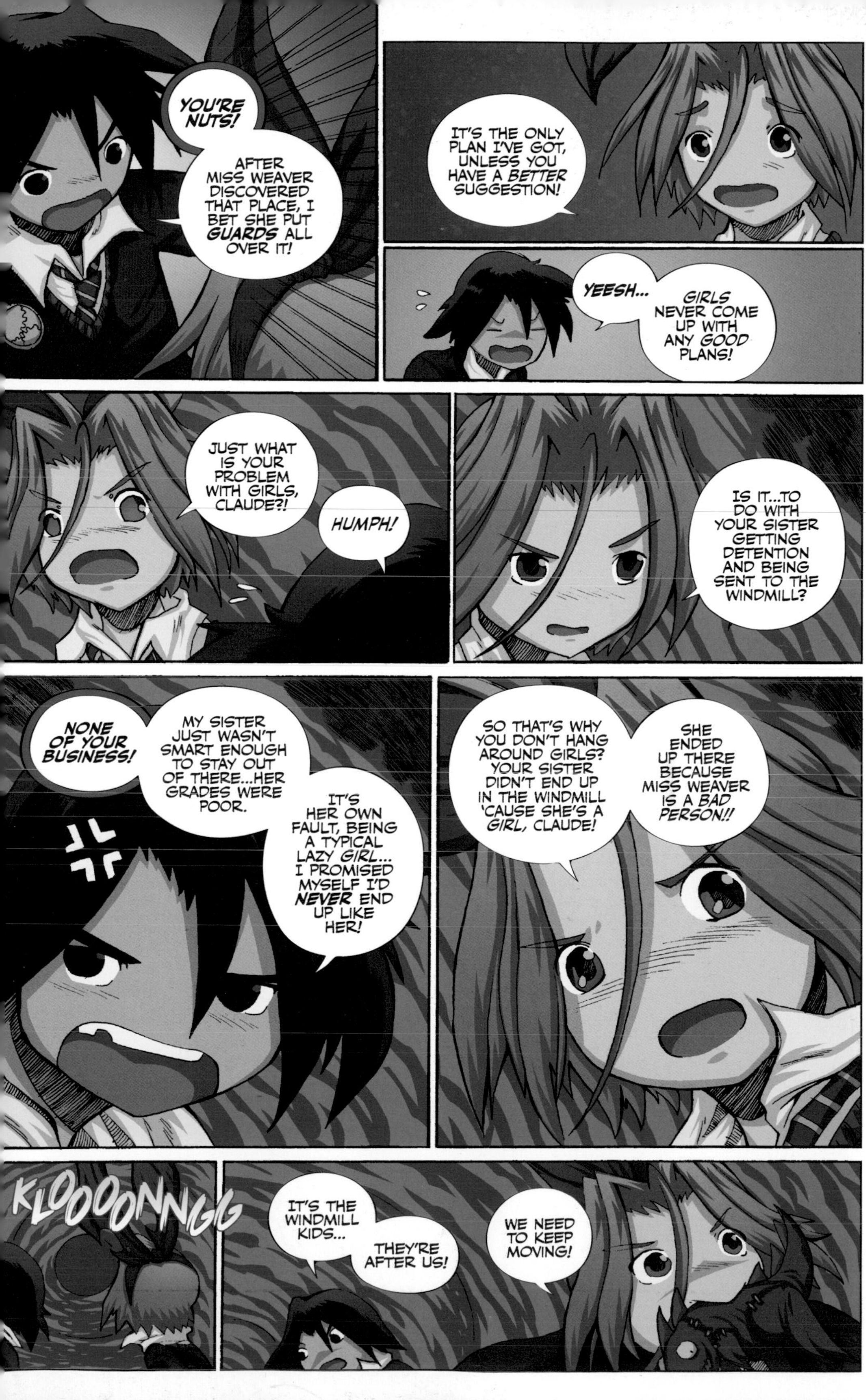
YOU'RE NUTS!
AFTER MISS WEAVER DISCOVERED THAT PLACE, I BET SHE PUT GUARDS ALL OVER IT!
IT'S THE ONLY PLAN I'VE GOT, UNLESS YOU HAVE A BETTER SUGGESTION!
YEESH...
GIRLS NEVER COME UP WITH ANY GOOD PLANS!
JUST WHAT IS YOUR PROBLEM WITH GIRLS, CLAUDE?!
HUMPH!
IS IT...TO DO WITH YOUR SISTER GETTING DETENTION AND BEING SENT TO THE WINDMILL?
NONE OF YOUR BUSINESS!
MY SISTER JUST WASN'T SMART ENOUGH TO STAY OUT OF THERE...HER GRADES WERE POOR.
IT'S HER OWN FAULT, BEING A TYPICAL LAZY GIRL... I PROMISED MYSELF I'D NEVER END UP LIKE HER!
SO THAT'S WHY YOU DON'T HANG AROUND GIRLS? YOUR SISTER DIDN'T END UP IN THE WINDMILL 'CAUSE SHE'S A GIRL, CLAUDE!
SHE ENDED UP THERE BECAUSE MISS WEAVER IS A BAD PERSON!!
KLOOOONNGG
IT'S THE WINDMILL KIDS...
THEY'RE AFTER US!
WE NEED TO KEEP MOVING!

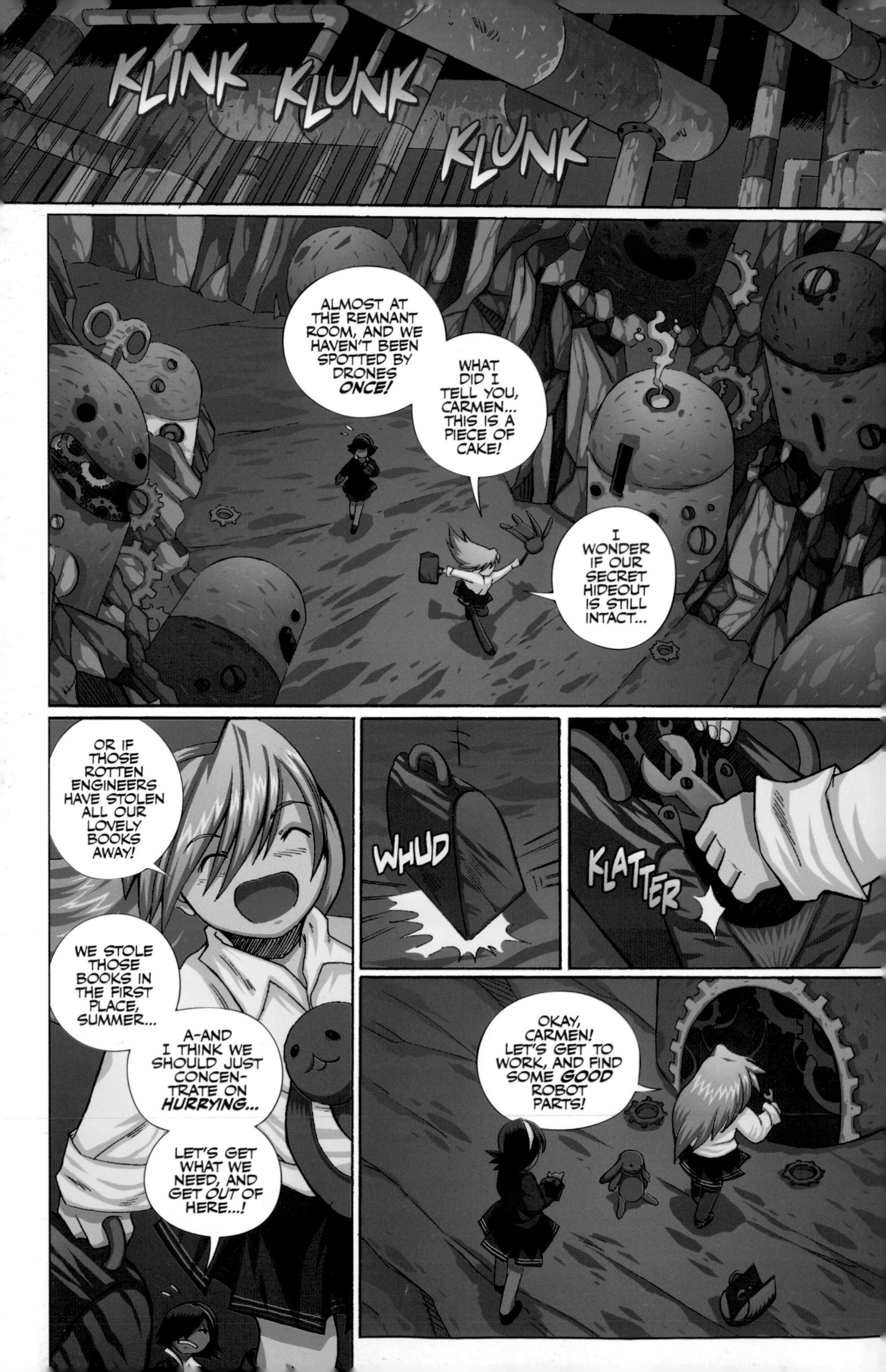
KLINK KLUNK
KLUNK
ALMOST AT THE REMNANT ROOM, AND WE HAVEN'T BEEN SPOTTED BY DRONES *ONCE!*
WHAT DID I TELL YOU, CARMEN... THIS IS A PIECE OF CAKE!
I WONDER IF OUR SECRET HIDEOUT IS STILL INTACT...
OR IF THOSE ROTTEN ENGINEERS HAVE STOLEN ALL OUR LOVELY BOOKS AWAY!
WE STOLE THOSE BOOKS IN THE FIRST PLACE, SUMMER...
A-AND I THINK WE SHOULD JUST CONCEN-TRATE ON *HURRYING...*
LET'S GET WHAT WE NEED, AND GET *OUT* OF HERE...!
WHUD
KLATTER
OKAY, CARMEN! LET'S GET TO WORK, AND FIND SOME *GOOD* ROBOT PARTS!

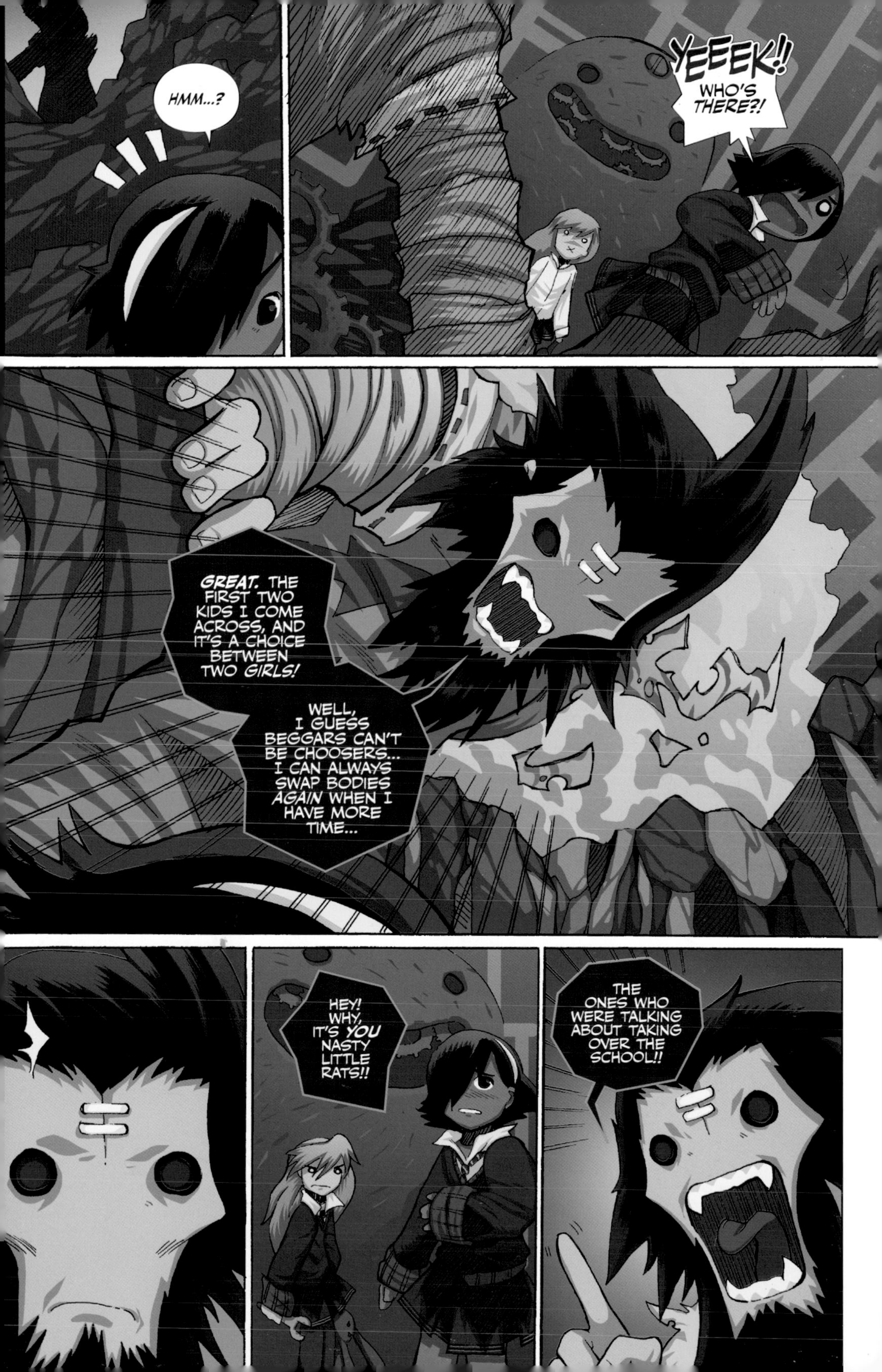
HMM...?
YEEEK!!
WHO'S THERE?!
GREAT. THE FIRST TWO KIDS I COME ACROSS, AND IT'S A CHOICE BETWEEN TWO GIRLS!
WELL, I GUESS BEGGARS CAN'T BE CHOOSERS... I CAN ALWAYS SWAP BODIES AGAIN WHEN I HAVE MORE TIME...
HEY! WHY, IT'S YOU NASTY LITTLE RATS!!
THE ONES WHO WERE TALKING ABOUT TAKING OVER THE SCHOOL!!

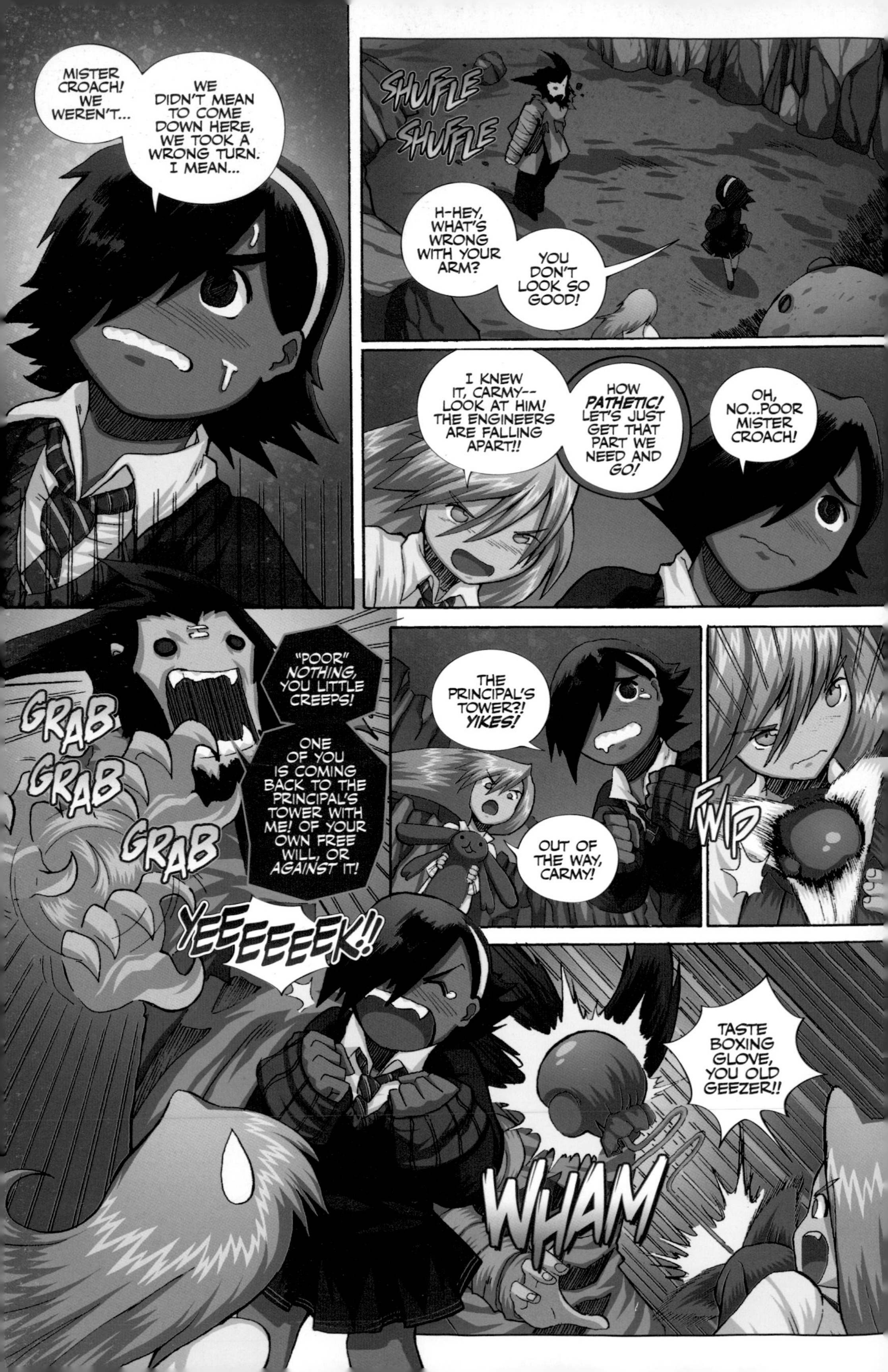
MISTER CROACH! WE WEREN'T...
WE DIDN'T MEAN TO COME DOWN HERE, WE TOOK A WRONG TURN. I MEAN...
SHUFFLE SHUFFLE
H-HEY, WHAT'S WRONG WITH YOUR ARM?
YOU DON'T LOOK SO GOOD!
I KNEW IT, CARMY-- LOOK AT HIM! THE ENGINEERS ARE FALLING APART!!
HOW *PATHETIC!* LET'S JUST GET THAT PART WE NEED AND *GO!*
OH, NO...POOR MISTER CROACH!
"POOR" *NOTHING,* YOU LITTLE CREEPS!
ONE OF YOU IS COMING BACK TO THE PRINCIPAL'S TOWER WITH ME! OF YOUR OWN FREE WILL, OR *AGAINST* IT!
GRAB GRAB GRAB
THE PRINCIPAL'S TOWER?! *YIKES!*
OUT OF THE WAY, CARMY!
FWIP
YEEEEEEK!!
TASTE BOXING GLOVE, YOU OLD GEEZER!!
WHAM

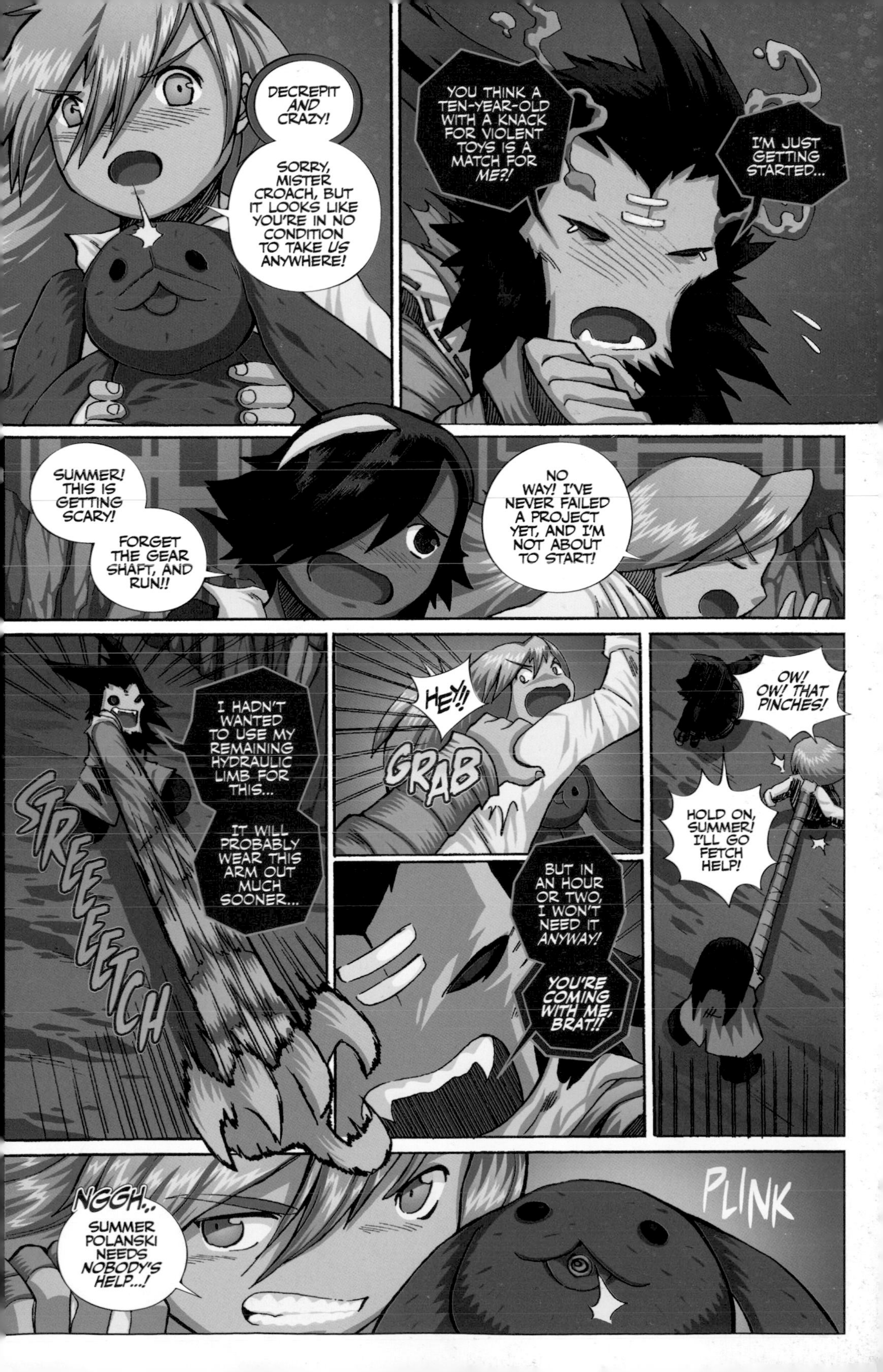
DECREPIT AND CRAZY!
SORRY, MISTER CROACH, BUT IT LOOKS LIKE YOU'RE IN NO CONDITION TO TAKE US ANYWHERE!
YOU THINK A TEN-YEAR-OLD WITH A KNACK FOR VIOLENT TOYS IS A MATCH FOR ME?!
I'M JUST GETTING STARTED...
SUMMER! THIS IS GETTING SCARY!
FORGET THE GEAR SHAFT, AND RUN!!
NO WAY! I'VE NEVER FAILED A PROJECT YET, AND I'M NOT ABOUT TO START!
I HADN'T WANTED TO USE MY REMAINING HYDRAULIC LIMB FOR THIS...
IT WILL PROBABLY WEAR THIS ARM OUT MUCH SOONER...
STREEEEETCH
HEY!!
GRAB
BUT IN AN HOUR OR TWO, I WON'T NEED IT ANYWAY!
YOU'RE COMING WITH ME, BRAT!!
OW! OW! THAT PINCHES!
HOLD ON, SUMMER! I'LL GO FETCH HELP!
NGGH...
SUMMER POLANSKI NEEDS NOBODY'S HELP...!
PLINK

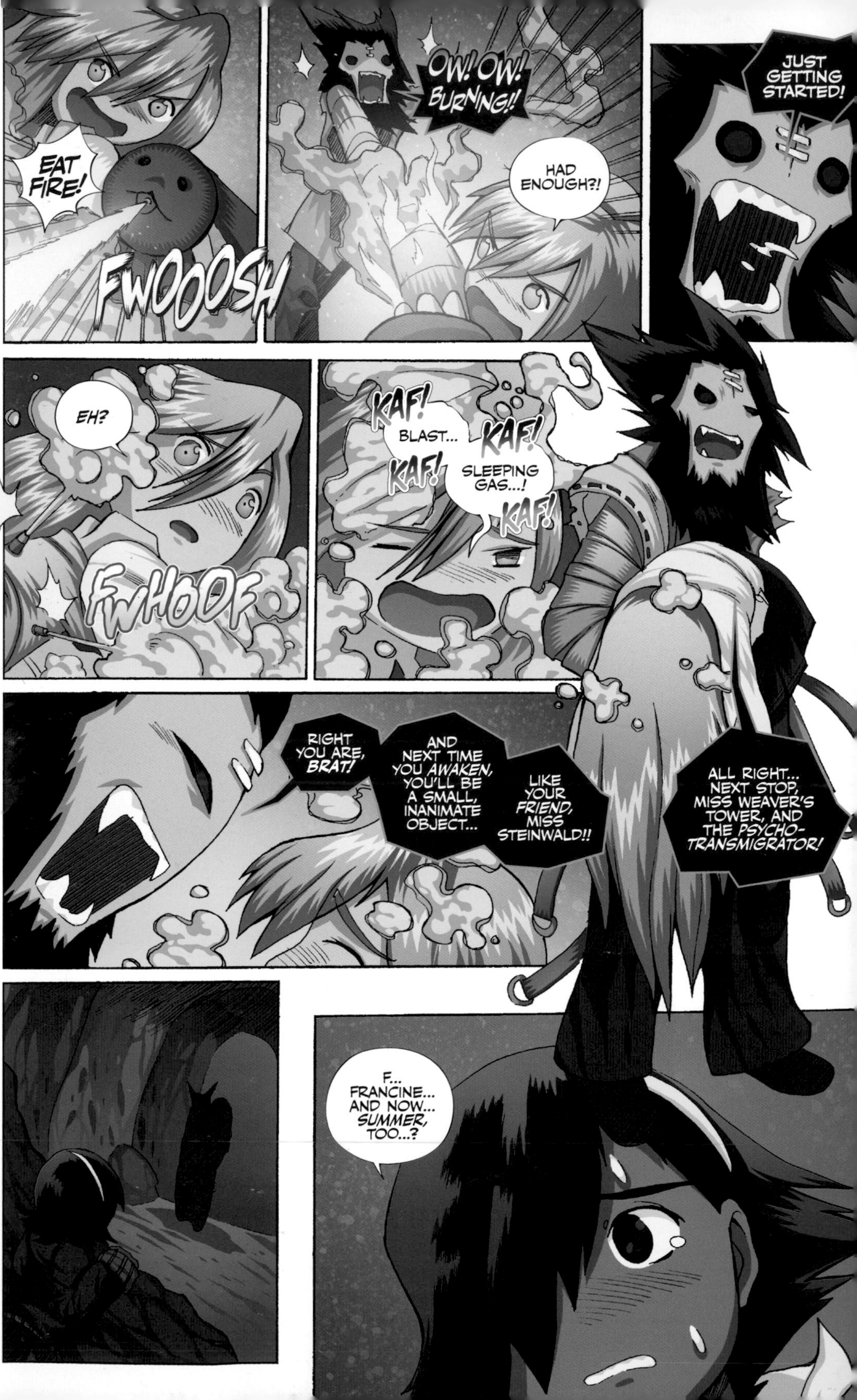
EAT FIRE!
FWOOOSH
OW! OW! BURNING!!
HAD ENOUGH?!
JUST GETTING STARTED!
EH?
FWHOOF
KAF!
BLAST...
KAF!
KAF!
SLEEPING GAS...!
KAF!
RIGHT YOU ARE, BRAT!
AND NEXT TIME YOU AWAKEN, YOU'LL BE A SMALL, INANIMATE OBJECT...
LIKE YOUR FRIEND, MISS STEINWALD!!
ALL RIGHT... NEXT STOP, MISS WEAVER'S TOWER, AND THE PSYCHO-TRANSMIGRATOR!
F... FRANCINE... AND NOW... SUMMER, TOO...?

CHAPTER THIRTEEN
Close to the Heart

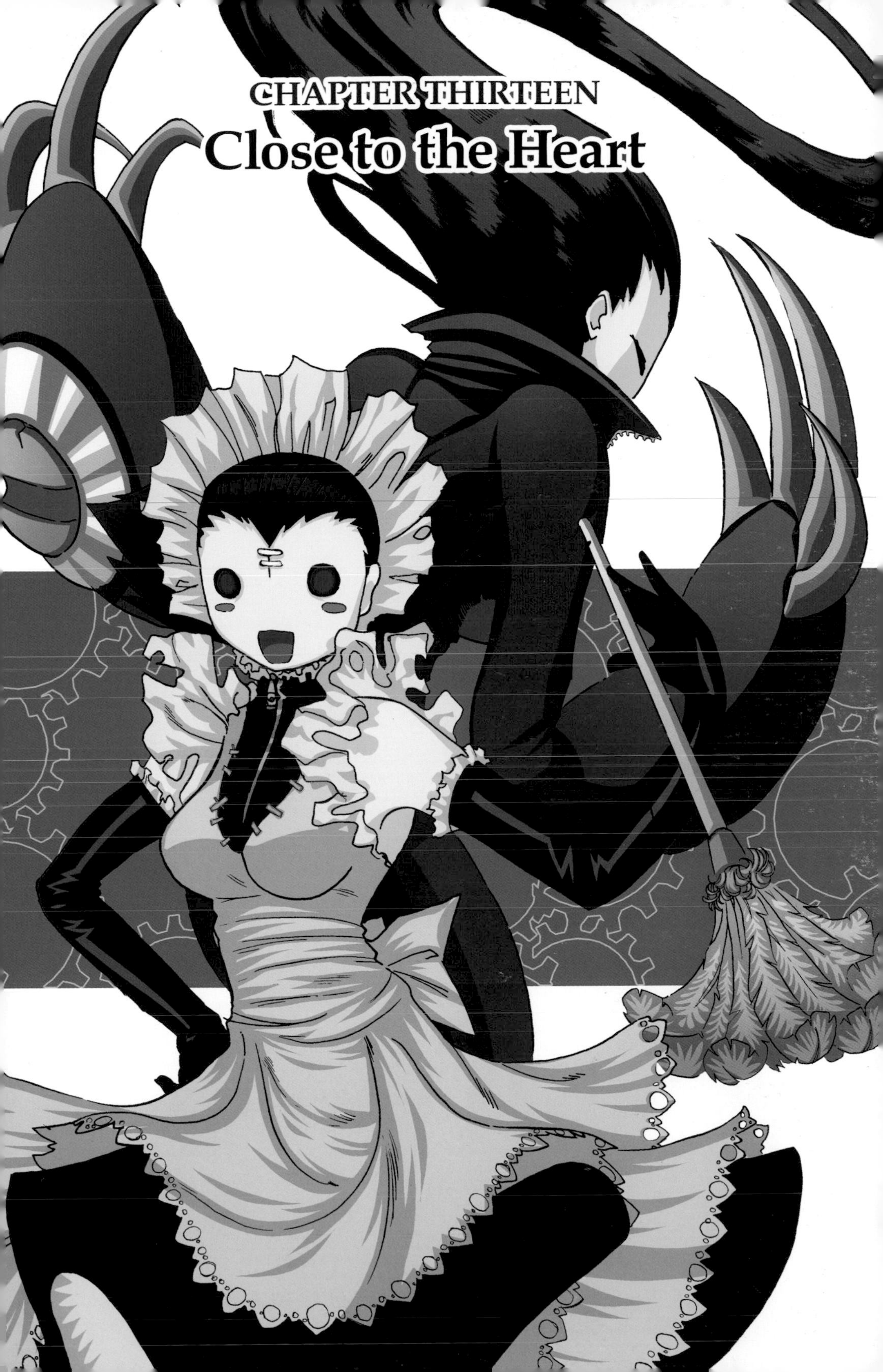

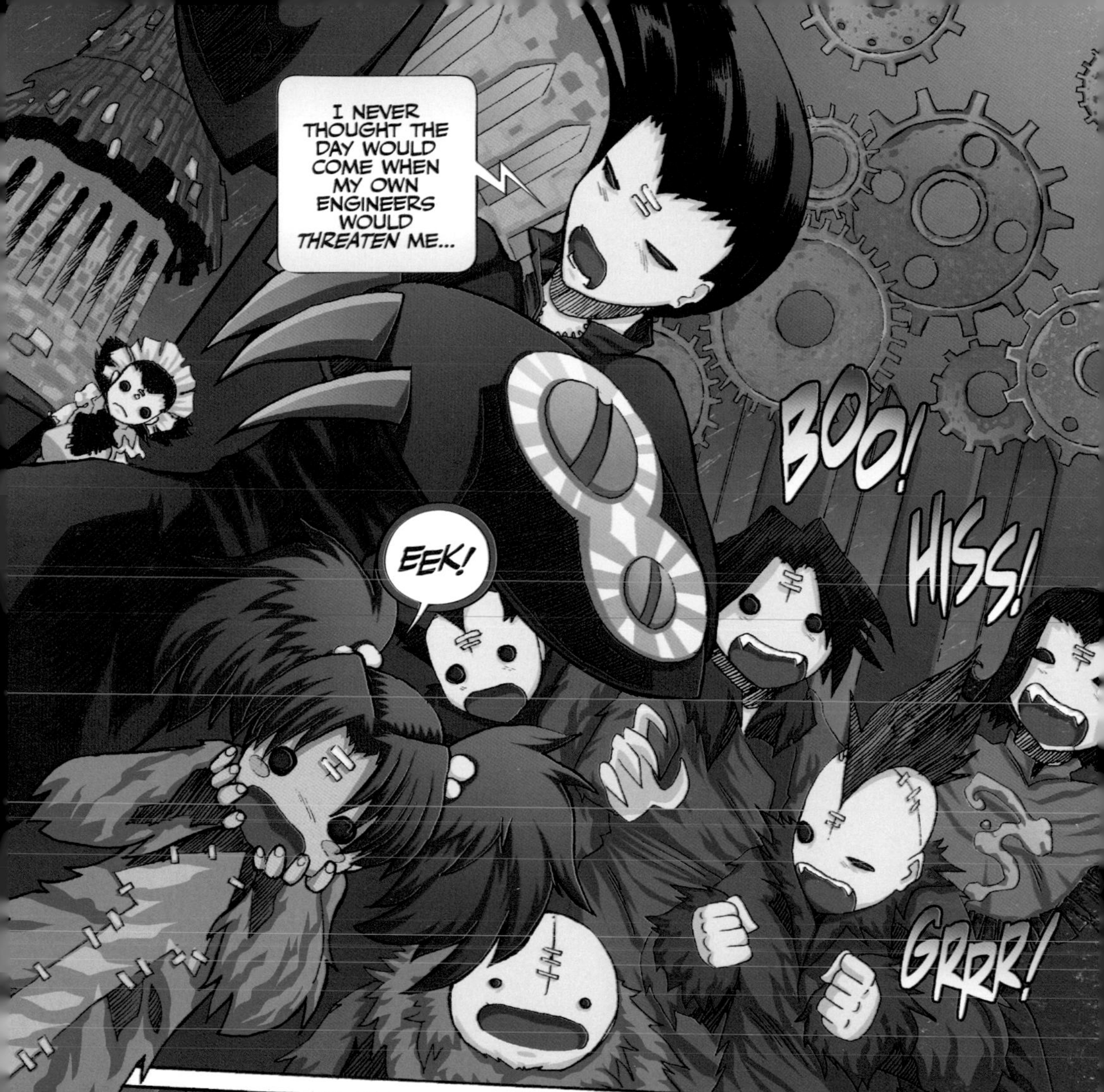
I NEVER THOUGHT THE DAY WOULD COME WHEN MY OWN ENGINEERS WOULD THREATEN ME...
EEK!
BOO!
HISS!
GRRR!

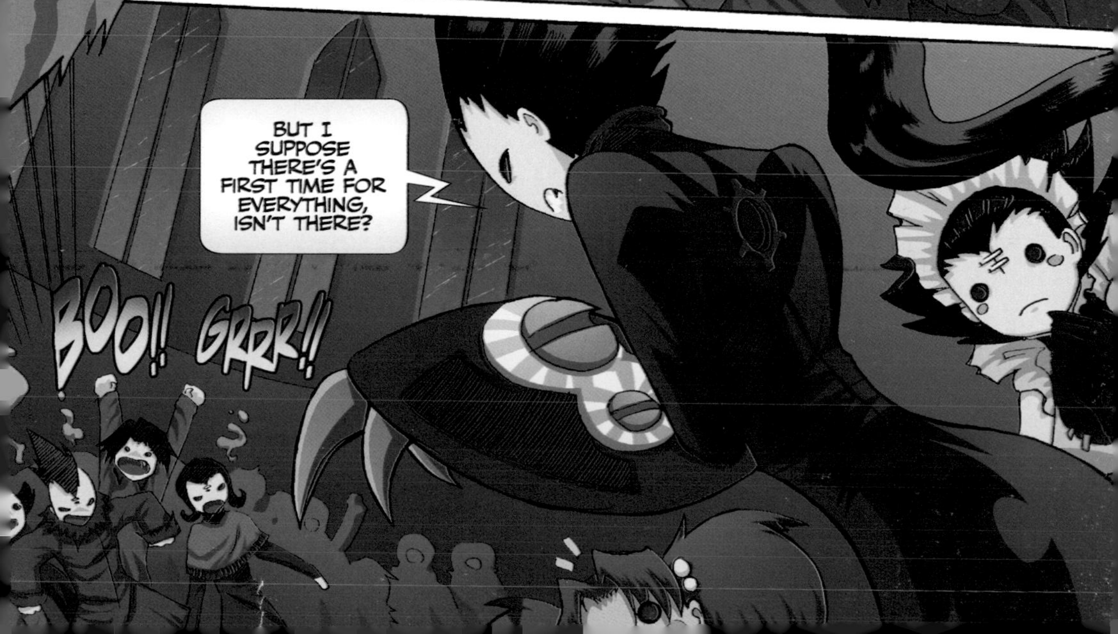
BUT I SUPPOSE THERE'S A FIRST TIME FOR EVERYTHING, ISN'T THERE?
BOO!! GRRR!!

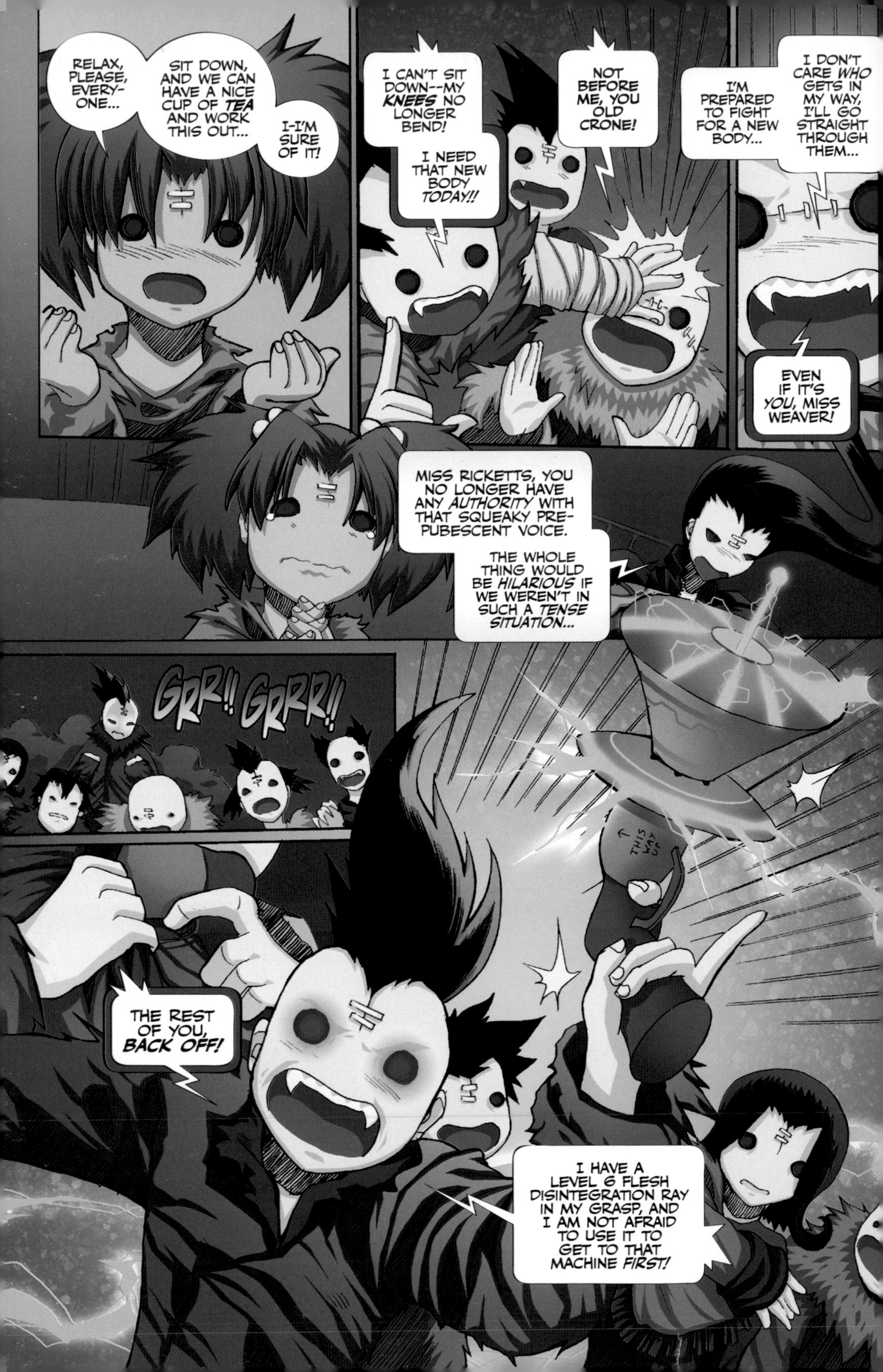
RELAX, PLEASE, EVERY-ONE...
SIT DOWN, AND WE CAN HAVE A NICE CUP OF *TEA* AND WORK THIS OUT...
I-I'M SURE OF IT!
I CAN'T SIT DOWN--MY ***KNEES*** NO LONGER BEND!
I NEED THAT NEW BODY *TODAY!!*
NOT BEFORE ME, YOU OLD CRONE!
I'M PREPARED TO FIGHT FOR A NEW BODY...
I DON'T CARE *WHO* GETS IN MY WAY, I'LL GO STRAIGHT THROUGH THEM...
EVEN IF IT'S *YOU*, MISS WEAVER!
MISS RICKETTS, YOU NO LONGER HAVE ANY *AUTHORITY* WITH THAT SQUEAKY PRE-PUBESCENT VOICE.
THE WHOLE THING WOULD BE *HILARIOUS* IF WE WEREN'T IN SUCH A *TENSE SITUATION*...
GRR!! GRRR!!
THIS WAY UP
THE REST OF YOU, ***BACK OFF!***
I HAVE A LEVEL 6 FLESH DISINTEGRATION RAY IN MY GRASP, AND I AM NOT AFRAID TO USE IT TO GET TO THAT MACHINE *FIRST!*

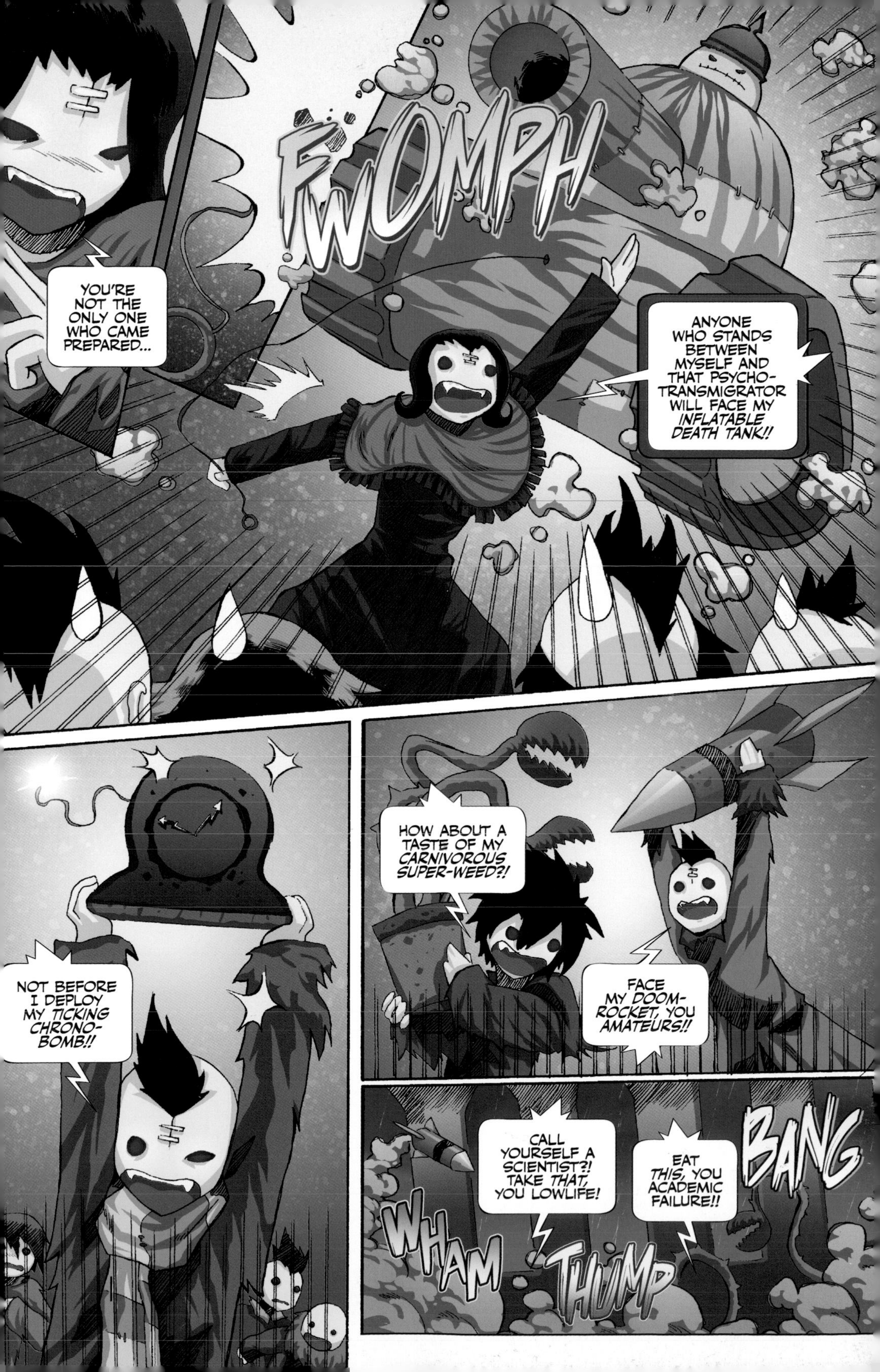
FWOMPH
YOU'RE NOT THE ONLY ONE WHO CAME PREPARED...
ANYONE WHO STANDS BETWEEN MYSELF AND THAT PSYCHO-TRANSMIGRATOR WILL FACE MY *INFLATABLE DEATH TANK!!*
NOT BEFORE I DEPLOY MY *TICKING CHRONO-BOMB!!*
HOW ABOUT A TASTE OF MY *CARNIVOROUS SUPER-WEED?!*
FACE MY *DOOM-ROCKET,* YOU *AMATEURS!!*
CALL YOURSELF A SCIENTIST?! TAKE *THAT,* YOU LOWLIFE!
EAT *THIS,* YOU ACADEMIC FAILURE!!
BANG
WHAM
THUMP

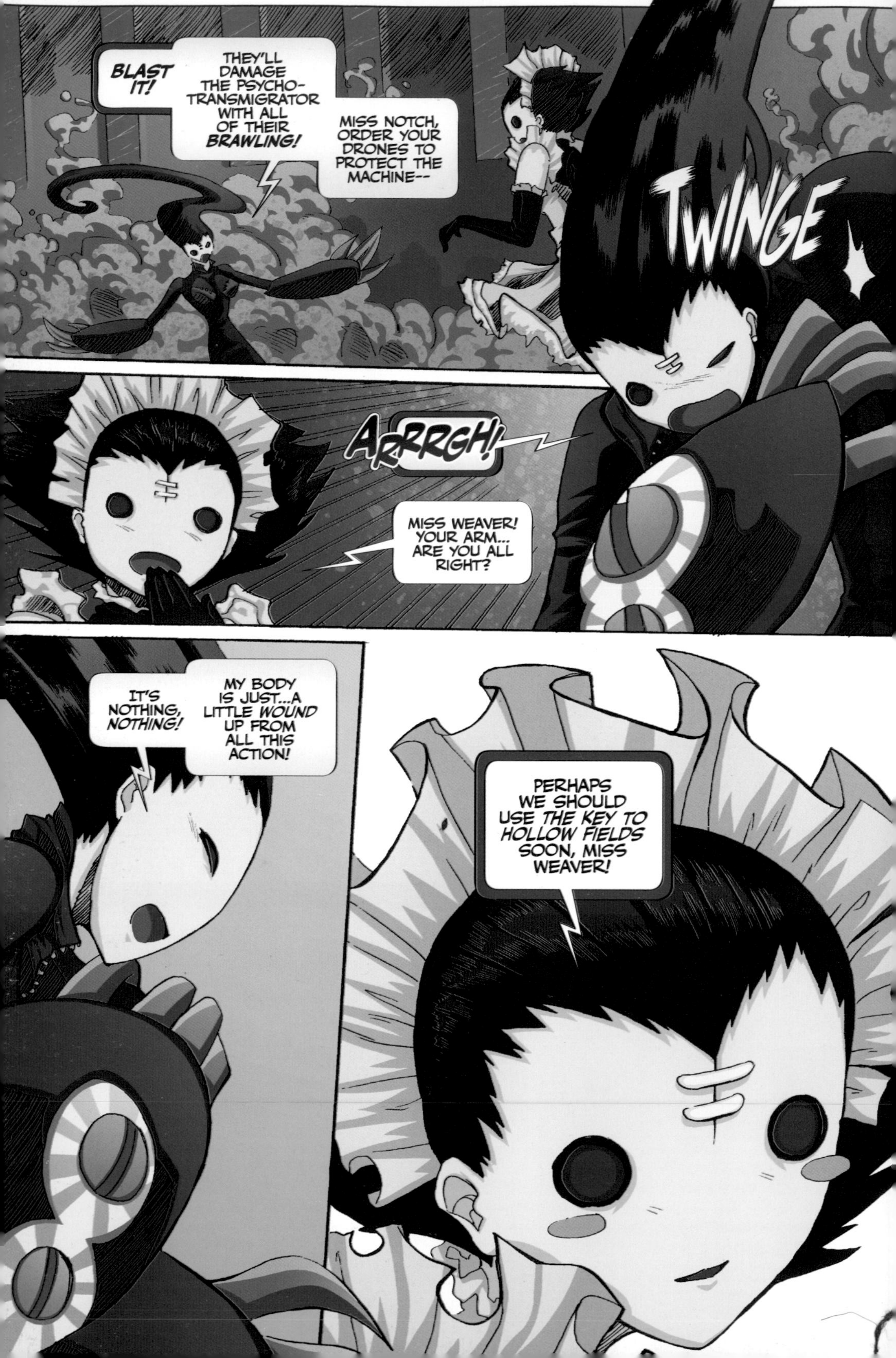
BLAST IT!
THEY'LL DAMAGE THE PSYCHO-TRANSMIGRATOR WITH ALL OF THEIR BRAWLING!
MISS NOTCH, ORDER YOUR DRONES TO PROTECT THE MACHINE--
TWINGE
ARRRGH!
MISS WEAVER! YOUR ARM... ARE YOU ALL RIGHT?
IT'S NOTHING, NOTHING!
MY BODY IS JUST...A LITTLE WOUND UP FROM ALL THIS ACTION!
PERHAPS WE SHOULD USE THE KEY TO HOLLOW FIELDS SOON, MISS WEAVER!

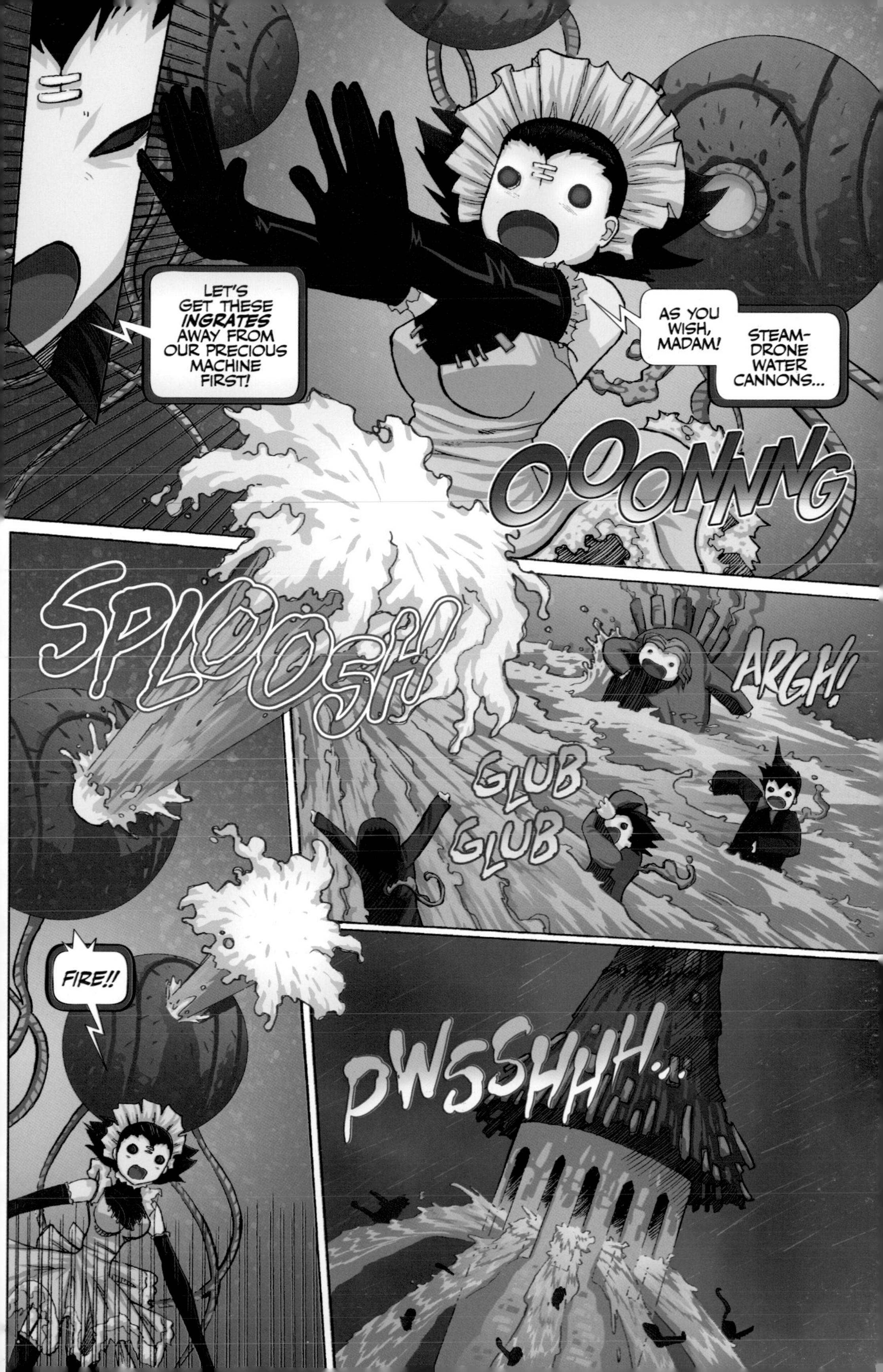
LET'S GET THESE INGRATES AWAY FROM OUR PRECIOUS MACHINE FIRST!
AS YOU WISH, MADAM!
STEAM-DRONE WATER CANNONS...
OOOONNNG
SPLOOOSH
ARGH!
GLUB GLUB
FIRE!!
PWSSHHH...

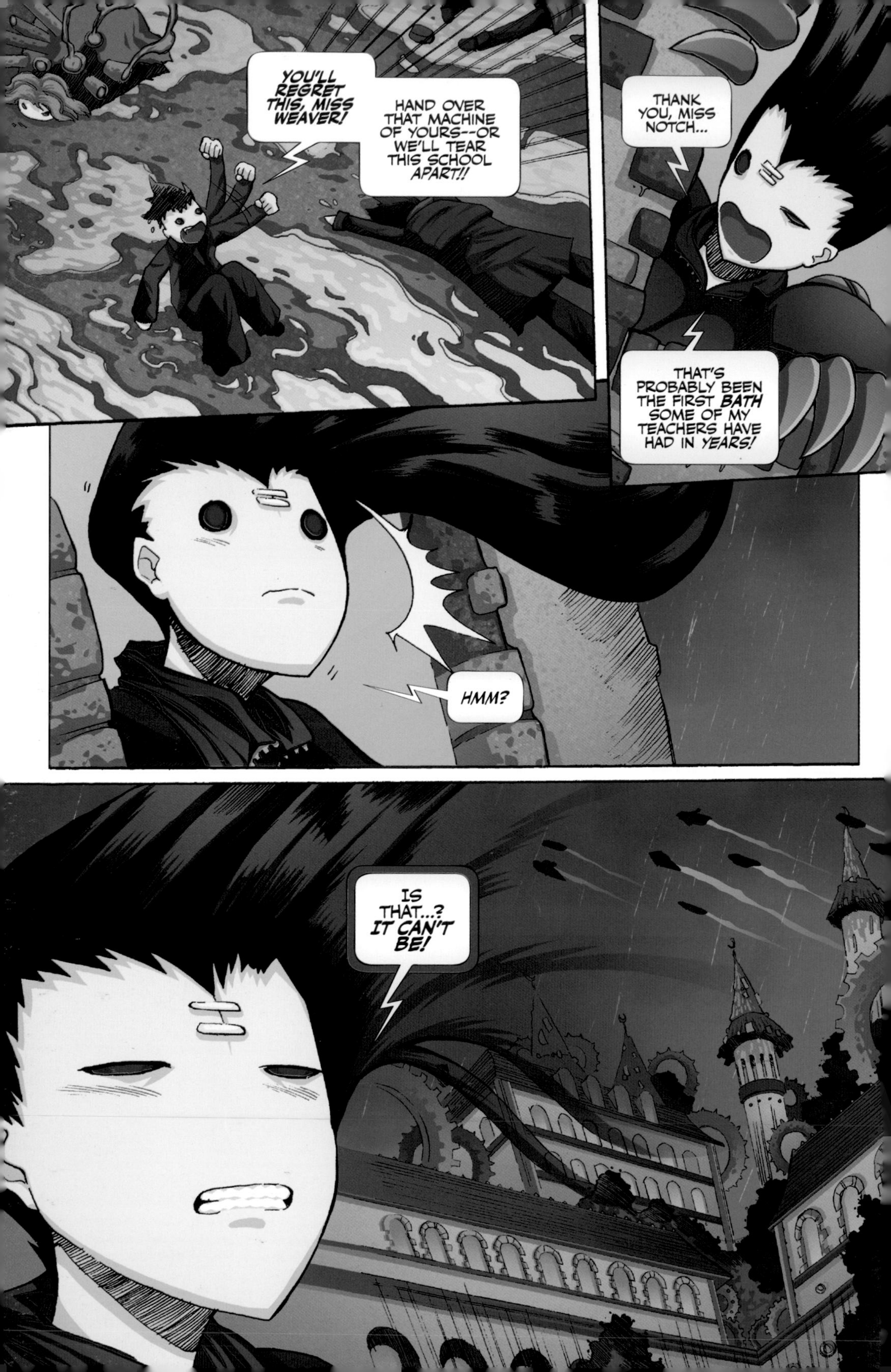
YOU'LL REGRET THIS, MISS WEAVER!
HAND OVER THAT MACHINE OF YOURS--OR WE'LL TEAR THIS SCHOOL APART!!
THANK YOU, MISS NOTCH...
THAT'S PROBABLY BEEN THE FIRST BATH SOME OF MY TEACHERS HAVE HAD IN YEARS!
HMM?
IS THAT...? IT CAN'T BE!

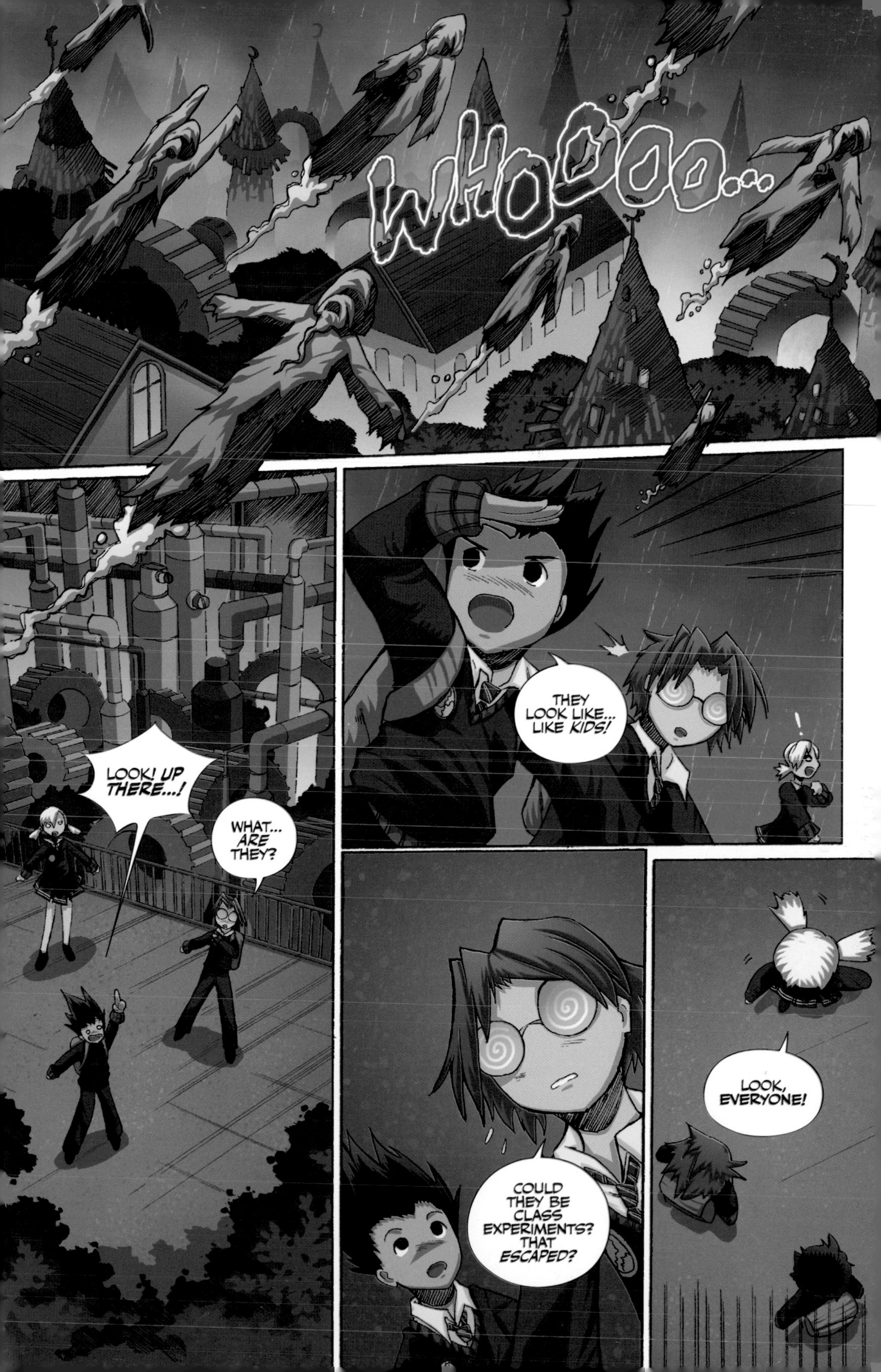
WHOOOOO...
LOOK! UP THERE...!
WHAT... ARE THEY?
THEY LOOK LIKE... LIKE KIDS!
COULD THEY BE CLASS EXPERIMENTS? THAT ESCAPED?
LOOK, EVERYONE!

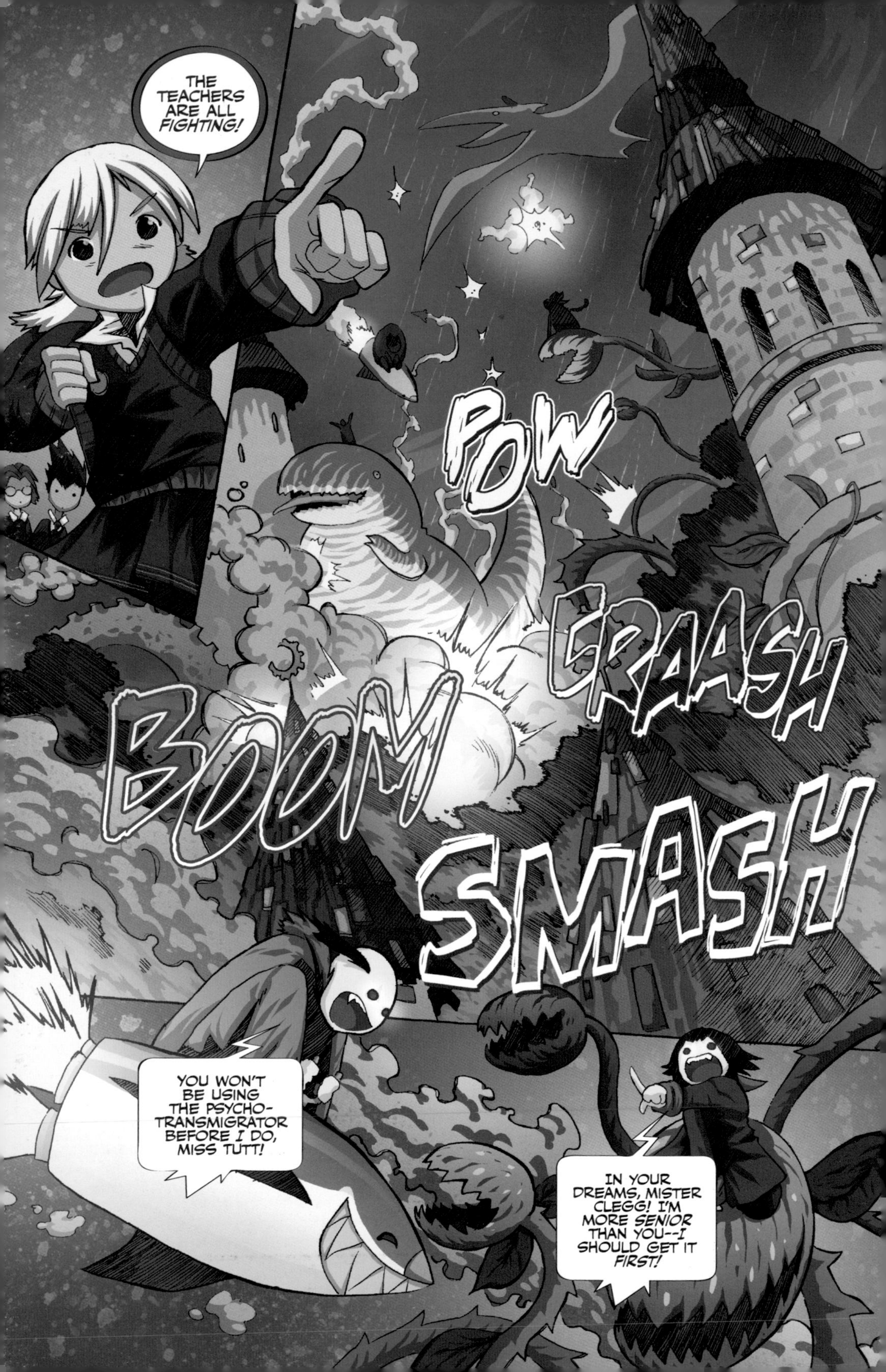
THE TEACHERS ARE ALL *FIGHTING!*
POW
CRAASH
BOOM
SMASH
YOU WON'T BE USING THE PSYCHO-TRANSMIGRATOR BEFORE *I* DO, MISS TUTT!
IN YOUR DREAMS, MISTER CLEGG! I'M MORE *SENIOR* THAN YOU--I SHOULD GET IT *FIRST!*

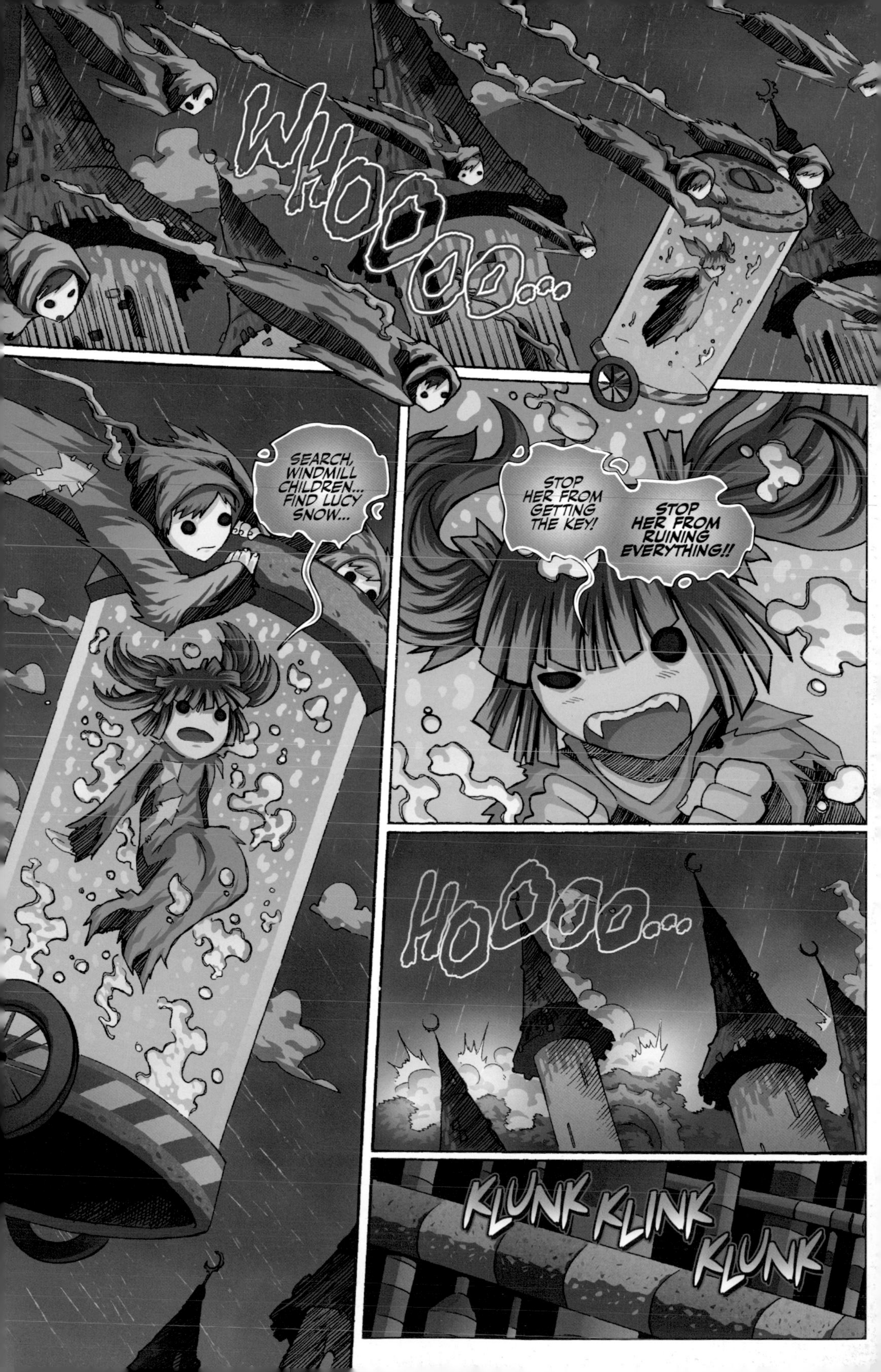
WHOOOOO...
SEARCH, WINDMILL CHILDREN... FIND LUCY SNOW...
STOP HER FROM GETTING THE KEY!
STOP HER FROM RUINING EVERYTHING!!
HOOOO...
KLUNK KLINK KLUNK

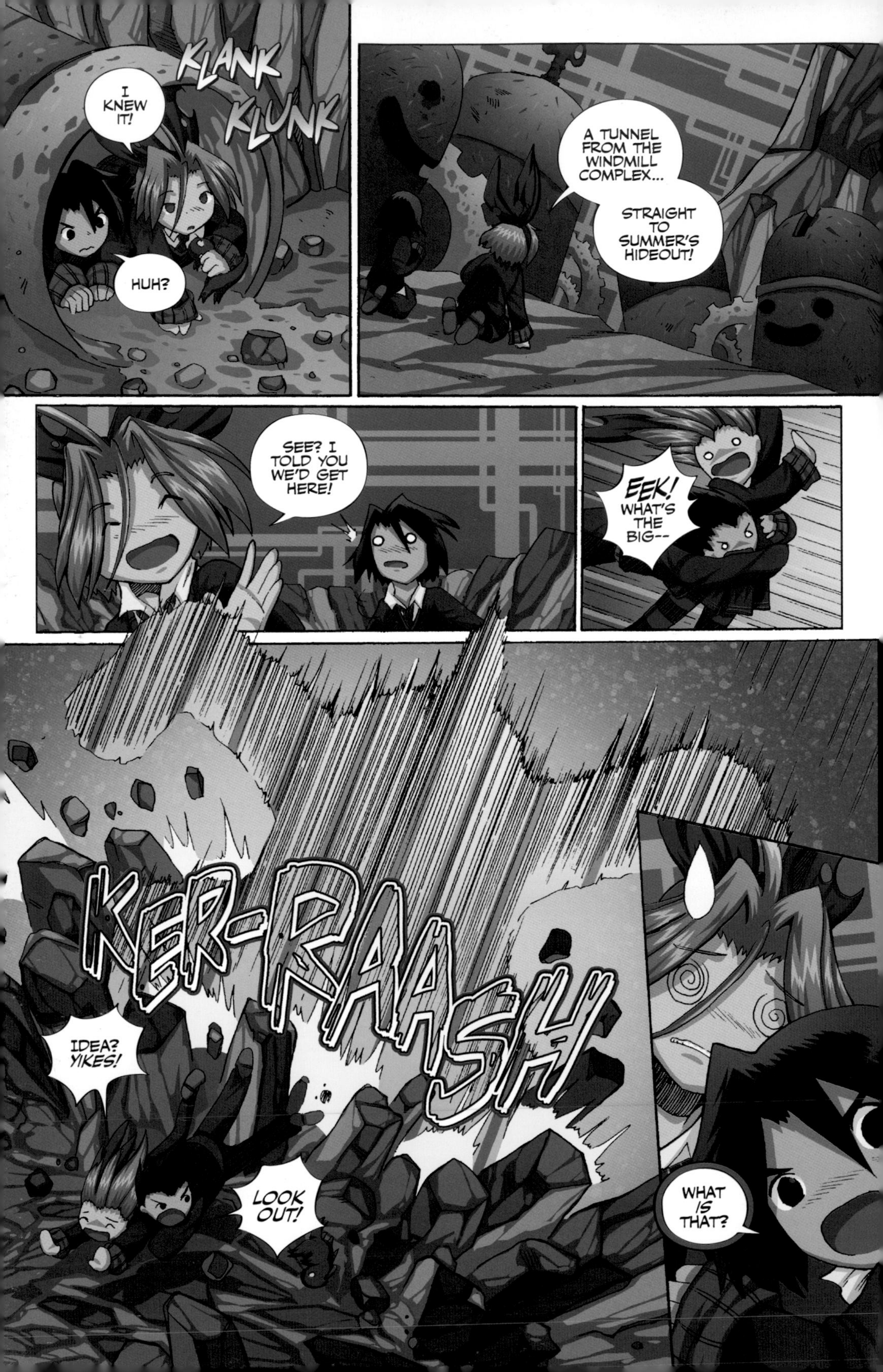
KLANK
KLUNK
I KNEW IT!
HUH?
A TUNNEL FROM THE WINDMILL COMPLEX...
STRAIGHT TO SUMMER'S HIDEOUT!
SEE? I TOLD YOU WE'D GET HERE!
EEK! WHAT'S THE BIG--
KER-RAASH
IDEA? YIKES!
LOOK OUT!
WHAT IS THAT?

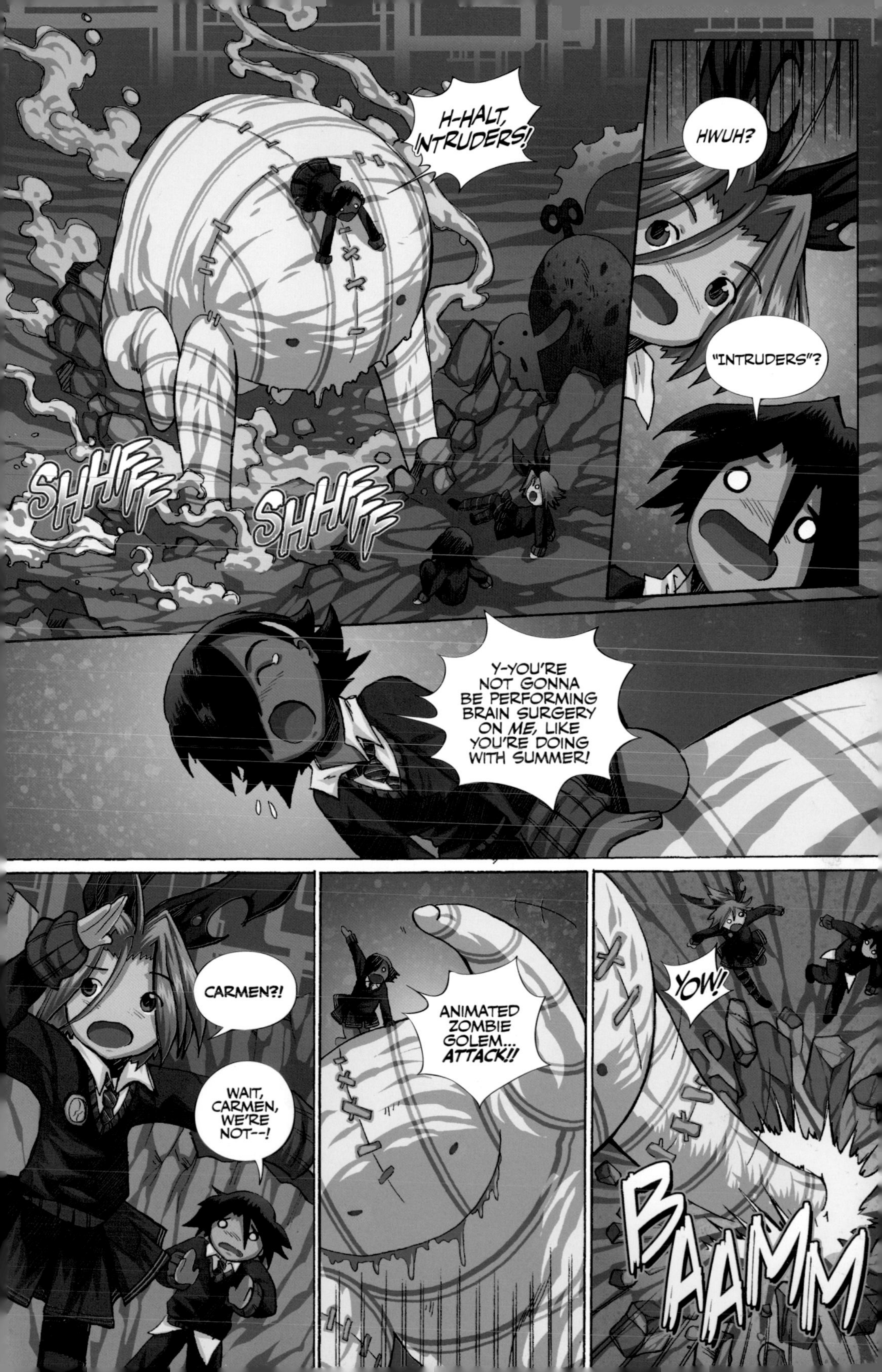
H-HALT, INTRUDERS!
SHHFFF
SHHFFF
HWUH?
"INTRUDERS"?
Y-YOU'RE NOT GONNA BE PERFORMING BRAIN SURGERY ON *ME*, LIKE YOU'RE DOING WITH SUMMER!
CARMEN?!
WAIT, CARMEN, WE'RE NOT--!
ANIMATED ZOMBIE GOLEM... *ATTACK!!*
YOW!
BAAMM

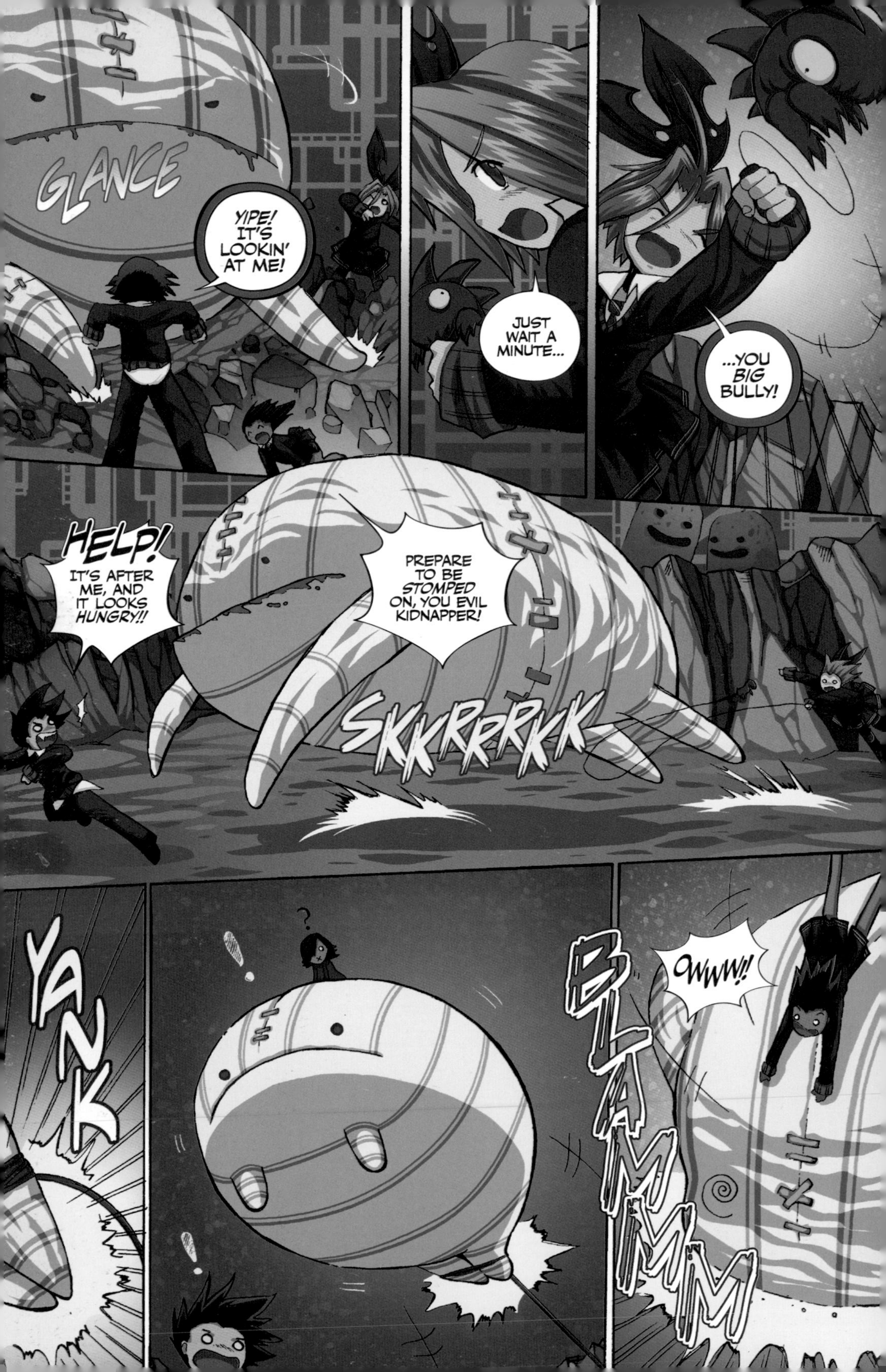
GLANCE
YIPE! IT'S LOOKIN' AT ME!
JUST WAIT A MINUTE...
...YOU BIG BULLY!
HELP! IT'S AFTER ME, AND IT LOOKS HUNGRY!!
PREPARE TO BE STOMPED ON, YOU EVIL KIDNAPPER!
SKKRRRKK
YANK
?
!
!
BLAMMMM
OWWW!!

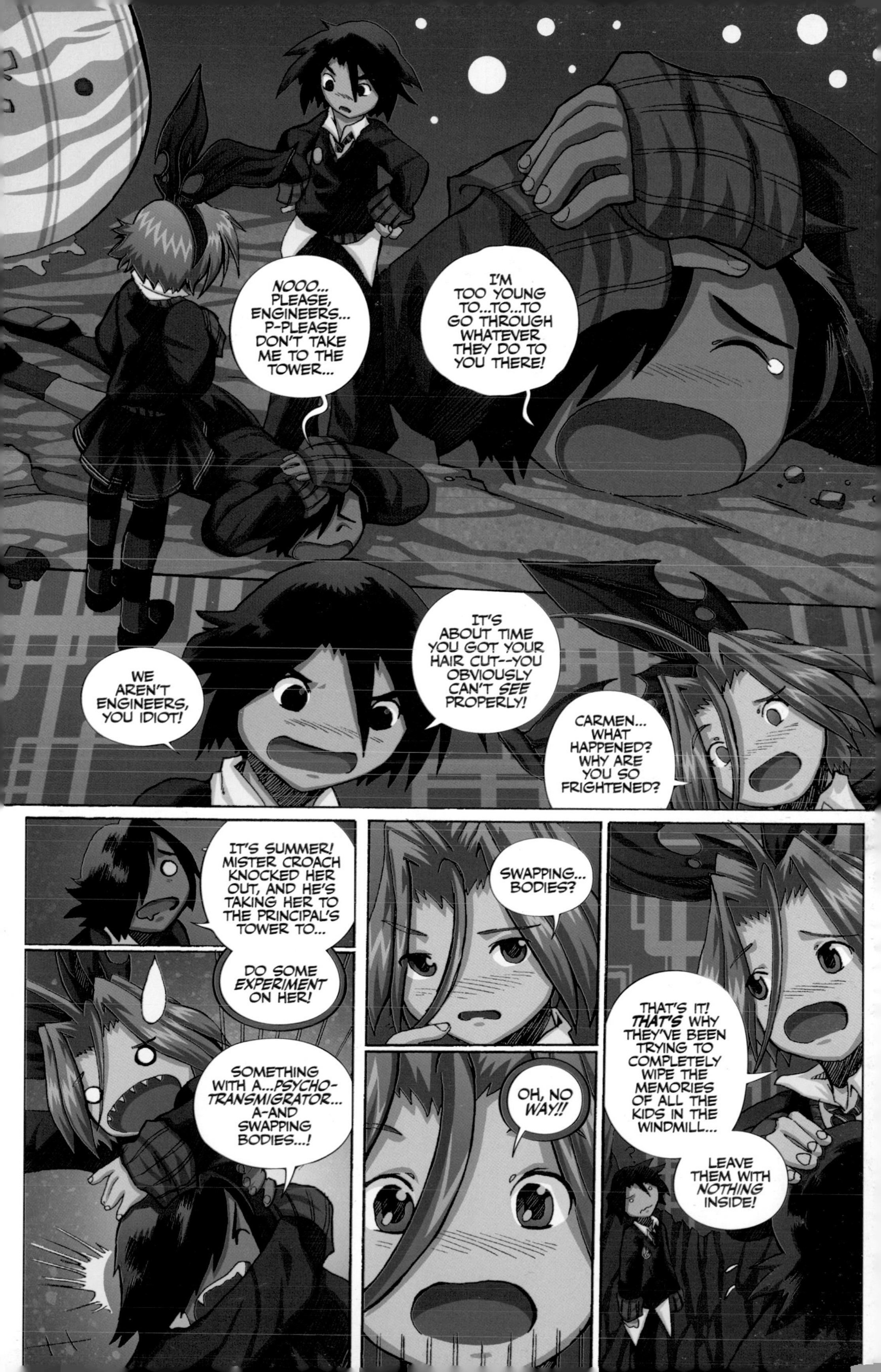

NOOO... PLEASE, ENGINEERS... P-PLEASE DON'T TAKE ME TO THE TOWER...
I'M TOO YOUNG TO...TO...TO GO THROUGH WHATEVER THEY DO TO YOU THERE!
WE AREN'T ENGINEERS, YOU IDIOT!
IT'S ABOUT TIME YOU GOT YOUR HAIR CUT--YOU OBVIOUSLY CAN'T *SEE* PROPERLY!
CARMEN... WHAT HAPPENED? WHY ARE YOU SO FRIGHTENED?
IT'S SUMMER! MISTER CROACH KNOCKED HER OUT, AND HE'S TAKING HER TO THE PRINCIPAL'S TOWER TO...
DO SOME *EXPERIMENT* ON HER!
SOMETHING WITH A...*PSYCHO-TRANSMIGRATOR*... A-AND SWAPPING BODIES...!
SWAPPING... BODIES?
OH, NO *WAY!!*
THAT'S IT! ***THAT'S*** WHY THEY'VE BEEN TRYING TO COMPLETELY WIPE THE MEMORIES OF ALL THE KIDS IN THE WINDMILL...
LEAVE THEM WITH *NOTHING* INSIDE!

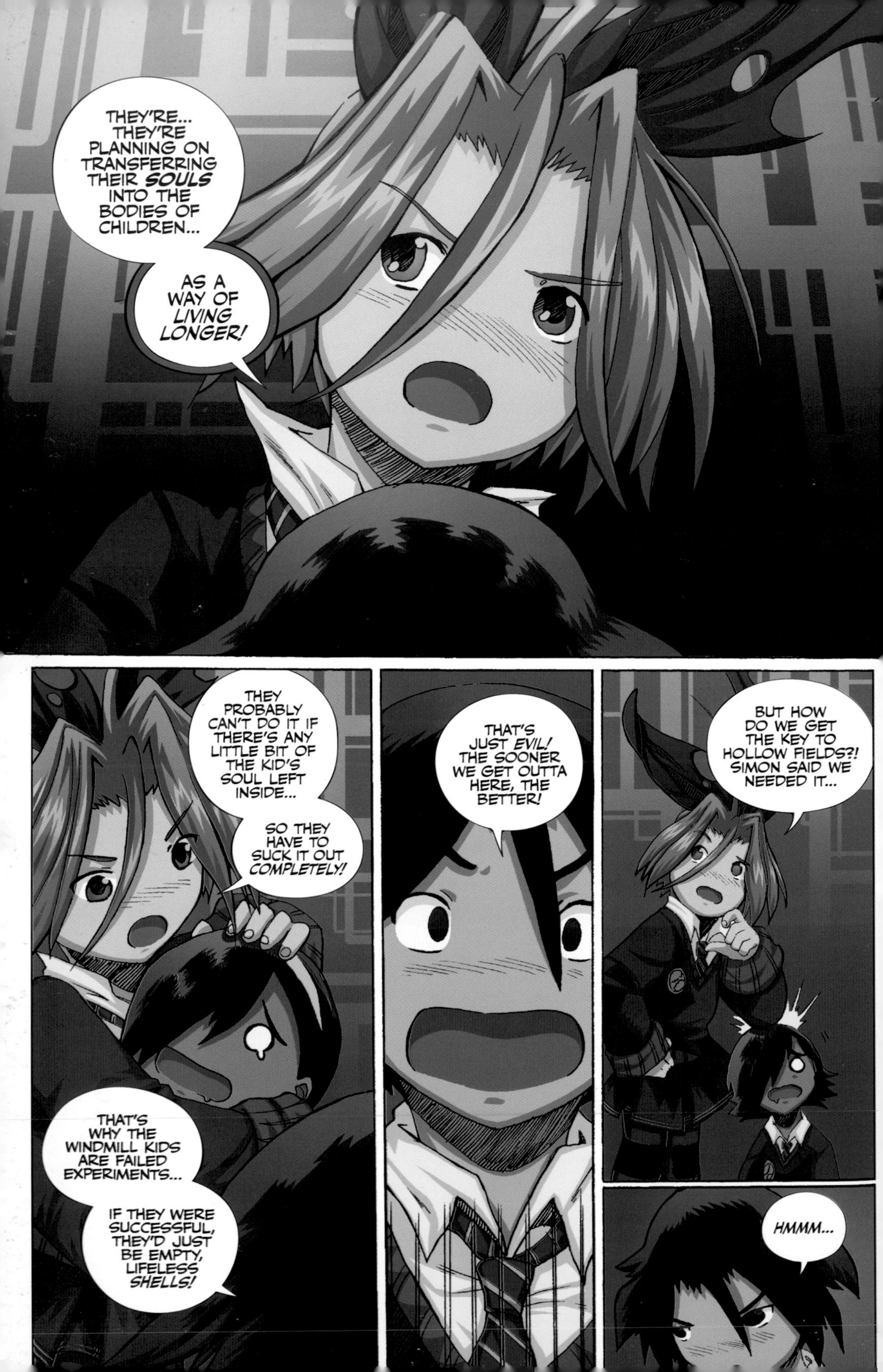
THEY'RE... THEY'RE PLANNING ON TRANSFERRING THEIR *SOULS* INTO THE BODIES OF CHILDREN...
AS A WAY OF *LIVING LONGER!*
THEY PROBABLY CAN'T DO IT IF THERE'S ANY LITTLE BIT OF THE KID'S SOUL LEFT INSIDE...
SO THEY HAVE TO SUCK IT OUT *COMPLETELY!*
THAT'S WHY THE WINDMILL KIDS ARE FAILED EXPERIMENTS...
IF THEY WERE SUCCESSFUL, THEY'D JUST BE EMPTY, LIFELESS *SHELLS!*
THAT'S JUST *EVIL!* THE SOONER WE GET OUTTA HERE, THE BETTER!
BUT HOW DO WE GET THE KEY TO HOLLOW FIELDS?! SIMON SAID WE NEEDED IT...
HMMM...

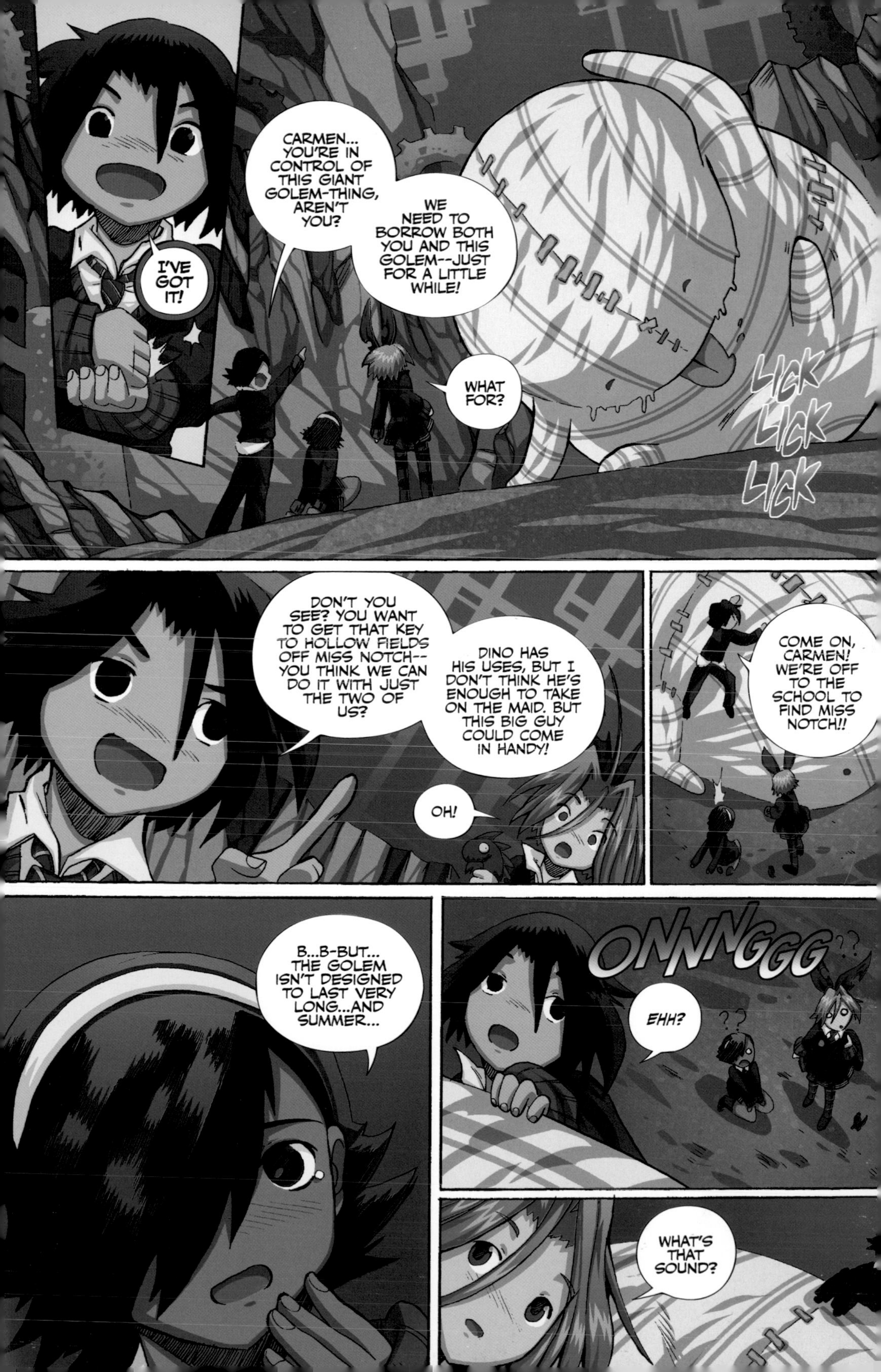
I'VE GOT IT!
CARMEN... YOU'RE IN CONTROL OF THIS GIANT GOLEM-THING, AREN'T YOU?
WE NEED TO BORROW BOTH YOU AND THIS GOLEM--JUST FOR A LITTLE WHILE!
WHAT FOR?
LICK LICK LICK
DON'T YOU SEE? YOU WANT TO GET THAT KEY TO HOLLOW FIELDS OFF MISS NOTCH--YOU THINK WE CAN DO IT WITH JUST THE TWO OF US?
DINO HAS HIS USES, BUT I DON'T THINK HE'S ENOUGH TO TAKE ON THE MAID. BUT THIS BIG GUY COULD COME IN HANDY!
OH!
COME ON, CARMEN! WE'RE OFF TO THE SCHOOL TO FIND MISS NOTCH!!
B...B-BUT... THE GOLEM ISN'T DESIGNED TO LAST VERY LONG...AND SUMMER...
ONNNGGG
EHH?
WHAT'S THAT SOUND?

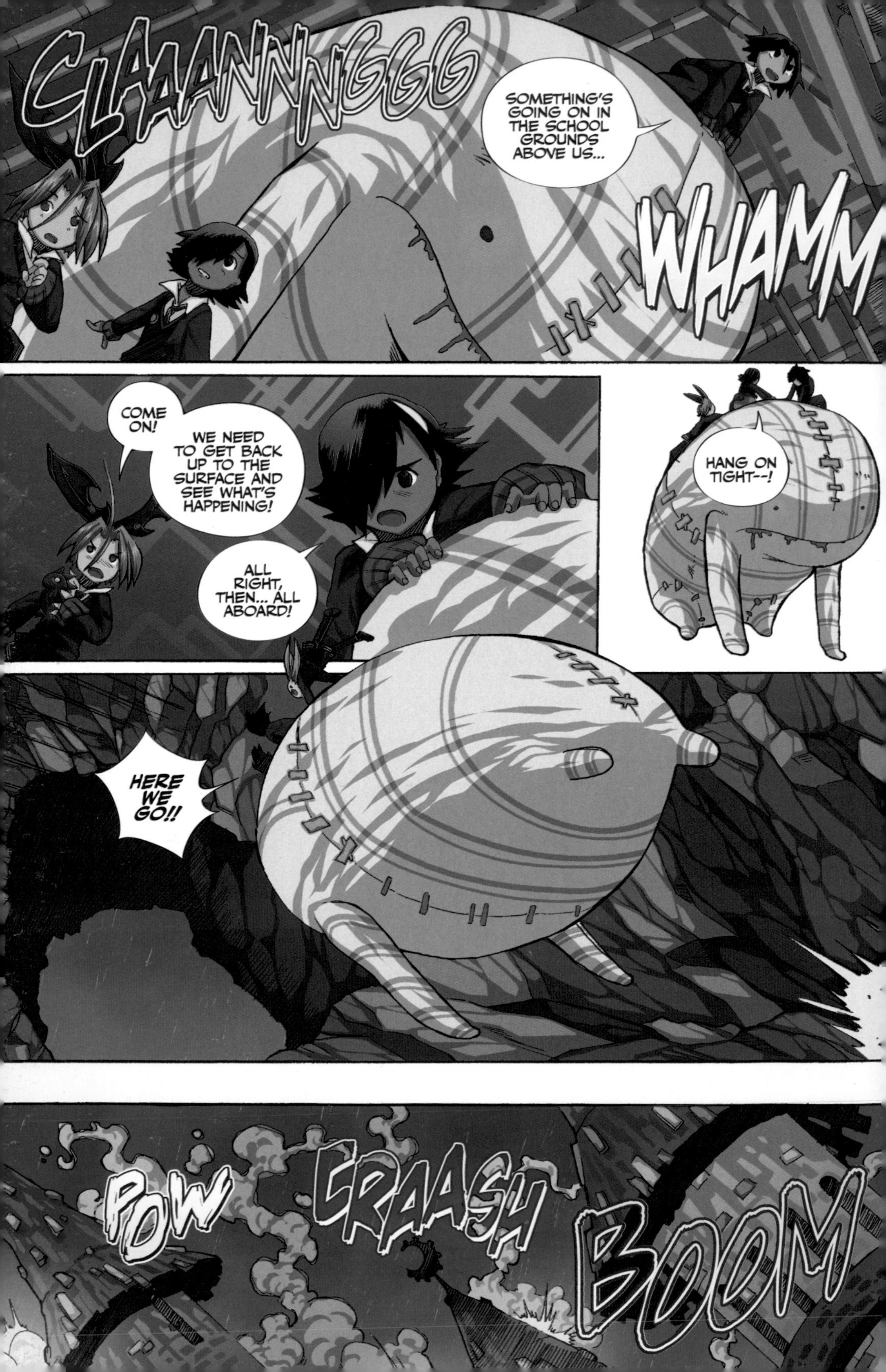
CLAAANNNGGG
SOMETHING'S GOING ON IN THE SCHOOL GROUNDS ABOVE US...
WHAMM
COME ON!
WE NEED TO GET BACK UP TO THE SURFACE AND SEE WHAT'S HAPPENING!
ALL RIGHT, THEN... ALL ABOARD!
HANG ON TIGHT--!
HERE WE GO!!
POW
CRAASH
BOOM

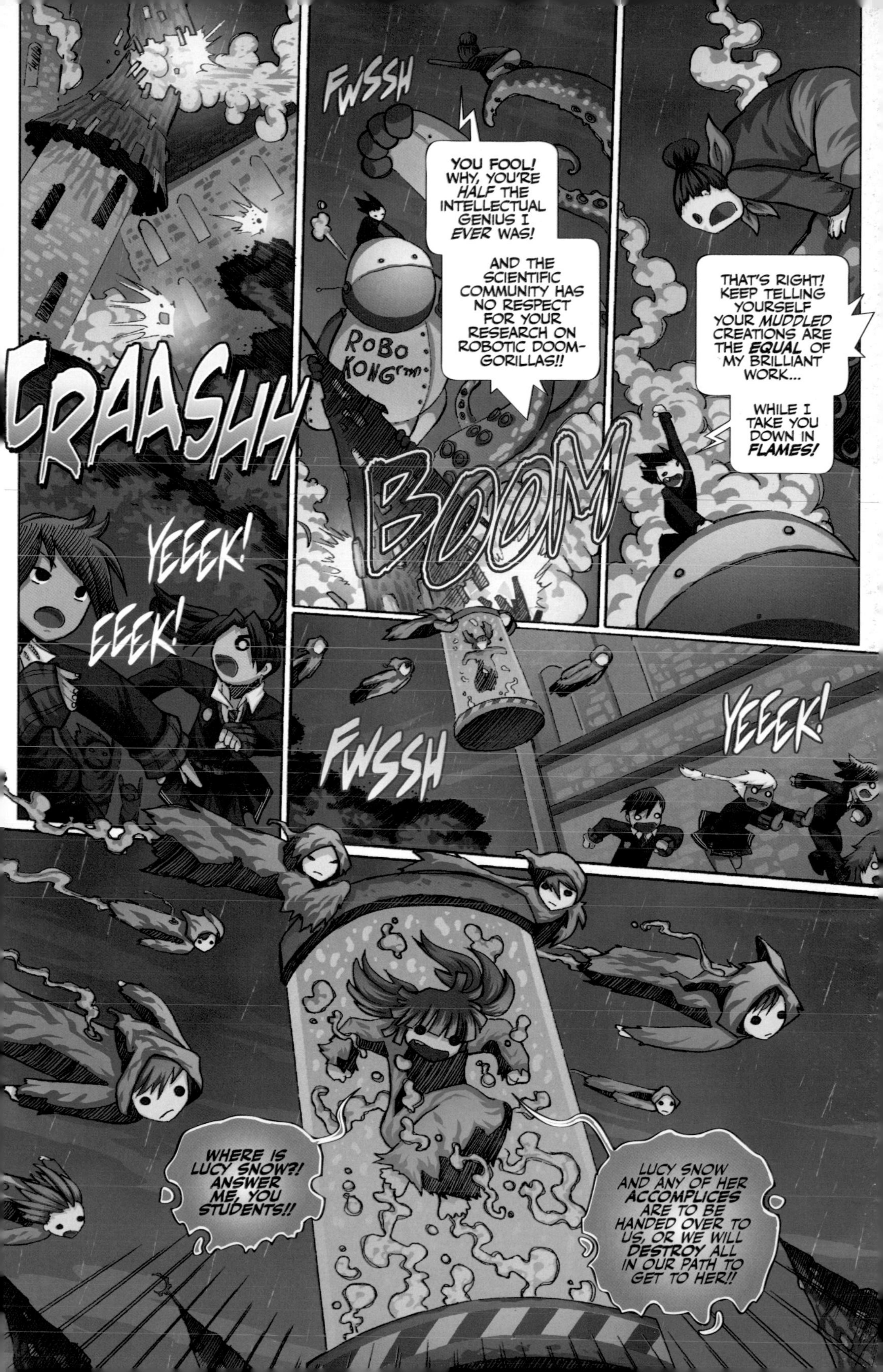
CRAASHH
YEEEK!
EEEK!
FWSSH
ROBO KONG™
YOU FOOL! WHY, YOU'RE HALF THE INTELLECTUAL GENIUS I EVER WAS!
AND THE SCIENTIFIC COMMUNITY HAS NO RESPECT FOR YOUR RESEARCH ON ROBOTIC DOOM-GORILLAS!!
BOOM
THAT'S RIGHT! KEEP TELLING YOURSELF YOUR MUDDLED CREATIONS ARE THE EQUAL OF MY BRILLIANT WORK...
WHILE I TAKE YOU DOWN IN FLAMES!
FWSSH
YEEEK!
WHERE IS LUCY SNOW?! ANSWER ME, YOU STUDENTS!!
LUCY SNOW AND ANY OF HER ACCOMPLICES ARE TO BE HANDED OVER TO US, OR WE WILL DESTROY ALL IN OUR PATH TO GET TO HER!!

OH MY...

OUR SCHOOL HAS NEVER FACED SUCH WIDESPREAD DESTRUCTION BEFORE!

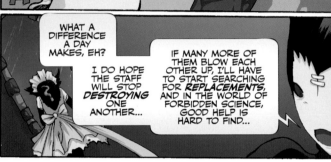

WHAT A DIFFERENCE A DAY MAKES, EH?

I DO HOPE THE STAFF WILL STOP *DESTROYING* ONE ANOTHER...

IF MANY MORE OF THEM BLOW EACH OTHER UP, I'LL HAVE TO START SEARCHING FOR *REPLACEMENTS*, AND IN THE WORLD OF FORBIDDEN SCIENCE, GOOD HELP IS HARD TO FIND...

OH DEAR, OH DEAR... THE ENGINEERS HAVE GONE MAD...THEY REFUSE TO WAIT!

EASY TO ACCUSE OTHERS OF BEING *IMPATIENT* WHEN YOU HAVE WHAT THEY DESIRE, MISS RICKETTS!

BUT YES, THIS IS DISAPPOINTING. NOT TO BE--

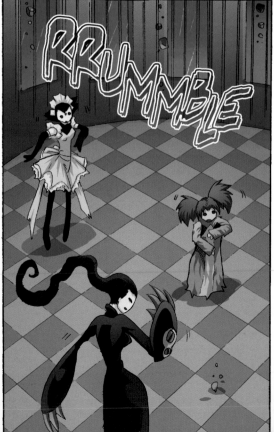

RRUMMBLE

MY JOINTS FEEL *STIFF* TODAY...MUST BE ALL THE *EXCITEMENT*...

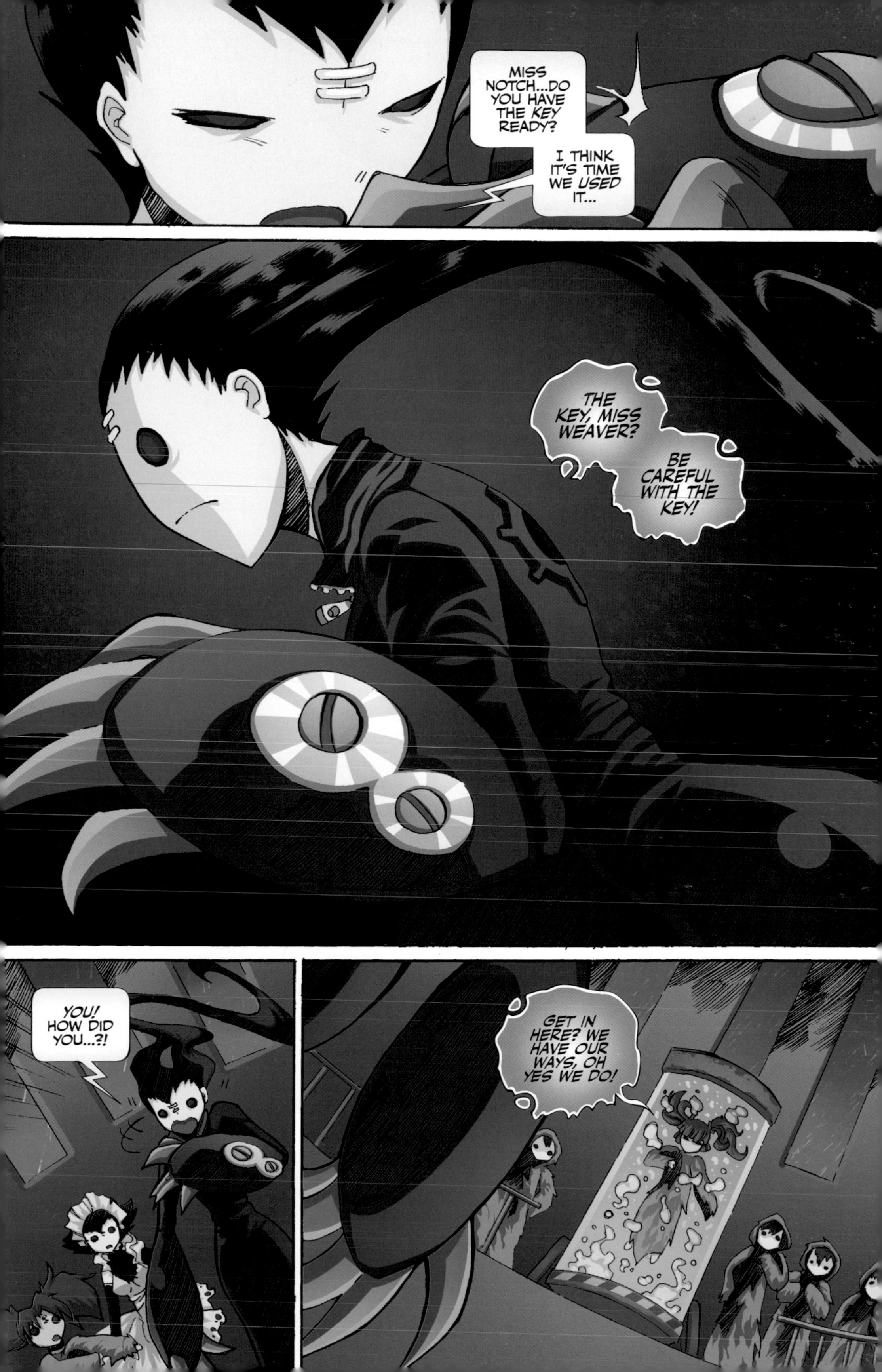
MISS NOTCH...DO YOU HAVE THE KEY READY?
I THINK IT'S TIME WE USED IT...
THE KEY, MISS WEAVER?
BE CAREFUL WITH THE KEY!
YOU! HOW DID YOU...?!
GET IN HERE? WE HAVE OUR WAYS, OH YES WE DO!

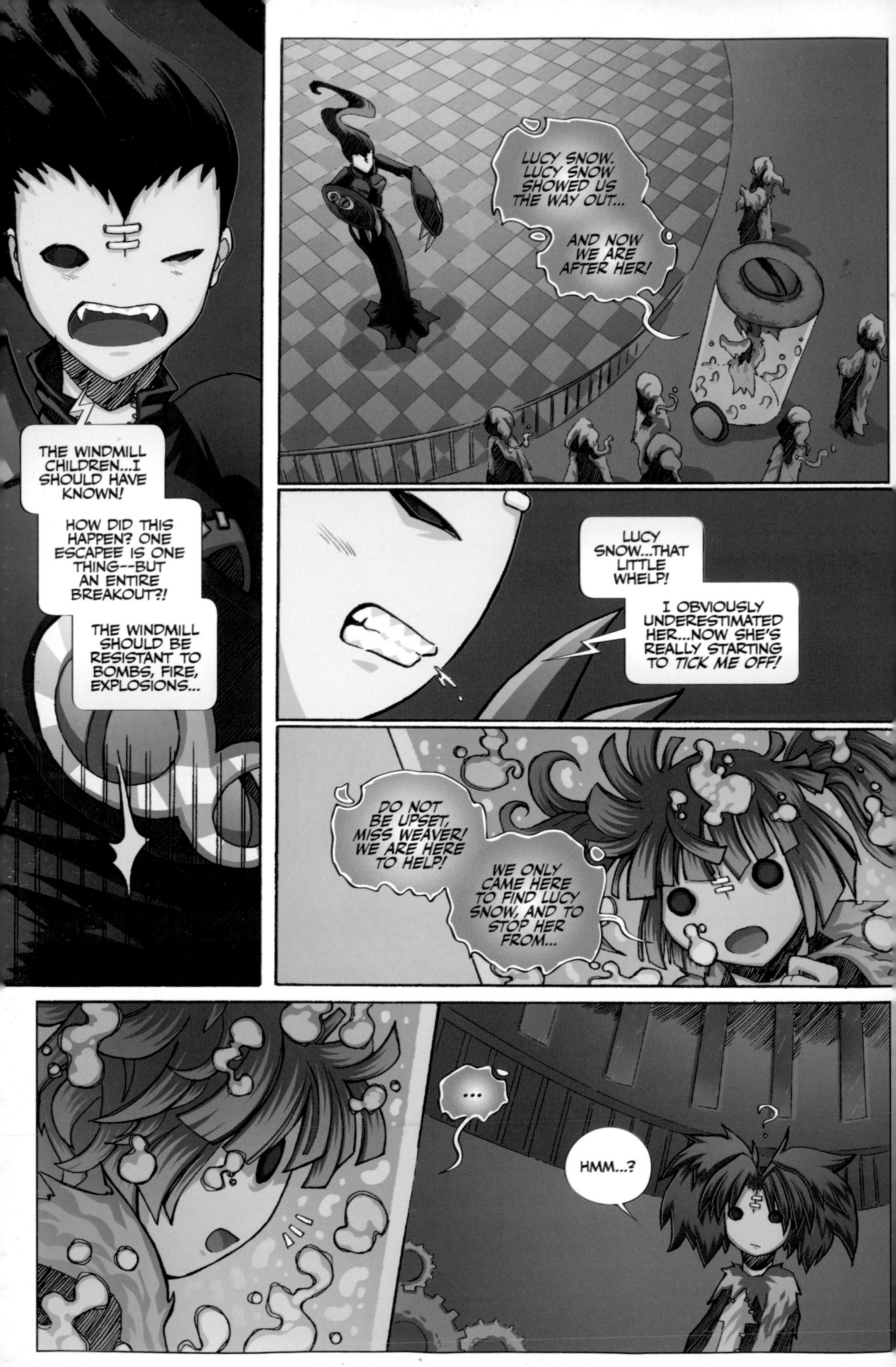
THE WINDMILL CHILDREN...I SHOULD HAVE KNOWN!
HOW DID THIS HAPPEN? ONE ESCAPEE IS ONE THING--BUT AN ENTIRE BREAKOUT?!
THE WINDMILL SHOULD BE RESISTANT TO BOMBS, FIRE, EXPLOSIONS...
LUCY SNOW. LUCY SNOW SHOWED US THE WAY OUT...
AND NOW WE ARE AFTER HER!
LUCY SNOW...THAT LITTLE WHELP!
I OBVIOUSLY UNDERESTIMATED HER...NOW SHE'S REALLY STARTING TO TICK ME OFF!
DO NOT BE UPSET, MISS WEAVER! WE ARE HERE TO HELP!
WE ONLY CAME HERE TO FIND LUCY SNOW, AND TO STOP HER FROM...
...
HMM...?
?

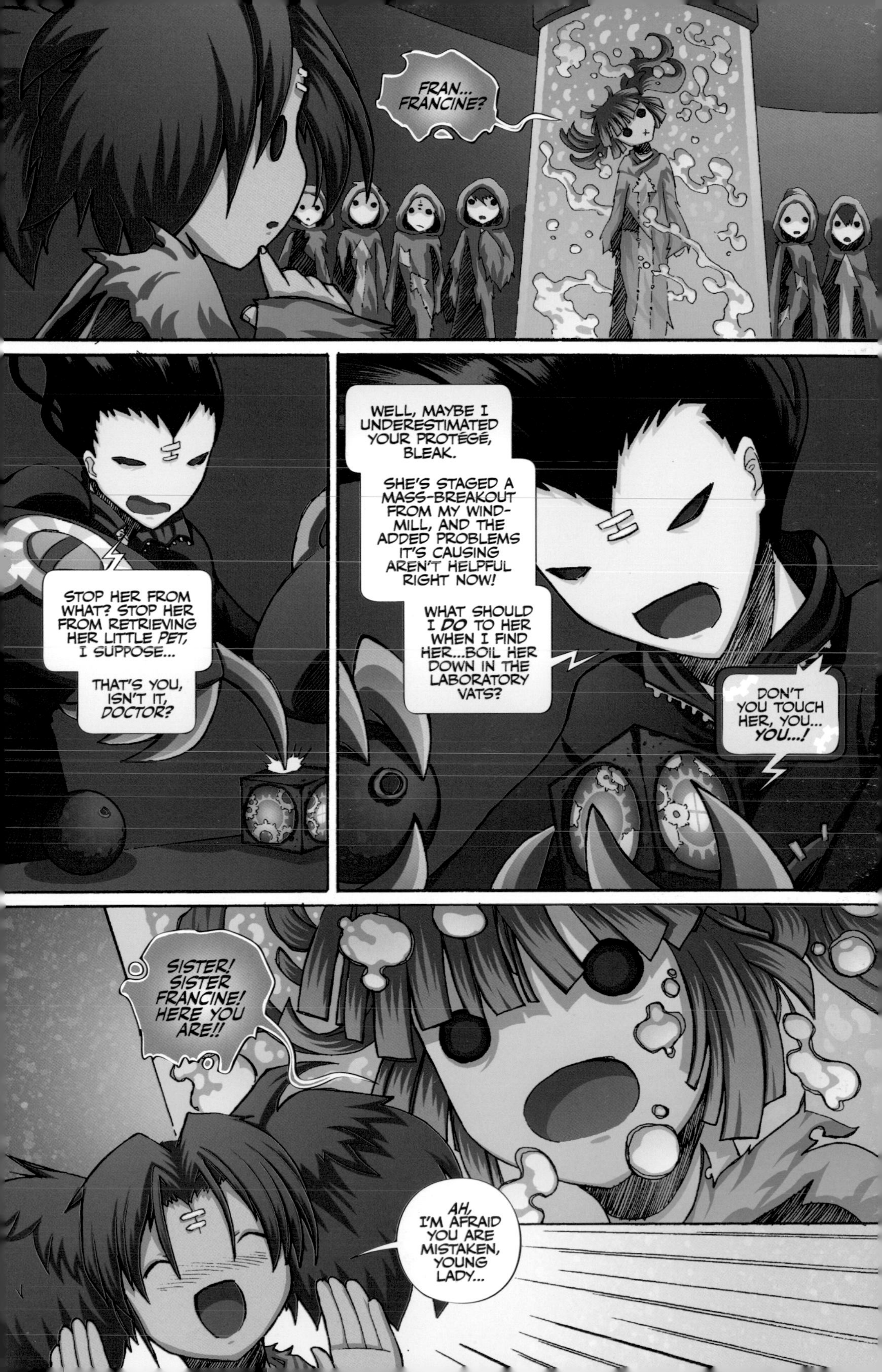
FRAN... FRANCINE?
STOP HER FROM WHAT? STOP HER FROM RETRIEVING HER LITTLE *PET*, I SUPPOSE...
THAT'S YOU, ISN'T IT, *DOCTOR*?
WELL, MAYBE I UNDERESTIMATED YOUR PROTÉGÉ, BLEAK.
SHE'S STAGED A MASS-BREAKOUT FROM MY WIND-MILL, AND THE ADDED PROBLEMS IT'S CAUSING AREN'T HELPFUL RIGHT NOW!
WHAT SHOULD I *DO* TO HER WHEN I FIND HER...BOIL HER DOWN IN THE LABORATORY VATS?
DON'T YOU TOUCH HER, YOU... *YOU...!*
SISTER! SISTER FRANCINE! HERE YOU ARE!!
AH, I'M AFRAID YOU ARE MISTAKEN, YOUNG LADY...

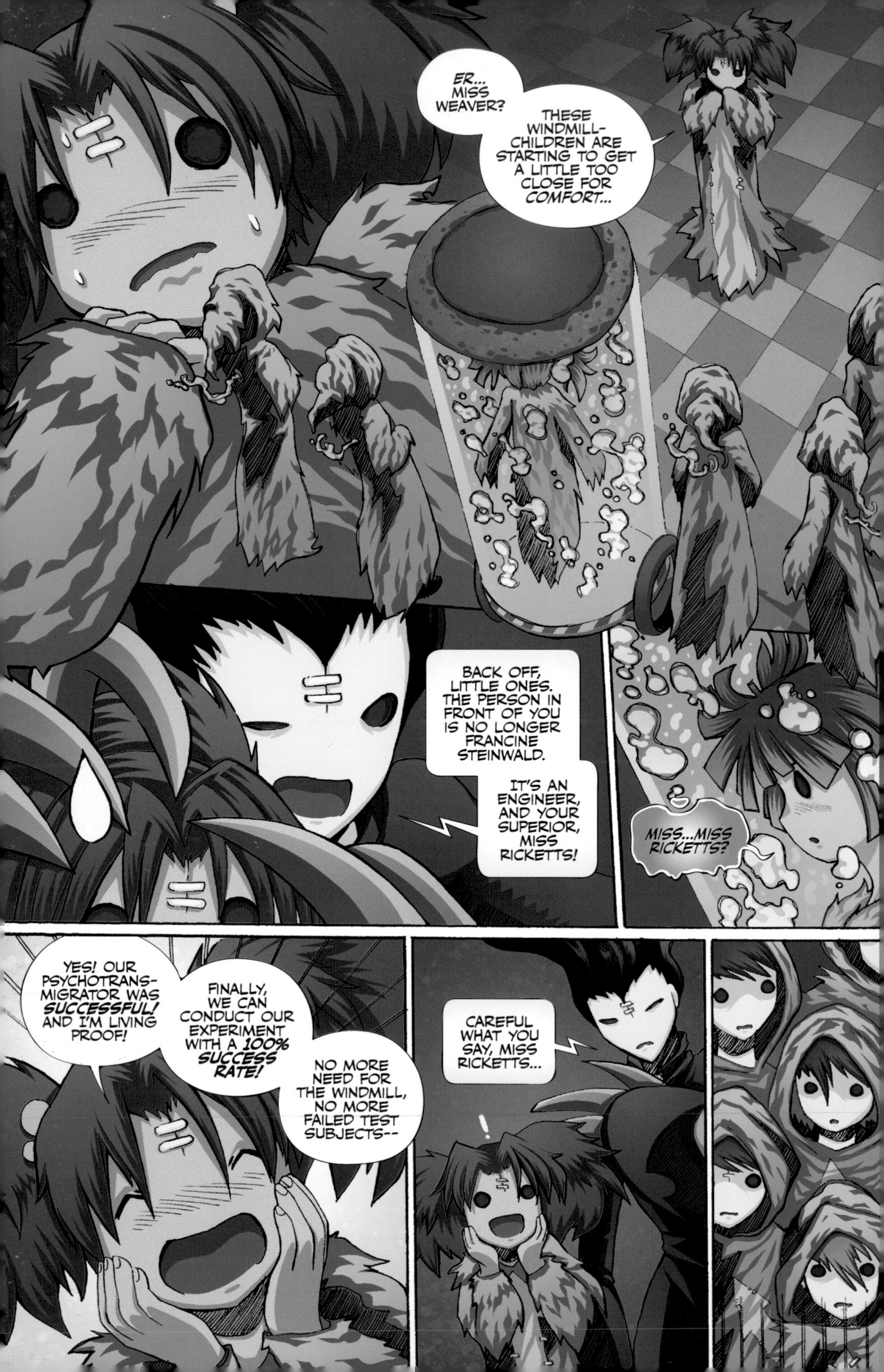
ER... MISS WEAVER?
THESE WINDMILL-CHILDREN ARE STARTING TO GET A LITTLE TOO CLOSE FOR *COMFORT*...
BACK OFF, LITTLE ONES. THE PERSON IN FRONT OF YOU IS NO LONGER FRANCINE STEINWALD.
IT'S AN ENGINEER, AND YOUR SUPERIOR, MISS RICKETTS!
MISS...MISS RICKETTS?
YES! OUR PSYCHOTRANS-MIGRATOR WAS ***SUCCESSFUL!*** AND I'M LIVING PROOF!
FINALLY, WE CAN CONDUCT OUR EXPERIMENT WITH A ***100% SUCCESS RATE!***
NO MORE NEED FOR THE WINDMILL, NO MORE FAILED TEST SUBJECTS--
CAREFUL WHAT YOU SAY, MISS RICKETTS...
!

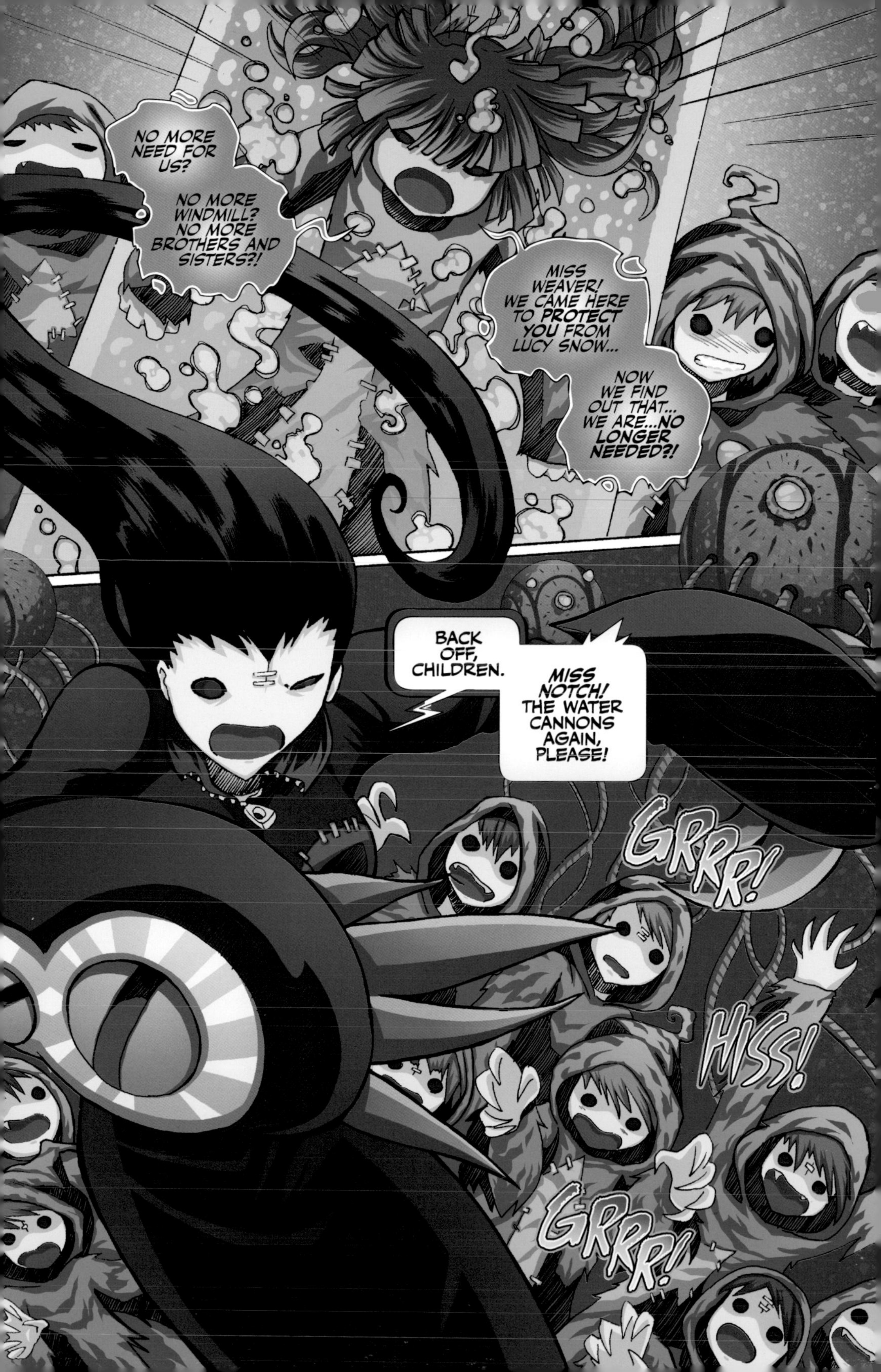

NO MORE NEED FOR US?
NO MORE WINDMILL? NO MORE BROTHERS AND SISTERS?!
MISS WEAVER! WE CAME HERE TO PROTECT YOU FROM LUCY SNOW...
NOW WE FIND OUT THAT... WE ARE...NO LONGER NEEDED?!
BACK OFF, CHILDREN.
MISS NOTCH! THE WATER CANNONS AGAIN, PLEASE!
GRRR!
HISS!
GRRR!

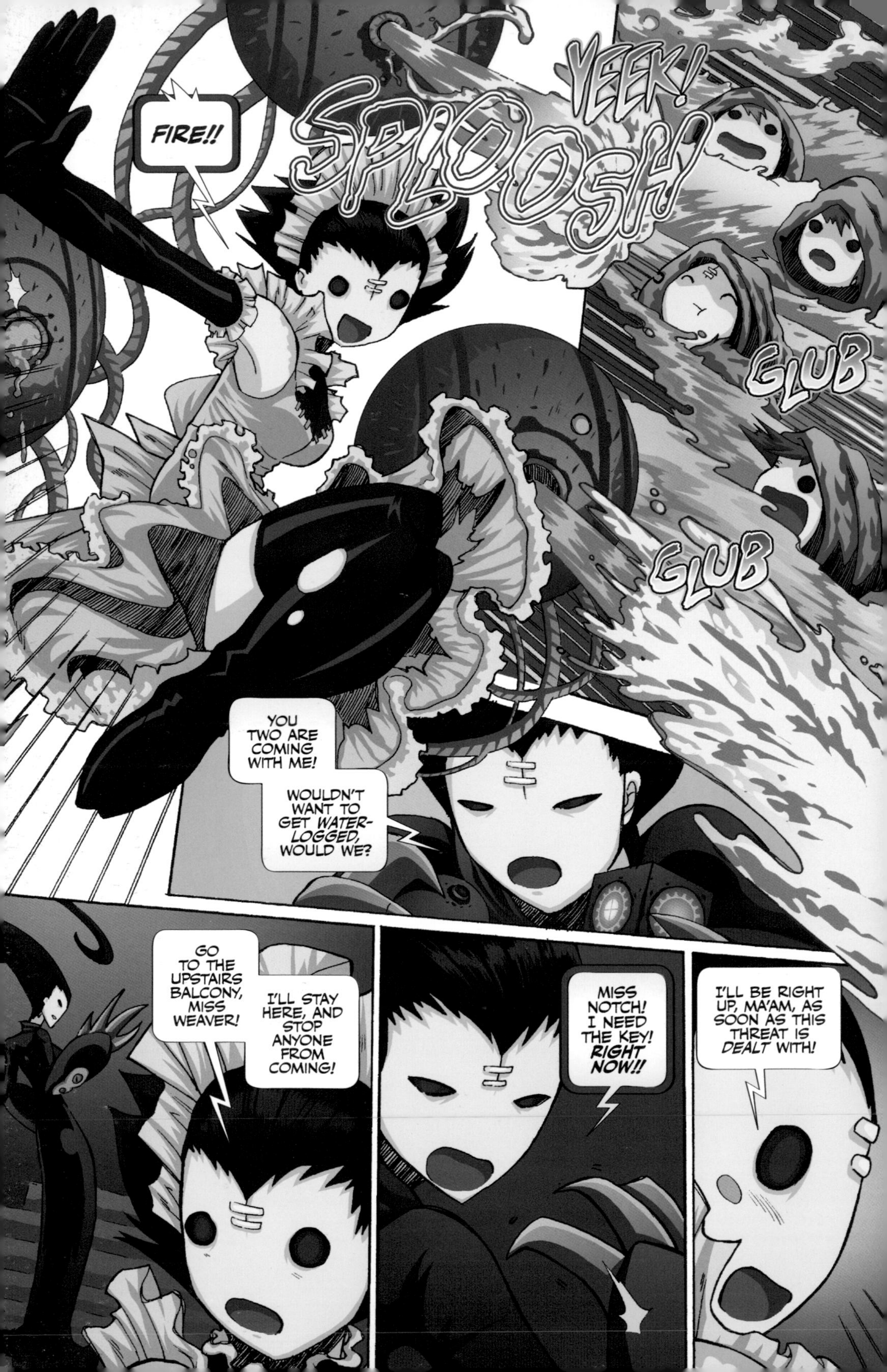
FIRE!!
SPLOOSH!
YEEK!
GLUB
GLUB
YOU TWO ARE COMING WITH ME!
WOULDN'T WANT TO GET WATER-LOGGED, WOULD WE?
GO TO THE UPSTAIRS BALCONY, MISS WEAVER!
I'LL STAY HERE, AND STOP ANYONE FROM COMING!
MISS NOTCH! I NEED THE KEY! RIGHT NOW!!
I'LL BE RIGHT UP, MA'AM, AS SOON AS THIS THREAT IS DEALT WITH!

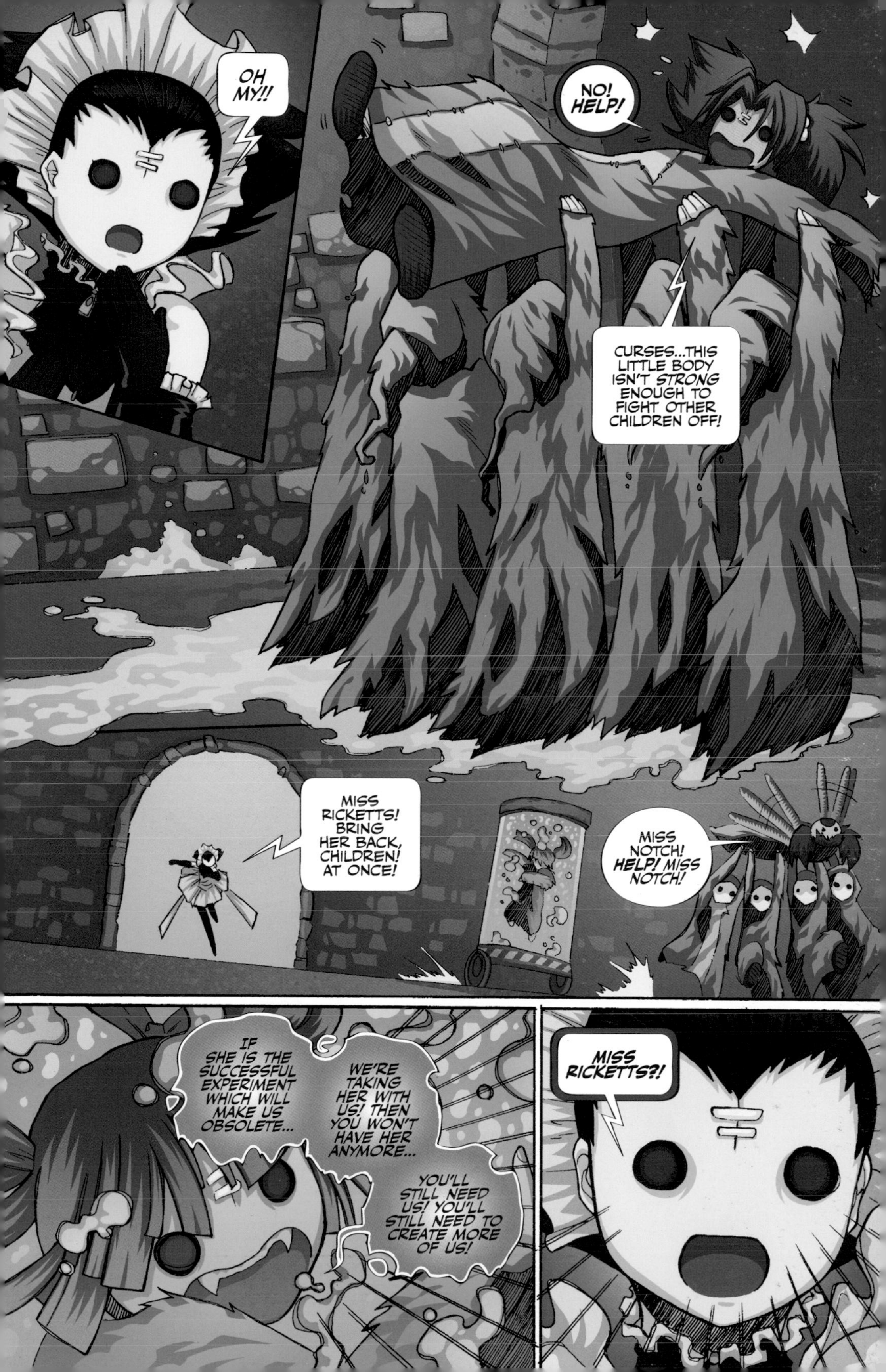
OH MY!!
NO! HELP!
CURSES...THIS LITTLE BODY ISN'T STRONG ENOUGH TO FIGHT OTHER CHILDREN OFF!
MISS RICKETTS! BRING HER BACK, CHILDREN! AT ONCE!
MISS NOTCH! HELP! MISS NOTCH!
IF SHE IS THE SUCCESSFUL EXPERIMENT WHICH WILL MAKE US OBSOLETE...
WE'RE TAKING HER WITH US! THEN YOU WON'T HAVE HER ANYMORE...
YOU'LL STILL NEED US! YOU'LL STILL NEED TO CREATE MORE OF US!
MISS RICKETTS?!

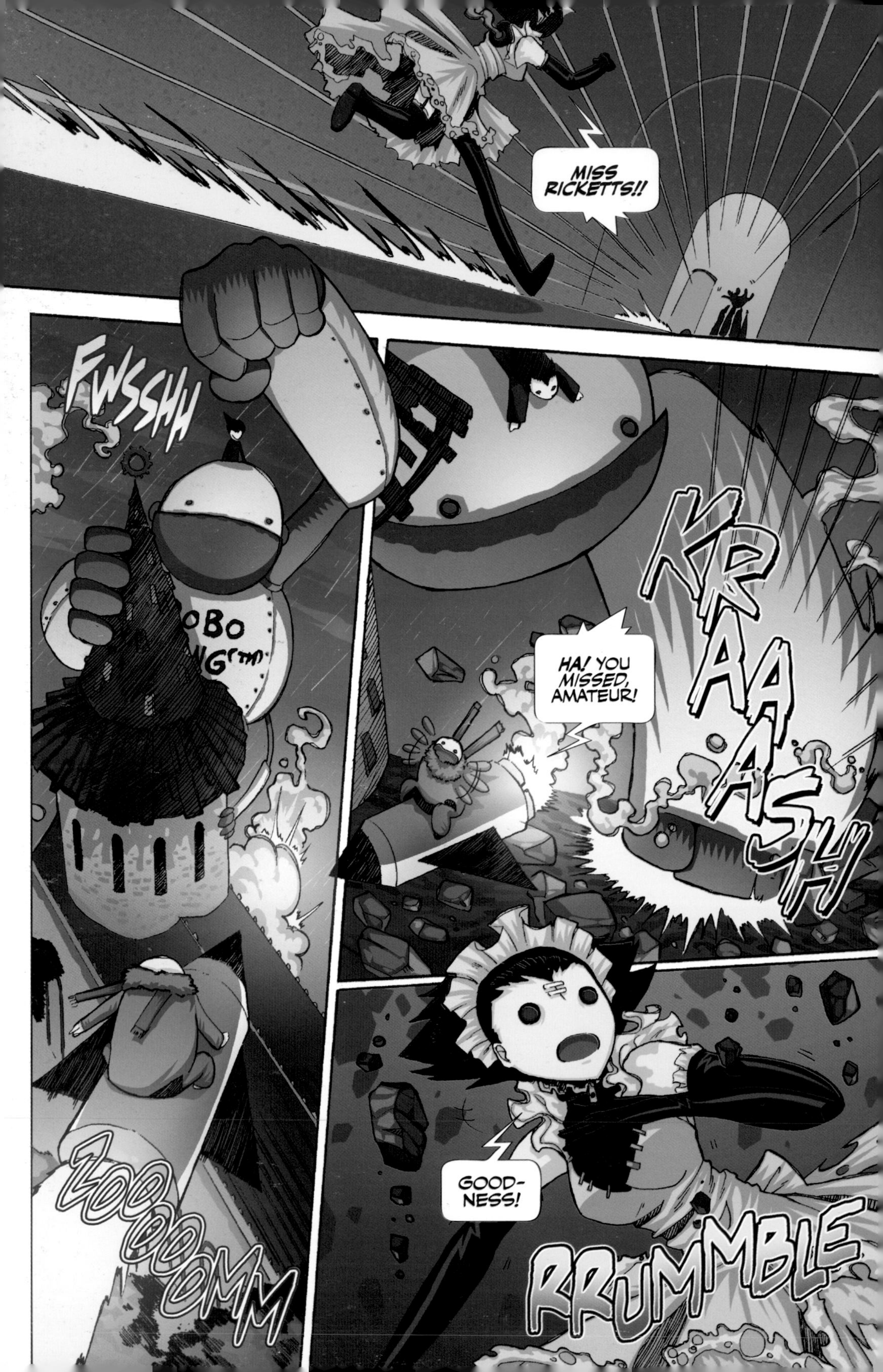
MISS RICKETTS!!
FWSSHH
ZOOOOOMM
KRAAAASH
HA! YOU MISSED, AMATEUR!
GOOD-NESS!
RRUMMBLE

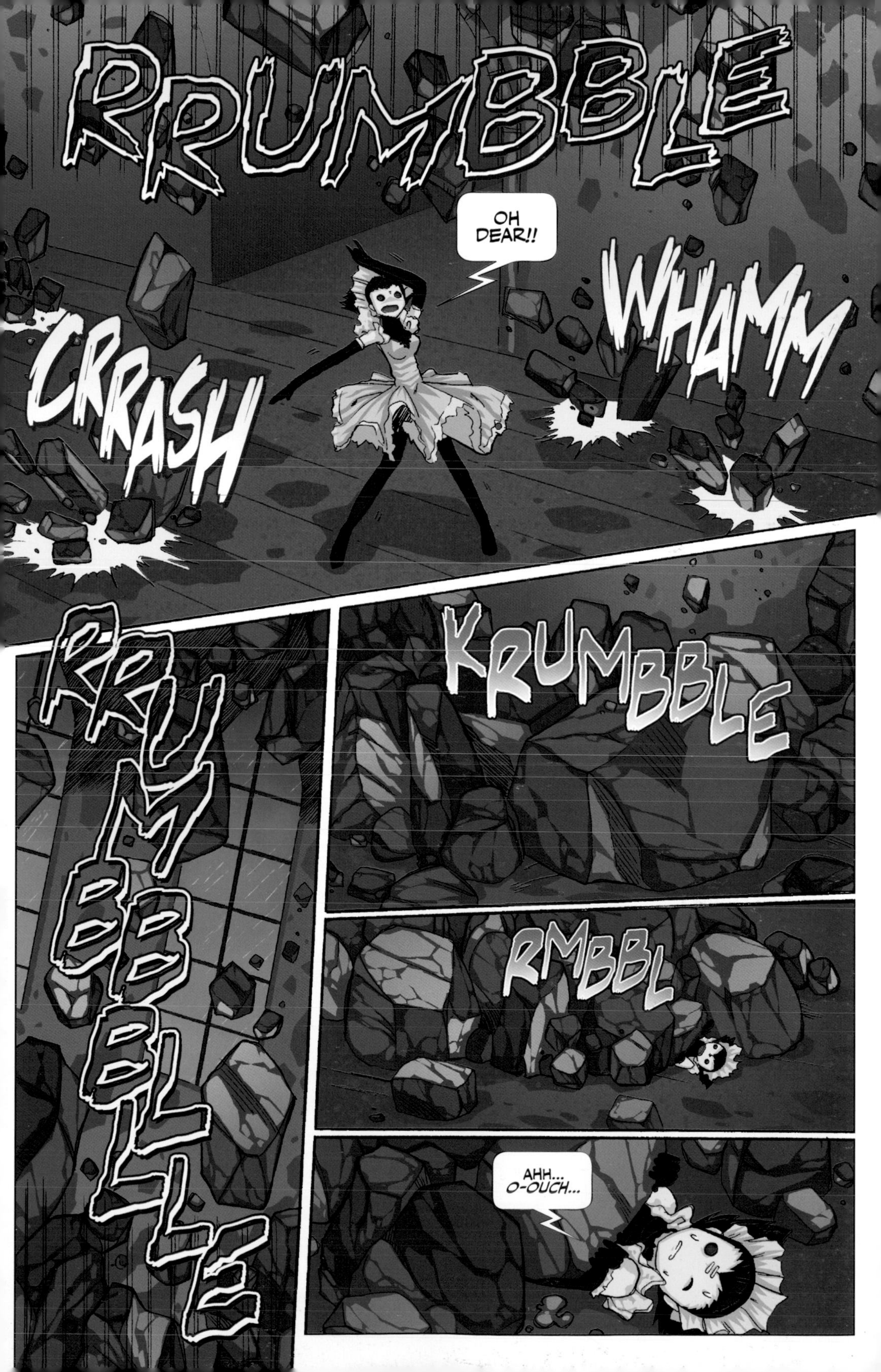
RRUMBBLE
OH DEAR!!
WHAMM
CRRASH
RRUMBBBLLE
KRUMBBLE
RMBBL
AHH... O-OUCH...

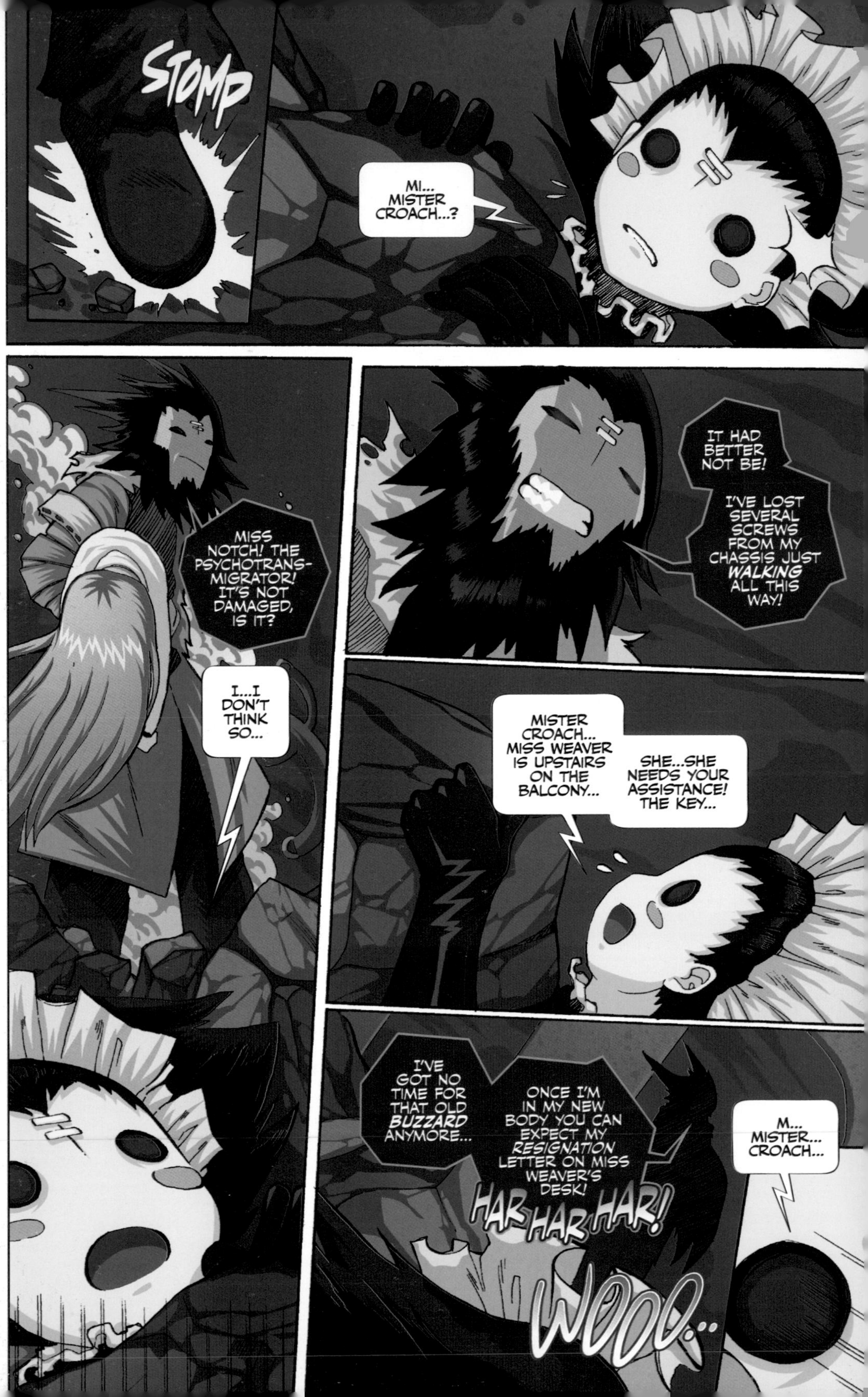
STOMP
MI... MISTER CROACH...?
MISS NOTCH! THE PSYCHOTRANS-MIGRATOR! IT'S NOT DAMAGED, IS IT?
I...I DON'T THINK SO...
IT HAD BETTER NOT BE!
I'VE LOST SEVERAL SCREWS FROM MY CHASSIS JUST *WALKING* ALL THIS WAY!
MISTER CROACH... MISS WEAVER IS UPSTAIRS ON THE BALCONY...
SHE...SHE NEEDS YOUR ASSISTANCE! THE KEY...
I'VE GOT NO TIME FOR THAT OLD *BUZZARD* ANYMORE...
ONCE I'M IN MY NEW BODY YOU CAN EXPECT MY *RESIGNATION* LETTER ON MISS WEAVER'S DESK!
HAR HAR HAR!
M... MISTER... CROACH...
WOOO...

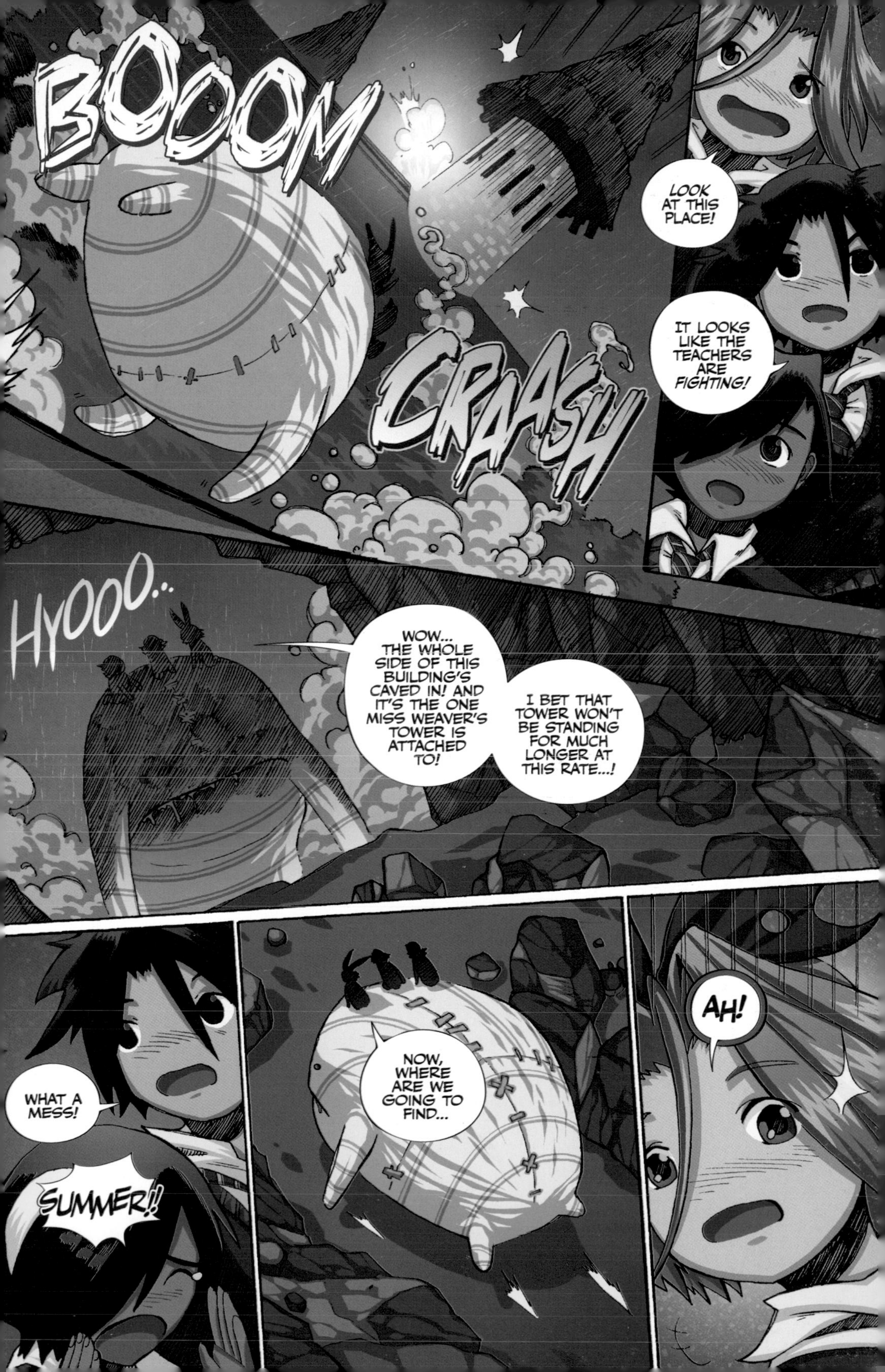
BOOOM
CRAASH
LOOK AT THIS PLACE!
IT LOOKS LIKE THE TEACHERS ARE FIGHTING!
HYOOO...
WOW... THE WHOLE SIDE OF THIS BUILDING'S CAVED IN! AND IT'S THE ONE MISS WEAVER'S TOWER IS ATTACHED TO!
I BET THAT TOWER WON'T BE STANDING FOR MUCH LONGER AT THIS RATE...!
WHAT A MESS!
SUMMER!!
NOW, WHERE ARE WE GOING TO FIND...
AH!

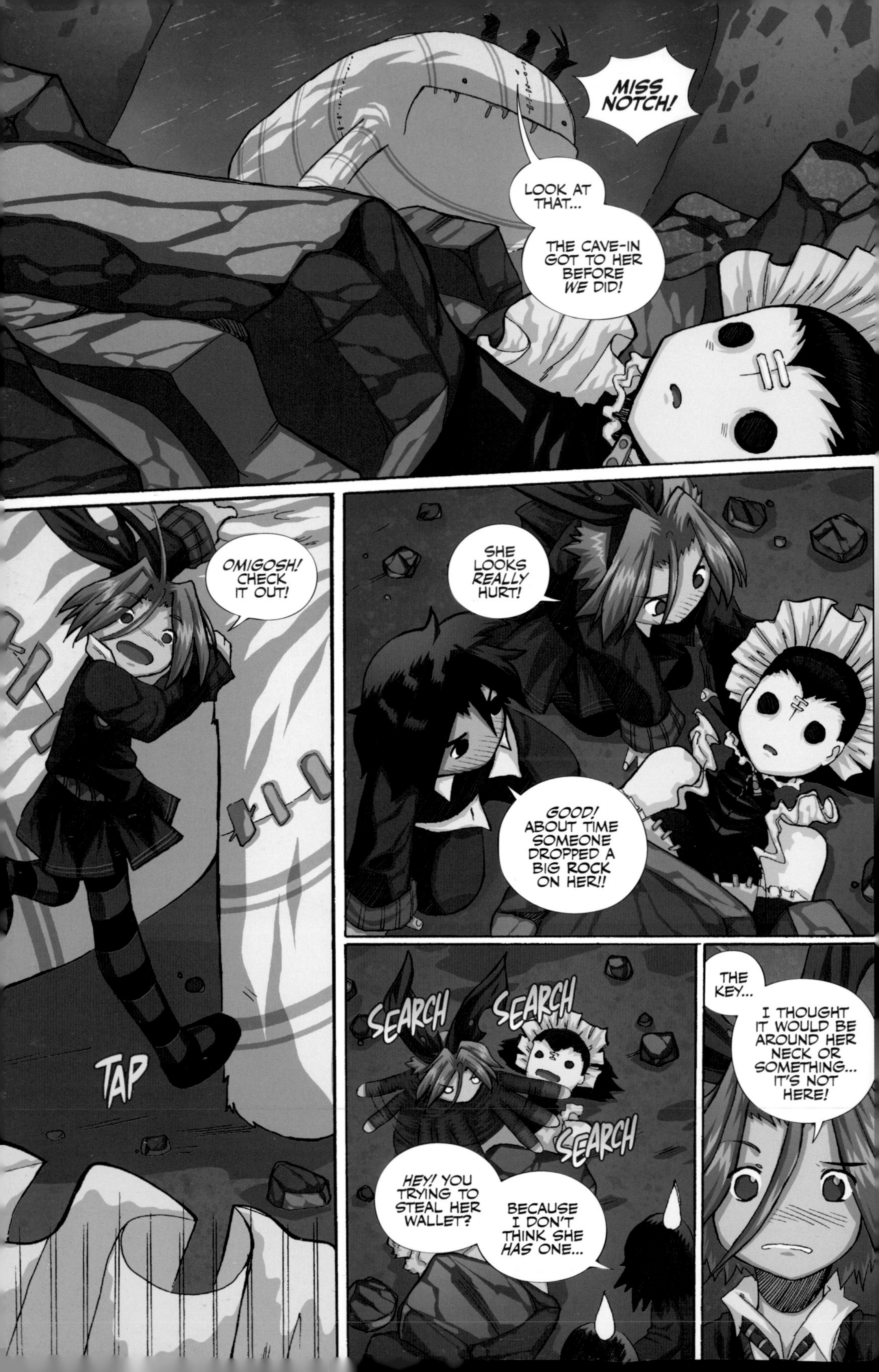
MISS NOTCH!
LOOK AT THAT...
THE CAVE-IN GOT TO HER BEFORE WE DID!
OMIGOSH! CHECK IT OUT!
TAP
SHE LOOKS REALLY HURT!
GOOD! ABOUT TIME SOMEONE DROPPED A BIG ROCK ON HER!!
SEARCH
SEARCH
SEARCH
HEY! YOU TRYING TO STEAL HER WALLET?
BECAUSE I DON'T THINK SHE HAS ONE...
THE KEY...
I THOUGHT IT WOULD BE AROUND HER NECK OR SOMETHING... IT'S NOT HERE!

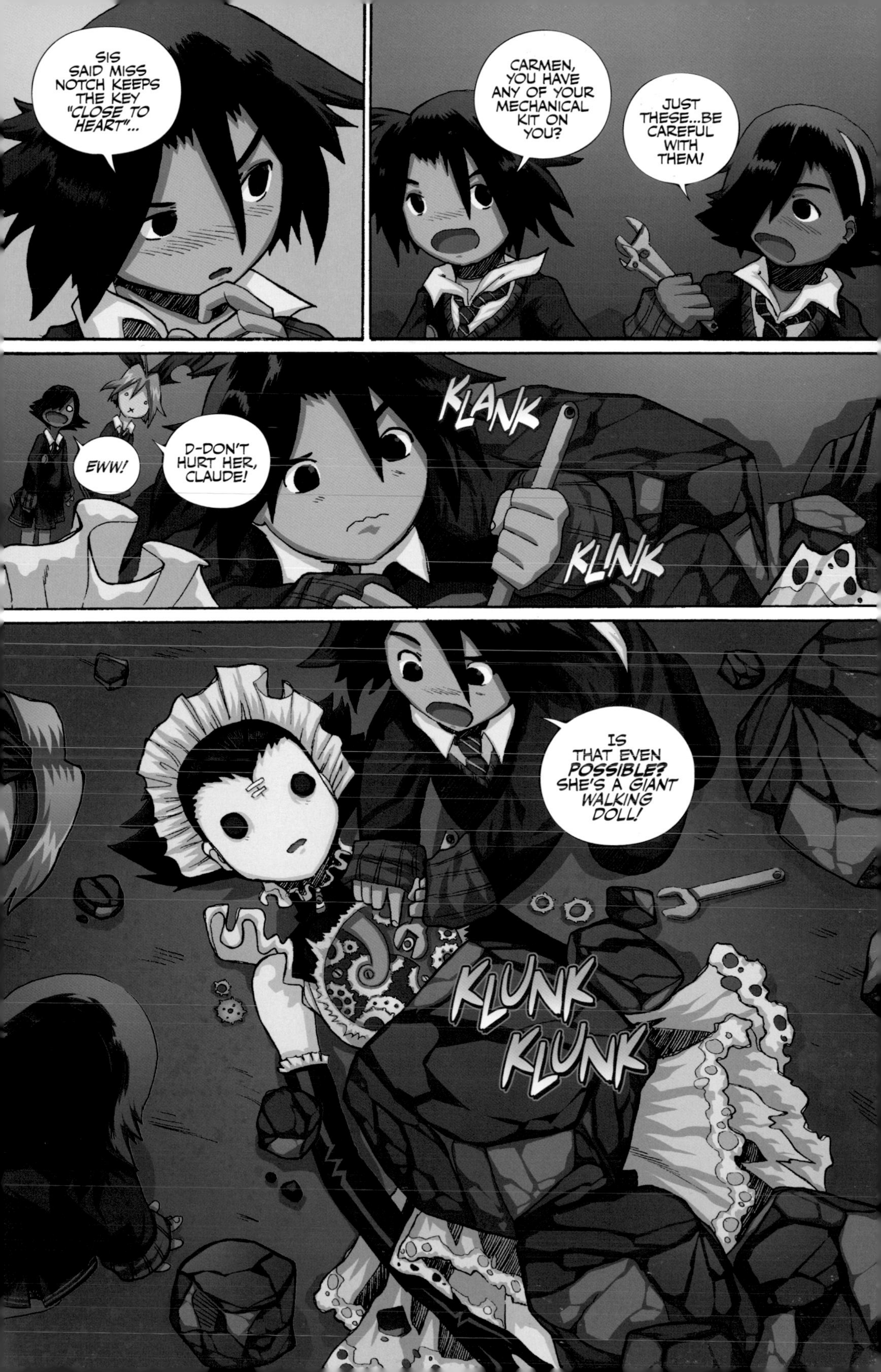
SIS SAID MISS NOTCH KEEPS THE KEY "CLOSE TO HEART"...
CARMEN, YOU HAVE ANY OF YOUR MECHANICAL KIT ON YOU?
JUST THESE...BE CAREFUL WITH THEM!
EWW!
D-DON'T HURT HER, CLAUDE!
KLANK
KLINK
IS THAT EVEN POSSIBLE? SHE'S A GIANT WALKING DOLL!
KLUNK
KLUNK

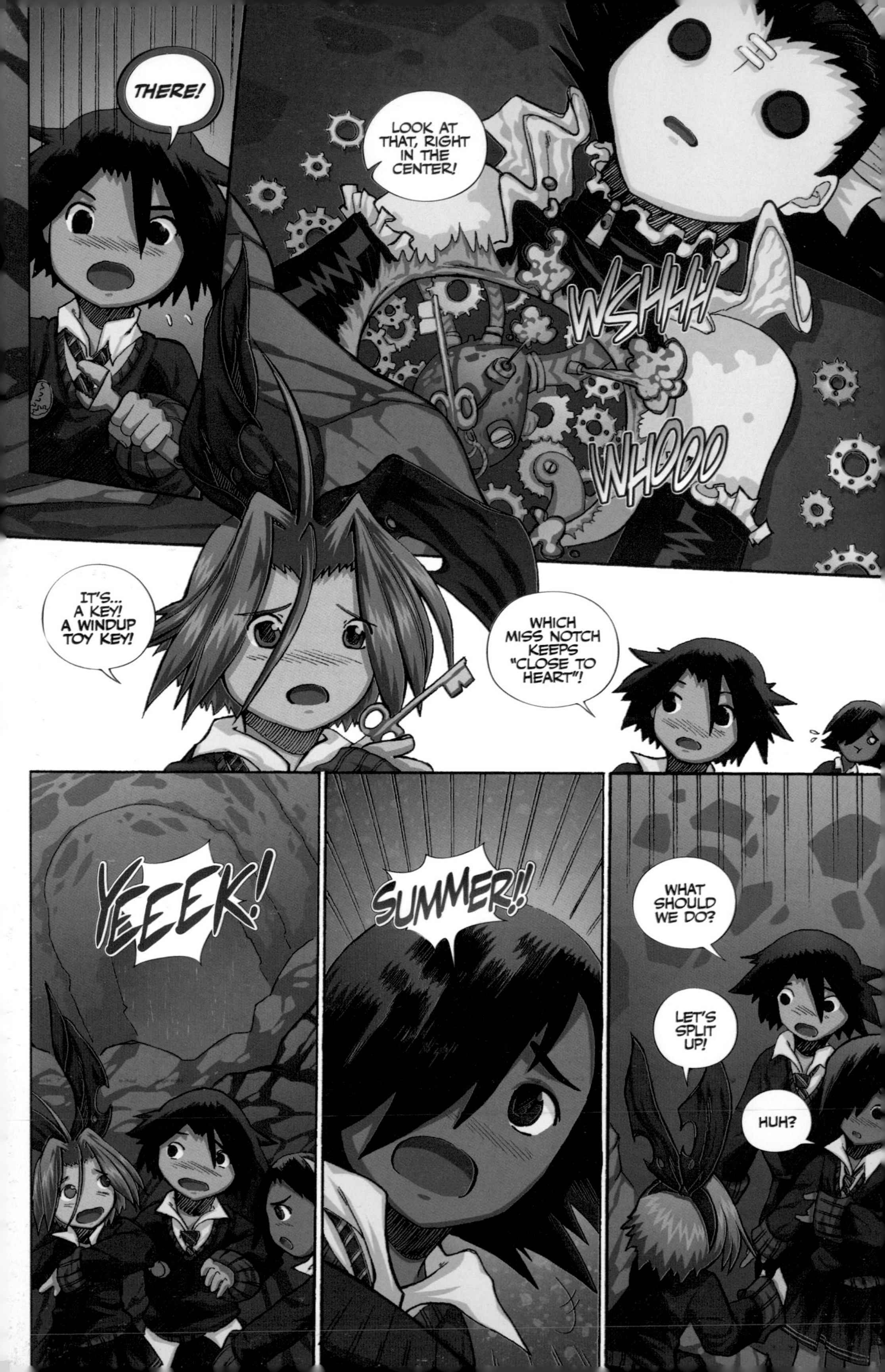
THERE!
LOOK AT THAT, RIGHT IN THE CENTER!
WSHHH
WHOOO
IT'S... A KEY! A WINDUP TOY KEY!
WHICH MISS NOTCH KEEPS "CLOSE TO HEART"!
YEEEK!
SUMMER!!
WHAT SHOULD WE DO?
LET'S SPLIT UP!
HUH?

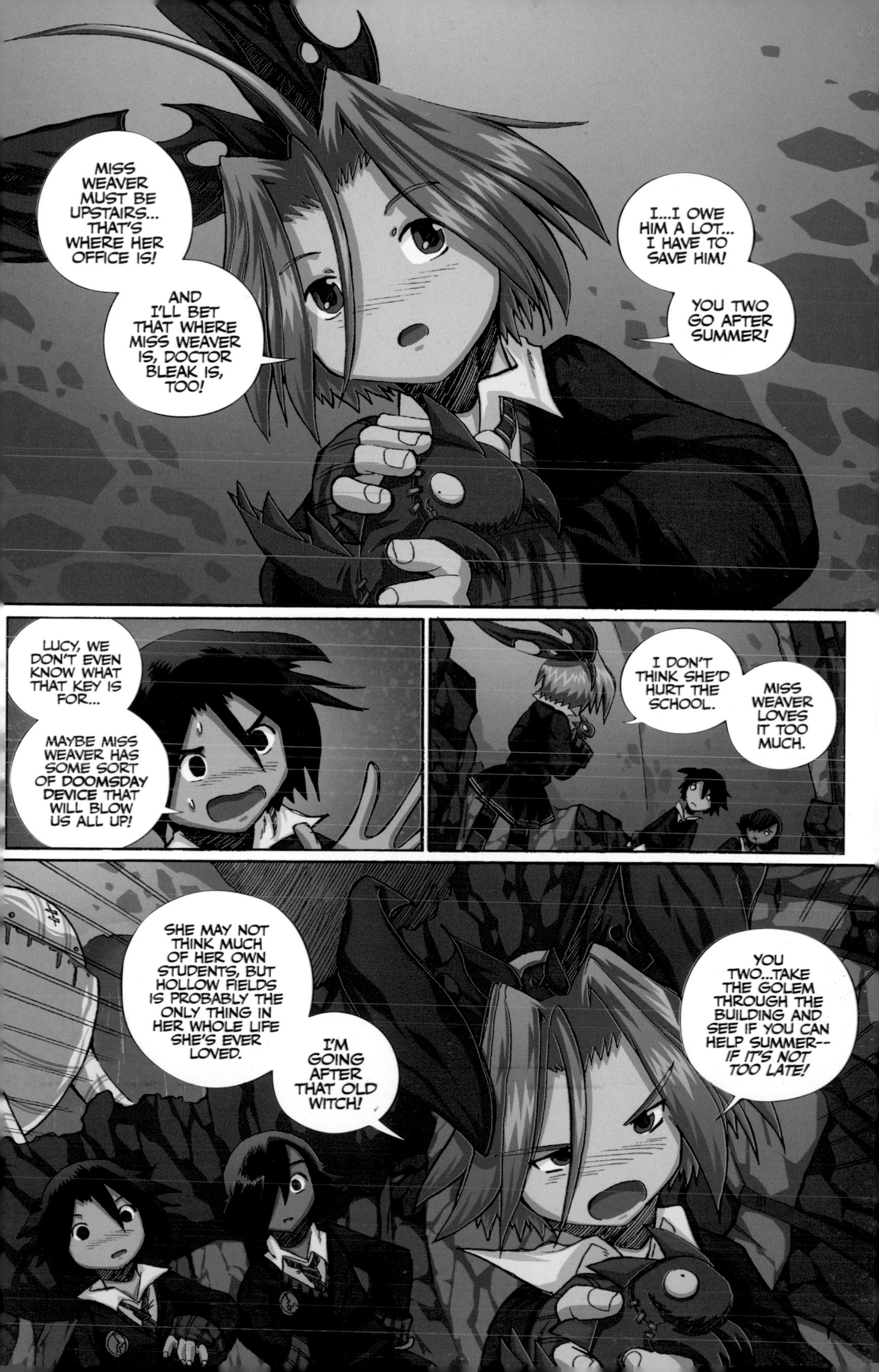
MISS WEAVER MUST BE UPSTAIRS... THAT'S WHERE HER OFFICE IS!
AND I'LL BET THAT WHERE MISS WEAVER IS, DOCTOR BLEAK IS, TOO!
I...I OWE HIM A LOT... I HAVE TO SAVE HIM!
YOU TWO GO AFTER SUMMER!
LUCY, WE DON'T EVEN KNOW WHAT THAT KEY IS FOR...
MAYBE MISS WEAVER HAS SOME SORT OF DOOMSDAY DEVICE THAT WILL BLOW US ALL UP!
I DON'T THINK SHE'D HURT THE SCHOOL.
MISS WEAVER LOVES IT TOO MUCH.
SHE MAY NOT THINK MUCH OF HER OWN STUDENTS, BUT HOLLOW FIELDS IS PROBABLY THE ONLY THING IN HER WHOLE LIFE SHE'S EVER LOVED.
I'M GOING AFTER THAT OLD WITCH!
YOU TWO...TAKE THE GOLEM THROUGH THE BUILDING AND SEE IF YOU CAN HELP SUMMER--*IF IT'S NOT TOO LATE!*

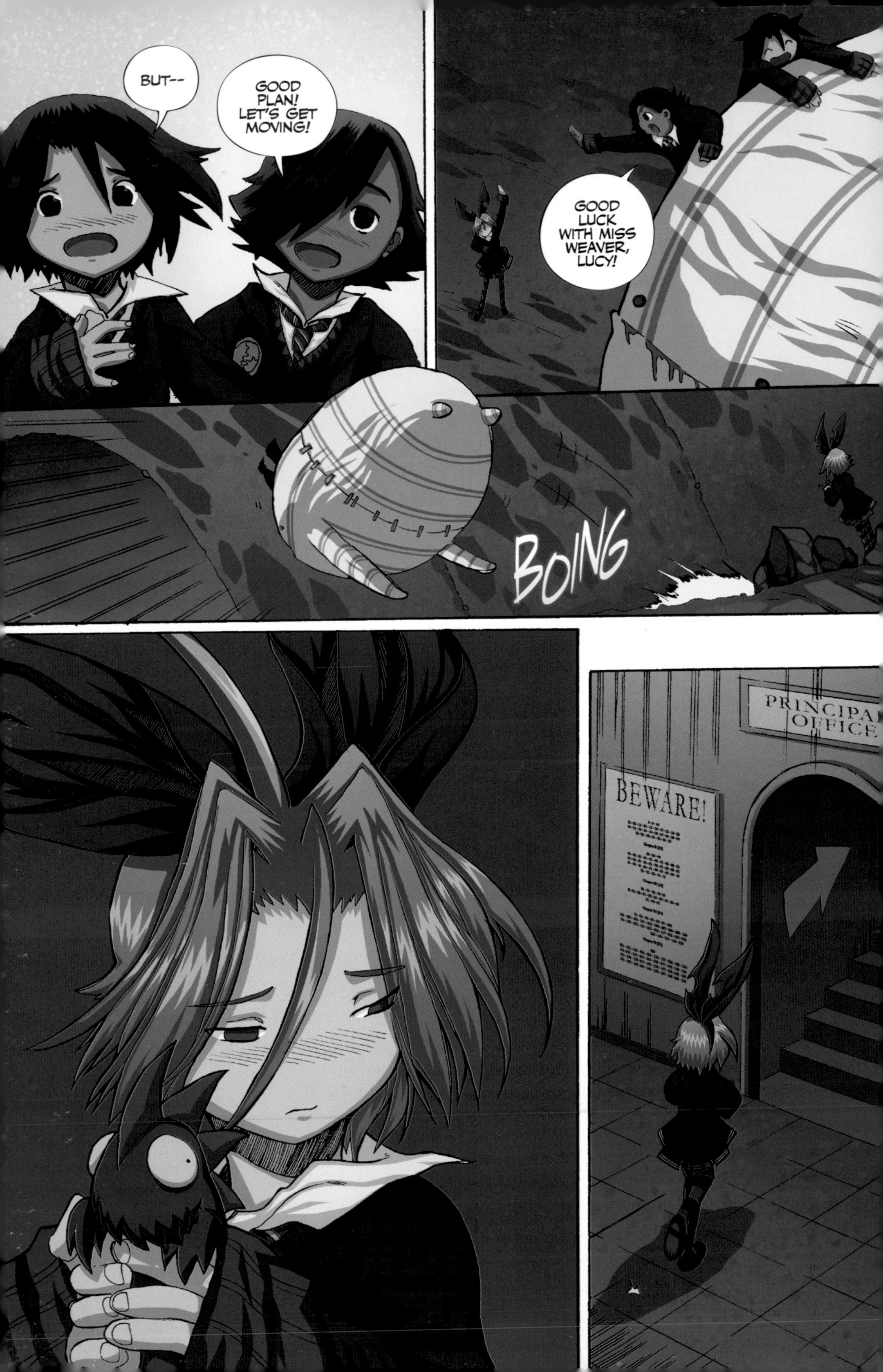
BUT--
GOOD PLAN! LET'S GET MOVING!
GOOD LUCK WITH MISS WEAVER, LUCY!
BOING
PRINCIPAL OFFICE
BEWARE!

CHAPTER FOURTEEN
Confrontations

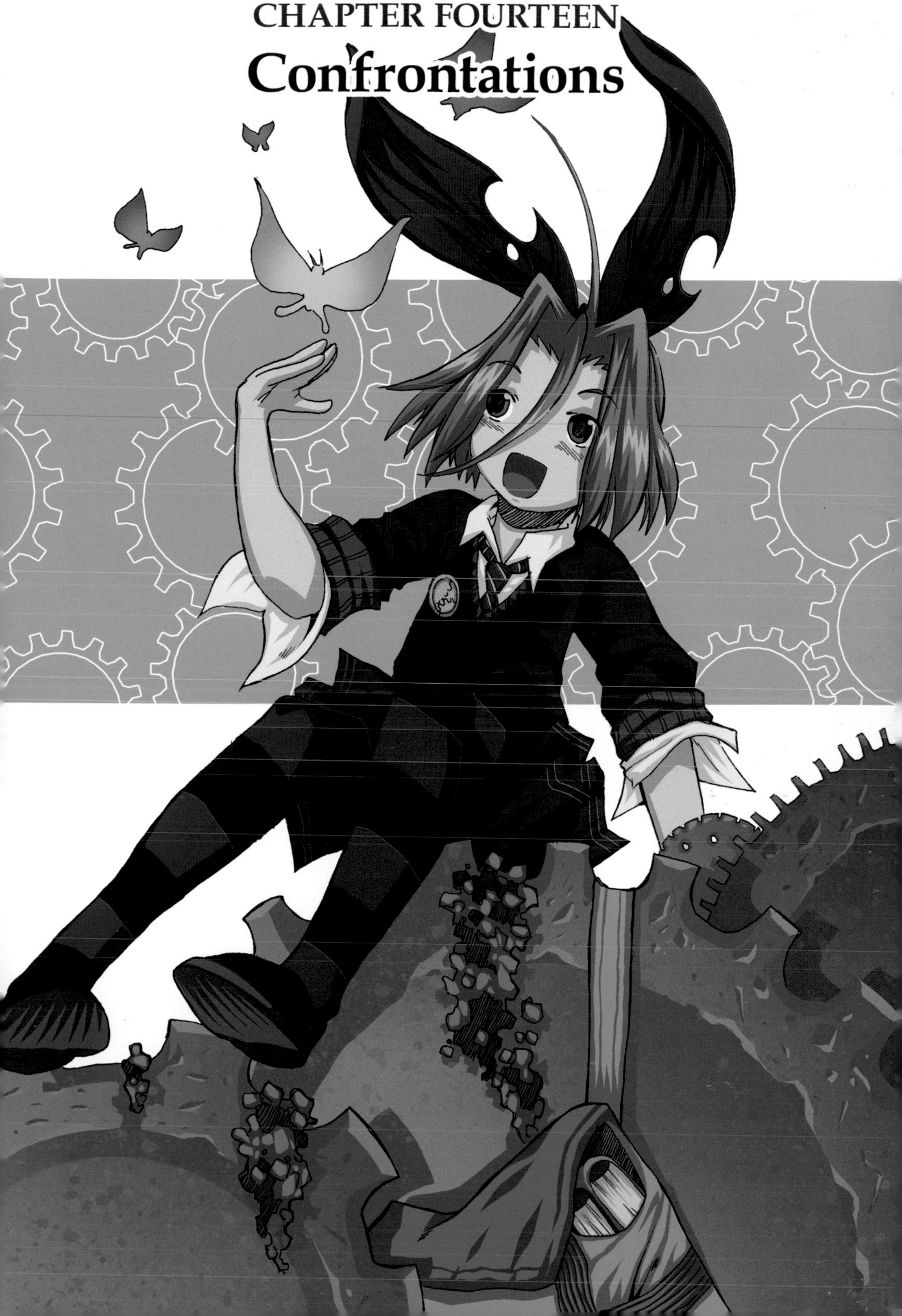

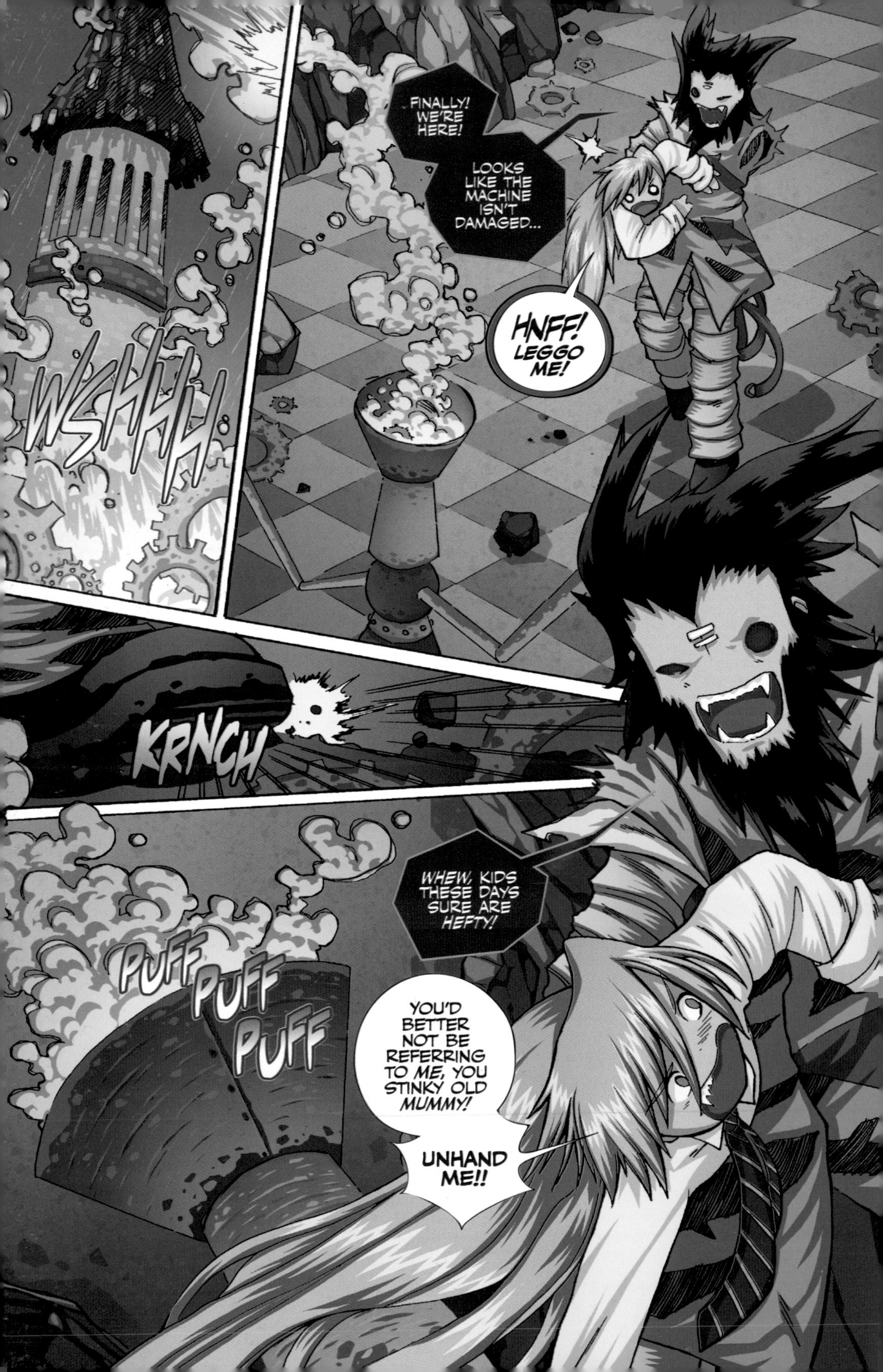
WSHHHH
FINALLY! WE'RE HERE!
LOOKS LIKE THE MACHINE ISN'T DAMAGED...
HNFF! LEGGO ME!
KRNCH
PUFF PUFF PUFF
WHEW, KIDS THESE DAYS SURE ARE HEFTY!
YOU'D BETTER NOT BE REFERRING TO ME, YOU STINKY OLD MUMMY!
UNHAND ME!!

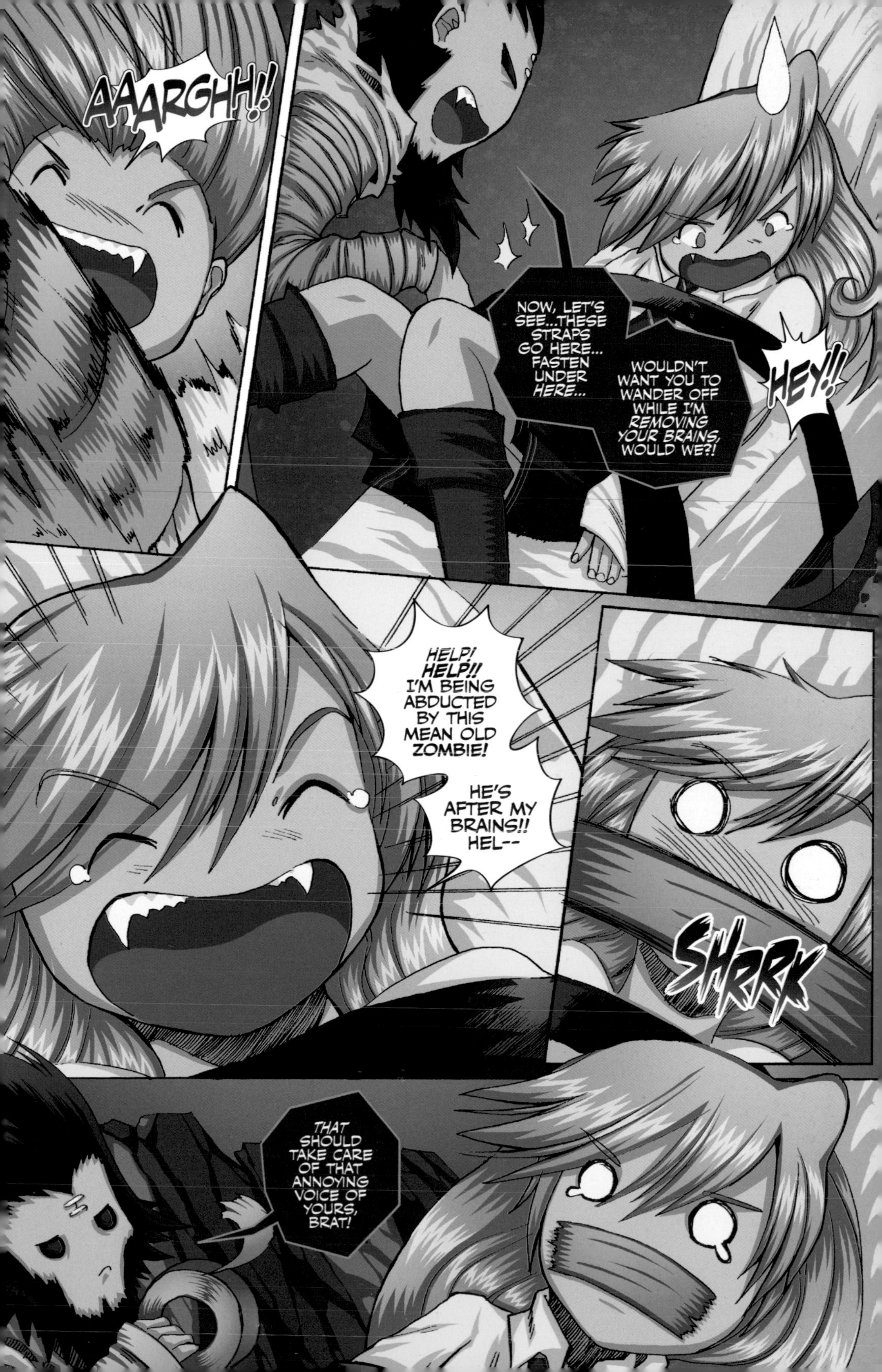
AAARGHH!!
NOW, LET'S SEE...THESE STRAPS GO HERE... FASTEN UNDER HERE...
WOULDN'T WANT YOU TO WANDER OFF WHILE I'M REMOVING YOUR BRAINS, WOULD WE?!
HEY!!
HELP! HELP!! I'M BEING ABDUCTED BY THIS MEAN OLD ZOMBIE!
HE'S AFTER MY BRAINS!! HEL--
SHRRK
THAT SHOULD TAKE CARE OF THAT ANNOYING VOICE OF YOURS, BRAT!

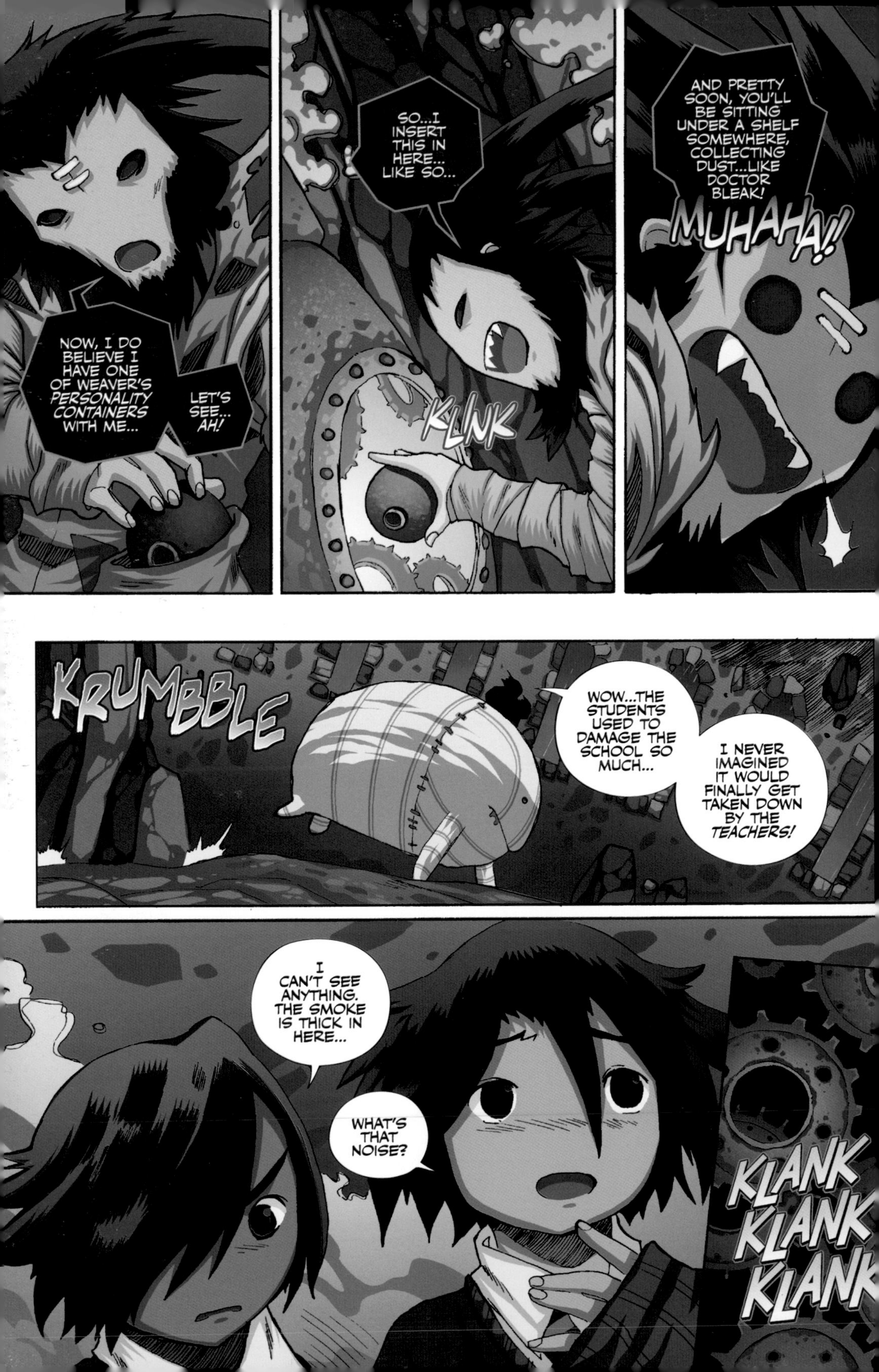
NOW, I DO BELIEVE I HAVE ONE OF WEAVER'S *PERSONALITY CONTAINERS* WITH ME...
LET'S SEE... *AH!*
SO...I INSERT THIS IN HERE... LIKE SO...
KLINK
AND PRETTY SOON, YOU'LL BE SITTING UNDER A SHELF SOMEWHERE, COLLECTING DUST...LIKE DOCTOR BLEAK!
MUHAHA!!
KRUMBBLE
WOW...THE STUDENTS USED TO DAMAGE THE SCHOOL SO MUCH...
I NEVER IMAGINED IT WOULD FINALLY GET TAKEN DOWN BY THE *TEACHERS!*
I CAN'T SEE ANYTHING. THE SMOKE IS THICK IN HERE...
WHAT'S THAT NOISE?
KLANK KLANK KLANK

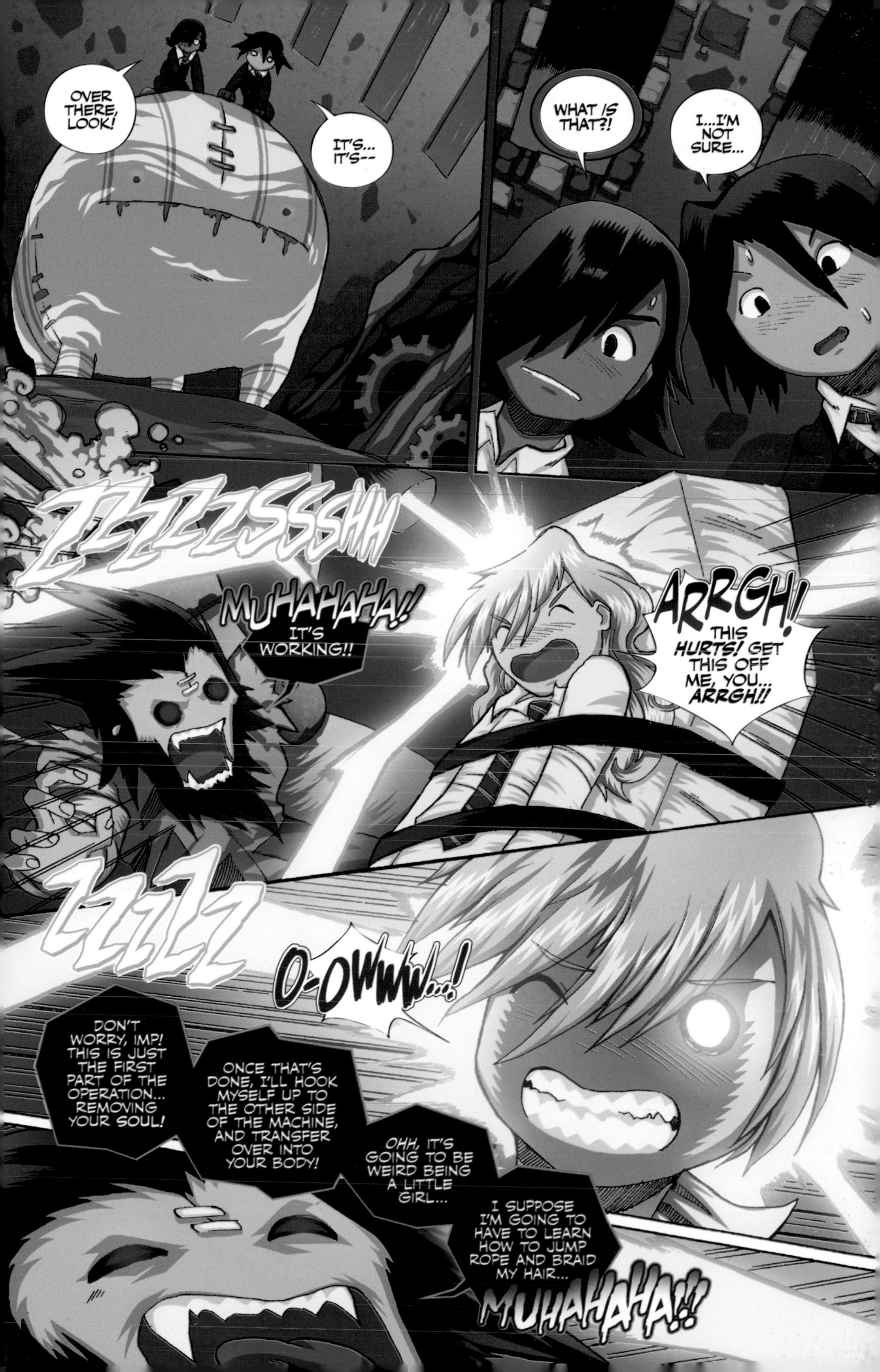
OVER THERE, LOOK!
IT'S... IT'S--
WHAT *IS* THAT?!
I...I'M NOT SURE...
ZZZZZZSSSSHH
MUHAHAHA!! IT'S WORKING!!
ARRGH! THIS *HURTS!* GET THIS OFF ME, YOU... *ARRGH!!*
ZZZZZ
O-OWWW...!
DON'T WORRY, IMP! THIS IS JUST THE FIRST PART OF THE OPERATION... REMOVING YOUR SOUL!
ONCE THAT'S DONE, I'LL HOOK MYSELF UP TO THE OTHER SIDE OF THE MACHINE, AND TRANSFER OVER INTO YOUR BODY!
OHH, IT'S GOING TO BE WEIRD BEING A LITTLE GIRL...
I SUPPOSE I'M GOING TO HAVE TO LEARN HOW TO JUMP ROPE AND BRAID MY HAIR...
MUHAHAHA!!

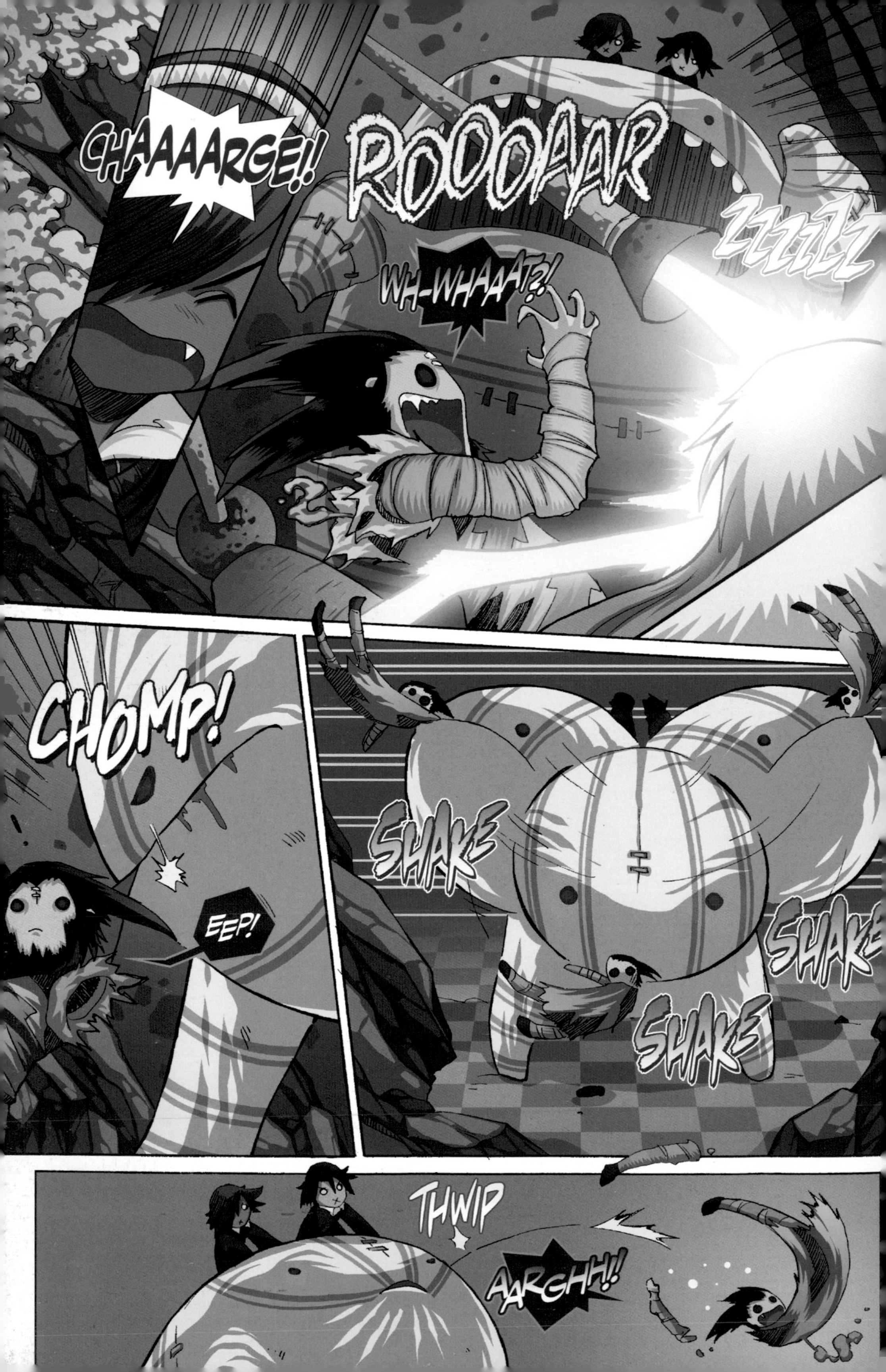
CHAAAARGE!!
ROOOAAR
ZZZZZZ
WH-WHAAAT?!
CHOMP!
EEP!
SHAKE
SHAKE
SHAKE
THWIP
AARGHH!!

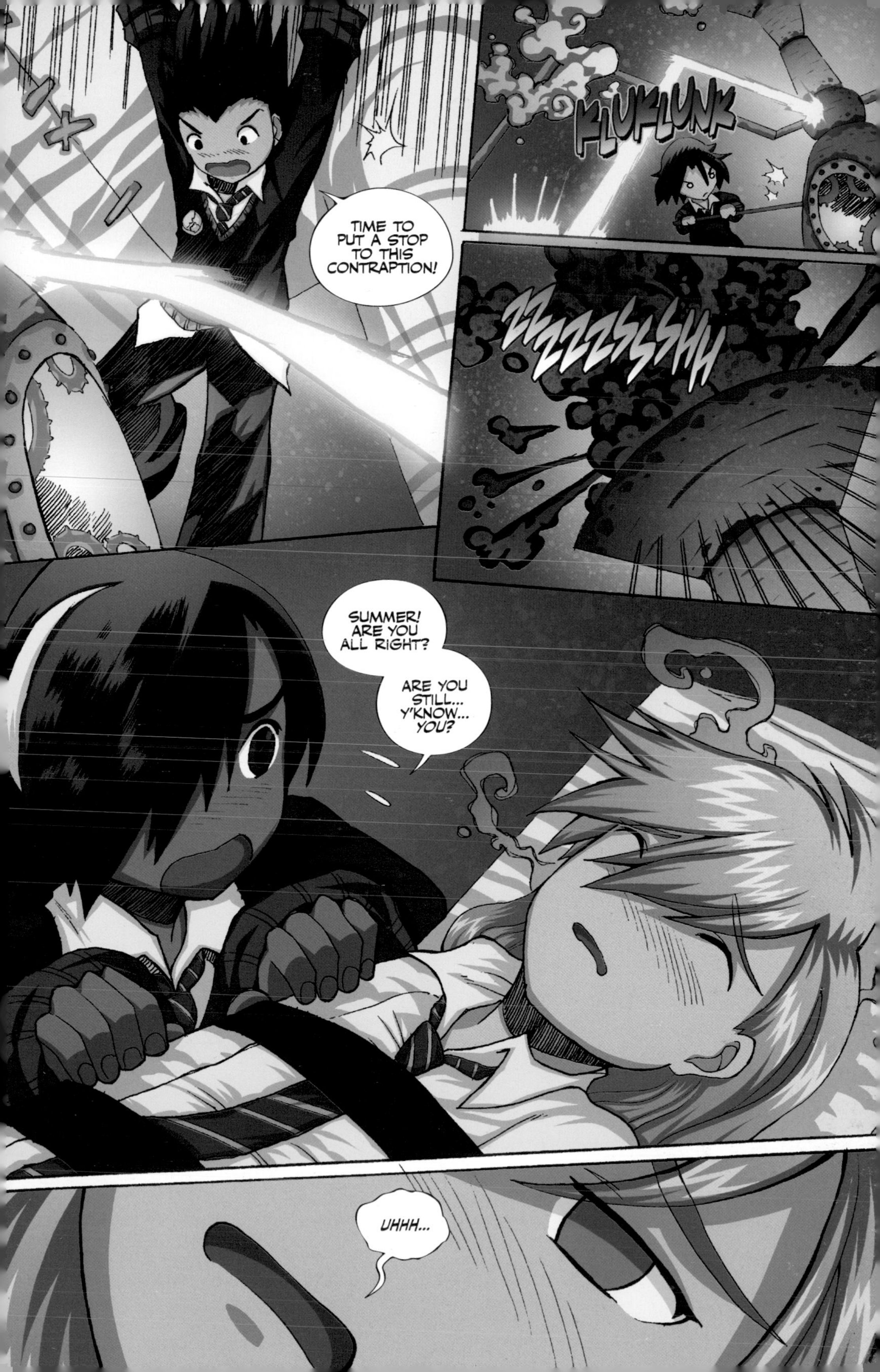
TIME TO PUT A STOP TO THIS CONTRAPTION!
KLUKLUNK
ZZZZZZSSSHH
SUMMER! ARE YOU ALL RIGHT?
ARE YOU STILL... Y'KNOW... YOU?
UHHH...

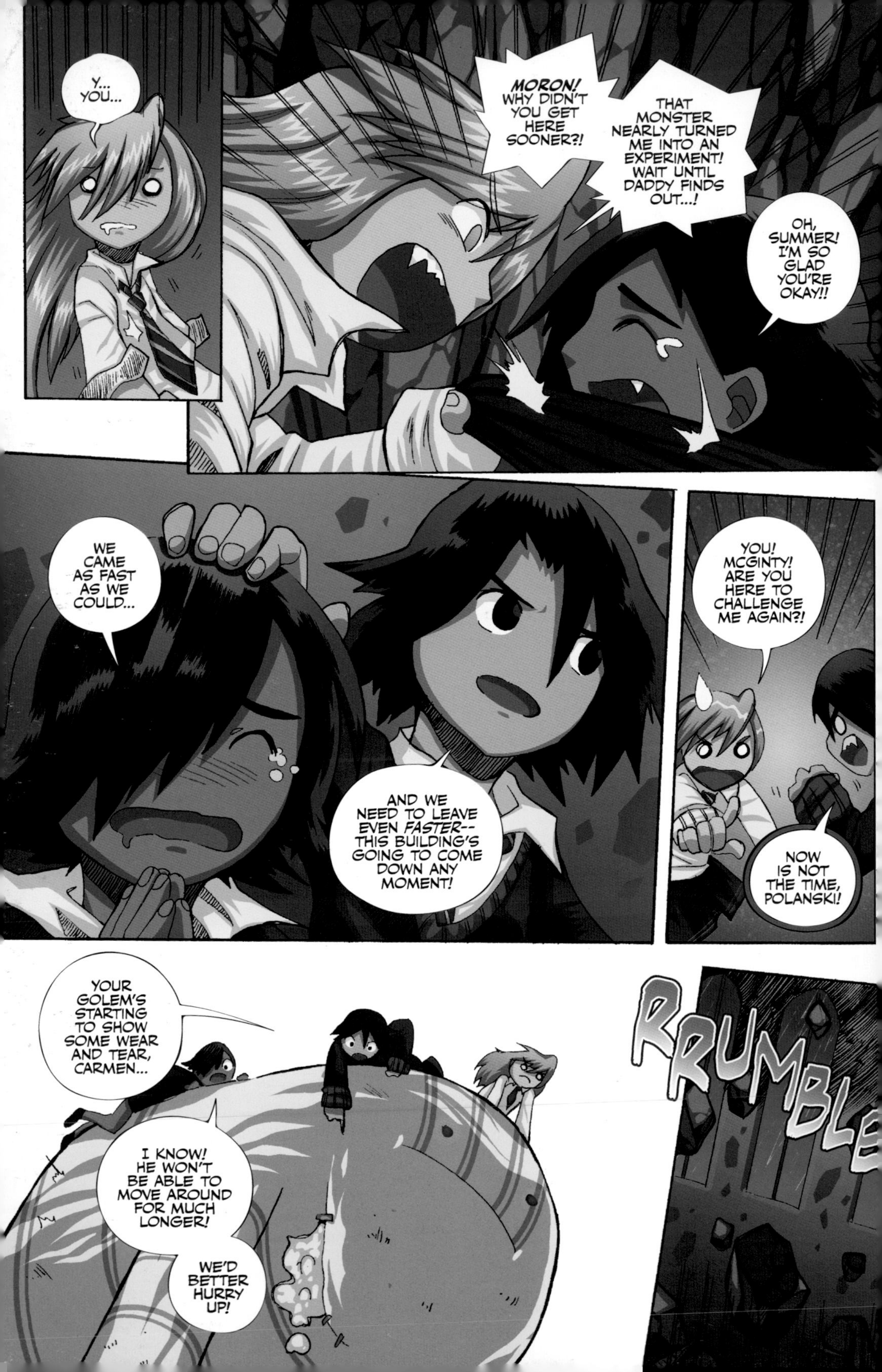
Y... YOU...
MORON! WHY DIDN'T YOU GET HERE SOONER?!
THAT MONSTER NEARLY TURNED ME INTO AN EXPERIMENT! WAIT UNTIL DADDY FINDS OUT...!
OH, SUMMER! I'M SO GLAD YOU'RE OKAY!!
WE CAME AS FAST AS WE COULD...
AND WE NEED TO LEAVE EVEN *FASTER*-- THIS BUILDING'S GOING TO COME DOWN ANY MOMENT!
YOU! MCGINTY! ARE YOU HERE TO CHALLENGE ME AGAIN?!
NOW IS NOT THE TIME, POLANSKI!
YOUR GOLEM'S STARTING TO SHOW SOME WEAR AND TEAR, CARMEN...
I KNOW! HE WON'T BE ABLE TO MOVE AROUND FOR MUCH LONGER!
WE'D BETTER HURRY UP!
RRUMBLE

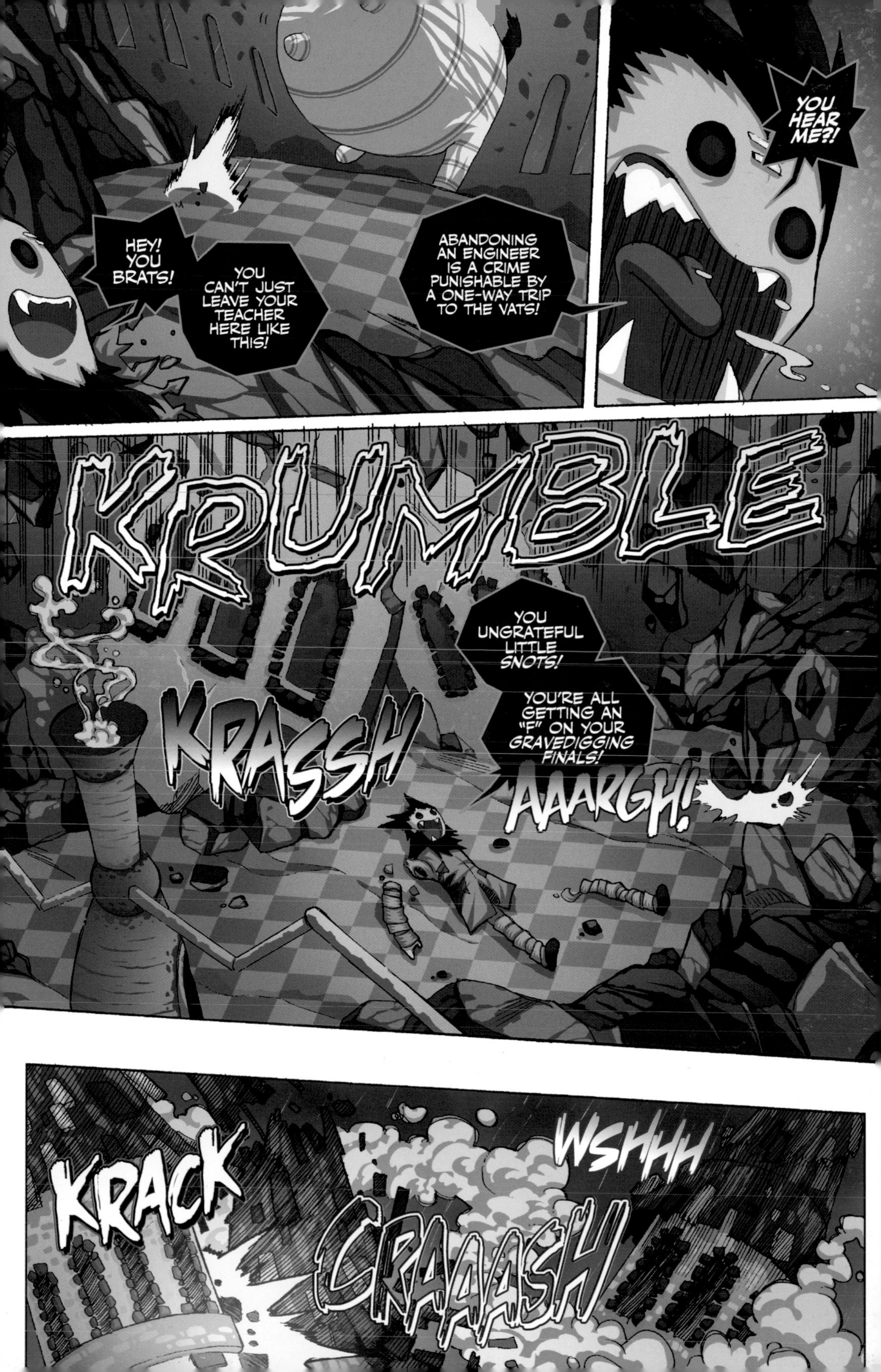
HEY! YOU BRATS!
YOU CAN'T JUST LEAVE YOUR TEACHER HERE LIKE THIS!
ABANDONING AN ENGINEER IS A CRIME PUNISHABLE BY A ONE-WAY TRIP TO THE VATS!
YOU HEAR ME?!
KRUMBLE
YOU UNGRATEFUL LITTLE SNOTS!
YOU'RE ALL GETTING AN "F" ON YOUR GRAVEDIGGING FINALS!
KRASSH
AAARGH!
WSHHH
KRACK
CRAAAASH

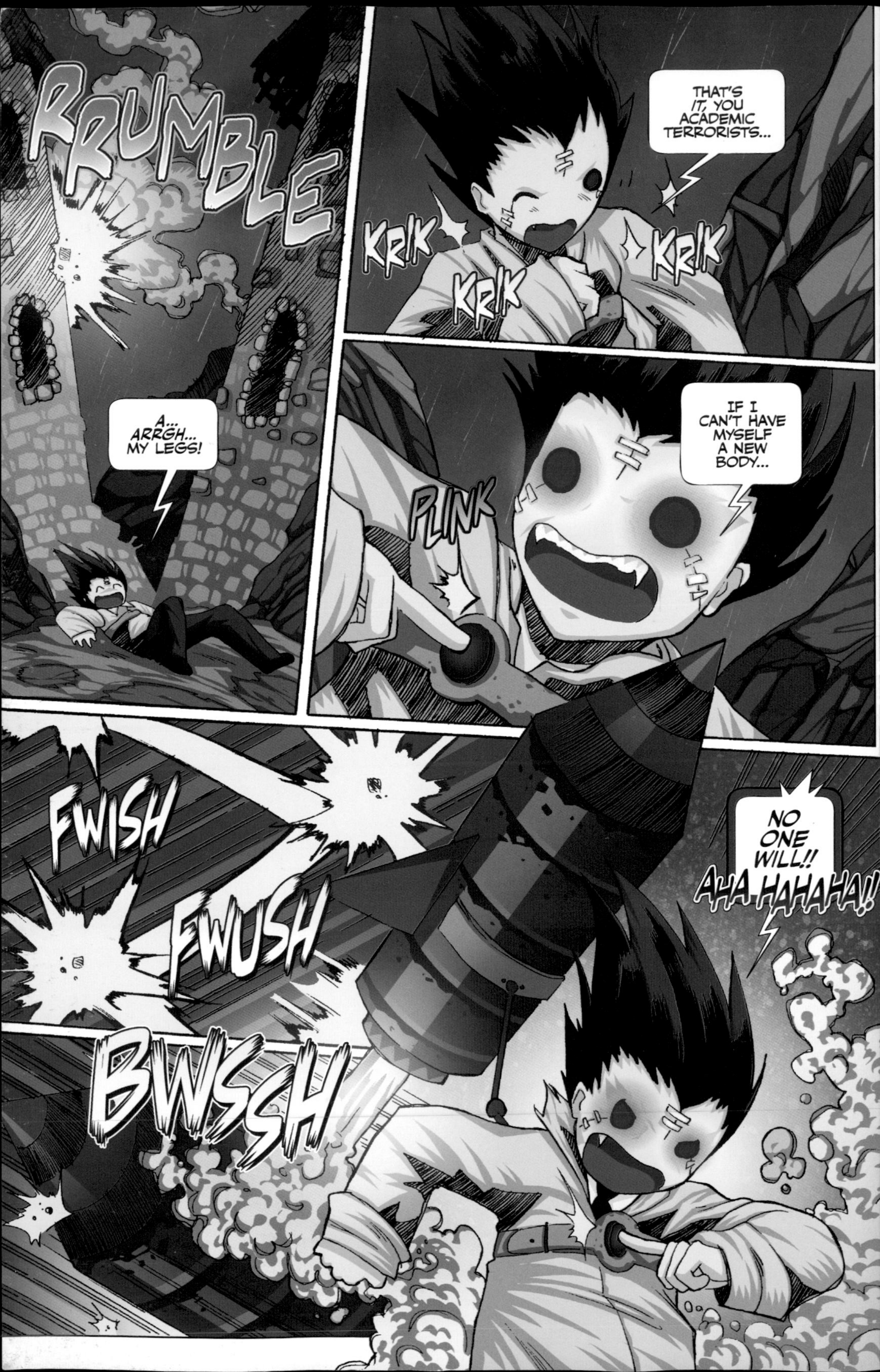
RRUMBLE
A... ARRGH... MY LEGS!
THAT'S IT, YOU ACADEMIC TERRORISTS...
KRIK
KRIK
KRIK
IF I CAN'T HAVE MYSELF A NEW BODY...
PLINK
FWISH
FWUSH
BWSSH
NO ONE WILL!!
AHA HAHAHA!!

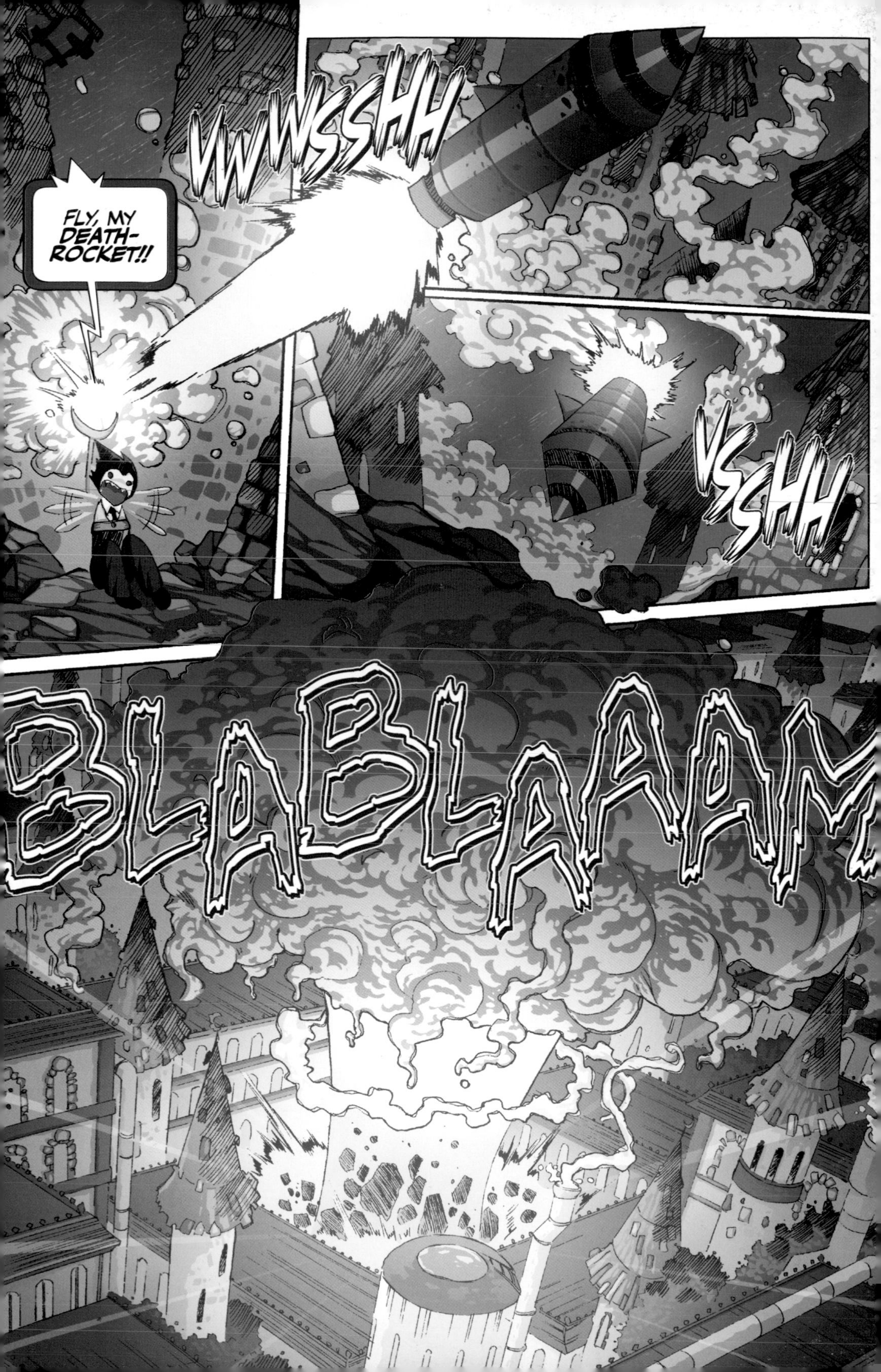
VWWSSHH
FLY, MY DEATH-ROCKET!!
VSSHH
BLABLAAAM

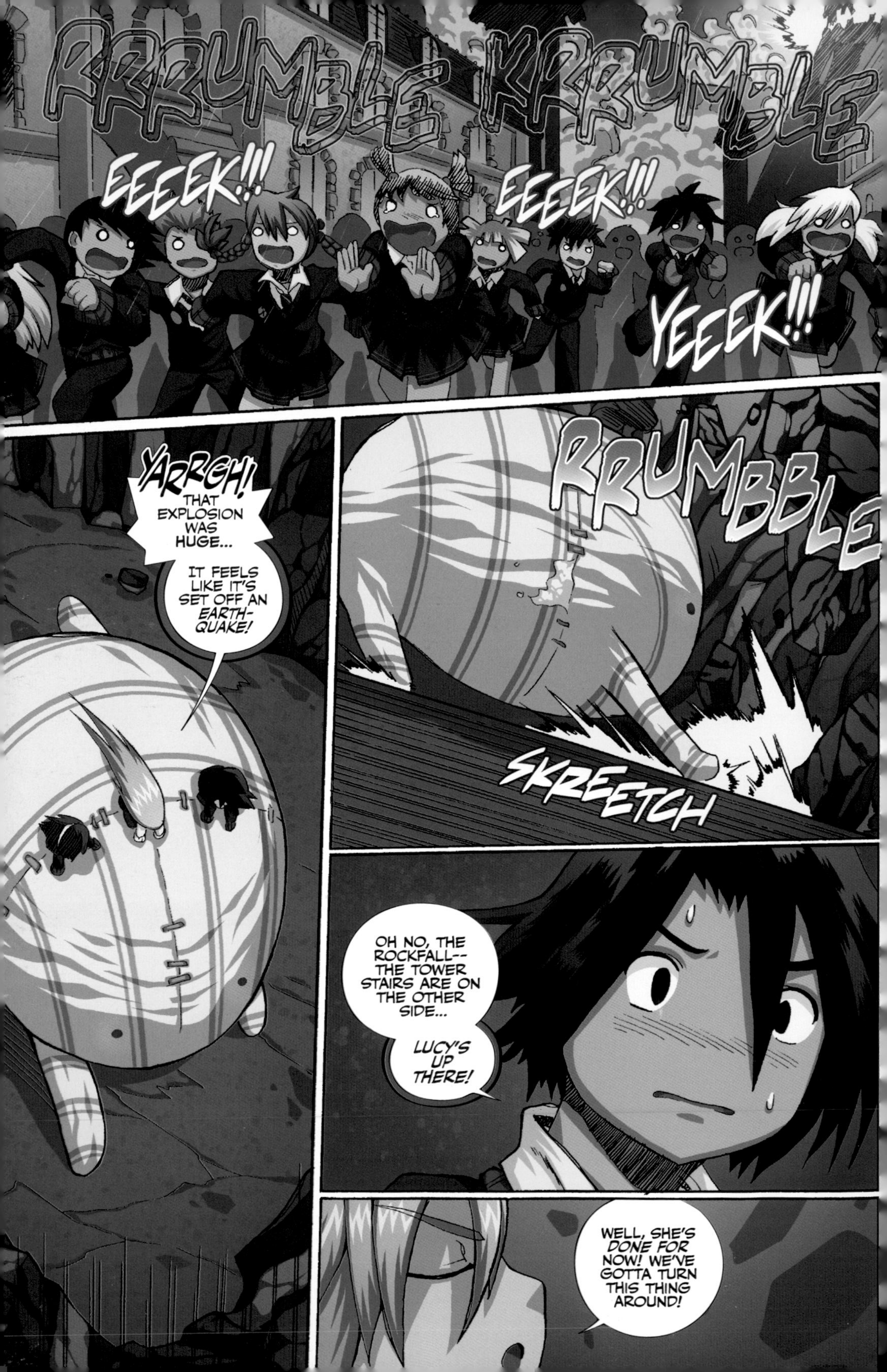
RRRUMBLE KRRRUMBLE
EEEEK!!!
EEEEK!!!
YEEEK!!!
YARRGH! THAT EXPLOSION WAS HUGE...
IT FEELS LIKE IT'S SET OFF AN EARTH-QUAKE!
RRUMBBLE
SKREETCH
OH NO, THE ROCKFALL-- THE TOWER STAIRS ARE ON THE OTHER SIDE...
LUCY'S UP THERE!
WELL, SHE'S DONE FOR NOW! WE'VE GOTTA TURN THIS THING AROUND!

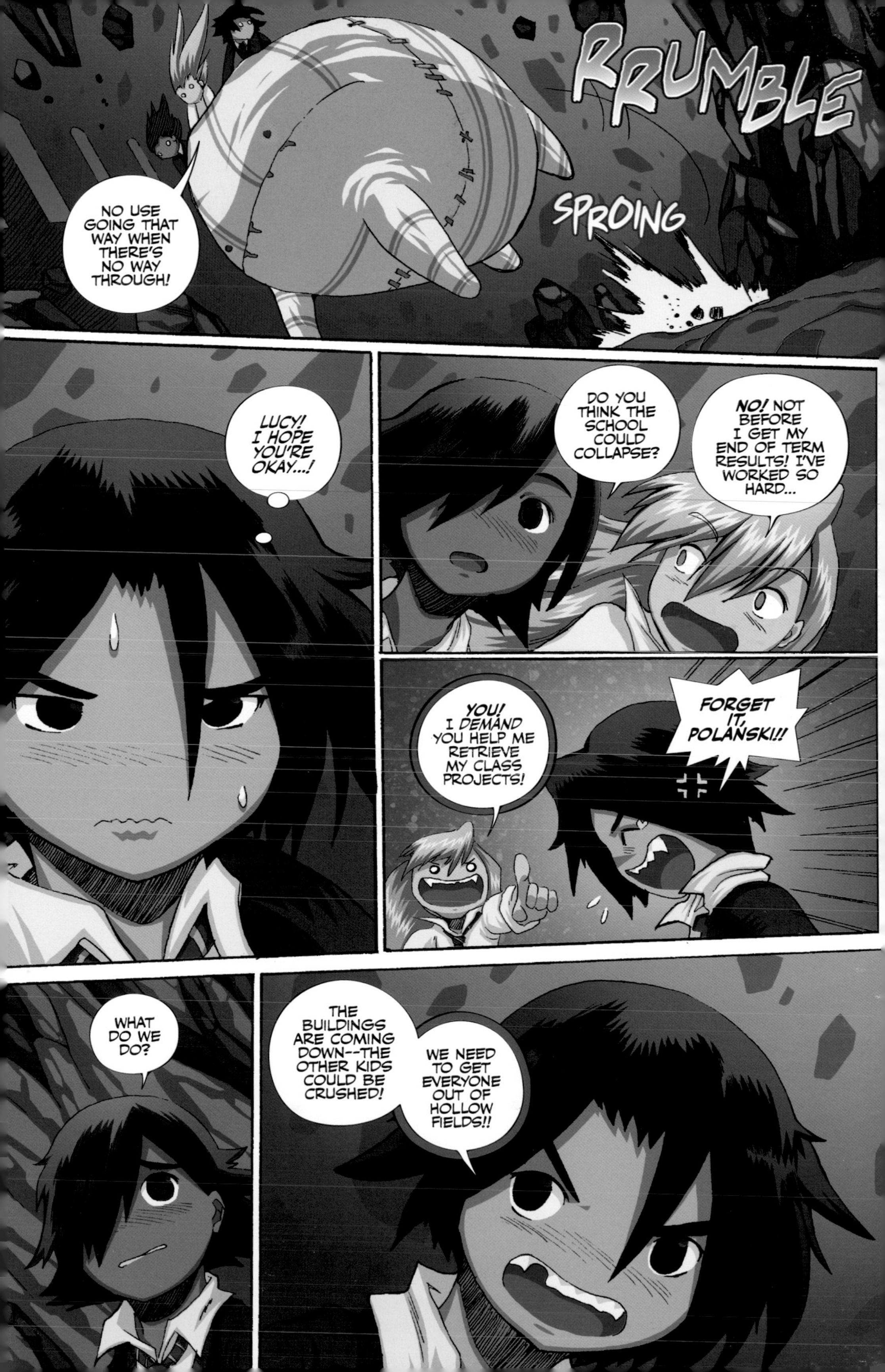
RRUMBLE
NO USE GOING THAT WAY WHEN THERE'S NO WAY THROUGH!
SPROING
LUCY! I HOPE YOU'RE OKAY...!
DO YOU THINK THE SCHOOL COULD COLLAPSE?
NO! NOT BEFORE I GET MY END OF TERM RESULTS! I'VE WORKED SO HARD...
YOU! I DEMAND YOU HELP ME RETRIEVE MY CLASS PROJECTS!
FORGET IT, POLANSKI!!
WHAT DO WE DO?
THE BUILDINGS ARE COMING DOWN--THE OTHER KIDS COULD BE CRUSHED!
WE NEED TO GET EVERYONE OUT OF HOLLOW FIELDS!!

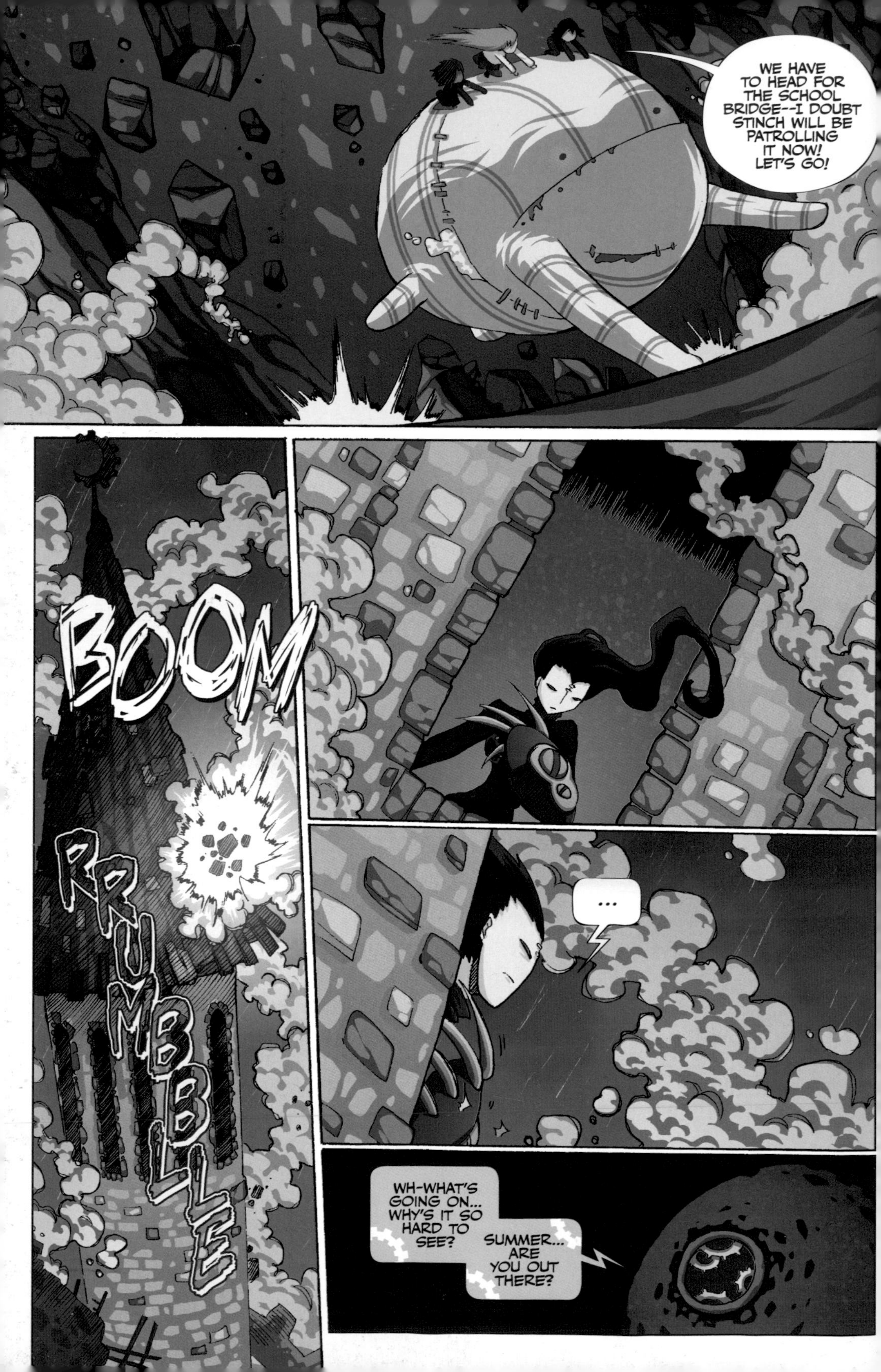
WE HAVE TO HEAD FOR THE SCHOOL BRIDGE--I DOUBT STINCH WILL BE PATROLLING IT NOW! LET'S GO!
BOOM
RRUMBBLE
...
WH-WHAT'S GOING ON... WHY'S IT SO HARD TO SEE?
SUMMER... ARE YOU OUT THERE?

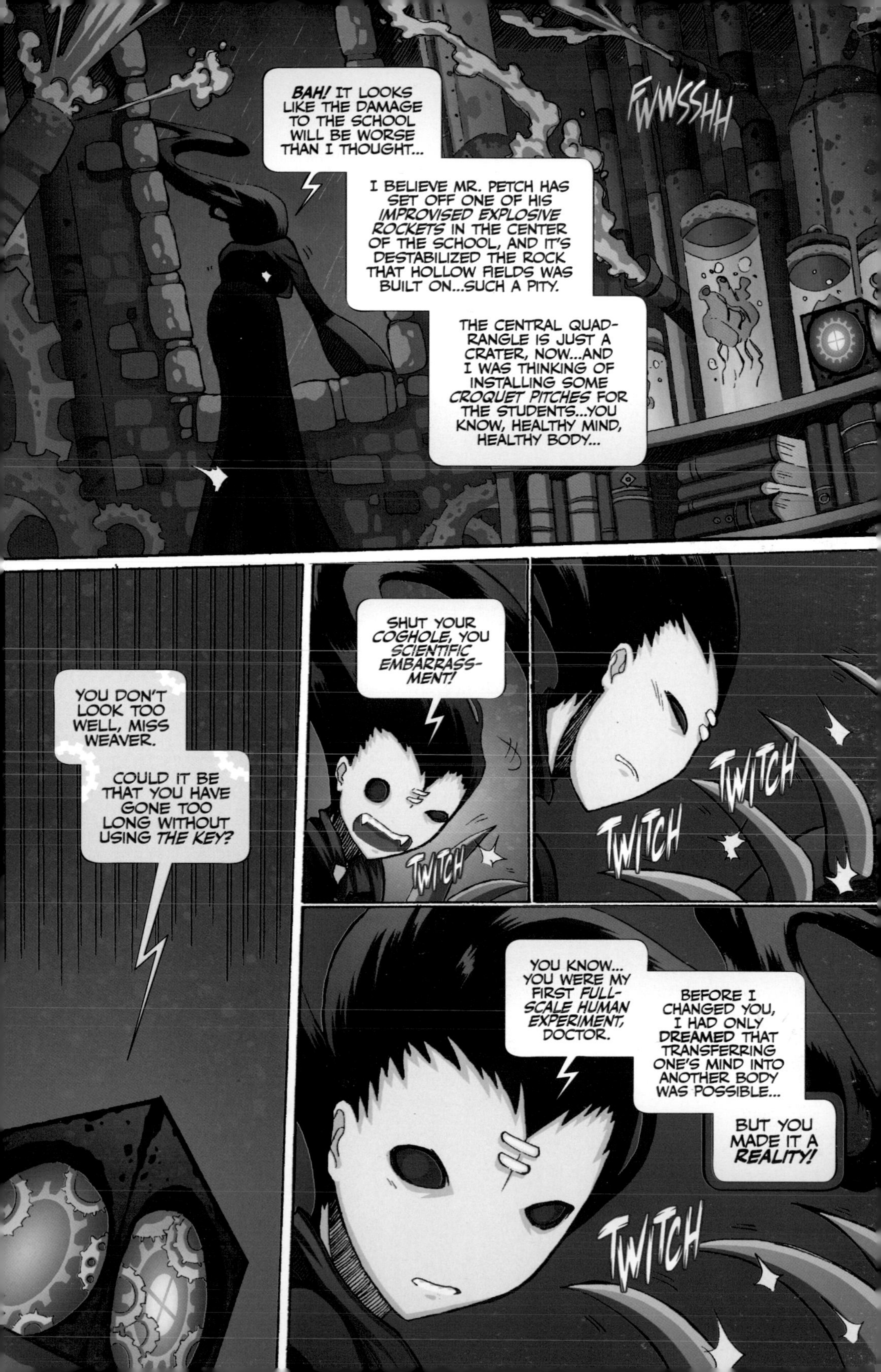
BAH! IT LOOKS LIKE THE DAMAGE TO THE SCHOOL WILL BE WORSE THAN I THOUGHT...
FWWSSHH
I BELIEVE MR. PETCH HAS SET OFF ONE OF HIS IMPROVISED EXPLOSIVE ROCKETS IN THE CENTER OF THE SCHOOL, AND IT'S DESTABILIZED THE ROCK THAT HOLLOW FIELDS WAS BUILT ON...SUCH A PITY.
THE CENTRAL QUAD-RANGLE IS JUST A CRATER, NOW...AND I WAS THINKING OF INSTALLING SOME CROQUET PITCHES FOR THE STUDENTS...YOU KNOW, HEALTHY MIND, HEALTHY BODY...
YOU DON'T LOOK TOO WELL, MISS WEAVER.
COULD IT BE THAT YOU HAVE GONE TOO LONG WITHOUT USING THE KEY?
SHUT YOUR COGHOLE, YOU SCIENTIFIC EMBARRASS-MENT!
TWITCH
TWITCH
TWITCH
YOU KNOW... YOU WERE MY FIRST FULL-SCALE HUMAN EXPERIMENT, DOCTOR.
BEFORE I CHANGED YOU, I HAD ONLY DREAMED THAT TRANSFERRING ONE'S MIND INTO ANOTHER BODY WAS POSSIBLE...
BUT YOU MADE IT A REALITY!
TWITCH

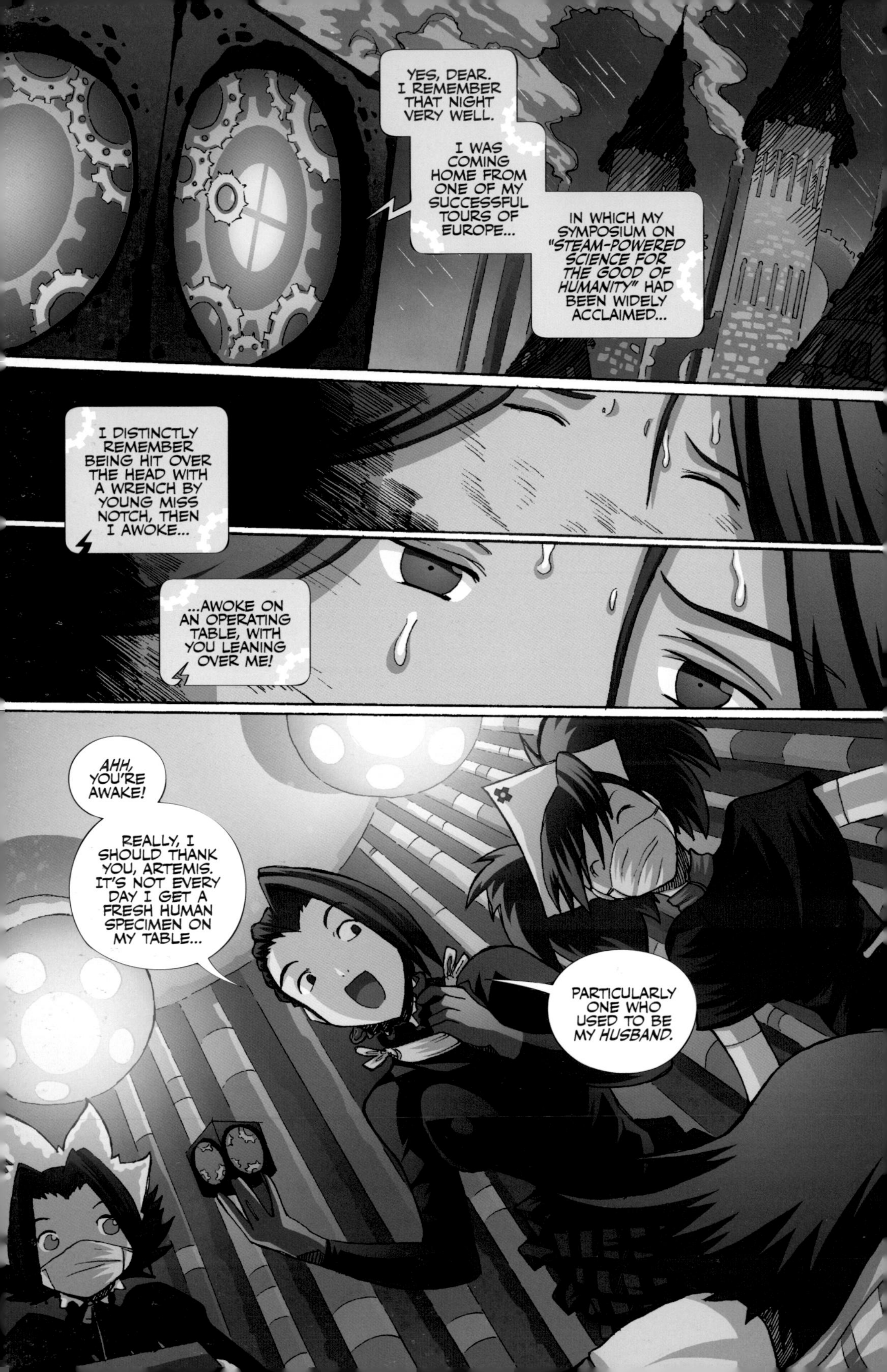
YES, DEAR. I REMEMBER THAT NIGHT VERY WELL.
I WAS COMING HOME FROM ONE OF MY SUCCESSFUL TOURS OF EUROPE...
IN WHICH MY SYMPOSIUM ON "STEAM-POWERED SCIENCE FOR THE GOOD OF HUMANITY" HAD BEEN WIDELY ACCLAIMED...
I DISTINCTLY REMEMBER BEING HIT OVER THE HEAD WITH A WRENCH BY YOUNG MISS NOTCH, THEN I AWOKE...
...AWOKE ON AN OPERATING TABLE, WITH YOU LEANING OVER ME!
AHH, YOU'RE AWAKE!
REALLY, I SHOULD THANK YOU, ARTEMIS. IT'S NOT EVERY DAY I GET A FRESH HUMAN SPECIMEN ON MY TABLE...
PARTICULARLY ONE WHO USED TO BE MY HUSBAND.

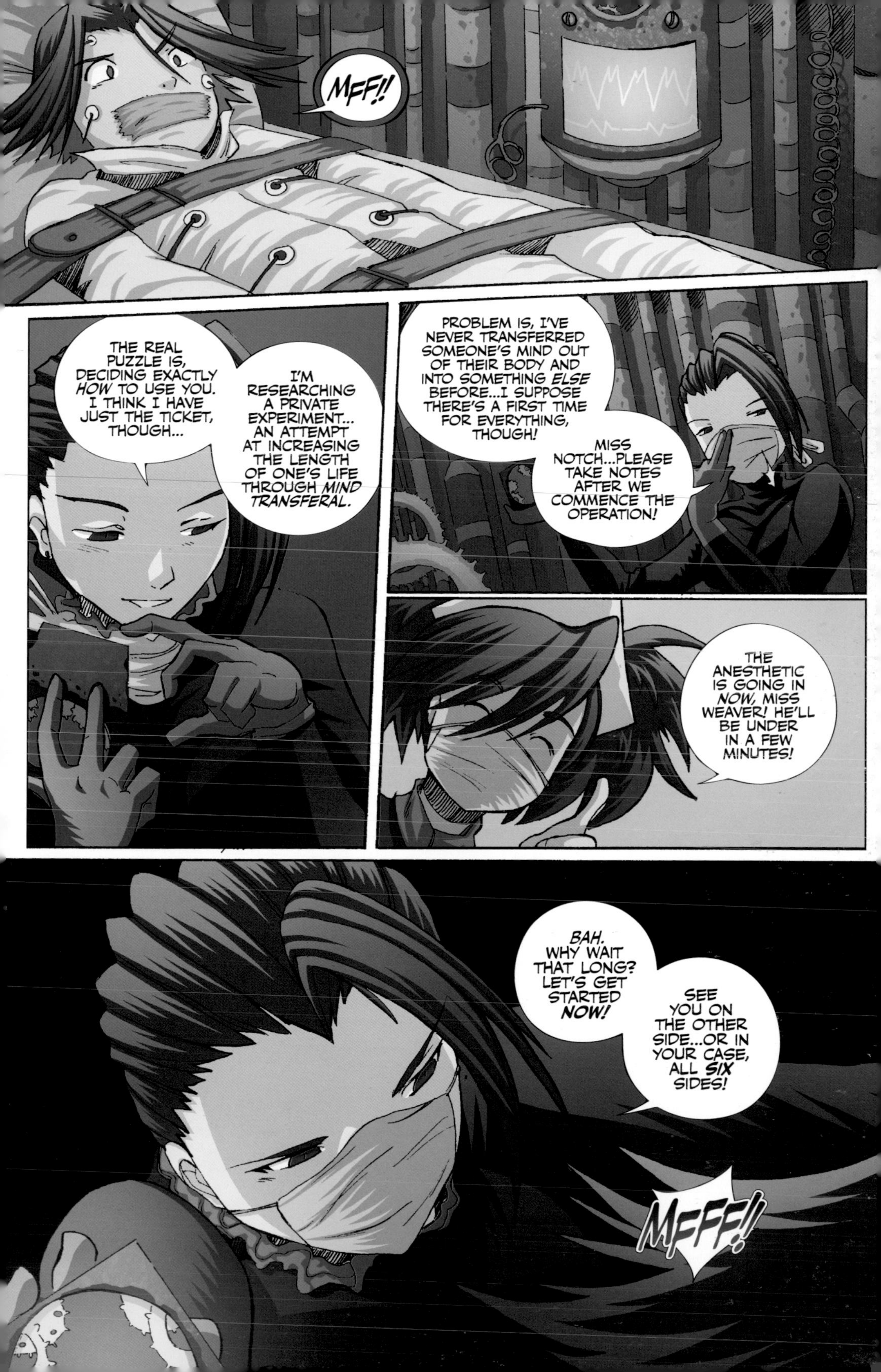
MFF!!
THE REAL PUZZLE IS, DECIDING EXACTLY *HOW* TO USE YOU. I THINK I HAVE JUST THE TICKET, THOUGH...
I'M RESEARCHING A PRIVATE EXPERIMENT... AN ATTEMPT AT INCREASING THE LENGTH OF ONE'S LIFE THROUGH *MIND TRANSFERAL.*
PROBLEM IS, I'VE NEVER TRANSFERRED SOMEONE'S MIND OUT OF THEIR BODY AND INTO SOMETHING *ELSE* BEFORE...I SUPPOSE THERE'S A FIRST TIME FOR EVERYTHING, THOUGH!
MISS NOTCH...PLEASE TAKE NOTES AFTER WE COMMENCE THE OPERATION!
THE ANESTHETIC IS GOING IN *NOW,* MISS WEAVER! HE'LL BE UNDER IN A FEW MINUTES!
BAH. WHY WAIT THAT LONG? LET'S GET STARTED ***NOW!***
SEE YOU ON THE OTHER SIDE...OR IN YOUR CASE, ALL ***SIX*** SIDES!
MFFF!!

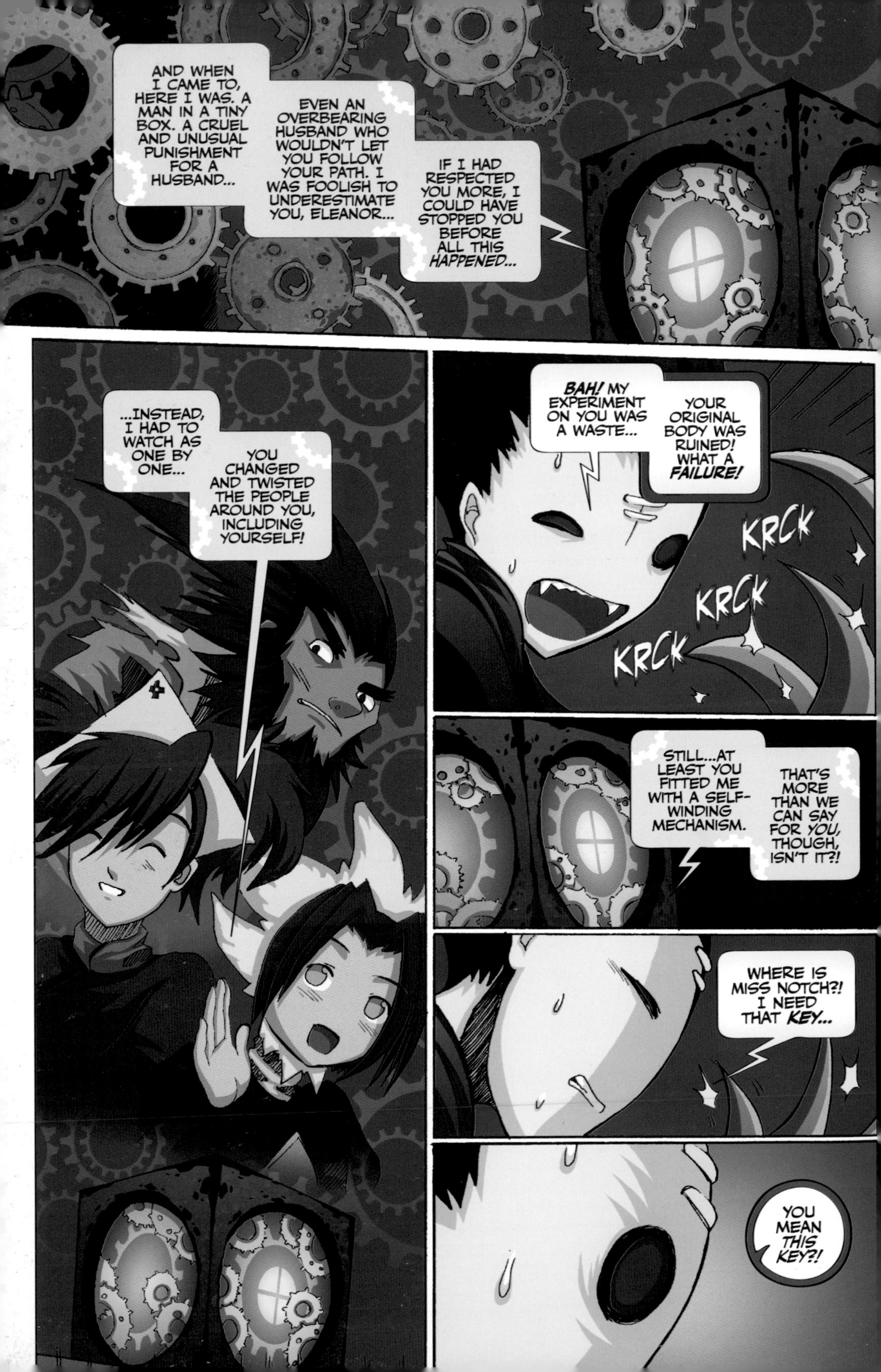

AND WHEN I CAME TO, HERE I WAS. A MAN IN A TINY BOX. A CRUEL AND UNUSUAL PUNISHMENT FOR A HUSBAND...
EVEN AN OVERBEARING HUSBAND WHO WOULDN'T LET YOU FOLLOW YOUR PATH. I WAS FOOLISH TO UNDERESTIMATE YOU, ELEANOR...
IF I HAD RESPECTED YOU MORE, I COULD HAVE STOPPED YOU BEFORE ALL THIS *HAPPENED...*
...INSTEAD, I HAD TO WATCH AS ONE BY ONE...
YOU CHANGED AND TWISTED THE PEOPLE AROUND YOU, INCLUDING YOURSELF!
BAH! MY EXPERIMENT ON YOU WAS A WASTE...
YOUR ORIGINAL BODY WAS RUINED! WHAT A *FAILURE!*
KRCK
KRCK
KRCK
STILL...AT LEAST YOU FITTED ME WITH A SELF-WINDING MECHANISM.
THAT'S MORE THAN WE CAN SAY FOR *YOU,* THOUGH, ISN'T IT?!
WHERE IS MISS NOTCH?! I NEED THAT *KEY...*
YOU MEAN *THIS KEY?!*

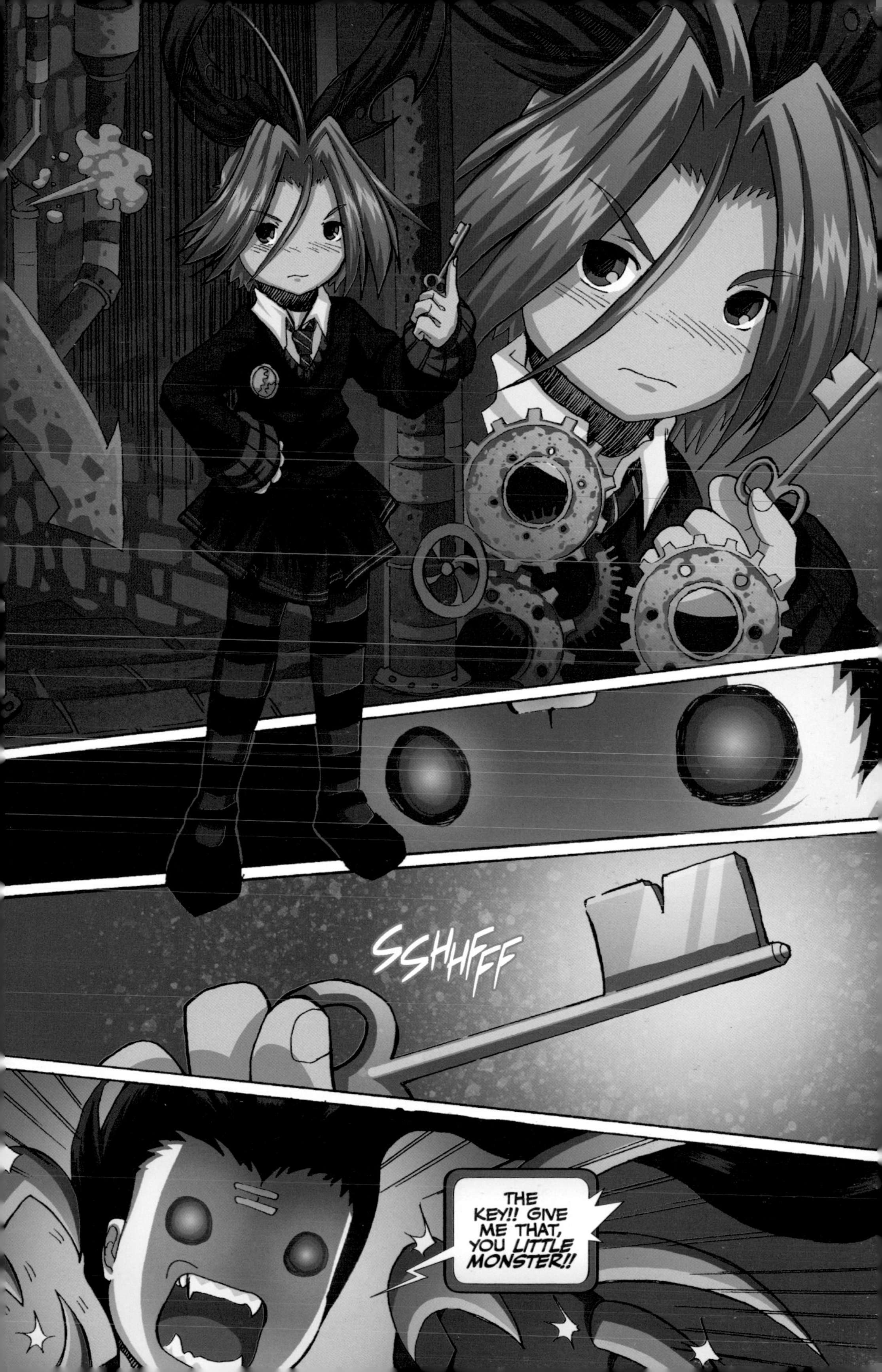
SSHHFFF
THE KEY!! GIVE ME THAT, YOU *LITTLE* MONSTER!!

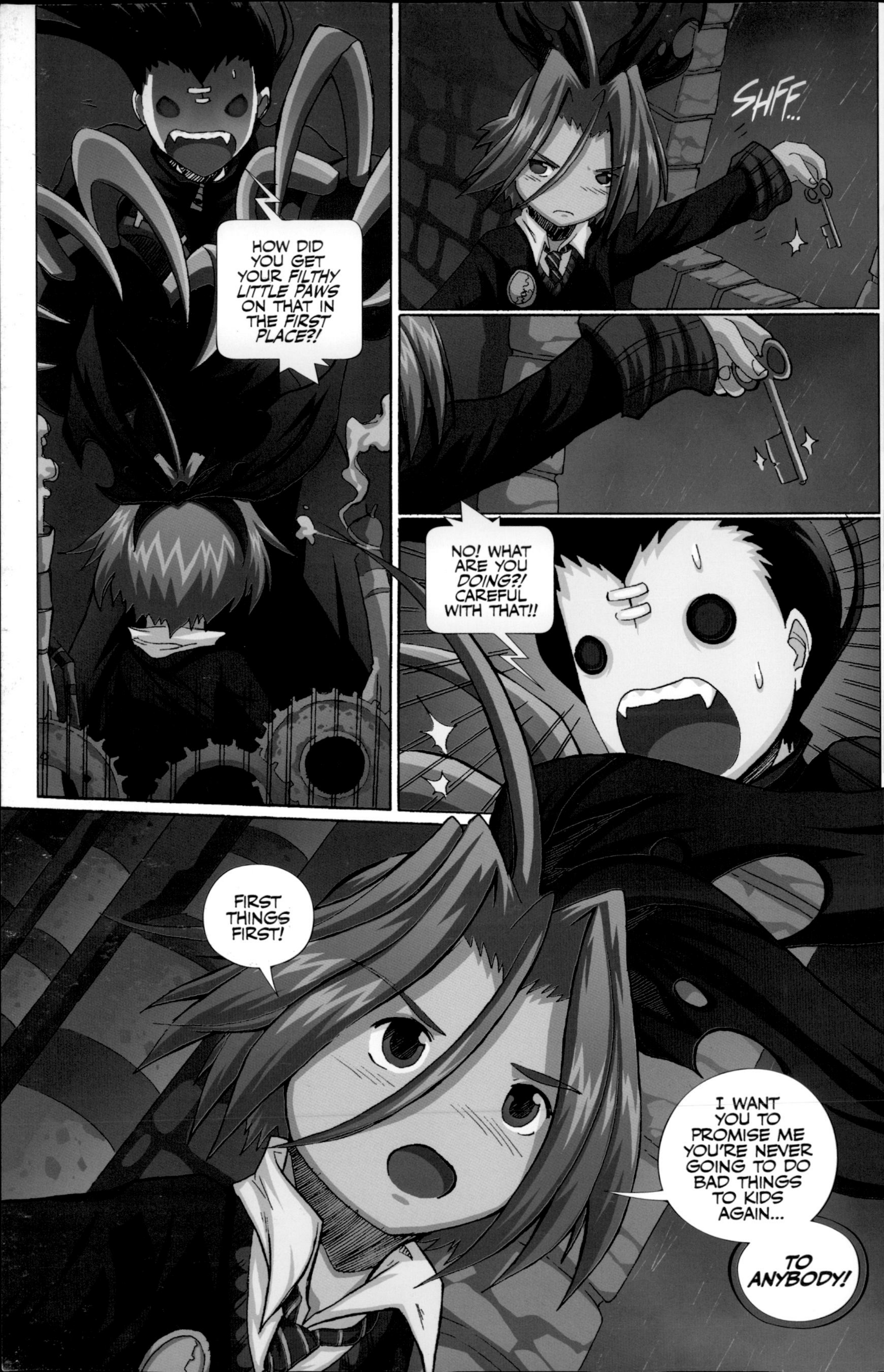
HOW DID YOU GET YOUR FILTHY LITTLE PAWS ON THAT IN THE FIRST PLACE?!
SHFF...
NO! WHAT ARE YOU DOING?! CAREFUL WITH THAT!!
FIRST THINGS FIRST!
I WANT YOU TO PROMISE ME YOU'RE NEVER GOING TO DO BAD THINGS TO KIDS AGAIN...
TO ANYBODY!

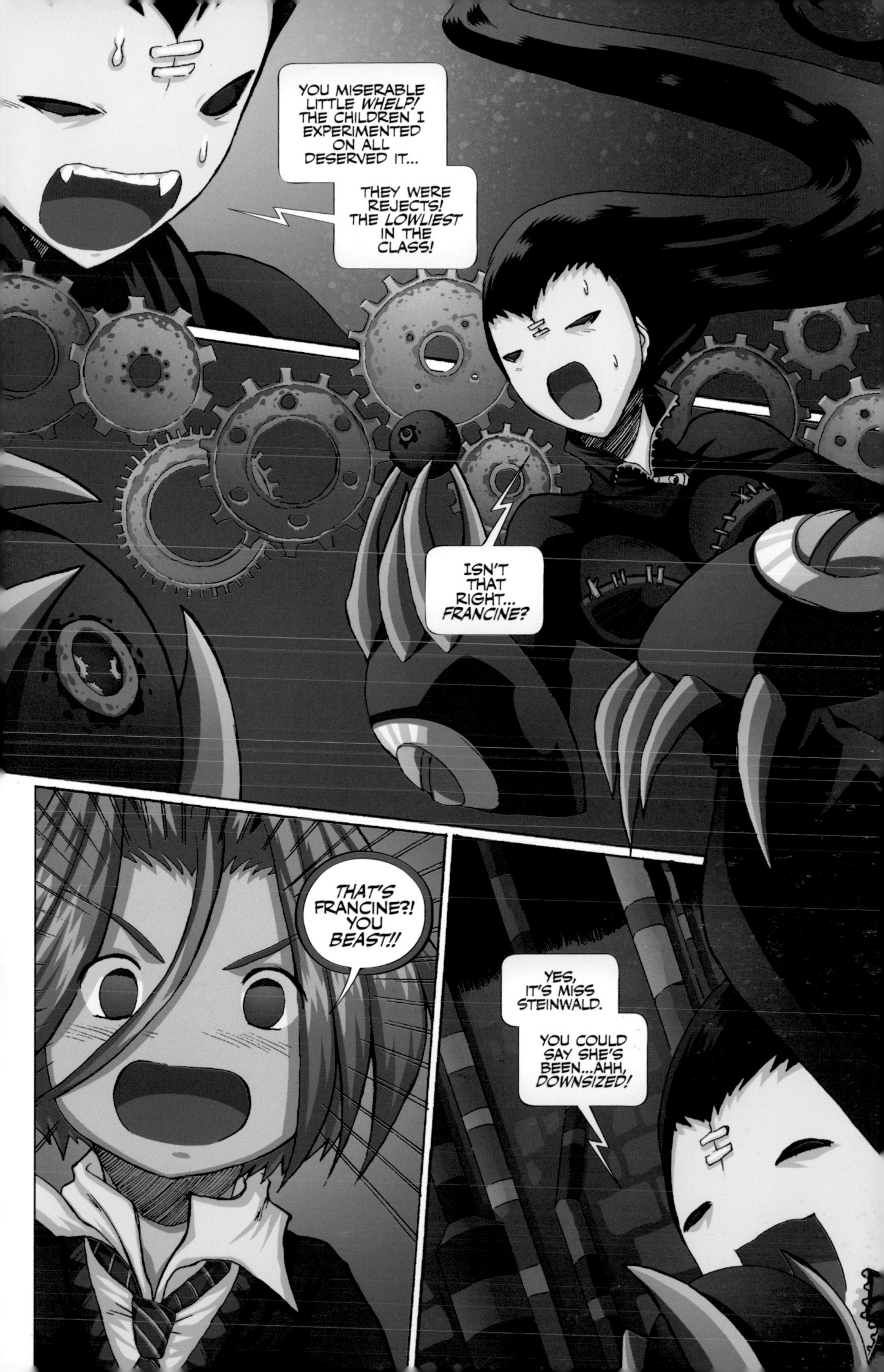
YOU MISERABLE LITTLE *WHELP!* THE CHILDREN I EXPERIMENTED ON ALL DESERVED IT...
THEY WERE REJECTS! THE *LOWLIEST* IN THE CLASS!
ISN'T THAT RIGHT... *FRANCINE?*
THAT'S FRANCINE?! YOU *BEAST!!*
YES, IT'S MISS STEINWALD.
YOU COULD SAY SHE'S BEEN...AHH, *DOWNSIZED!*

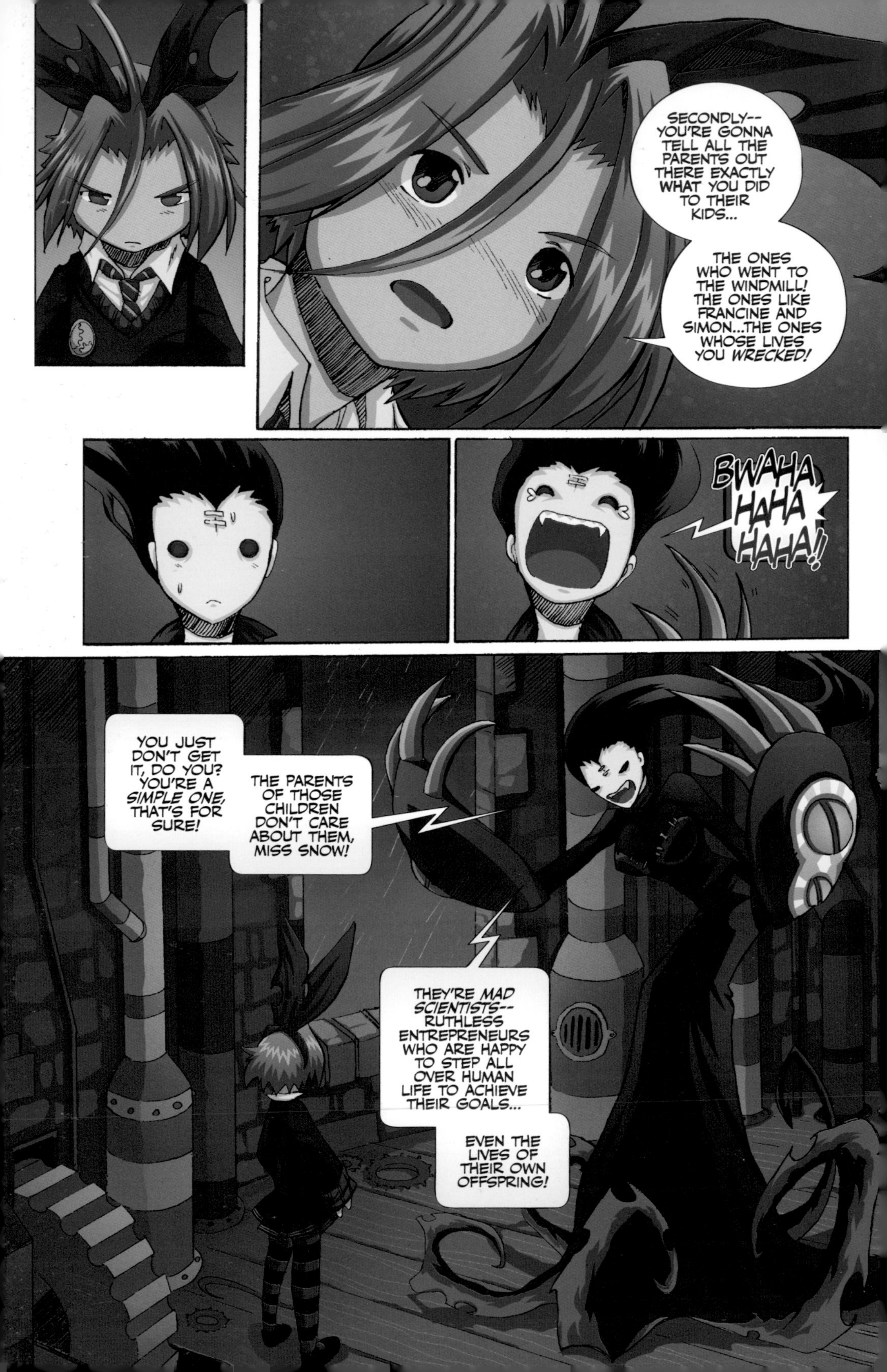
SECONDLY--YOU'RE GONNA TELL ALL THE PARENTS OUT THERE EXACTLY WHAT YOU DID TO THEIR KIDS...
THE ONES WHO WENT TO THE WINDMILL! THE ONES LIKE FRANCINE AND SIMON...THE ONES WHOSE LIVES YOU *WRECKED!*
BWAHA HAHA HAHA!!
YOU JUST DON'T GET IT, DO YOU? YOU'RE A *SIMPLE ONE,* THAT'S FOR SURE!
THE PARENTS OF THOSE CHILDREN DON'T CARE ABOUT THEM, MISS SNOW!
THEY'RE *MAD SCIENTISTS*--RUTHLESS ENTREPRENEURS WHO ARE HAPPY TO STEP ALL OVER HUMAN LIFE TO ACHIEVE THEIR GOALS...
EVEN THE LIVES OF THEIR OWN OFFSPRING!

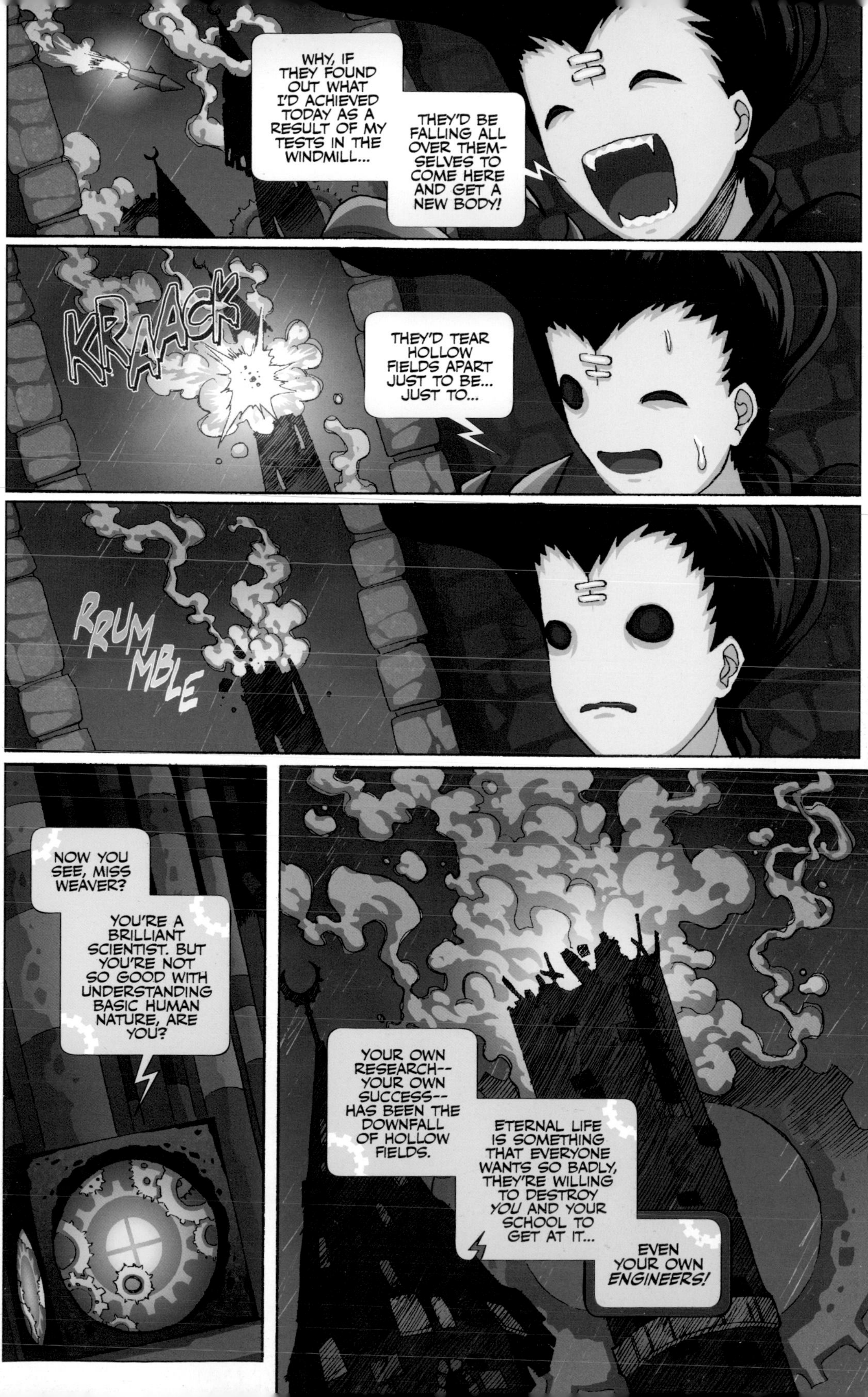
WHY, IF THEY FOUND OUT WHAT I'D ACHIEVED TODAY AS A RESULT OF MY TESTS IN THE WINDMILL...
THEY'D BE FALLING ALL OVER THEM-SELVES TO COME HERE AND GET A NEW BODY!
KRAACK
THEY'D TEAR HOLLOW FIELDS APART JUST TO BE... JUST TO...
RRUMMBLE
NOW YOU SEE, MISS WEAVER?
YOU'RE A BRILLIANT SCIENTIST. BUT YOU'RE NOT SO GOOD WITH UNDERSTANDING BASIC HUMAN NATURE, ARE YOU?
YOUR OWN RESEARCH-- YOUR OWN SUCCESS-- HAS BEEN THE DOWNFALL OF HOLLOW FIELDS.
ETERNAL LIFE IS SOMETHING THAT EVERYONE WANTS SO BADLY, THEY'RE WILLING TO DESTROY *YOU* AND YOUR SCHOOL TO GET AT IT...
EVEN YOUR OWN *ENGINEERS!*

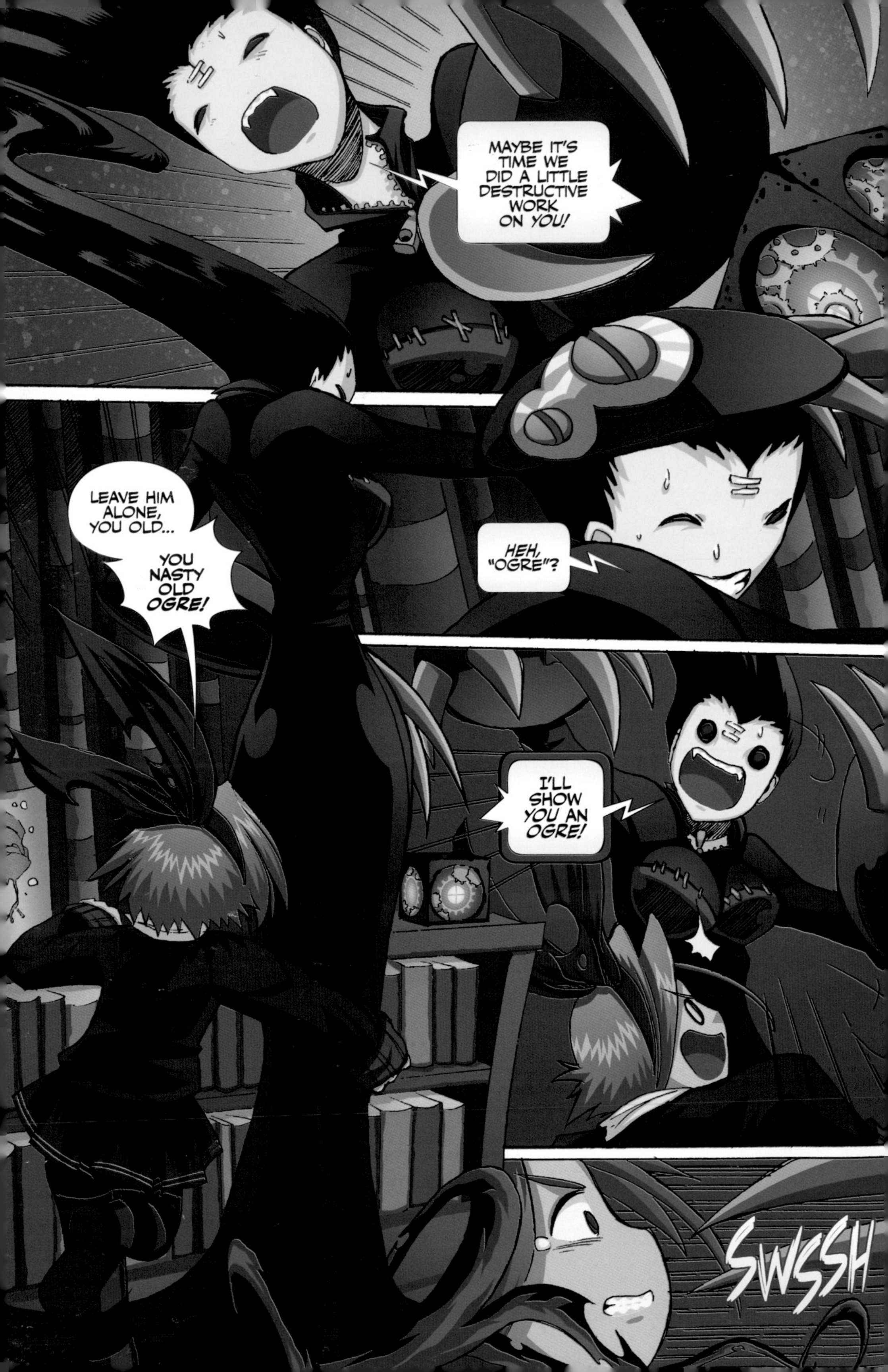

MAYBE IT'S TIME WE DID A LITTLE DESTRUCTIVE WORK ON YOU!
LEAVE HIM ALONE, YOU OLD...
YOU NASTY OLD OGRE!
HEH, "OGRE"?
I'LL SHOW YOU AN OGRE!
SWSSH

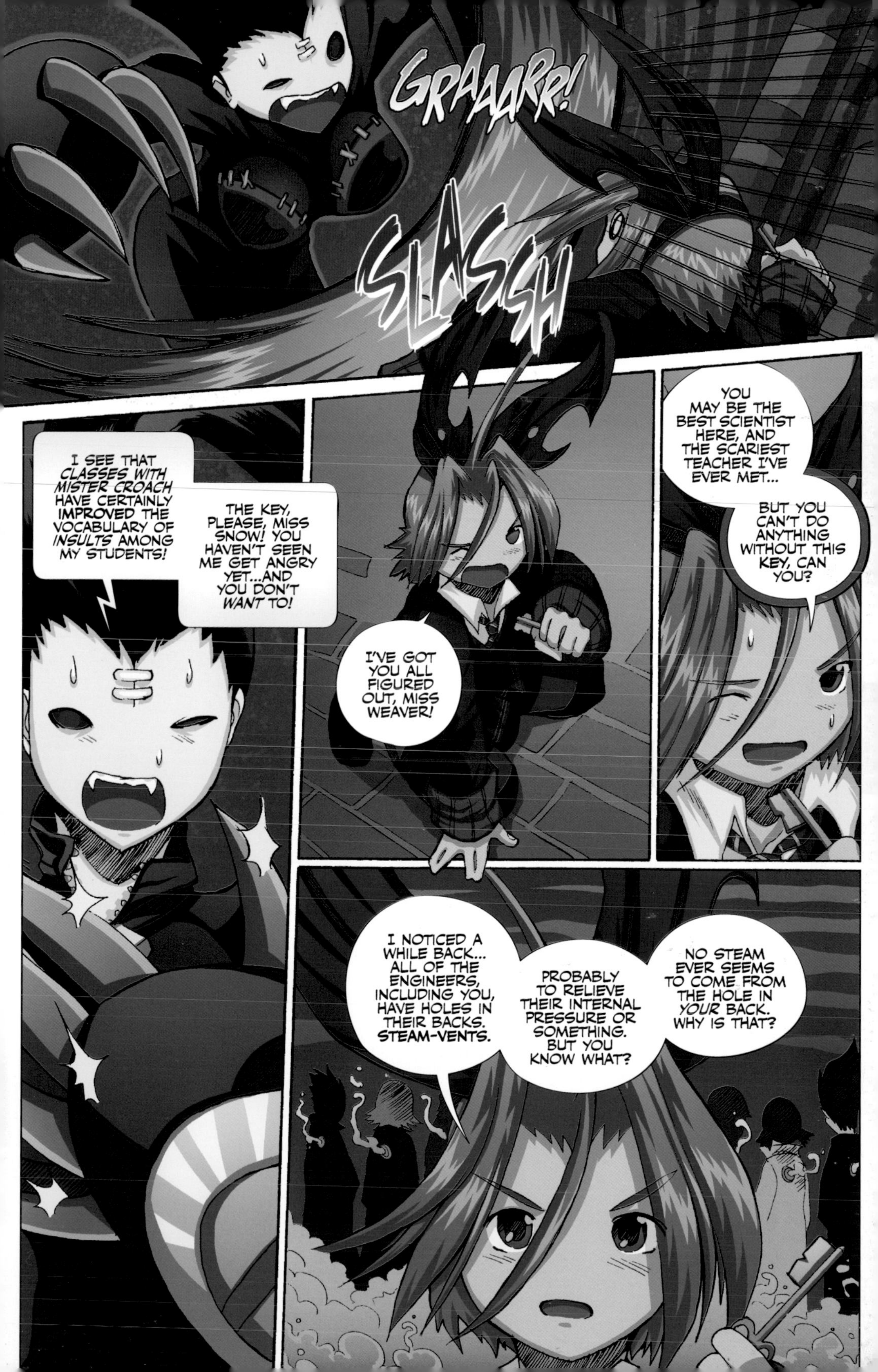
GRAAARR!
SLASSH
I SEE THAT *CLASSES WITH MISTER CROACH* HAVE CERTAINLY IMPROVED THE VOCABULARY OF *INSULTS* AMONG MY STUDENTS!
THE KEY, PLEASE, MISS SNOW! YOU HAVEN'T SEEN ME GET ANGRY YET...AND YOU DON'T *WANT* TO!
I'VE GOT YOU ALL FIGURED OUT, MISS WEAVER!
YOU MAY BE THE BEST SCIENTIST HERE, AND THE SCARIEST TEACHER I'VE EVER MET...
BUT YOU CAN'T DO ANYTHING WITHOUT THIS KEY, CAN YOU?
I NOTICED A WHILE BACK... ALL OF THE ENGINEERS, INCLUDING YOU, HAVE HOLES IN THEIR BACKS. STEAM-VENTS.
PROBABLY TO RELIEVE THEIR INTERNAL PRESSURE OR SOMETHING. BUT YOU KNOW WHAT?
NO STEAM EVER SEEMS TO COME FROM THE HOLE IN *YOUR* BACK. WHY IS THAT?

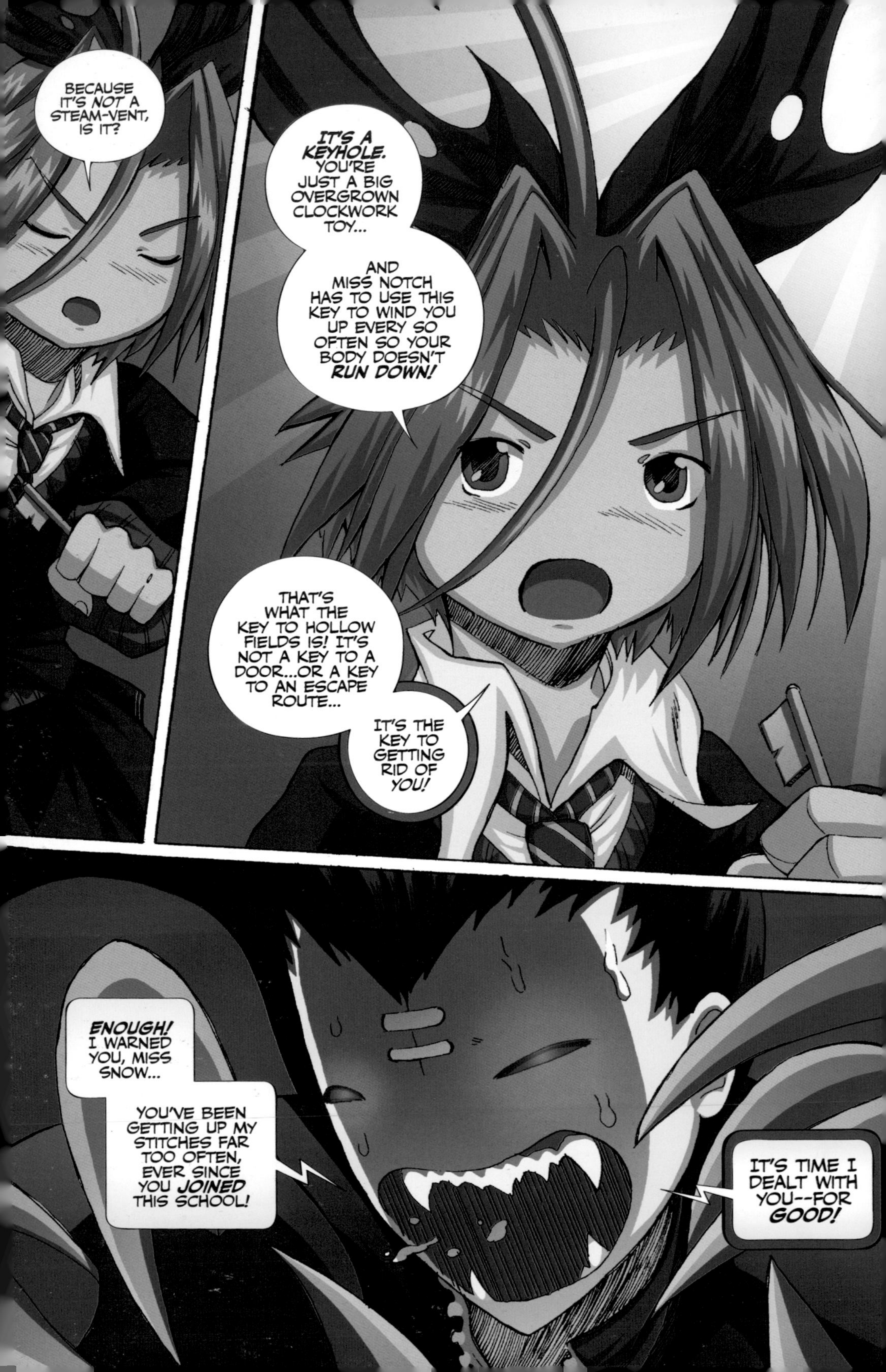
BECAUSE IT'S *NOT* A STEAM-VENT, IS IT?
IT'S A KEYHOLE. YOU'RE JUST A BIG OVERGROWN CLOCKWORK TOY...
AND MISS NOTCH HAS TO USE THIS KEY TO WIND YOU UP EVERY SO OFTEN SO YOUR BODY DOESN'T ***RUN DOWN!***
THAT'S WHAT THE KEY TO HOLLOW FIELDS IS! IT'S NOT A KEY TO A DOOR...OR A KEY TO AN ESCAPE ROUTE...
IT'S THE KEY TO GETTING RID OF *YOU!*
ENOUGH! I WARNED YOU, MISS SNOW...
YOU'VE BEEN GETTING UP MY STITCHES FAR TOO OFTEN, EVER SINCE YOU ***JOINED*** THIS SCHOOL!
IT'S TIME I DEALT WITH YOU--FOR ***GOOD!***

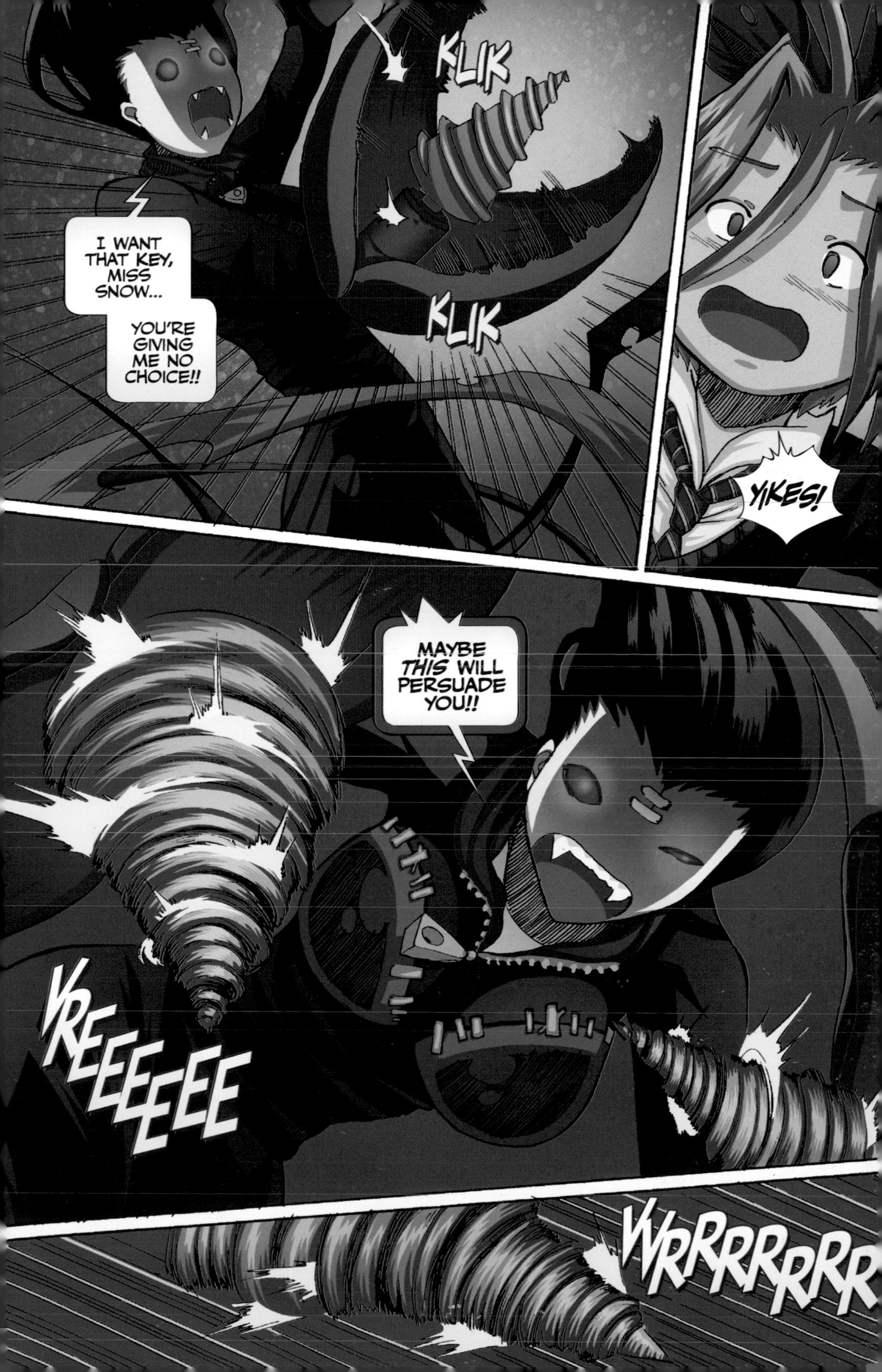
KLIK
I WANT THAT KEY, MISS SNOW...
YOU'RE GIVING ME NO CHOICE!!
KLIK
YIKES!
MAYBE *THIS* WILL PERSUADE YOU!!
VREEEEEEE
VVRRRRRRR

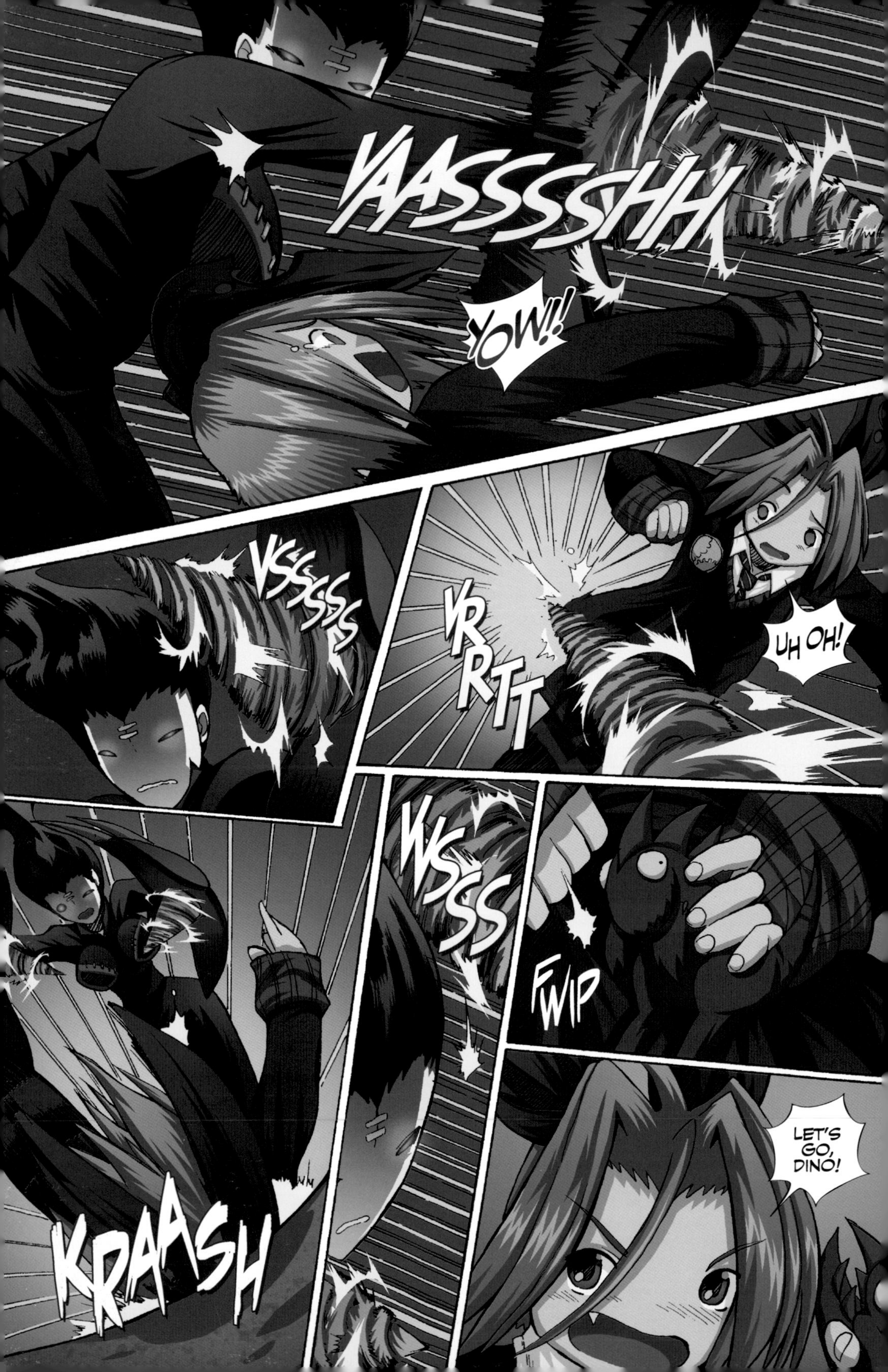
YAASSSHH
YOW!!
VSSSSSS
VRRTTT
UH OH!
KRAASH
WSSSS
FWIP
LET'S GO, DINO!

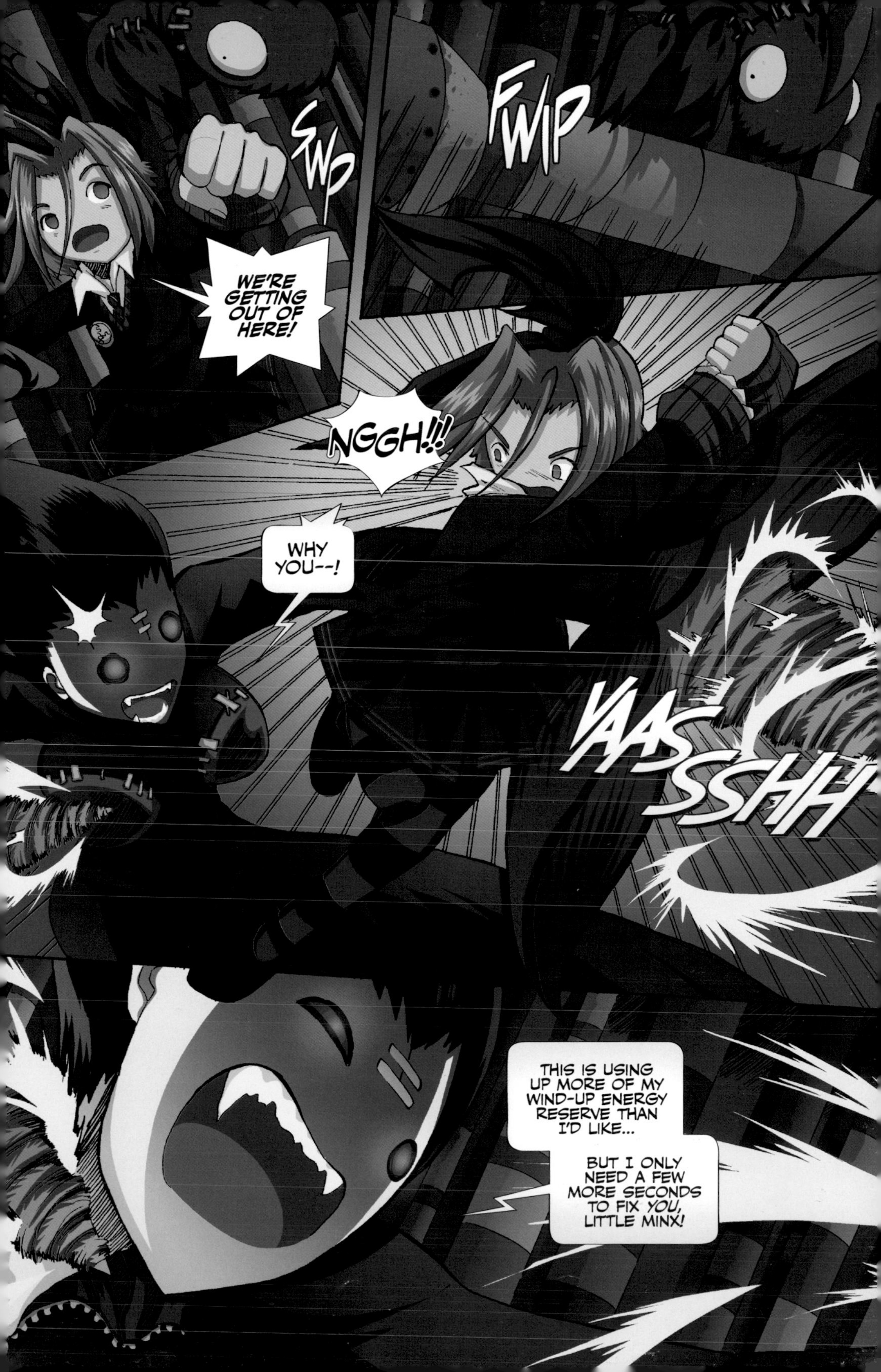
SWP
FWIP
WE'RE GETTING OUT OF HERE!
NGGH!!!
WHY YOU--!
YAAS SSHH
THIS IS USING UP MORE OF MY WIND-UP ENERGY RESERVE THAN I'D LIKE...
BUT I ONLY NEED A FEW MORE SECONDS TO FIX YOU, LITTLE MINX!

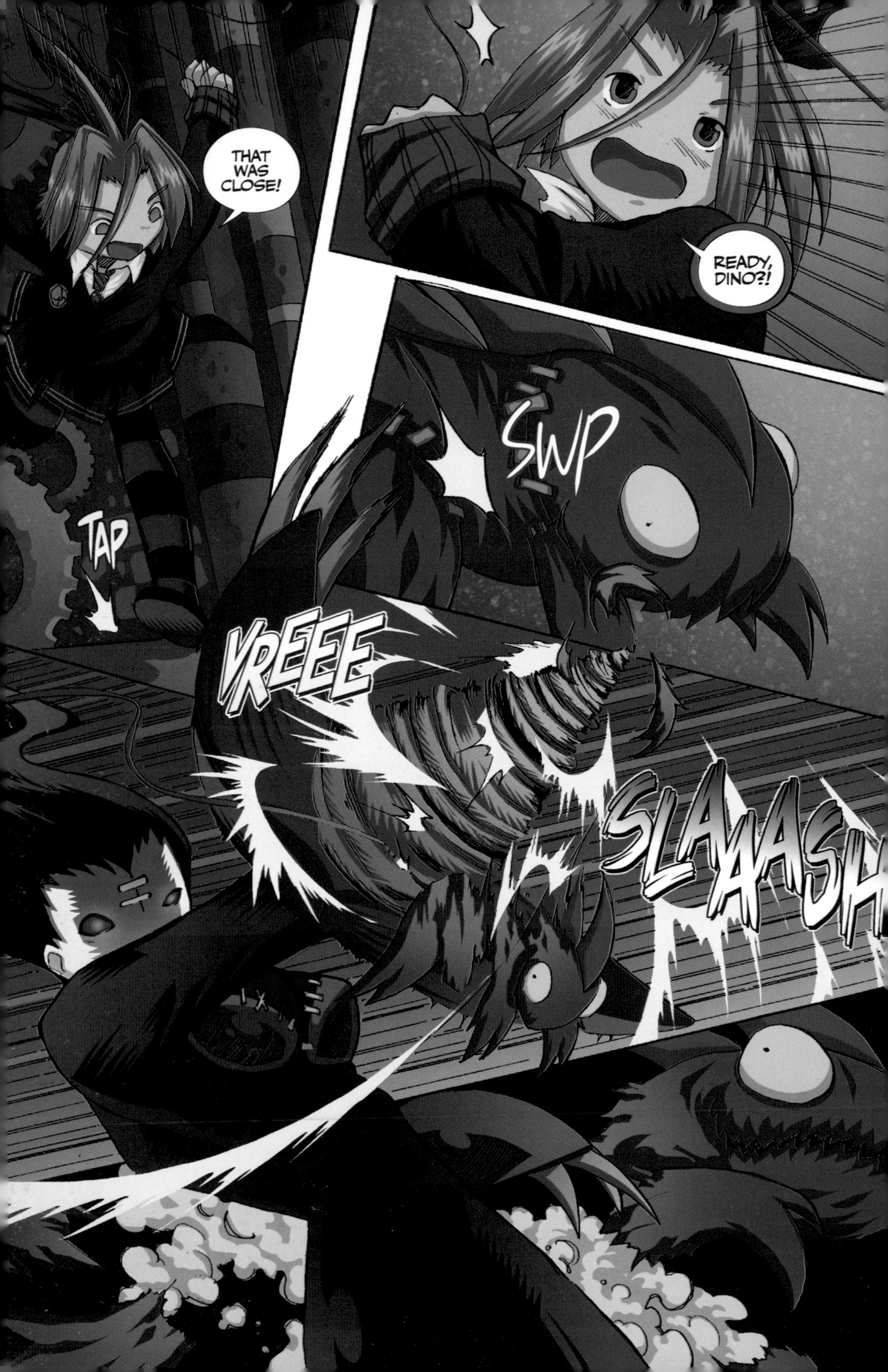
THAT WAS CLOSE!
TAP
READY, DINO?!
SWP
VREEE
SLAAASH

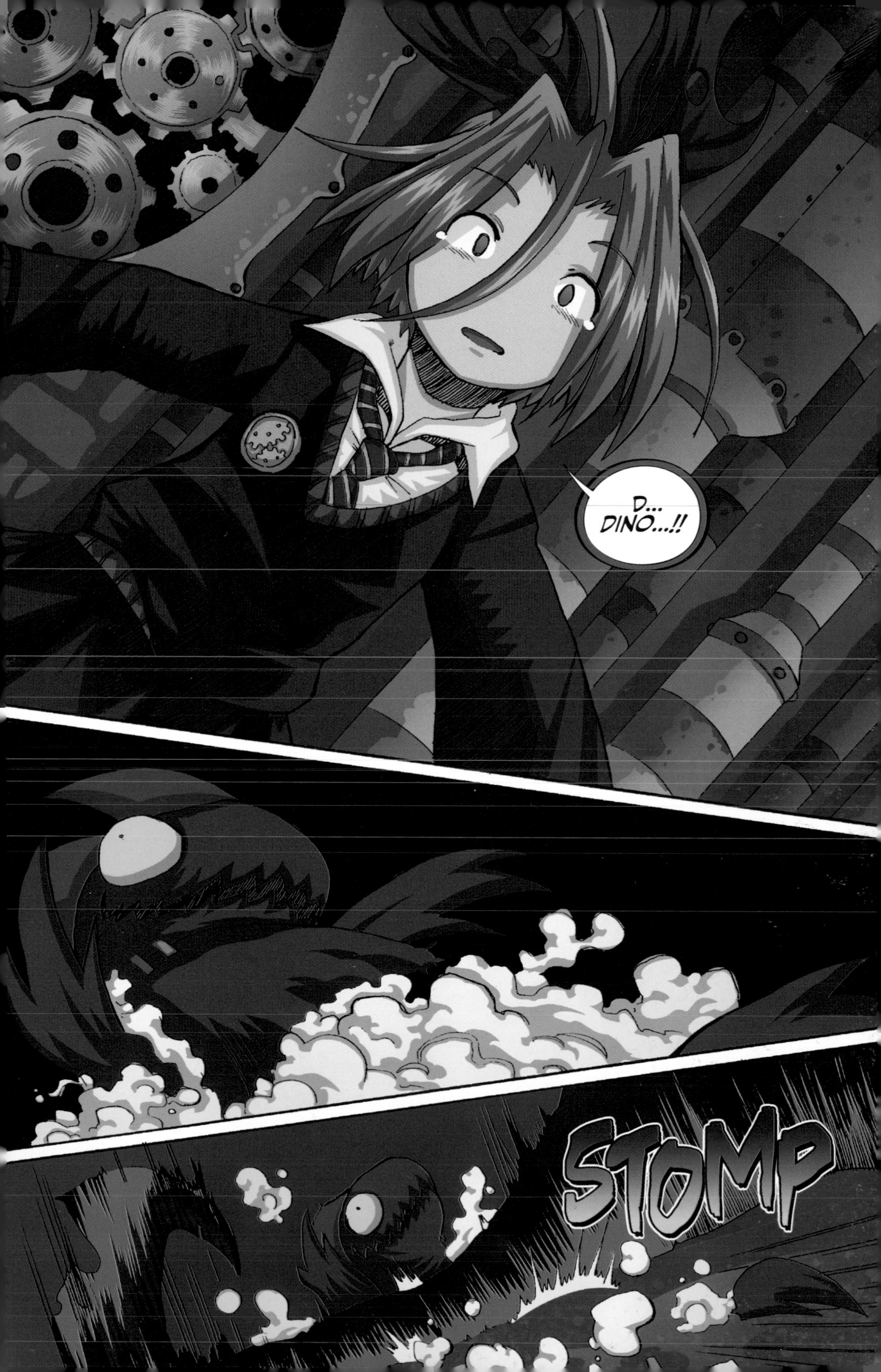
D... DINO...!!
STOMP

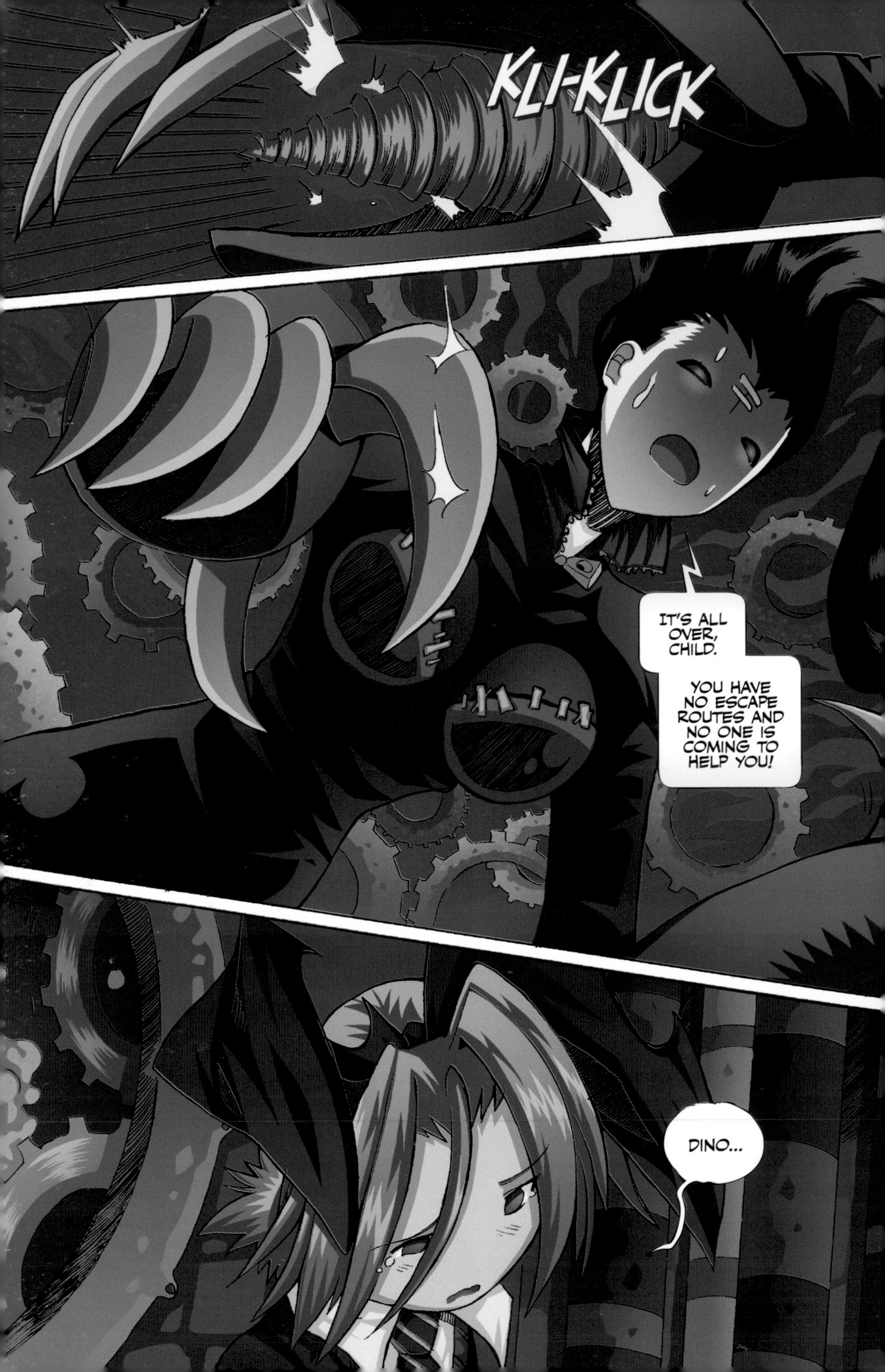
KLI-KLICK
IT'S ALL OVER, CHILD.
YOU HAVE NO ESCAPE ROUTES AND NO ONE IS COMING TO HELP YOU!
DINO...

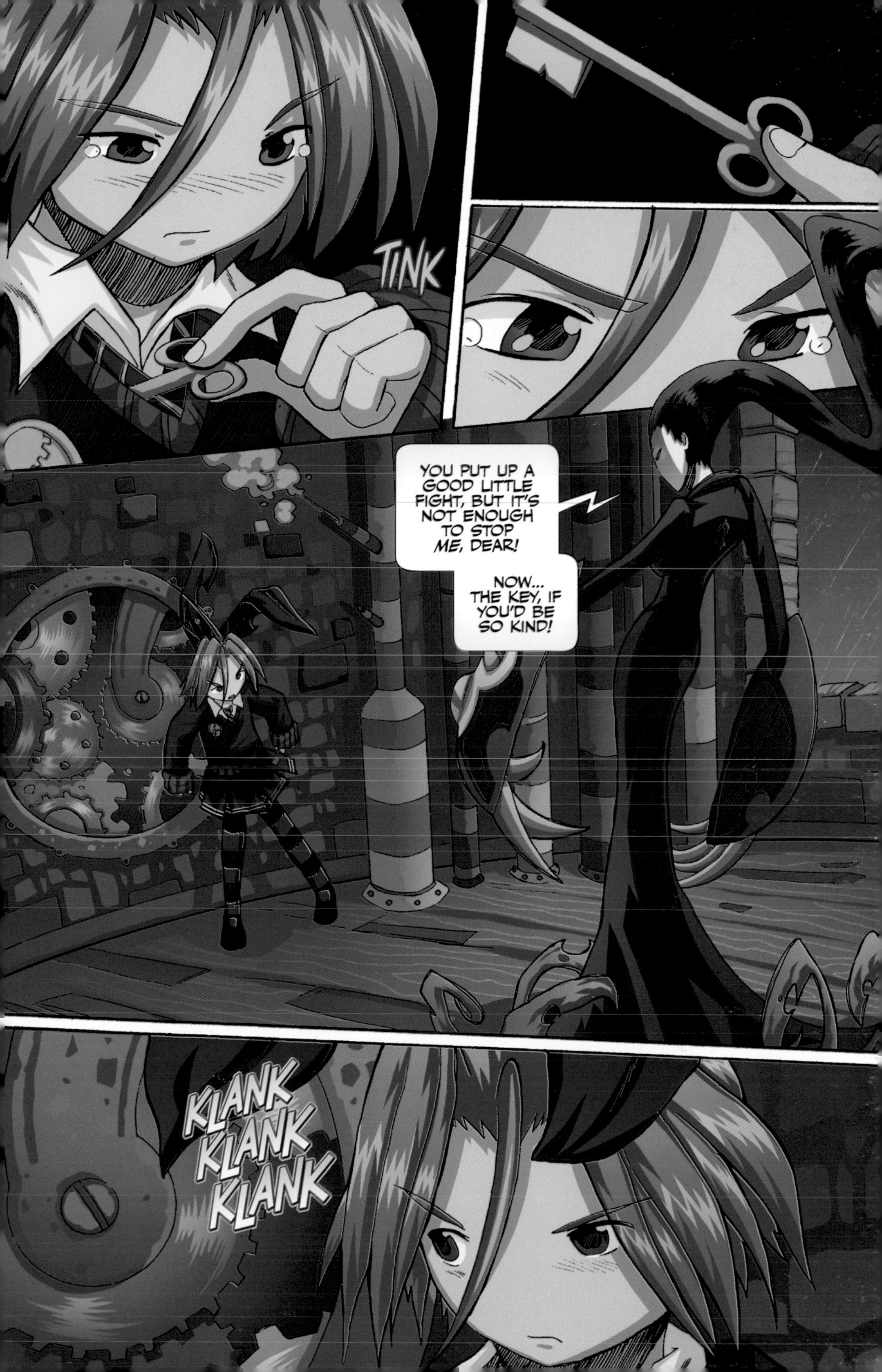
TINK
YOU PUT UP A GOOD LITTLE FIGHT, BUT IT'S NOT ENOUGH TO STOP *ME*, DEAR!
NOW... THE KEY, IF YOU'D BE SO KIND!
KLANK KLANK KLANK

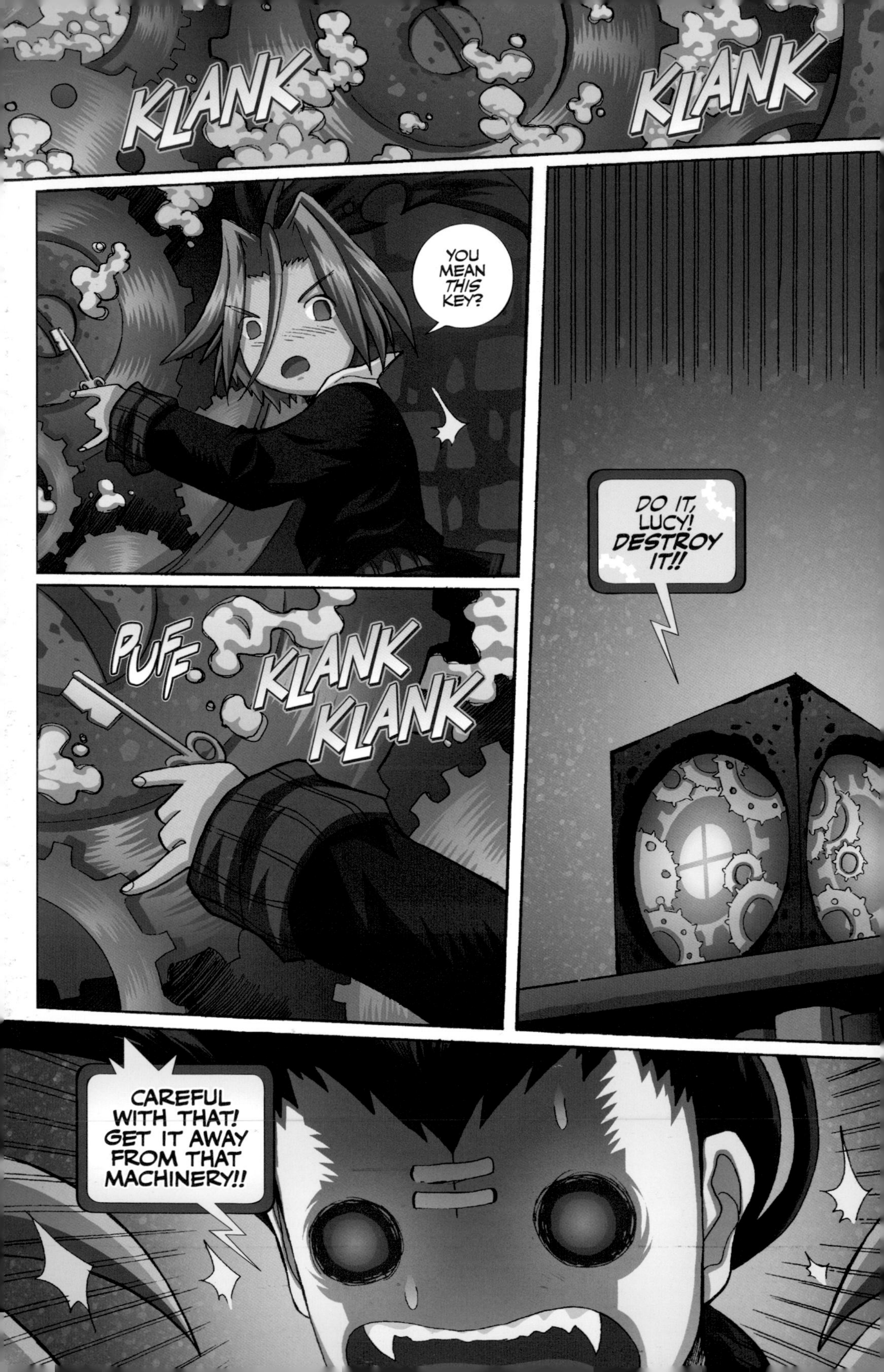
KLANK
KLANK
YOU MEAN THIS KEY?
DO IT, LUCY! DESTROY IT!!
PUFF
KLANK
KLANK
CAREFUL WITH THAT! GET IT AWAY FROM THAT MACHINERY!!

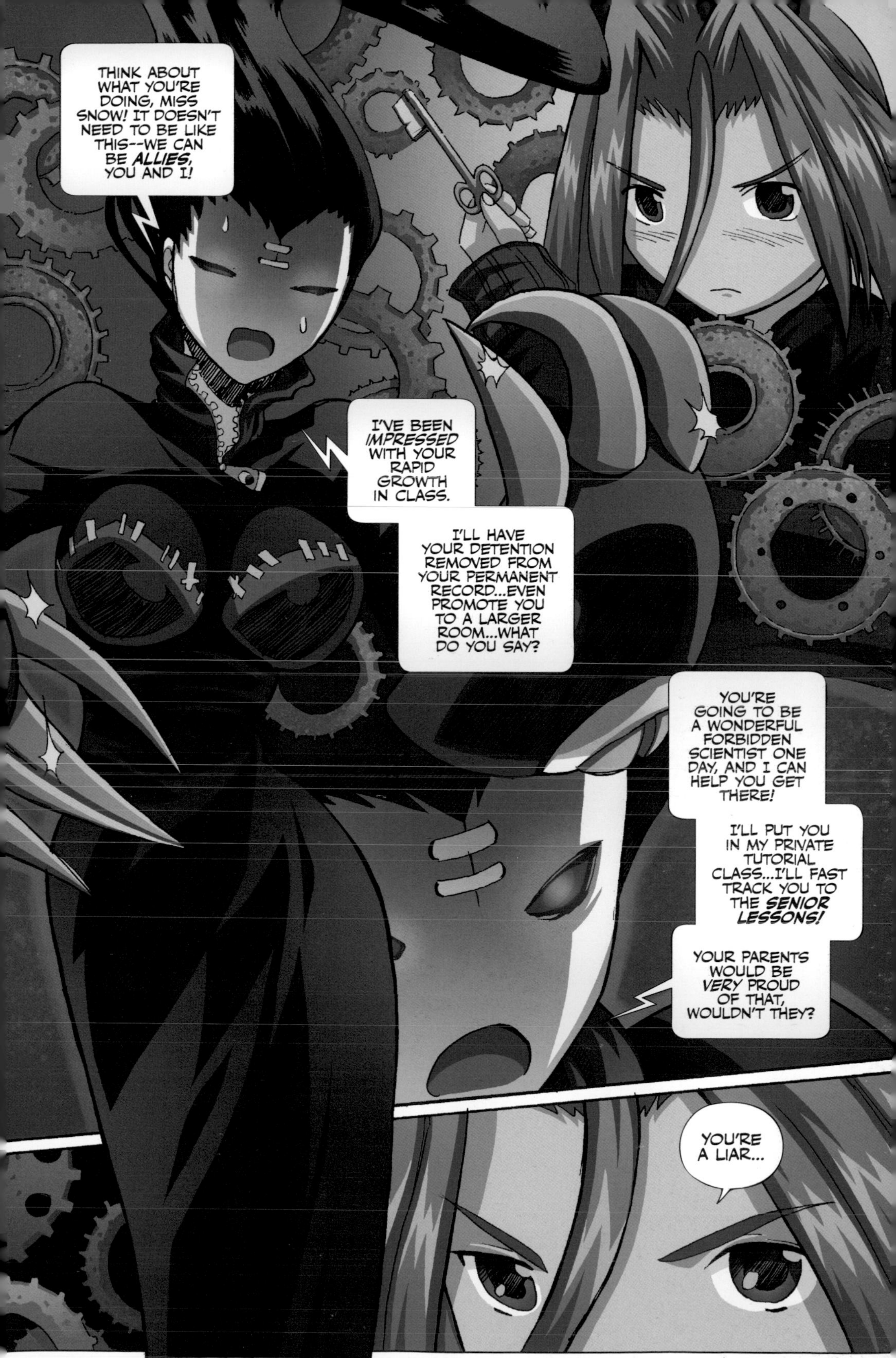
THINK ABOUT WHAT YOU'RE DOING, MISS SNOW! IT DOESN'T NEED TO BE LIKE THIS--WE CAN BE *ALLIES,* YOU AND I!
I'VE BEEN *IMPRESSED* WITH YOUR RAPID GROWTH IN CLASS.
I'LL HAVE YOUR DETENTION REMOVED FROM YOUR PERMANENT RECORD...EVEN PROMOTE YOU TO A LARGER ROOM...WHAT DO YOU SAY?
YOU'RE GOING TO BE A WONDERFUL FORBIDDEN SCIENTIST ONE DAY, AND I CAN HELP YOU GET THERE!
I'LL PUT YOU IN MY PRIVATE TUTORIAL CLASS...I'LL FAST TRACK YOU TO THE ***SENIOR LESSONS!***
YOUR PARENTS WOULD BE *VERY* PROUD OF THAT, WOULDN'T THEY?
YOU'RE A LIAR...

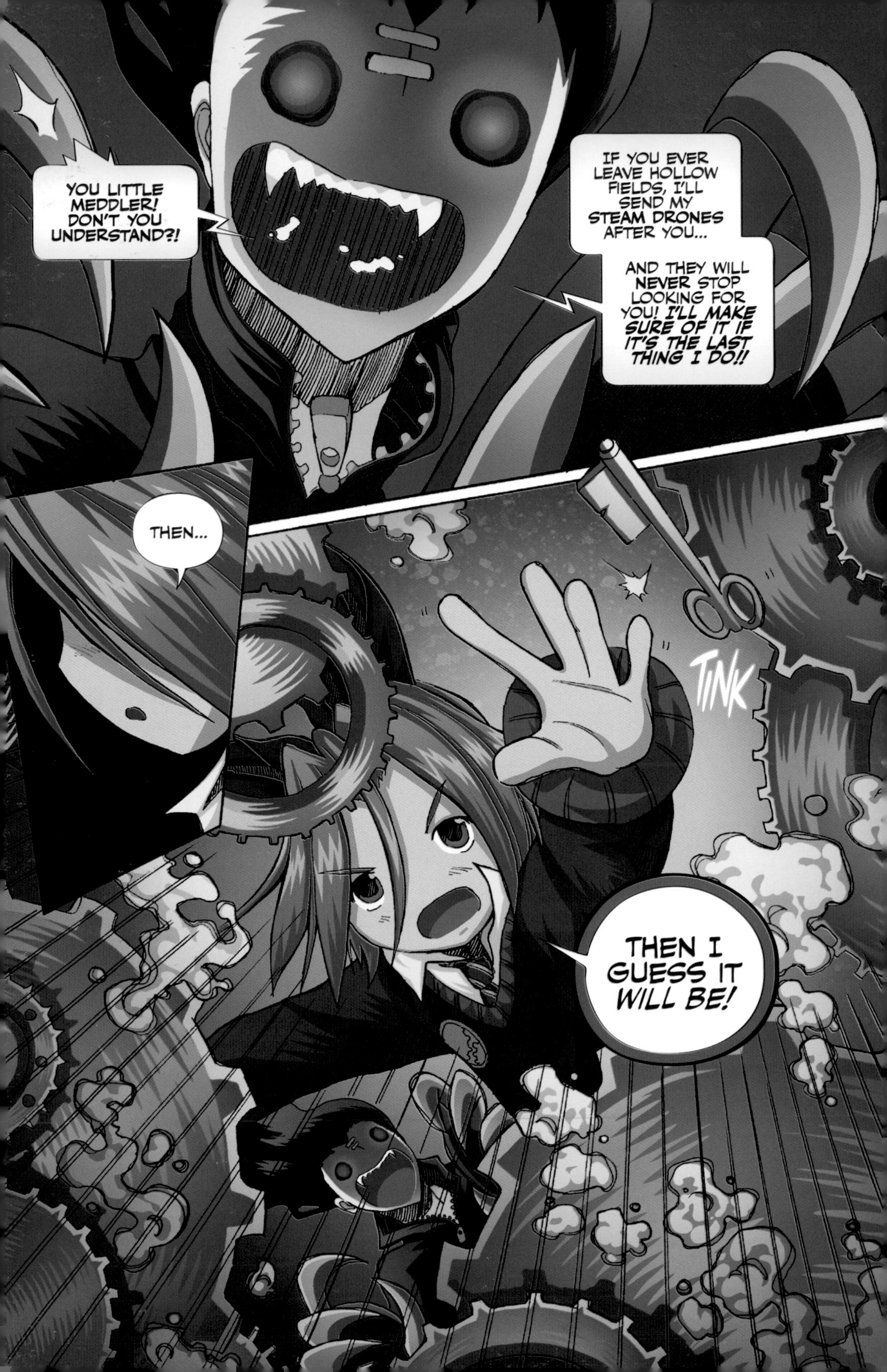
YOU LITTLE MEDDLER! DON'T YOU UNDERSTAND?!
IF YOU EVER LEAVE HOLLOW FIELDS, I'LL SEND MY STEAM DRONES AFTER YOU...
AND THEY WILL NEVER STOP LOOKING FOR YOU! I'LL MAKE SURE OF IT IF IT'S THE LAST THING I DO!!
THEN...
TINK
THEN I GUESS IT WILL BE!

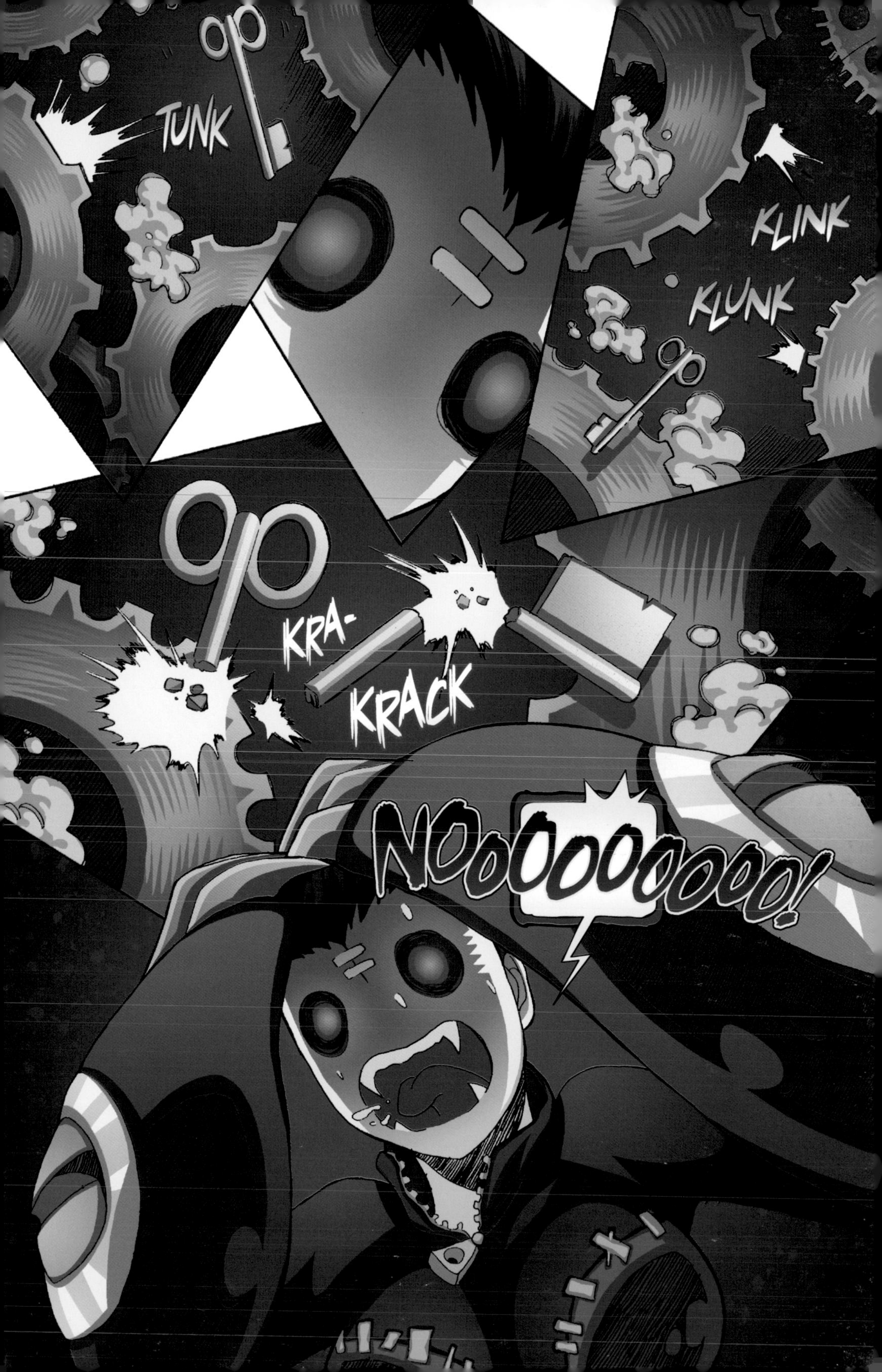
TUNK
KLINK
KLUNK
KRA-
KRACK
NOOOOOOOOOO!

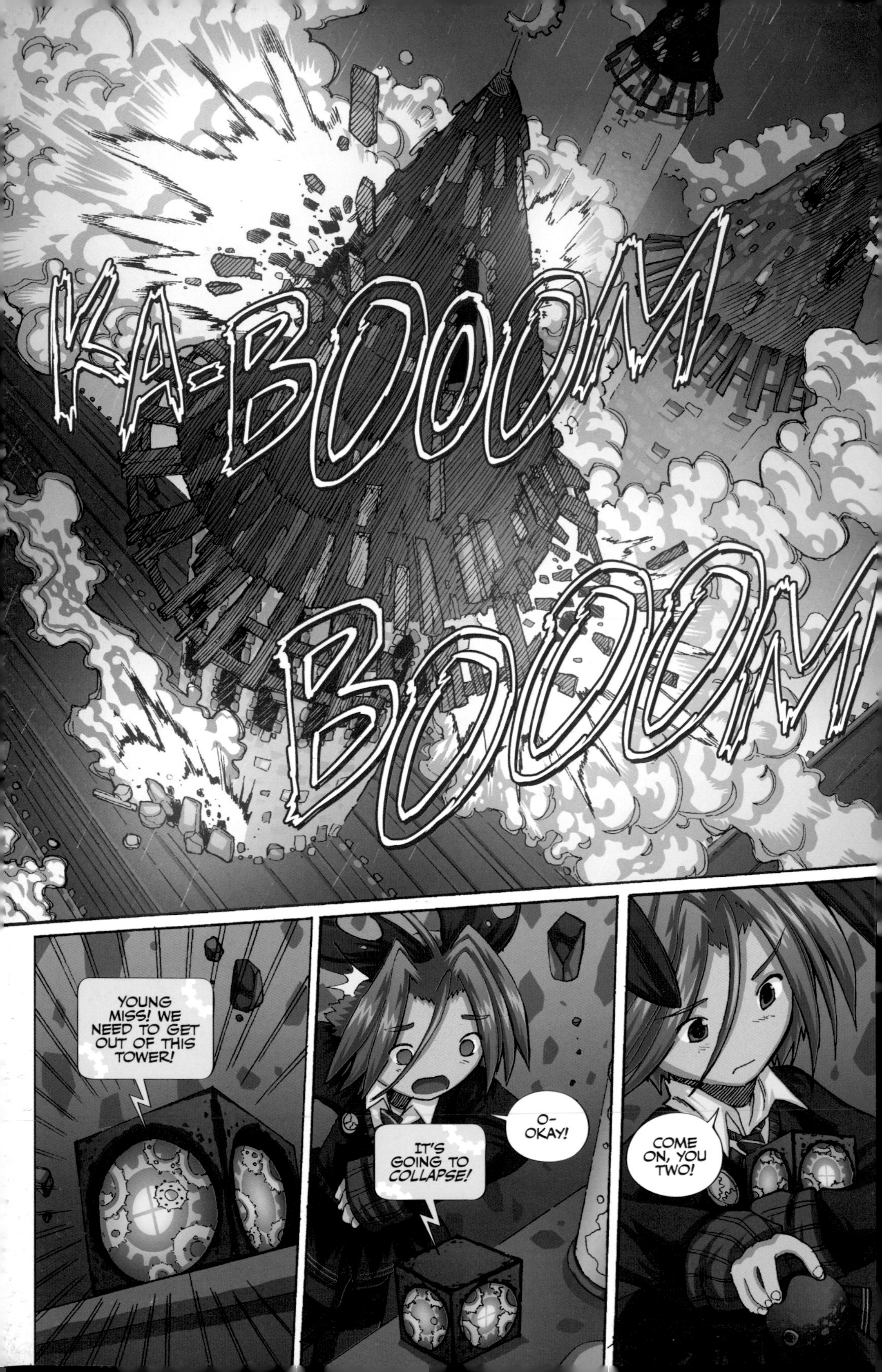
KA-BOOOM
BOOOOM
YOUNG MISS! WE NEED TO GET OUT OF THIS TOWER!
O-OKAY!
IT'S GOING TO COLLAPSE!
COME ON, YOU TWO!

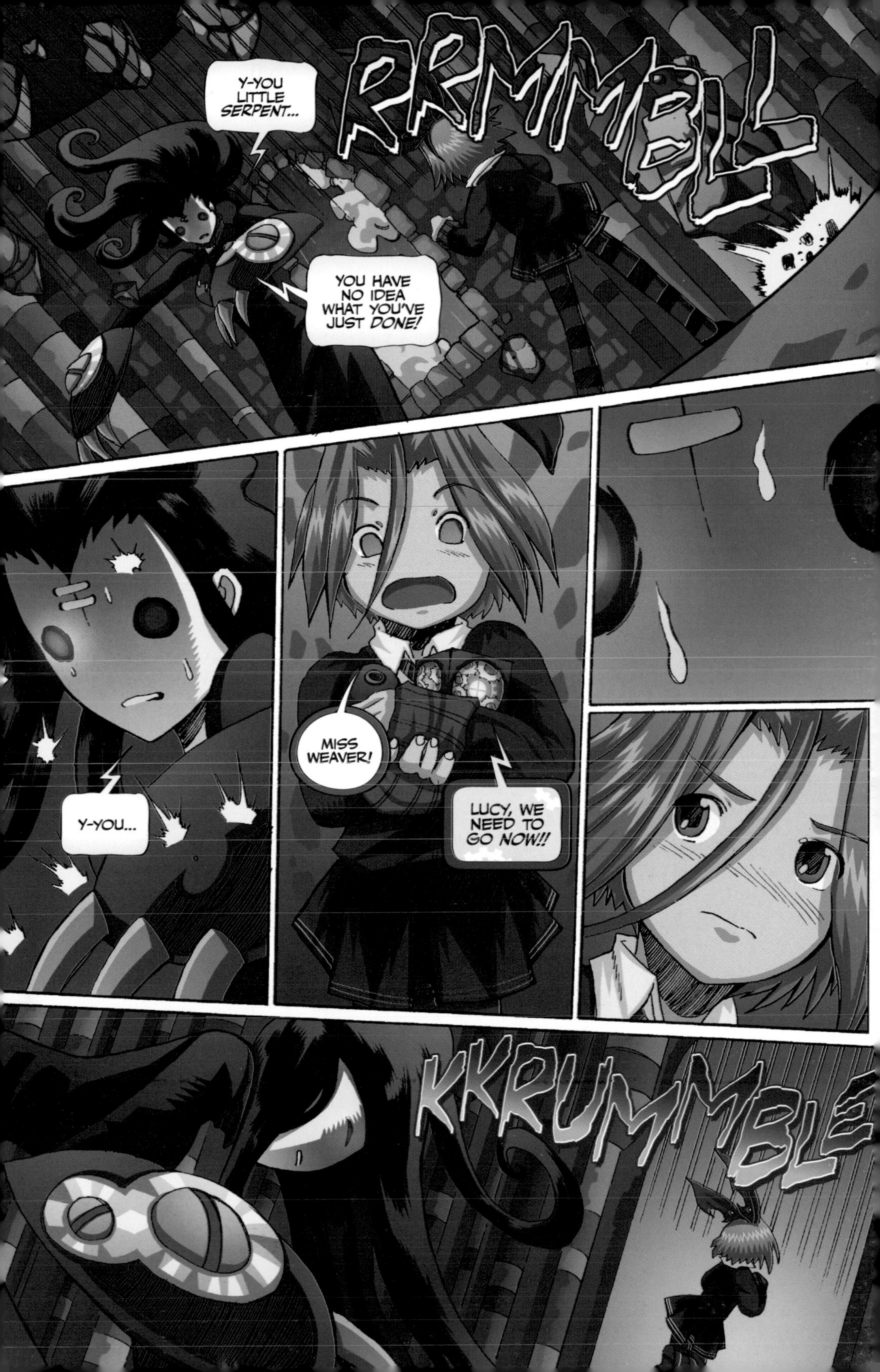
Y-YOU LITTLE SERPENT...
RRMMBLL
YOU HAVE NO IDEA WHAT YOU'VE JUST *DONE!*
Y-YOU...
MISS WEAVER!
LUCY, WE NEED TO GO *NOW!!*
KKRUMMBLE

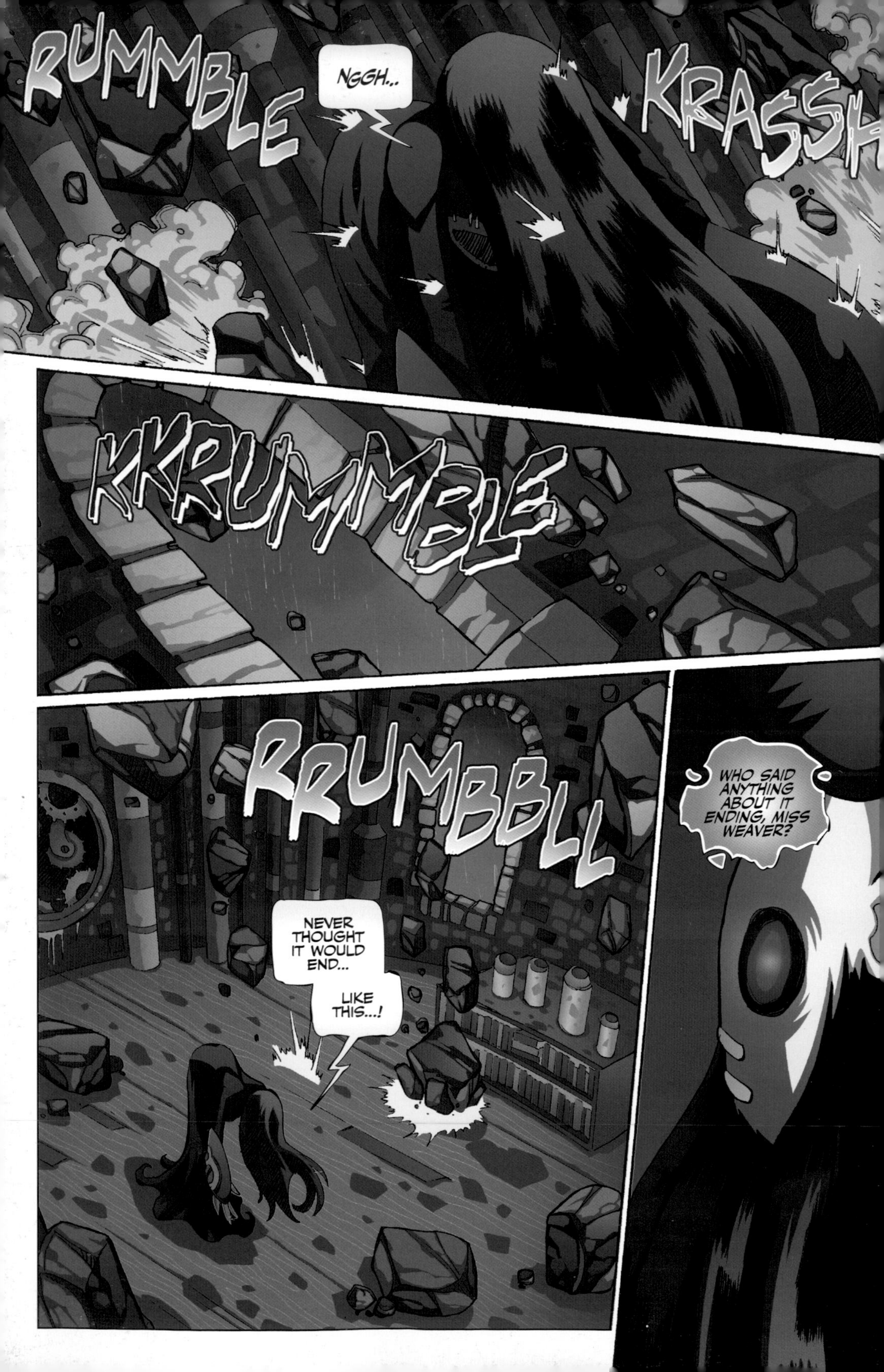
RUMMBLE
NGGH..
KRASSH
KKRUMMBLE
RRUMBBLL
NEVER THOUGHT IT WOULD END...
LIKE THIS...!
WHO SAID ANYTHING ABOUT IT ENDING, MISS WEAVER?

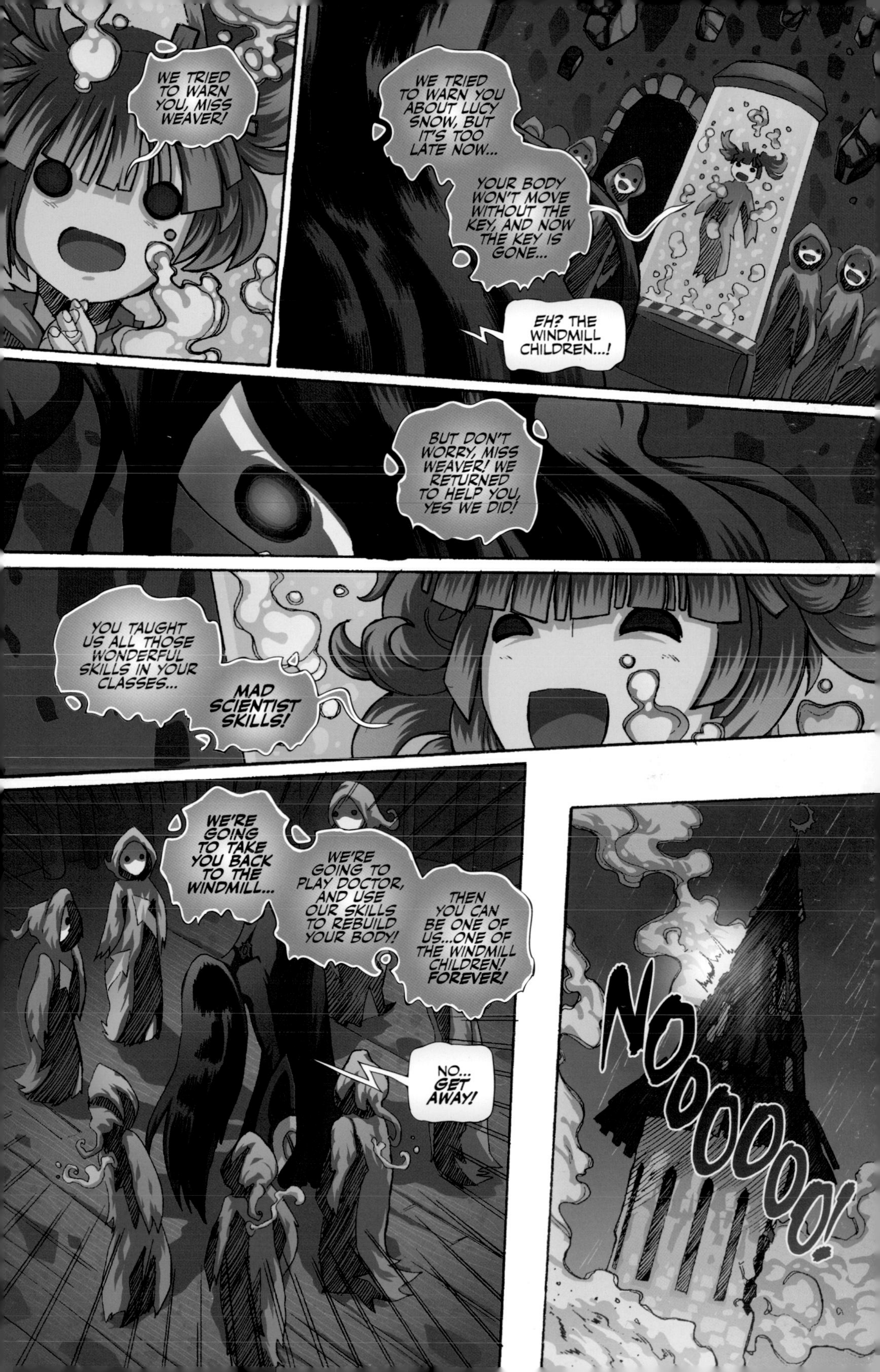
WE TRIED TO WARN YOU, MISS WEAVER!
WE TRIED TO WARN YOU ABOUT LUCY SNOW, BUT IT'S TOO LATE NOW...
YOUR BODY WON'T MOVE WITHOUT THE KEY, AND NOW THE KEY IS GONE...
EH? THE WINDMILL CHILDREN...!
BUT DON'T WORRY, MISS WEAVER! WE RETURNED TO HELP YOU, YES WE DID!
YOU TAUGHT US ALL THOSE WONDERFUL SKILLS IN YOUR CLASSES...
MAD SCIENTIST SKILLS!
WE'RE GOING TO TAKE YOU BACK TO THE WINDMILL...
WE'RE GOING TO PLAY DOCTOR, AND USE OUR SKILLS TO REBUILD YOUR BODY!
THEN YOU CAN BE ONE OF US...ONE OF THE WINDMILL CHILDREN! FOREVER!
NO... GET AWAY!
NOOOOOOO!

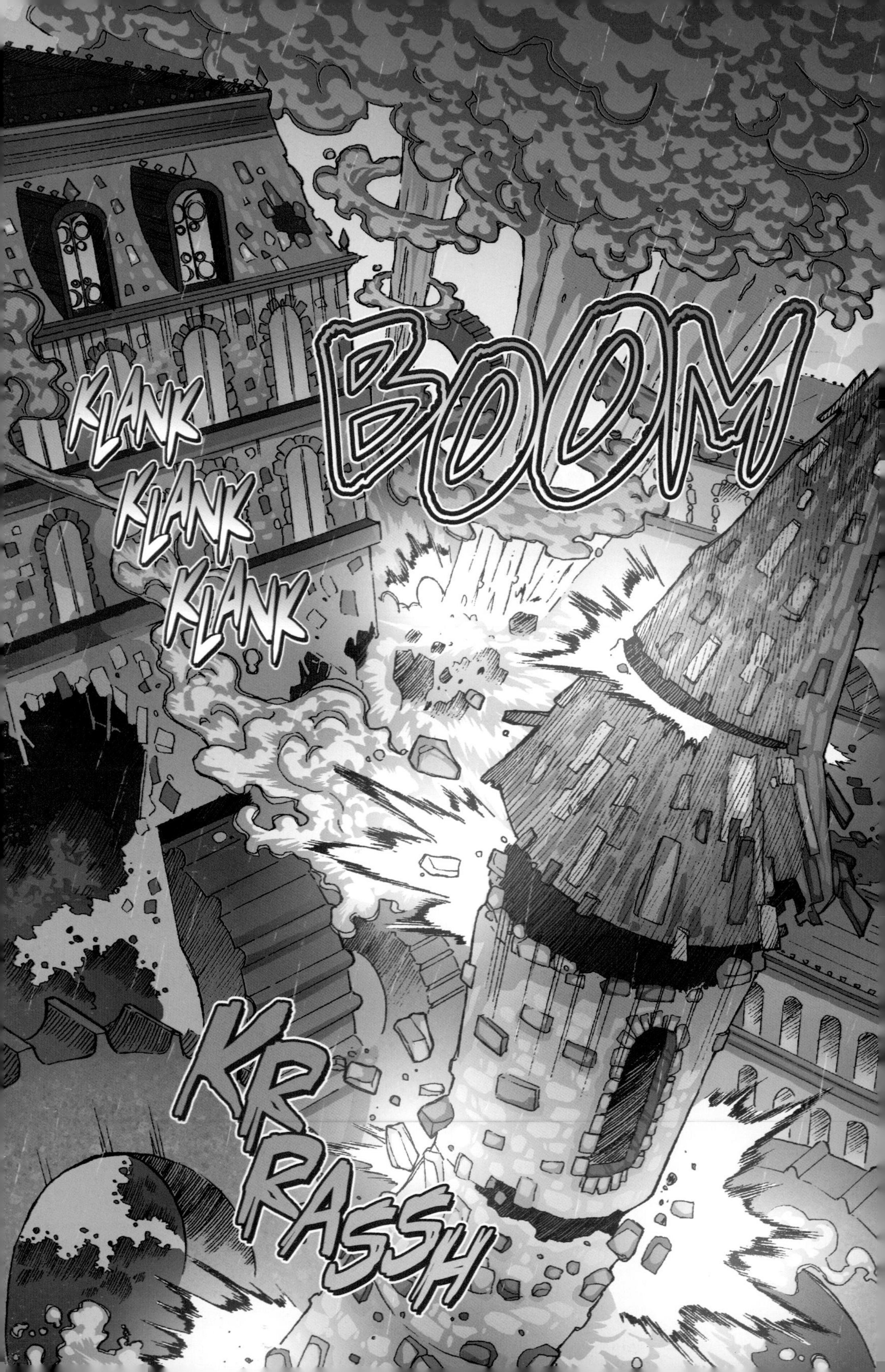
KLANK
KLANK
KLANK
BOOM
KR
RASSH

FINAL CHAPTER
School's Out

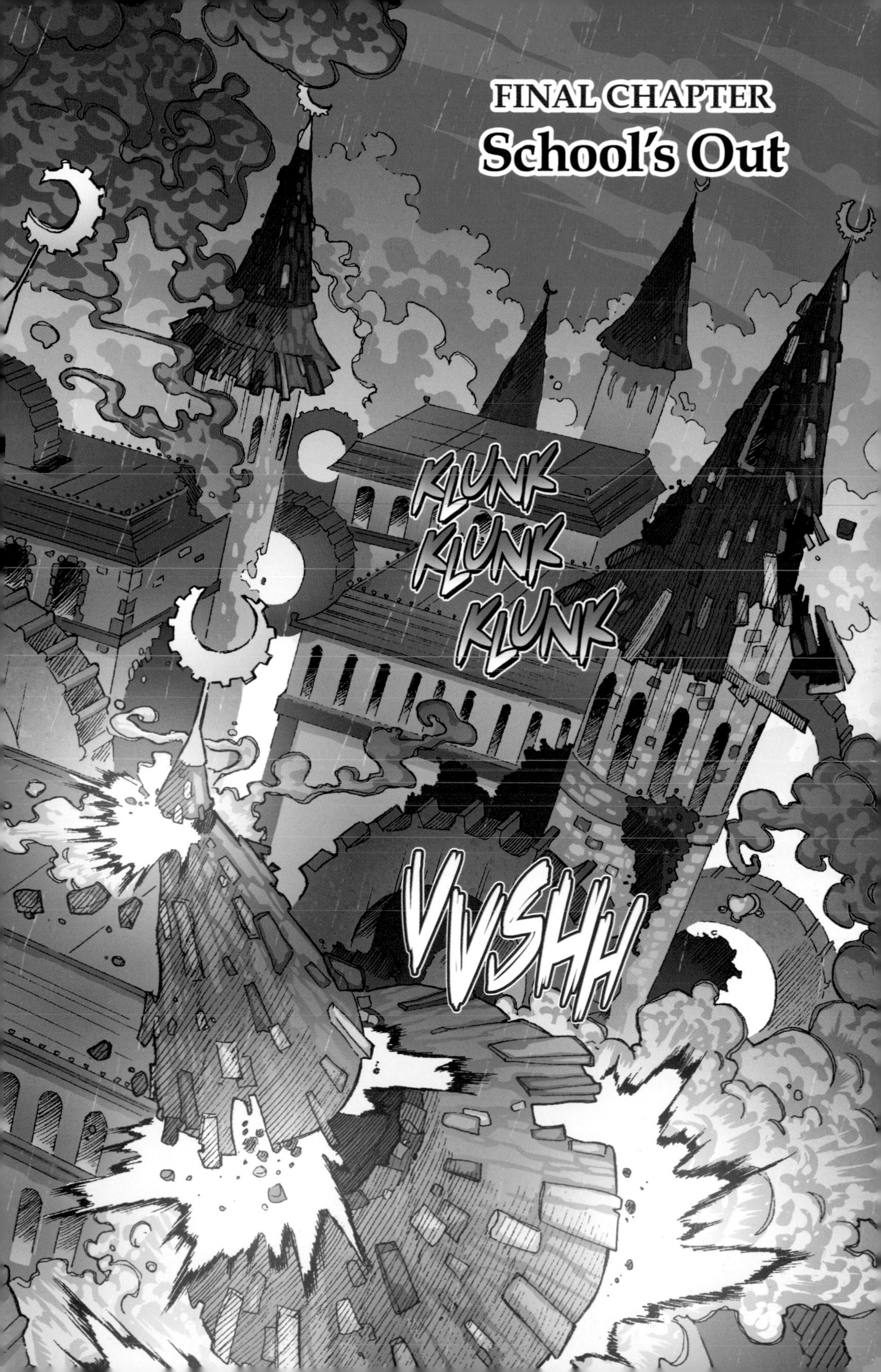
KLUNK
KLUNK
KLUNK
VVSHH

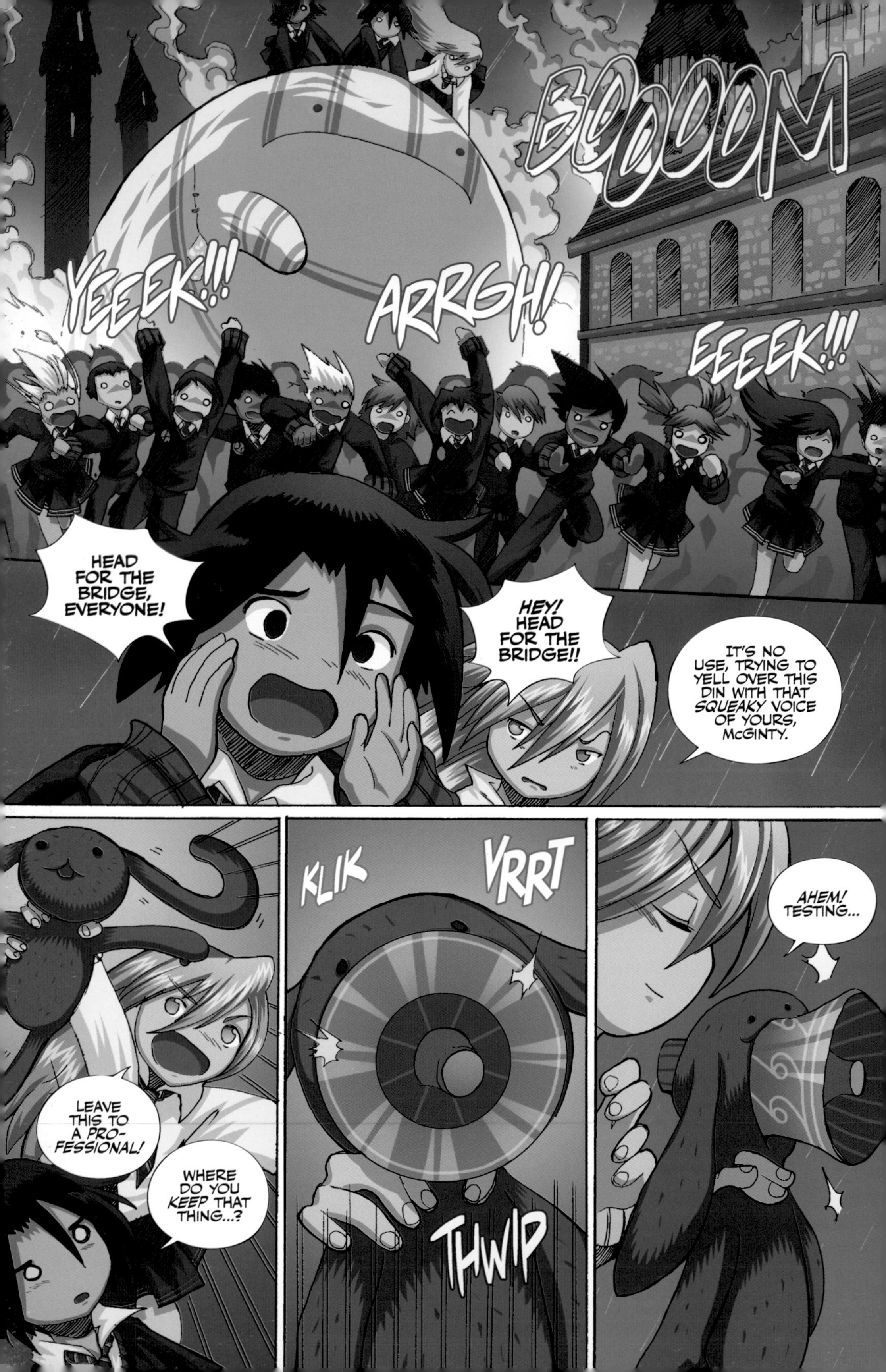
BOOOOOM
YEEEK!!!
ARRGH!
EEEEK!!!
HEAD FOR THE BRIDGE, EVERYONE!
HEY! HEAD FOR THE BRIDGE!!
IT'S NO USE, TRYING TO YELL OVER THIS DIN WITH THAT SQUEAKY VOICE OF YOURS, McGINTY.
LEAVE THIS TO A PRO-FESSIONAL!
WHERE DO YOU KEEP THAT THING...?
KLIK
VRRT
THWIP
AHEM! TESTING...

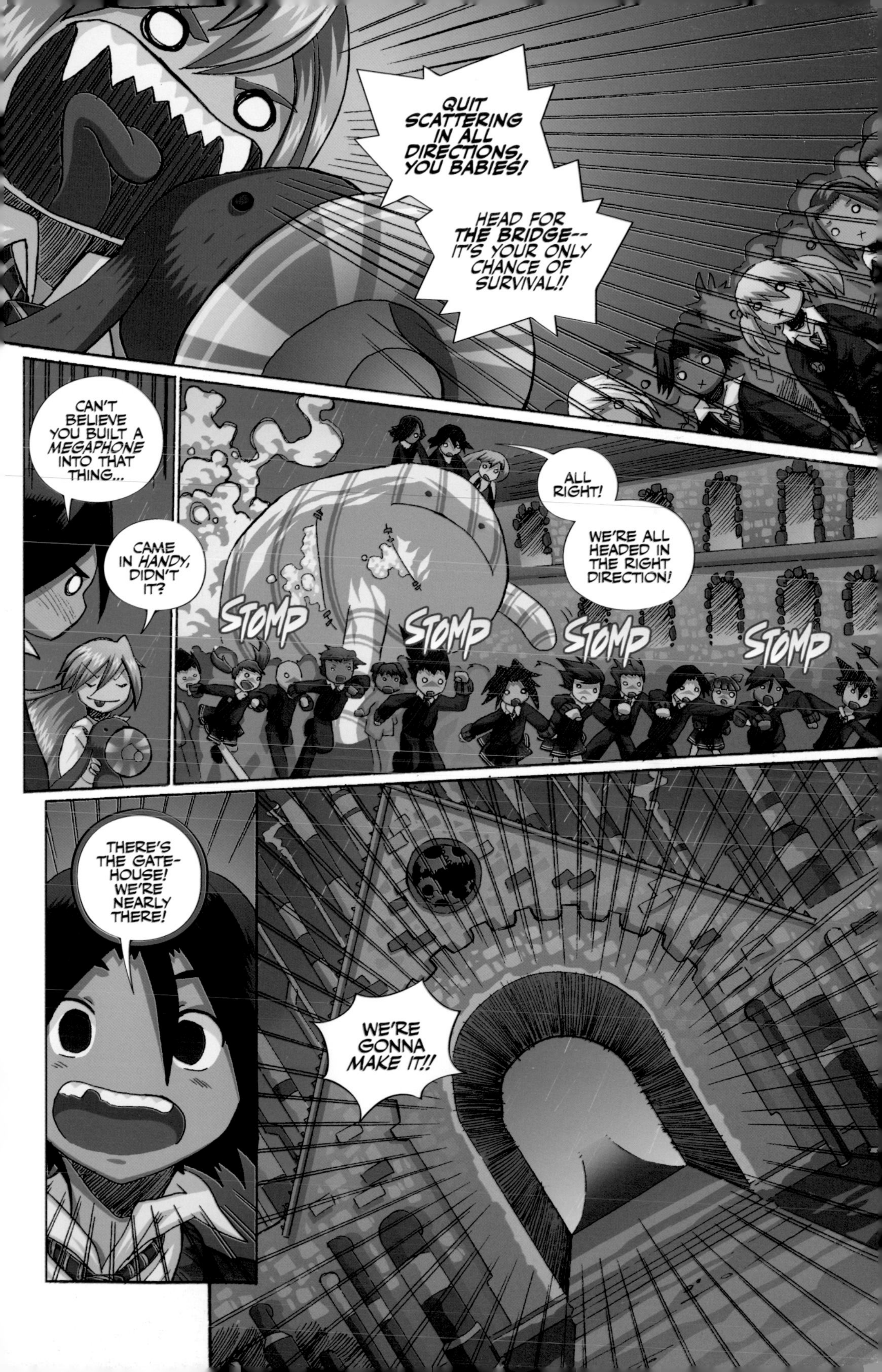
QUIT SCATTERING IN ALL DIRECTIONS, YOU BABIES!
HEAD FOR THE BRIDGE-- IT'S YOUR ONLY CHANCE OF SURVIVAL!!
CAN'T BELIEVE YOU BUILT A MEGAPHONE INTO THAT THING...
CAME IN HANDY, DIDN'T IT?
ALL RIGHT!
WE'RE ALL HEADED IN THE RIGHT DIRECTION!
STOMP
STOMP
STOMP
STOMP
THERE'S THE GATE-HOUSE! WE'RE NEARLY THERE!
WE'RE GONNA MAKE IT!!

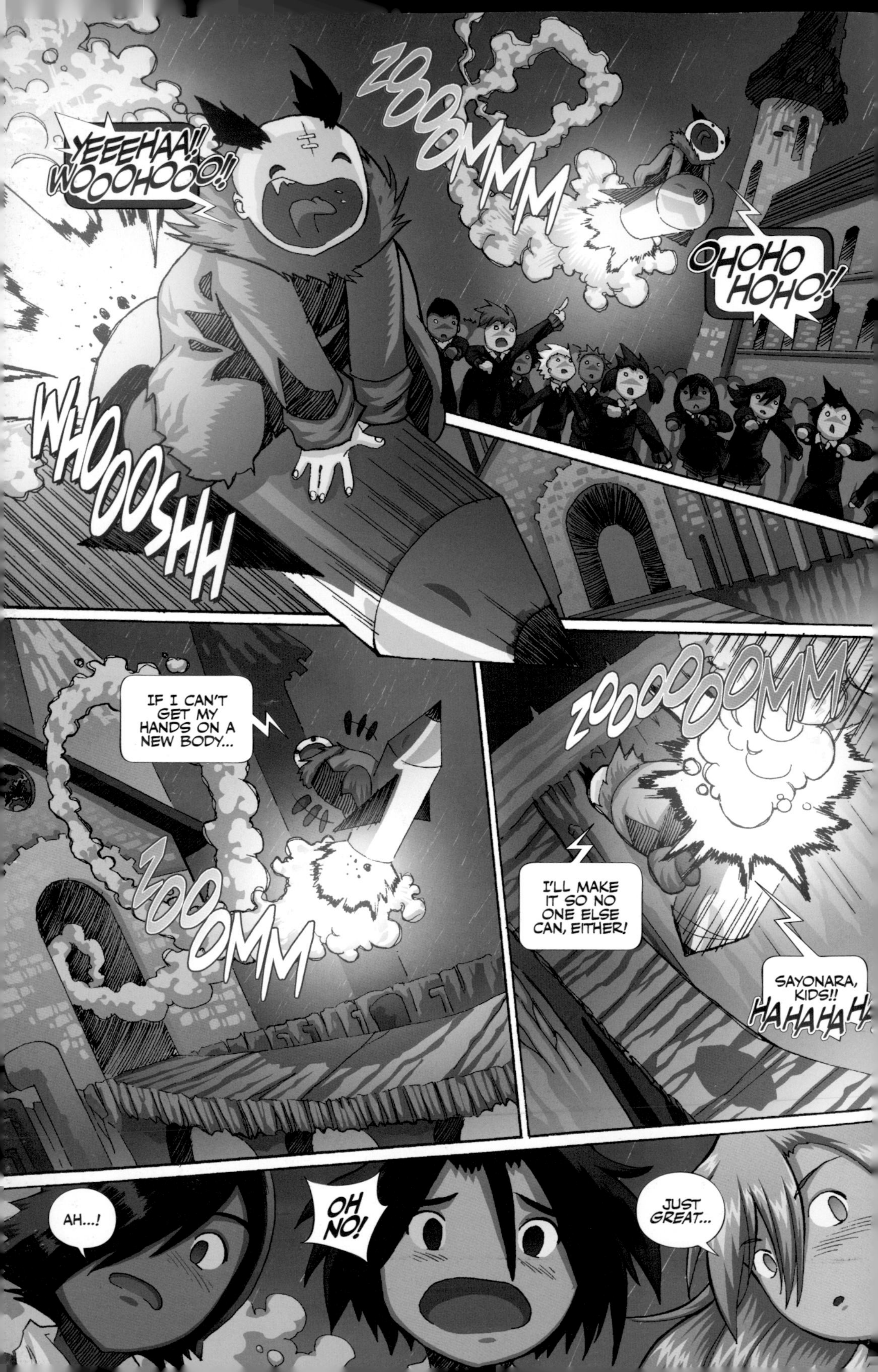
YEEEHAA!! WOOOHOOOO!!
ZOOOOMMMM
OHOHO HOHO!!
WHOOOOSHH
IF I CAN'T GET MY HANDS ON A NEW BODY...
ZOOOOMM
ZOOOOOOOMM
I'LL MAKE IT SO NO ONE ELSE CAN, EITHER!
SAYONARA, KIDS!! HAHAHAHA
AH...!
OH NO!
JUST GREAT...

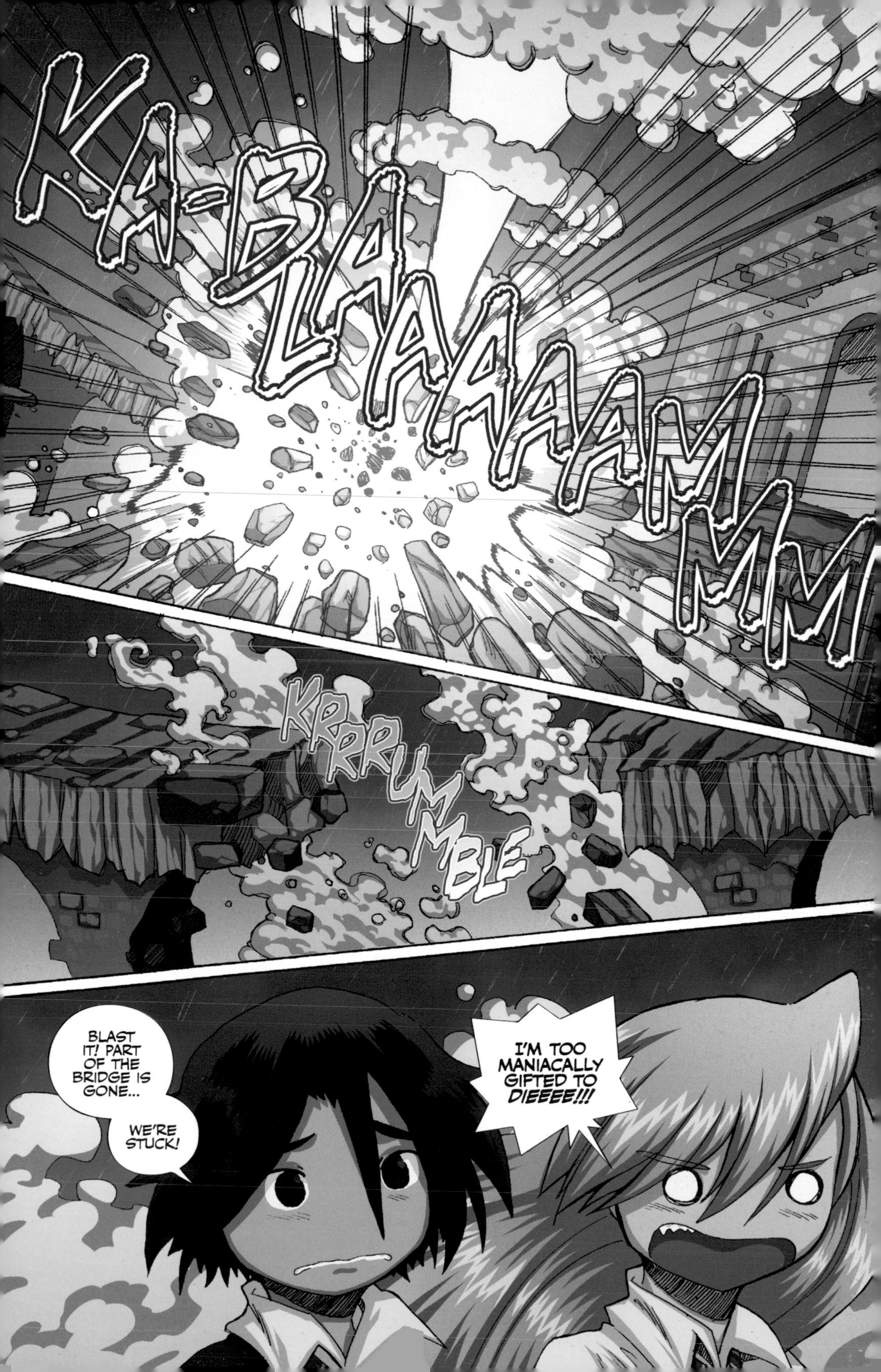
KA-BLAAAAAMMMM
KRRRUMMBLE
BLAST IT! PART OF THE BRIDGE IS GONE...
WE'RE STUCK!
I'M TOO MANIACALLY GIFTED TO *DIEEEE!!!*

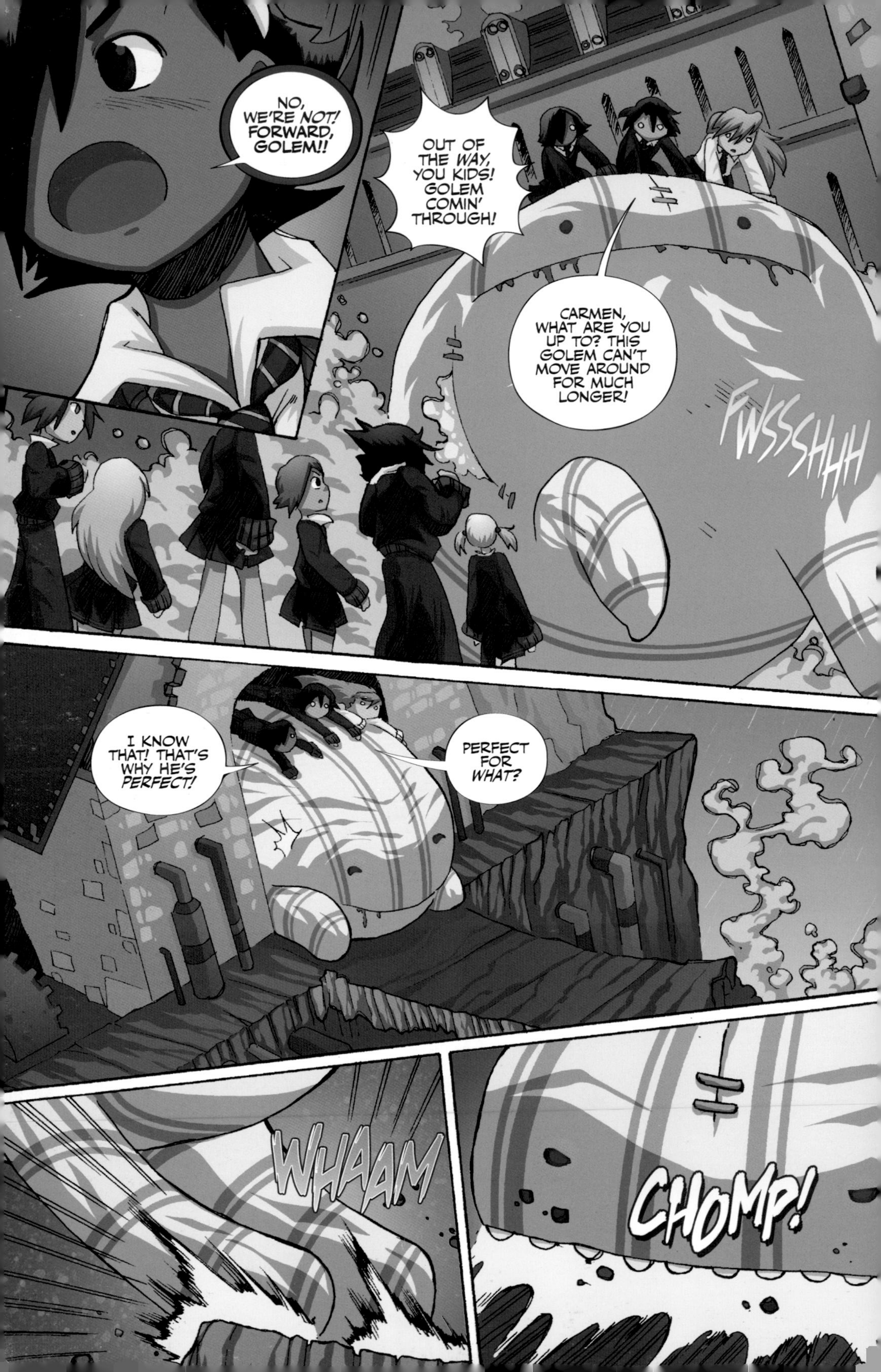
NO, WE'RE *NOT!* FORWARD, GOLEM!!
OUT OF THE *WAY,* YOU KIDS! GOLEM COMIN' THROUGH!
CARMEN, WHAT ARE YOU UP TO? THIS GOLEM CAN'T MOVE AROUND FOR MUCH LONGER!
FWSSSHHH
I KNOW THAT! THAT'S WHY HE'S *PERFECT!*
PERFECT FOR *WHAT?*
WHAAM
CHOMP!

PERFECT FOR MAKING A *BRIDGE*, SEE?

WOW!

PRETTY SMART, HUH?

NOT BAD!

YAMMER YAMMER

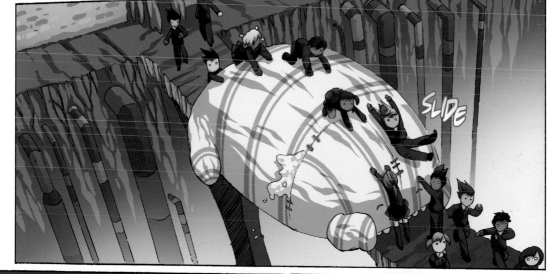

SLIDE

SHFF

KRUMBLE

EH?

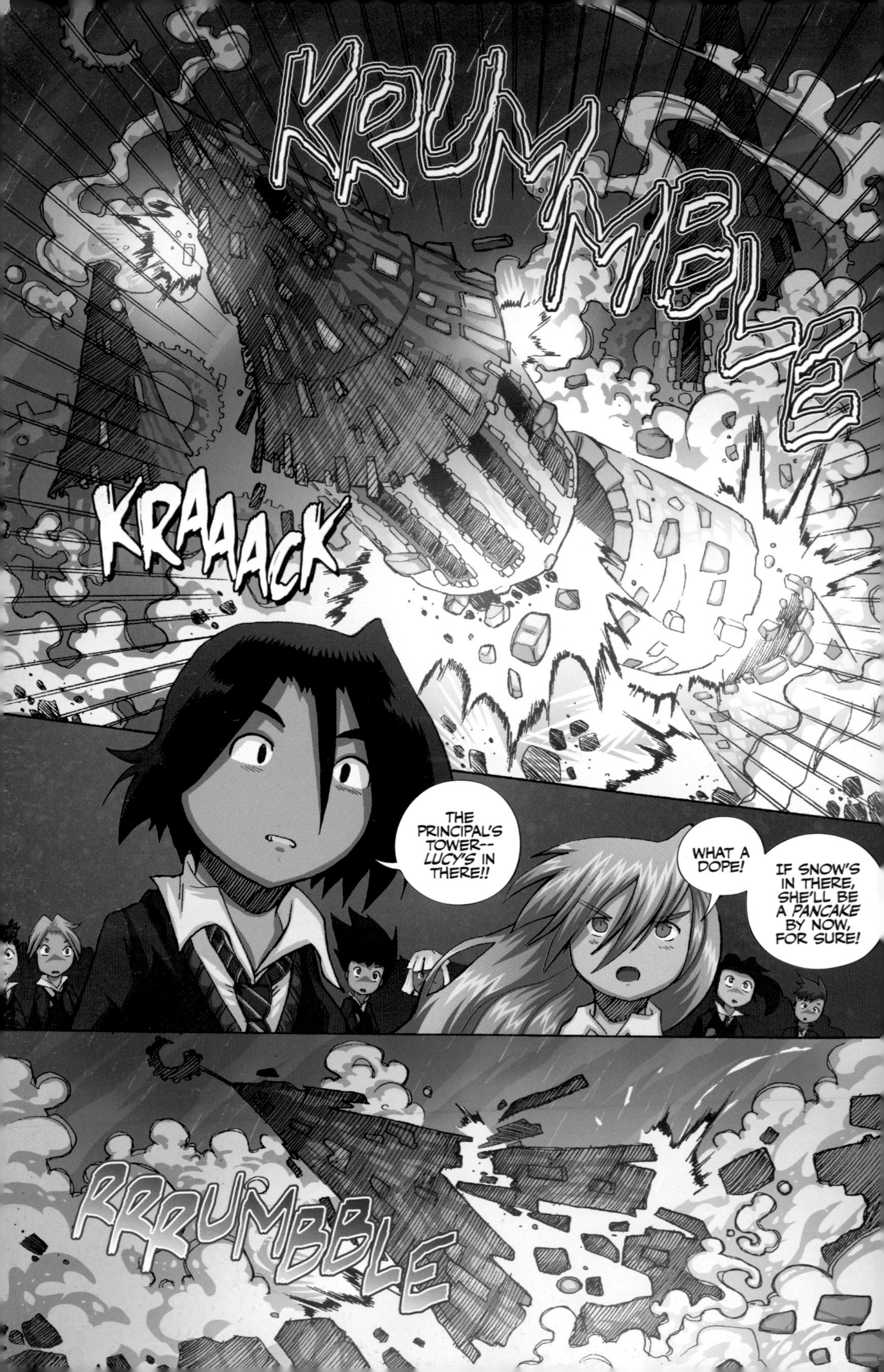
KRUMMBLE
KRAAAACK
THE PRINCIPAL'S TOWER-- *LUCY'S* IN THERE!!
WHAT A DOPE!
IF SNOW'S IN THERE, SHE'LL BE A *PANCAKE* BY NOW, FOR SURE!
RRRUMBBLE

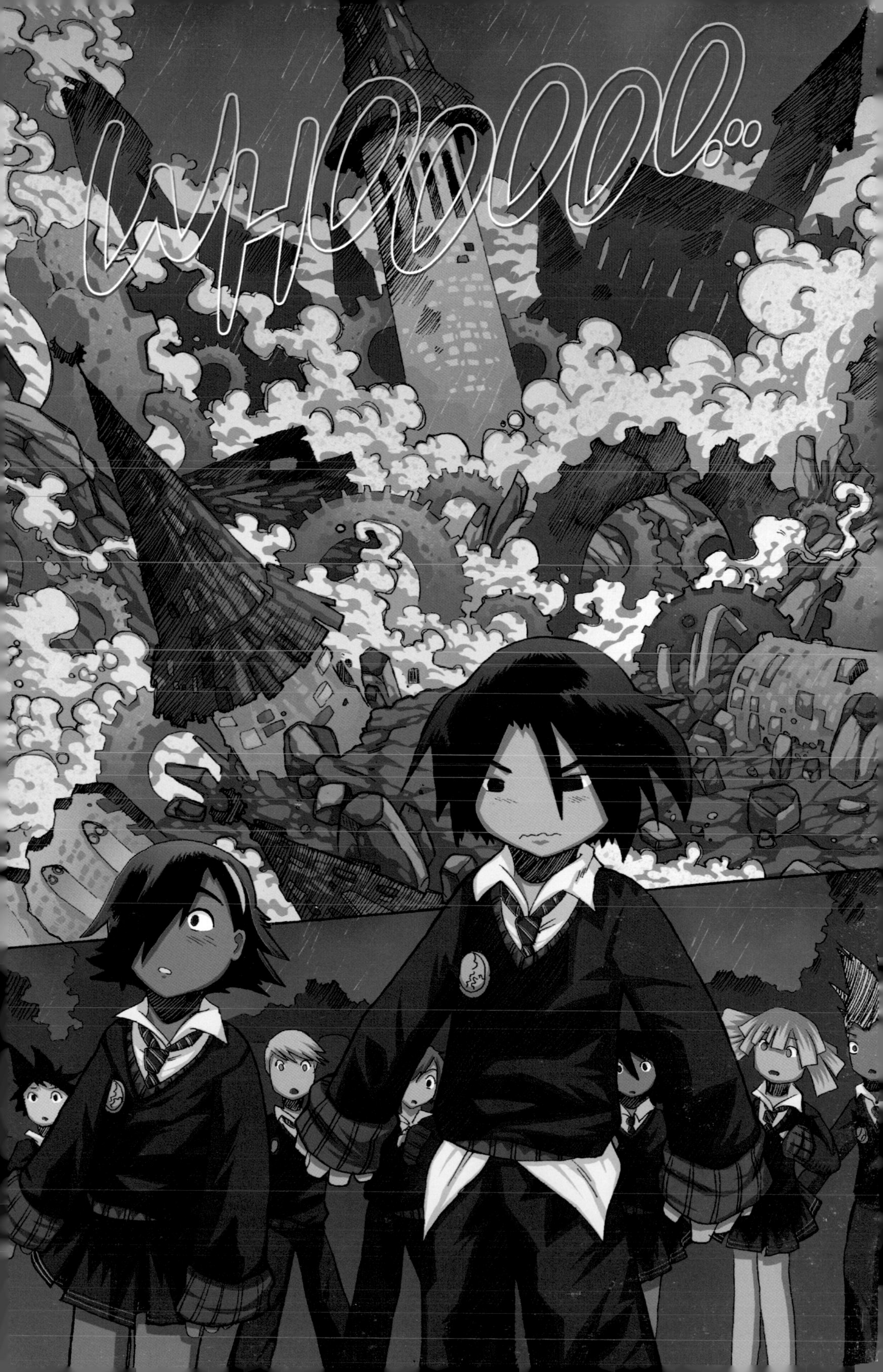
WHOOOOOL...

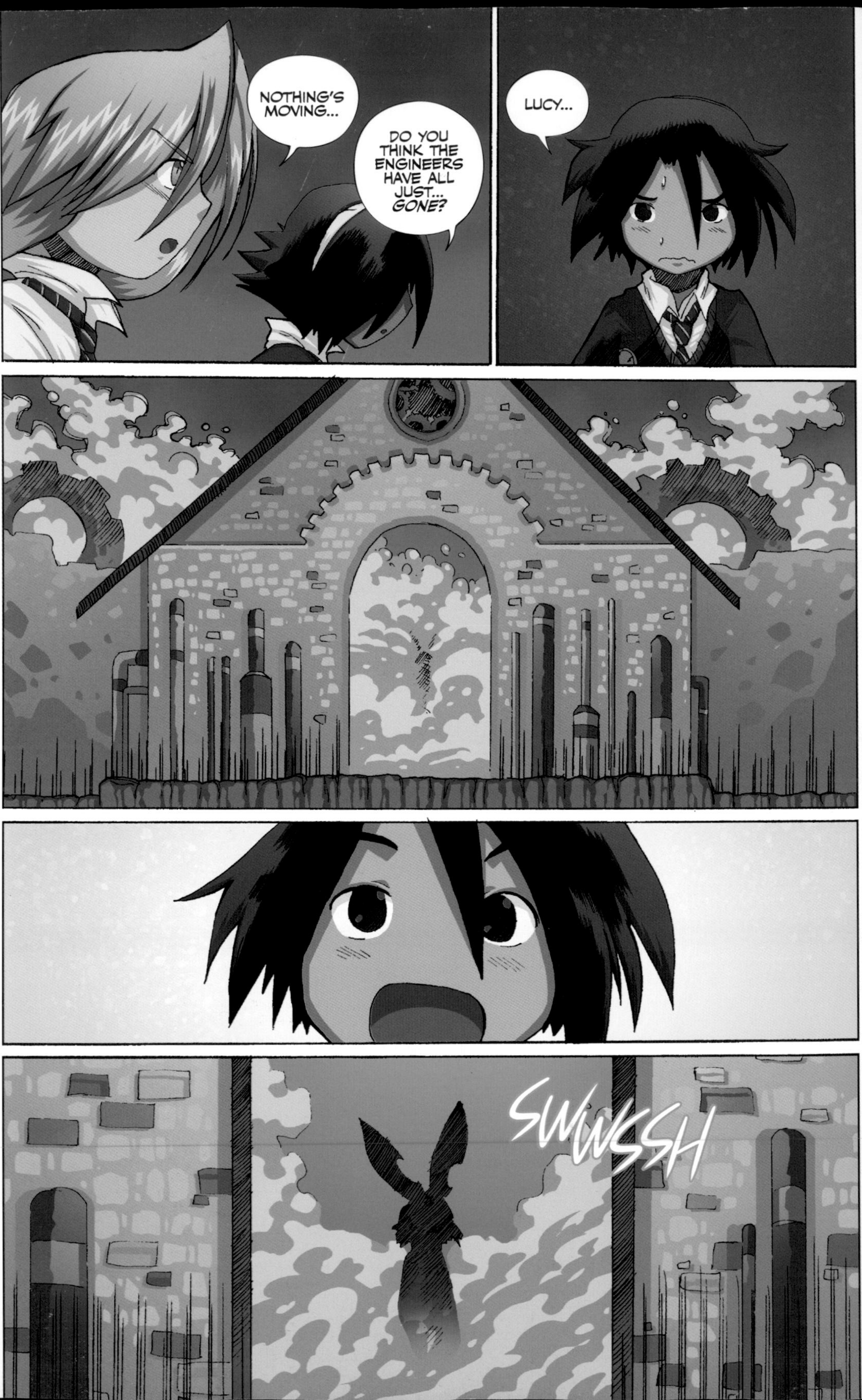
NOTHING'S MOVING...
DO YOU THINK THE ENGINEERS HAVE ALL JUST... GONE?
LUCY...
SWWSSH

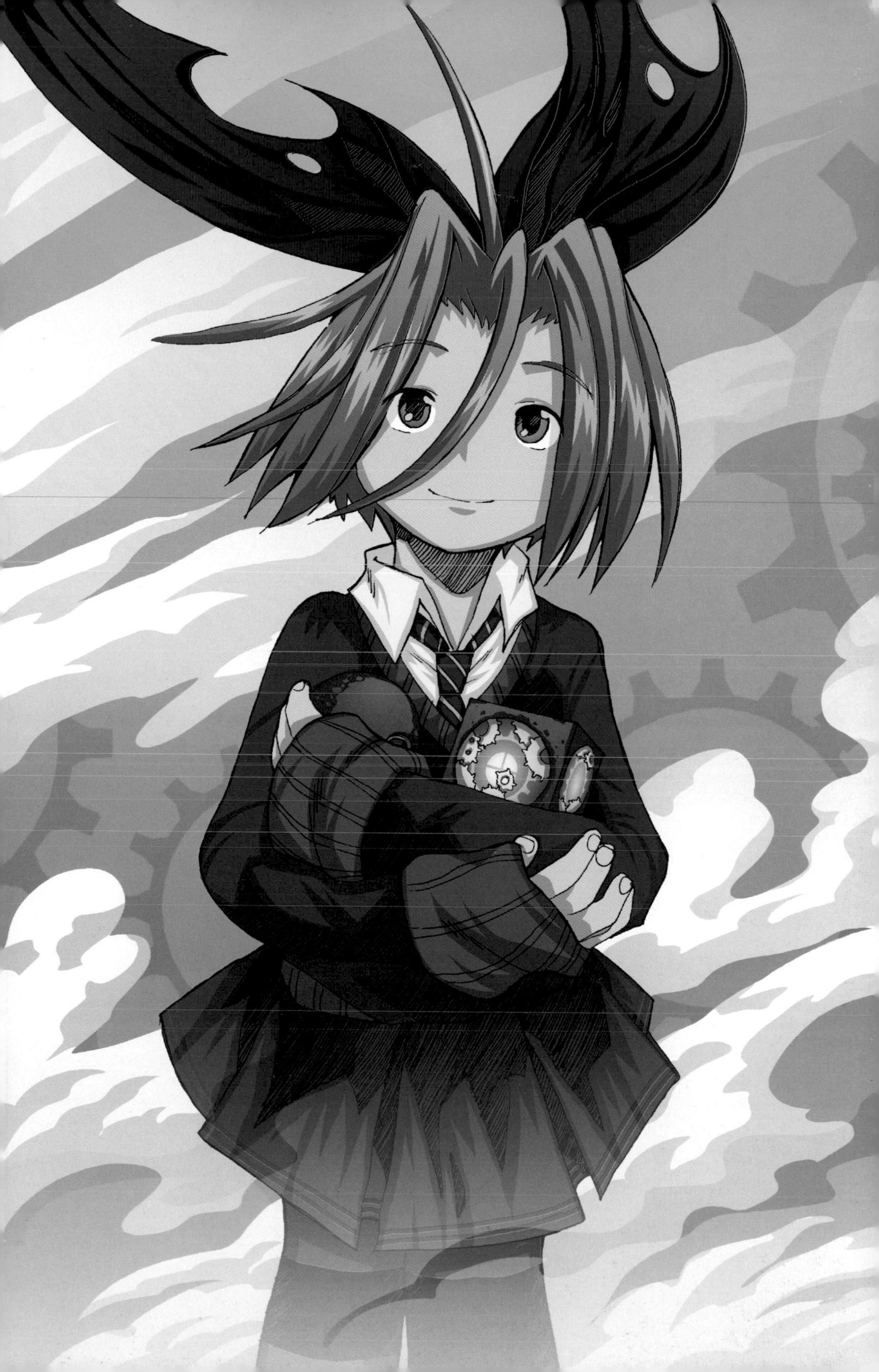

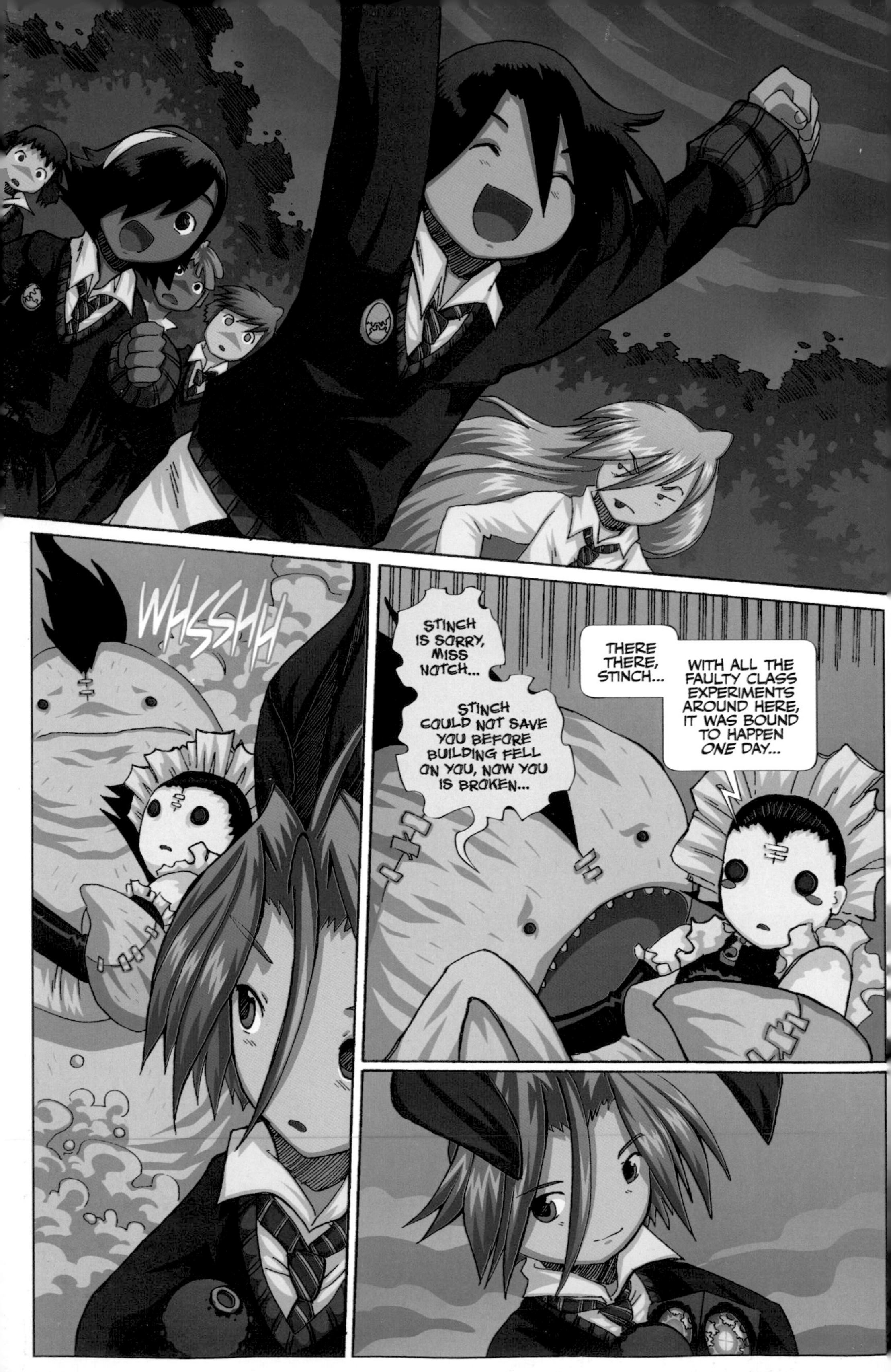
WHSSHH
STINCH IS SORRY, MISS NATCH...
STINCH COULD NOT SAVE YOU BEFORE BUILDING FELL ON YOU, NOW YOU IS BROKEN...
THERE THERE, STINCH...
WITH ALL THE FAULTY CLASS EXPERIMENTS AROUND HERE, IT WAS BOUND TO HAPPEN *ONE* DAY...

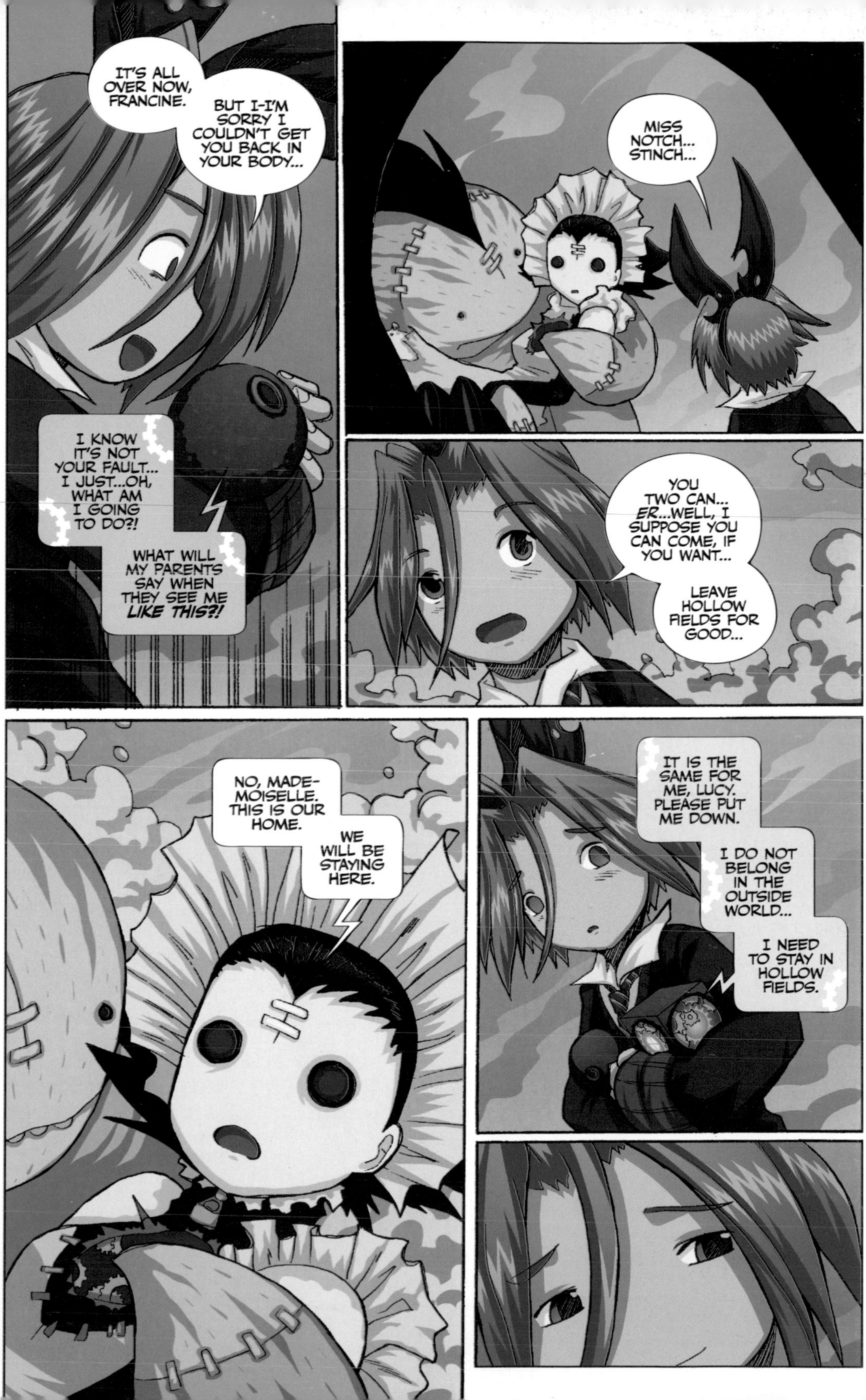
IT'S ALL OVER NOW, FRANCINE.
BUT I-I'M SORRY I COULDN'T GET YOU BACK IN YOUR BODY...
I KNOW IT'S NOT YOUR FAULT... I JUST...OH, WHAT AM I GOING TO DO?!
WHAT WILL MY PARENTS SAY WHEN THEY SEE ME *LIKE THIS?!*
MISS NOTCH... STINCH...
YOU TWO CAN... *ER*...WELL, I SUPPOSE YOU CAN COME, IF YOU WANT...
LEAVE HOLLOW FIELDS FOR GOOD...
NO, MADE-MOISELLE. THIS IS OUR HOME.
WE WILL BE STAYING HERE.
IT IS THE SAME FOR ME, LUCY. PLEASE PUT ME DOWN.
I DO NOT BELONG IN THE OUTSIDE WORLD...
I NEED TO STAY IN HOLLOW FIELDS.

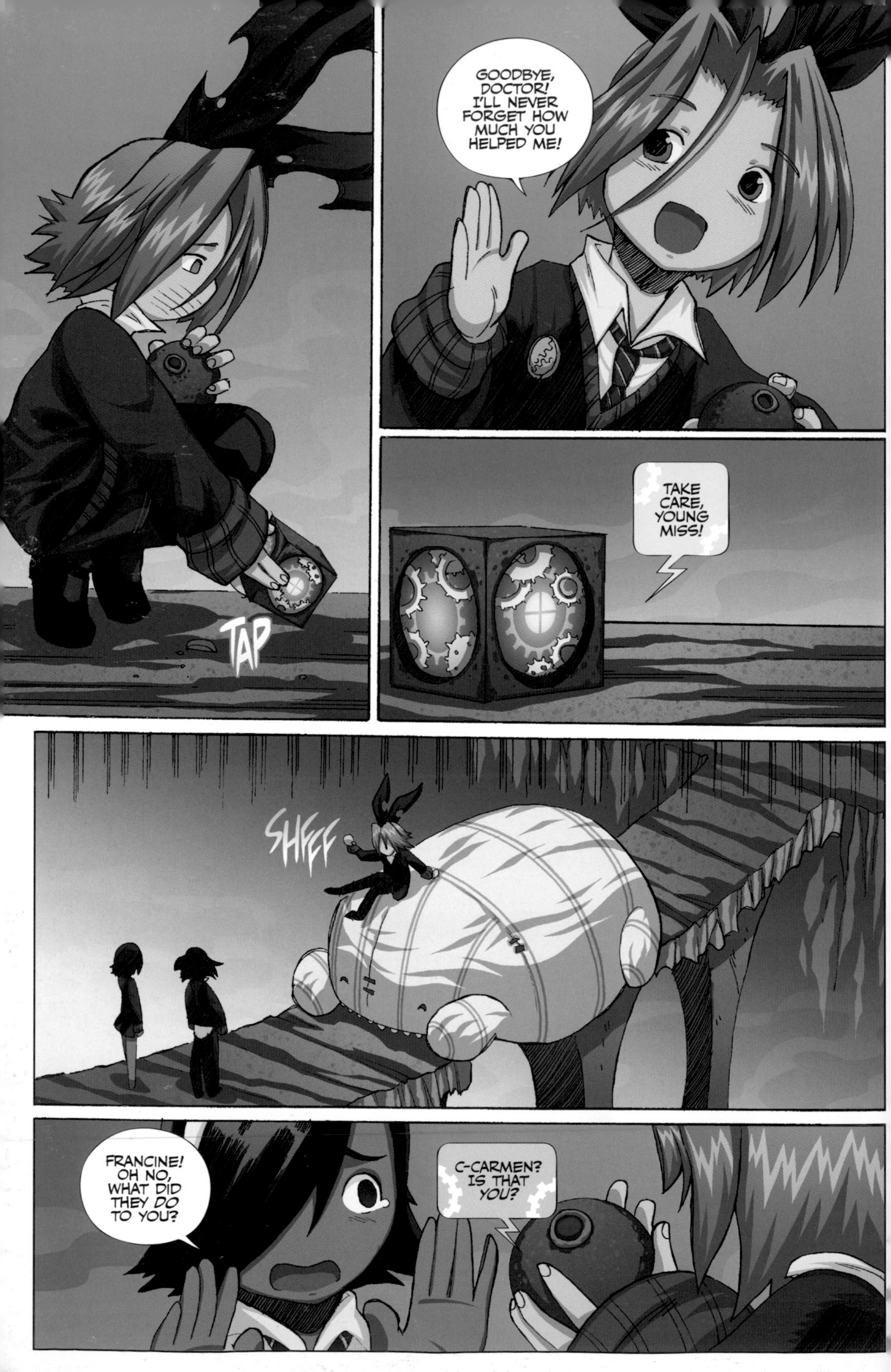
TAP
GOODBYE, DOCTOR! I'LL NEVER FORGET HOW MUCH YOU HELPED ME!
TAKE CARE, YOUNG MISS!
SHFFF
FRANCINE! OH NO, WHAT DID THEY DO TO YOU?
C-CARMEN? IS THAT YOU?

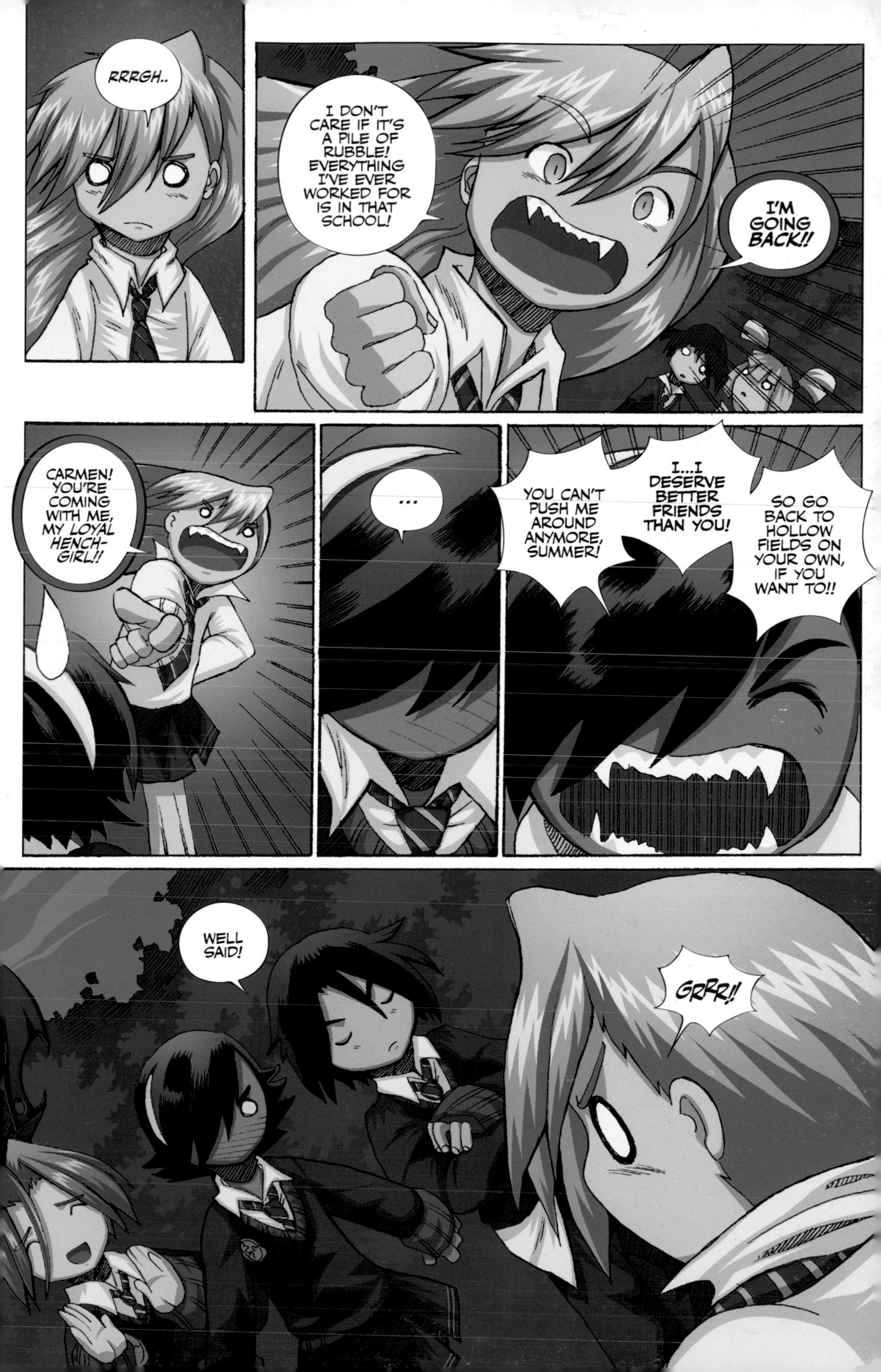
RRRGH..
I DON'T CARE IF IT'S A PILE OF RUBBLE! EVERYTHING I'VE EVER WORKED FOR IS IN THAT SCHOOL!
I'M GOING BACK!!
CARMEN! YOU'RE COMING WITH ME, MY LOYAL HENCH-GIRL!!
...
YOU CAN'T PUSH ME AROUND ANYMORE, SUMMER!
I...I DESERVE BETTER FRIENDS THAN YOU!
SO GO BACK TO HOLLOW FIELDS ON YOUR OWN, IF YOU WANT TO!!
WELL SAID!
GRRR!!

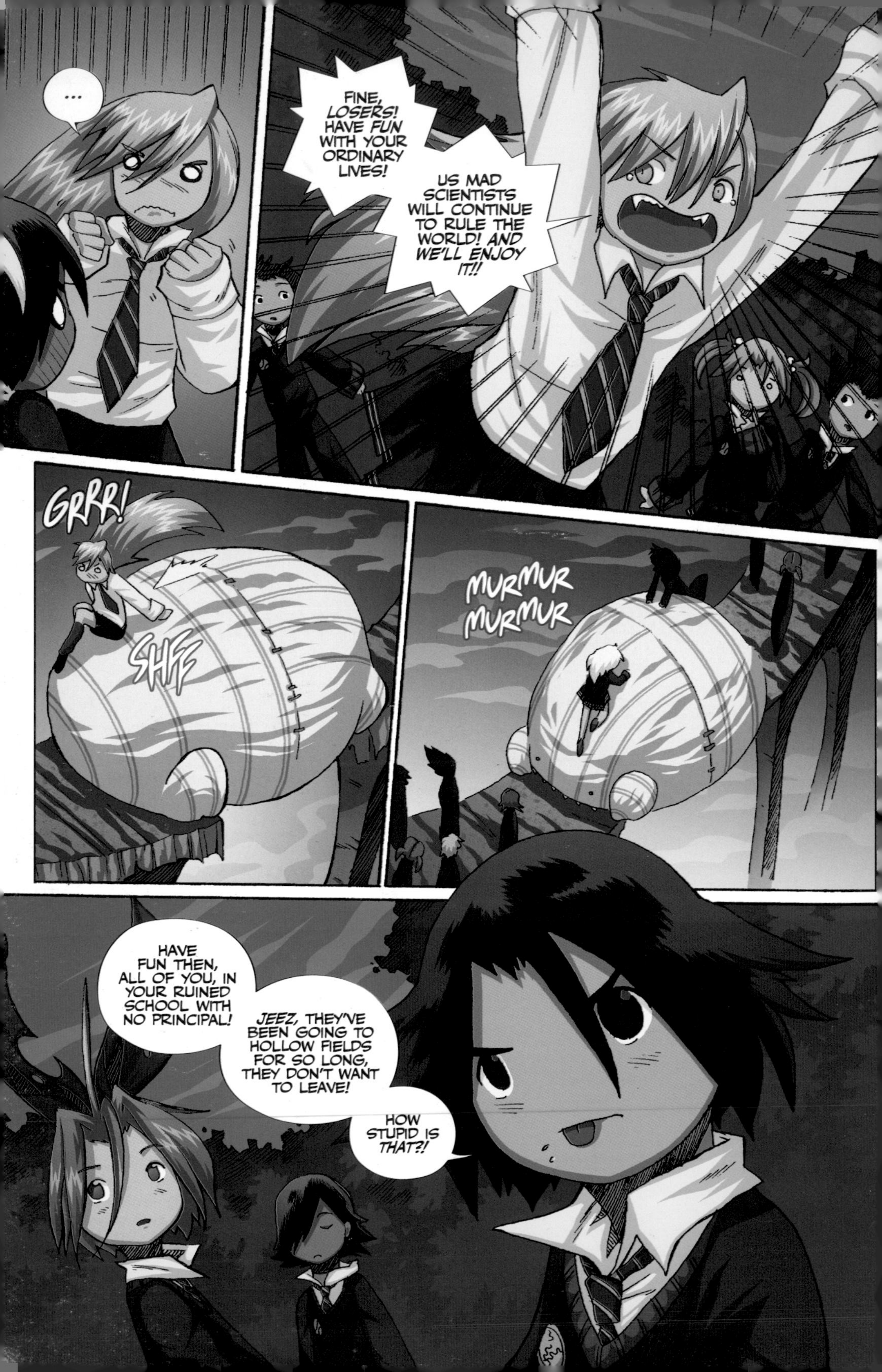
...
FINE, LOSERS! HAVE FUN WITH YOUR ORDINARY LIVES!
US MAD SCIENTISTS WILL CONTINUE TO RULE THE WORLD! AND WE'LL ENJOY IT!!
GRRR!
SHFF
MURMUR MURMUR
HAVE FUN THEN, ALL OF YOU, IN YOUR RUINED SCHOOL WITH NO PRINCIPAL!
JEEZ, THEY'VE BEEN GOING TO HOLLOW FIELDS FOR SO LONG, THEY DON'T WANT TO LEAVE!
HOW STUPID IS THAT?!

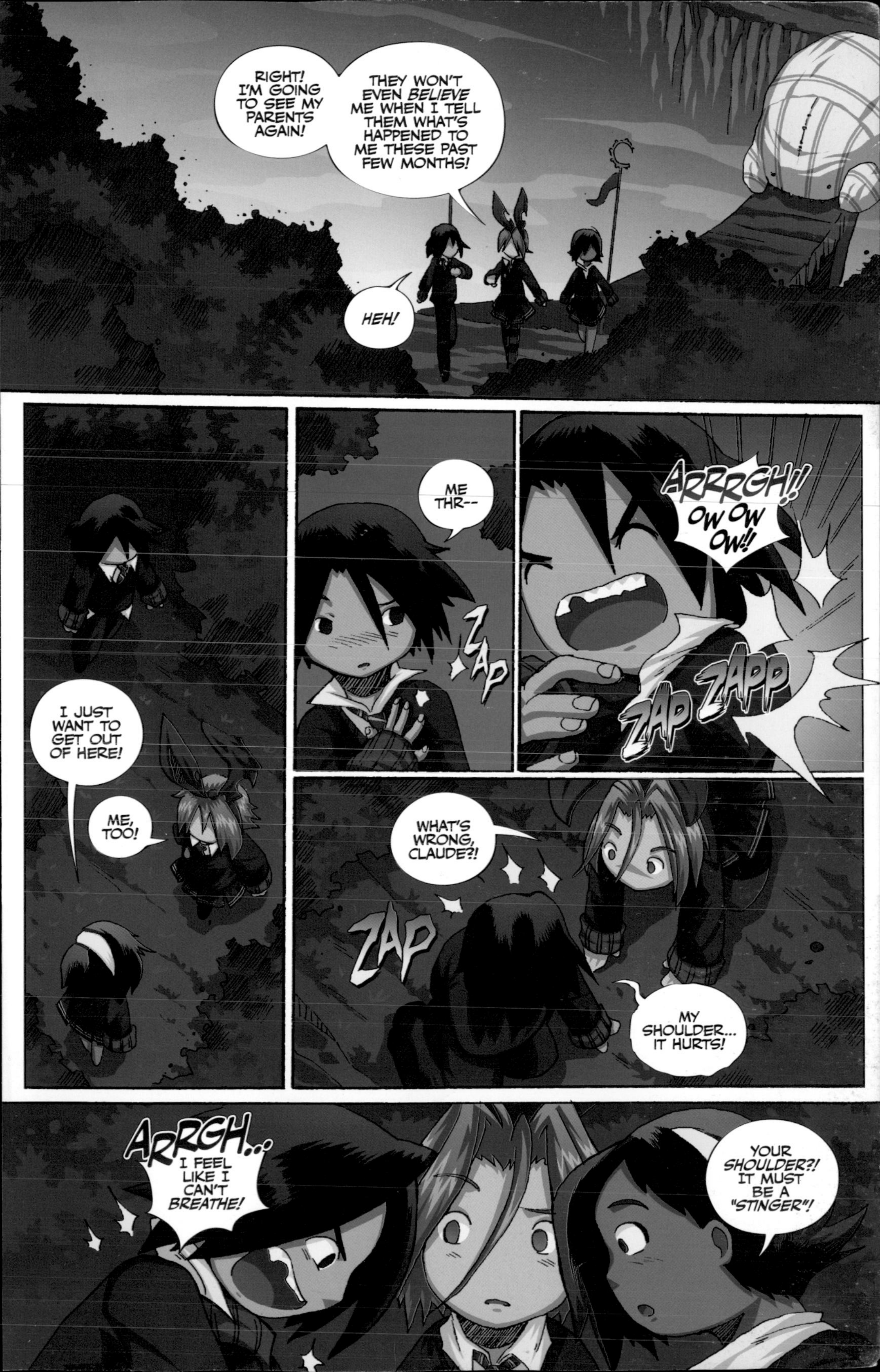

RIGHT! I'M GOING TO SEE MY PARENTS AGAIN!
THEY WON'T EVEN *BELIEVE* ME WHEN I TELL THEM WHAT'S HAPPENED TO ME THESE PAST FEW MONTHS!
HEH!
I JUST WANT TO GET OUT OF HERE!
ME, TOO!
ME THR--
ZAP
ARRRGH!! OW OW OW!!
ZAP ZAPP
WHAT'S WRONG, CLAUDE?!
ZAP
MY SHOULDER... IT HURTS!
ARRGH...
I FEEL LIKE I CAN'T BREATHE!
YOUR SHOULDER?! IT MUST BE A "STINGER"!

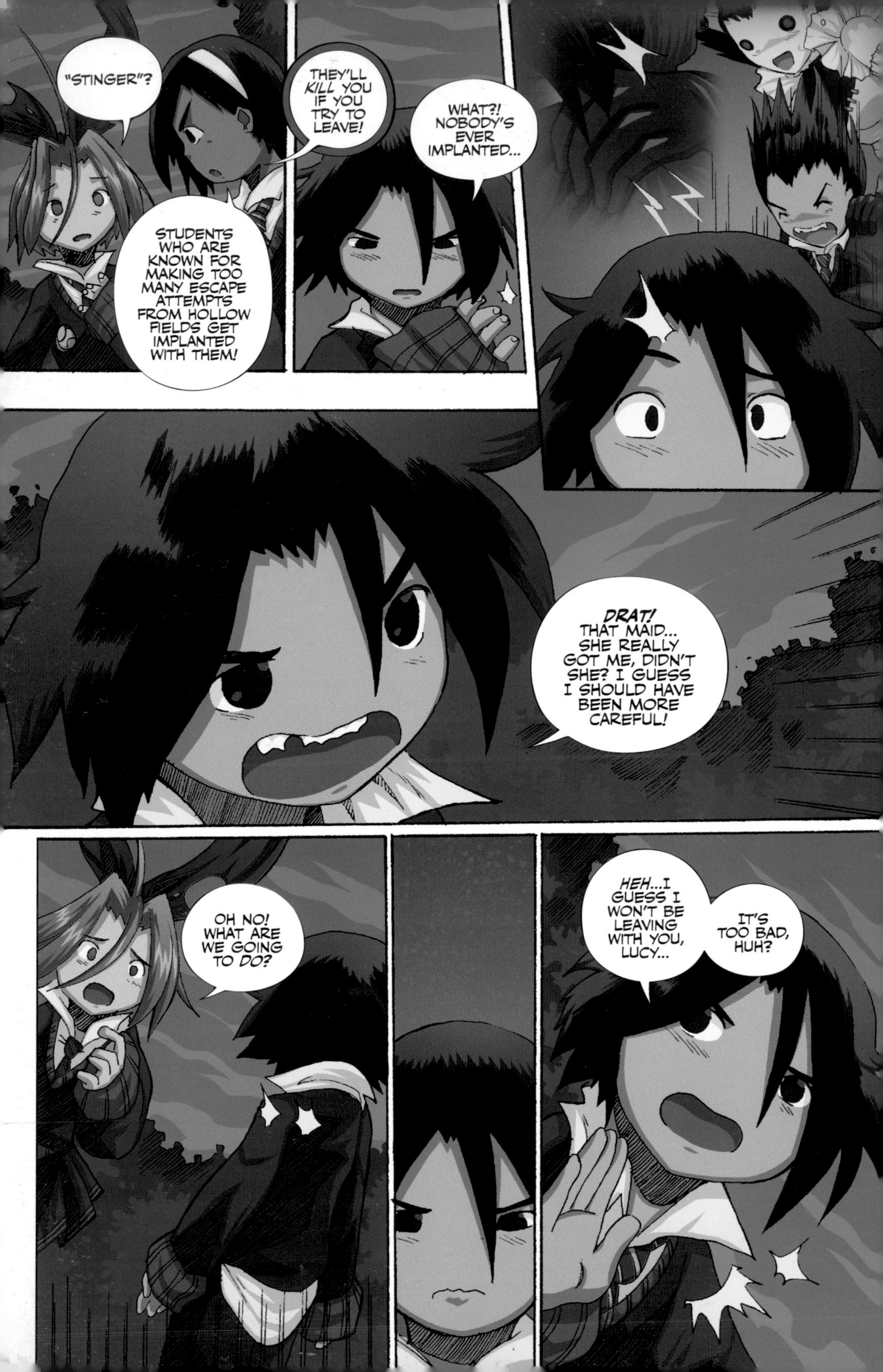
"STINGER"?
STUDENTS WHO ARE KNOWN FOR MAKING TOO MANY ESCAPE ATTEMPTS FROM HOLLOW FIELDS GET IMPLANTED WITH THEM!
THEY'LL *KILL* YOU IF YOU TRY TO LEAVE!
WHAT?! NOBODY'S EVER IMPLANTED...
DRAT! THAT MAID... SHE REALLY GOT ME, DIDN'T SHE? I GUESS I SHOULD HAVE BEEN MORE CAREFUL!
OH NO! WHAT ARE WE GOING TO *DO*?
HEH...I GUESS I WON'T BE LEAVING WITH YOU, LUCY...
IT'S TOO BAD, HUH?

BUT, CLAUDE...

GO ON, GET MOVING! YOUR PARENTS ARE WAITING FOR YOU, RIGHT?

GET LOST! STOP MAKING THIS HARD!

W-WELL... GOODBYE, THEN...

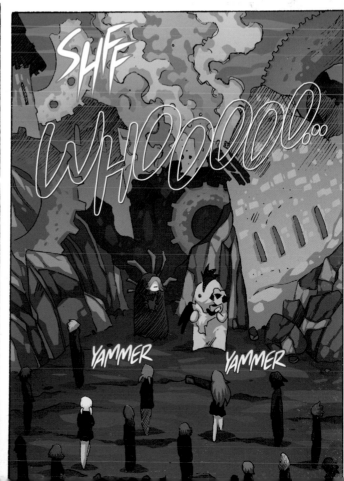

SHF

WHOOOOOO...

YAMMER

YAMMER

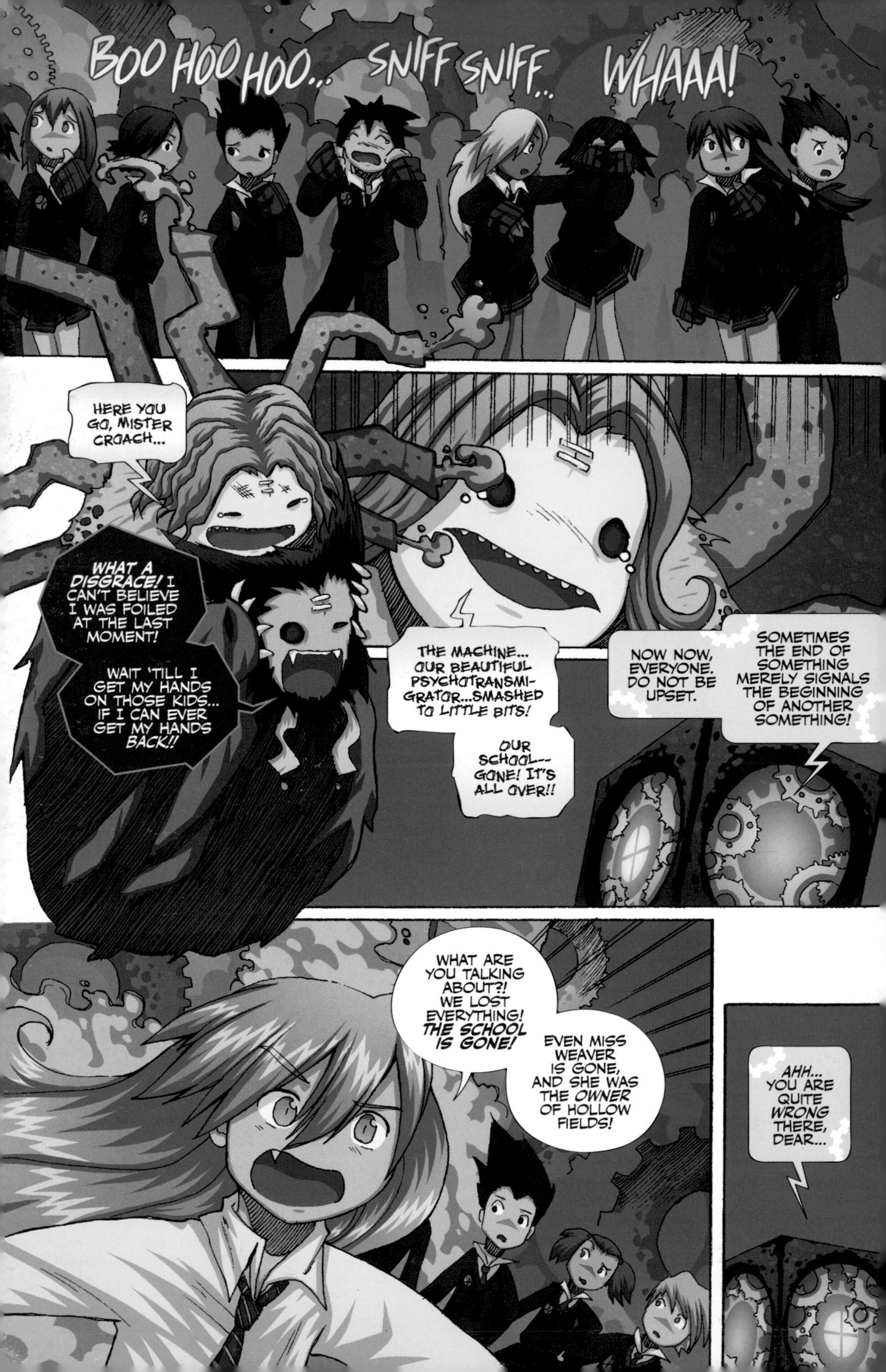
BOO HOO HOO... SNIFF SNIFF... WHAAA!
HERE YOU GO, MISTER CROACH...
WHAT A DISGRACE! I CAN'T BELIEVE I WAS FOILED AT THE LAST MOMENT!
WAIT 'TILL I GET MY HANDS ON THOSE KIDS... IF I CAN EVER GET MY HANDS BACK!!
THE MACHINE... OUR BEAUTIFUL PSYCHOTRANSMI-GRATOR...SMASHED TO LITTLE BITS!
OUR SCHOOL-- GONE! IT'S ALL OVER!!
NOW NOW, EVERYONE. DO NOT BE UPSET.
SOMETIMES THE END OF SOMETHING MERELY SIGNALS THE BEGINNING OF ANOTHER SOMETHING!
WHAT ARE YOU TALKING ABOUT?! WE LOST EVERYTHING! THE SCHOOL IS GONE!
EVEN MISS WEAVER IS GONE, AND SHE WAS THE OWNER OF HOLLOW FIELDS!
AHH... YOU ARE QUITE WRONG THERE, DEAR...

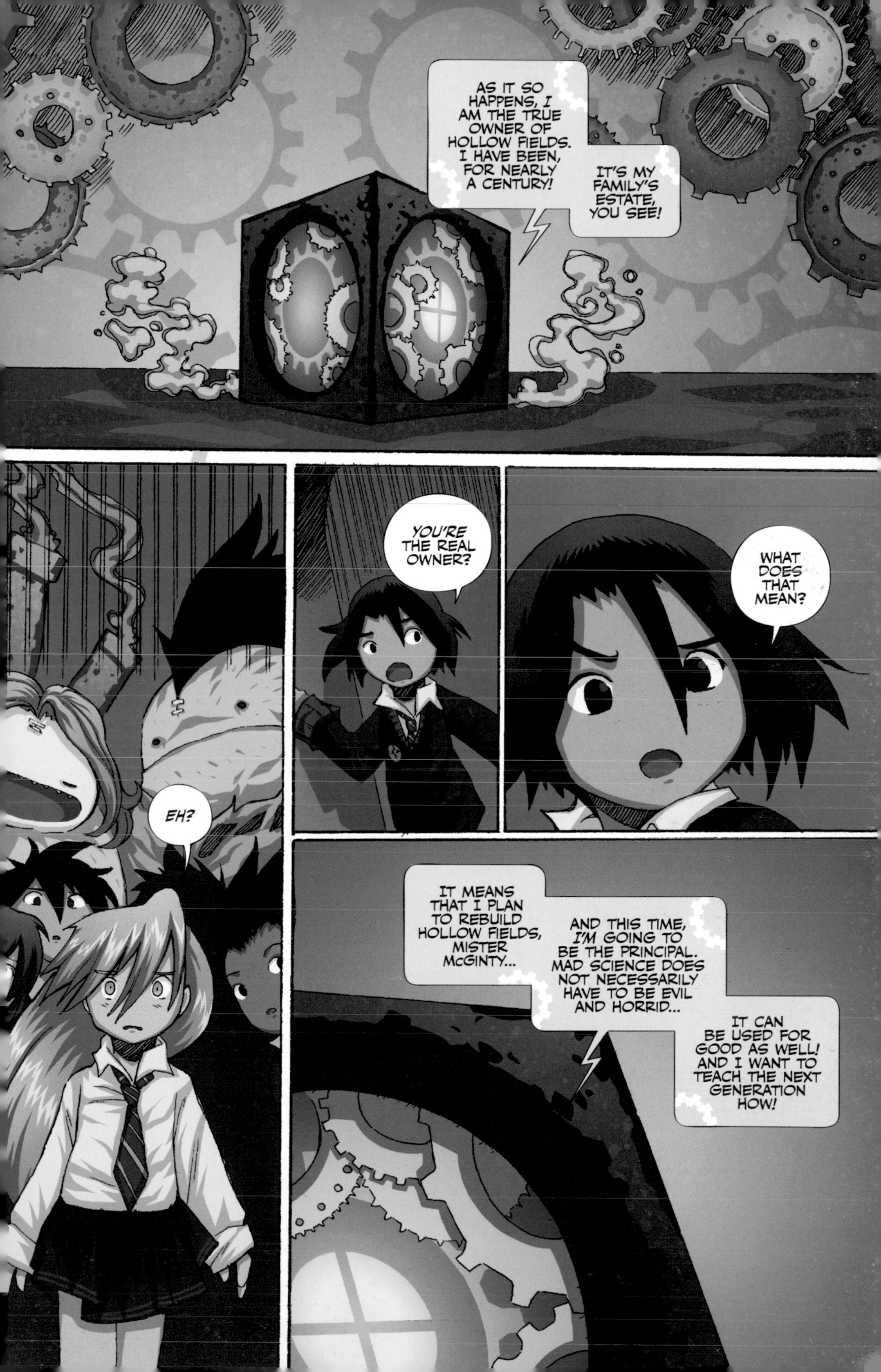
AS IT SO HAPPENS, *I* AM THE TRUE OWNER OF HOLLOW FIELDS. I HAVE BEEN, FOR NEARLY A CENTURY!
IT'S MY FAMILY'S ESTATE, YOU SEE!
EH?
YOU'RE THE REAL OWNER?
WHAT DOES THAT MEAN?
IT MEANS THAT I PLAN TO REBUILD HOLLOW FIELDS, MISTER McGINTY...
AND THIS TIME, *I'M* GOING TO BE THE PRINCIPAL. MAD SCIENCE DOES NOT NECESSARILY HAVE TO BE EVIL AND HORRID...
IT CAN BE USED FOR GOOD AS WELL! AND I WANT TO TEACH THE NEXT GENERATION HOW!

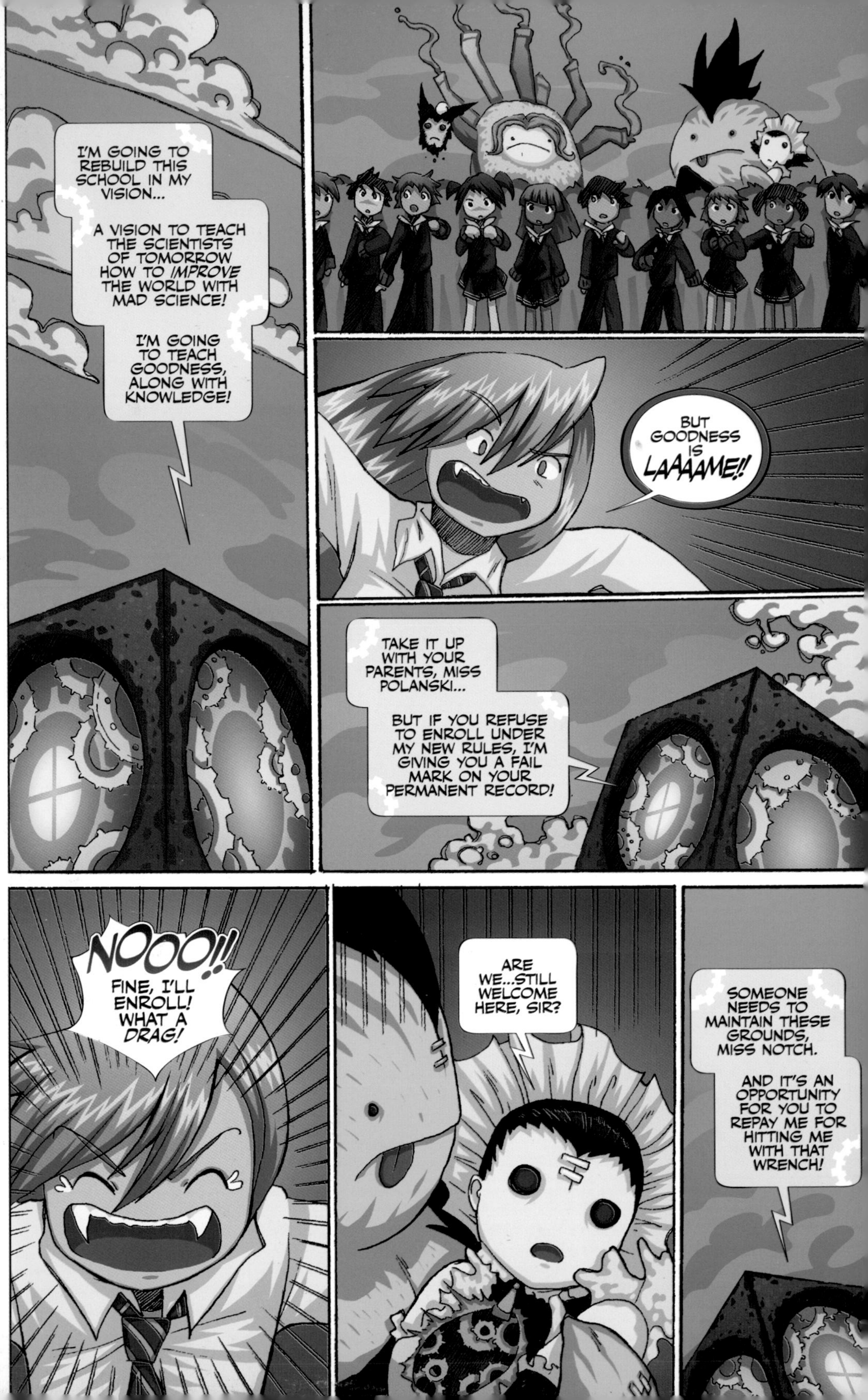
I'M GOING TO REBUILD THIS SCHOOL IN MY VISION...
A VISION TO TEACH THE SCIENTISTS OF TOMORROW HOW TO *IMPROVE* THE WORLD WITH MAD SCIENCE!
I'M GOING TO TEACH GOODNESS, ALONG WITH KNOWLEDGE!
BUT GOODNESS IS *LAAAAME!!*
TAKE IT UP WITH YOUR PARENTS, MISS POLANSKI...
BUT IF YOU REFUSE TO ENROLL UNDER MY NEW RULES, I'M GIVING YOU A FAIL MARK ON YOUR PERMANENT RECORD!
NOOO!!
FINE, I'LL ENROLL! WHAT A *DRAG!*
ARE WE...STILL WELCOME HERE, SIR?
SOMEONE NEEDS TO MAINTAIN THESE GROUNDS, MISS NOTCH.
AND IT'S AN OPPORTUNITY FOR YOU TO REPAY ME FOR HITTING ME WITH THAT WRENCH!

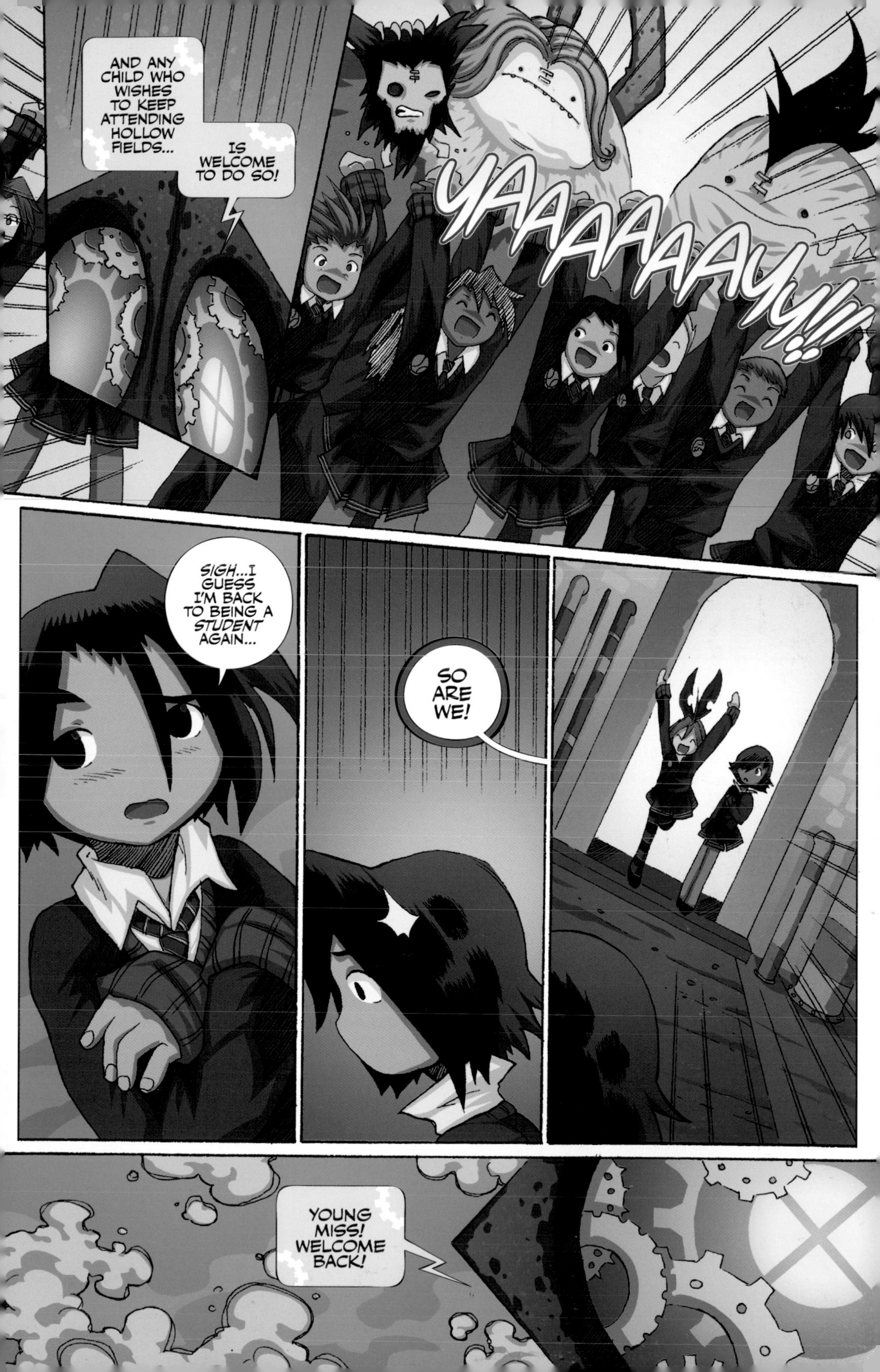
AND ANY CHILD WHO WISHES TO KEEP ATTENDING HOLLOW FIELDS...
IS WELCOME TO DO SO!
YAAAAAAAY!!!
SIGH...I GUESS I'M BACK TO BEING A *STUDENT* AGAIN...
SO ARE WE!
YOUNG MISS! WELCOME BACK!

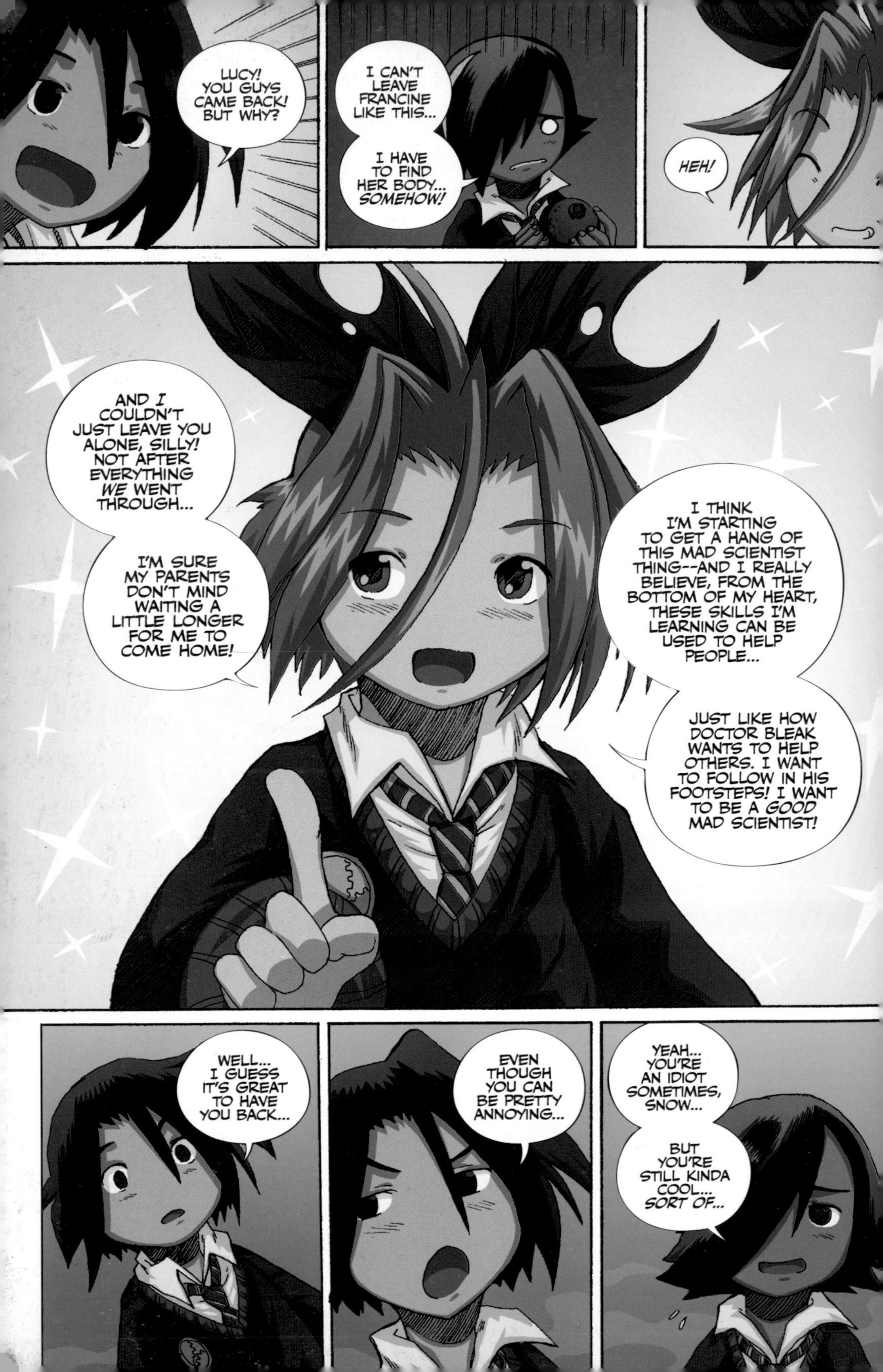
LUCY! YOU GUYS CAME BACK! BUT WHY?
I CAN'T LEAVE FRANCINE LIKE THIS...
I HAVE TO FIND HER BODY... *SOMEHOW!*
HEH!
AND *I* COULDN'T JUST LEAVE YOU ALONE, SILLY! NOT AFTER EVERYTHING *WE* WENT THROUGH...
I'M SURE MY PARENTS DON'T MIND WAITING A LITTLE LONGER FOR ME TO COME HOME!
I THINK I'M STARTING TO GET A HANG OF THIS MAD SCIENTIST THING--AND I REALLY BELIEVE, FROM THE BOTTOM OF MY HEART, THESE SKILLS I'M LEARNING CAN BE USED TO HELP PEOPLE...
JUST LIKE HOW DOCTOR BLEAK WANTS TO HELP OTHERS. I WANT TO FOLLOW IN HIS FOOTSTEPS! I WANT TO BE A *GOOD* MAD SCIENTIST!
WELL... I GUESS IT'S GREAT TO HAVE YOU BACK...
EVEN THOUGH YOU CAN BE PRETTY ANNOYING...
YEAH... YOU'RE AN IDIOT SOMETIMES, SNOW...
BUT YOU'RE STILL KINDA COOL... *SORT OF...*

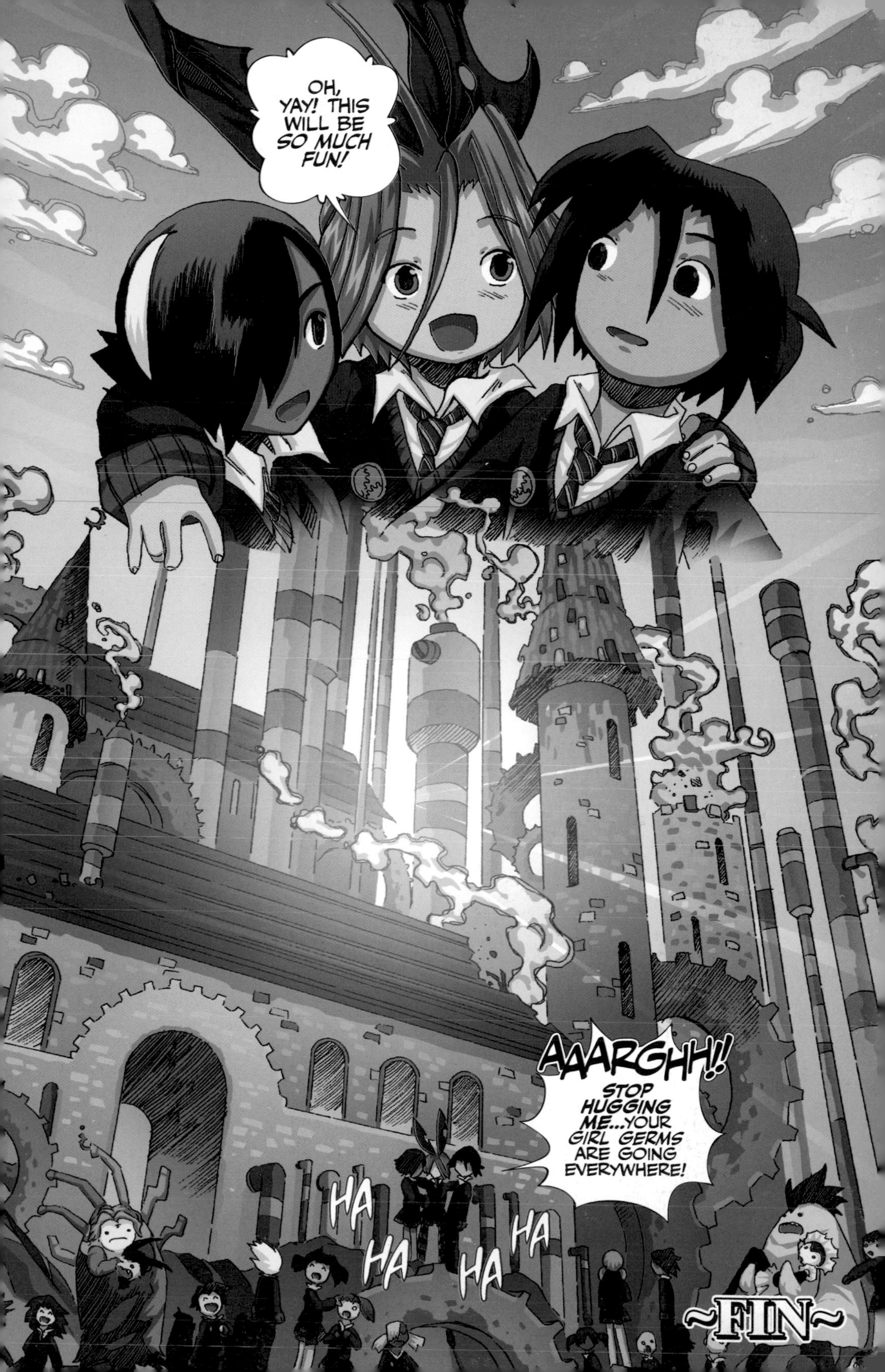
OH, YAY! THIS WILL BE SO MUCH FUN!
AAARGHH!!
STOP HUGGING ME...YOUR GIRL GERMS ARE GOING EVERYWHERE!
HA
HA
HA
HA
~FIN~

Hollow Fields BONUS COMICS

Graveyard Grumblings

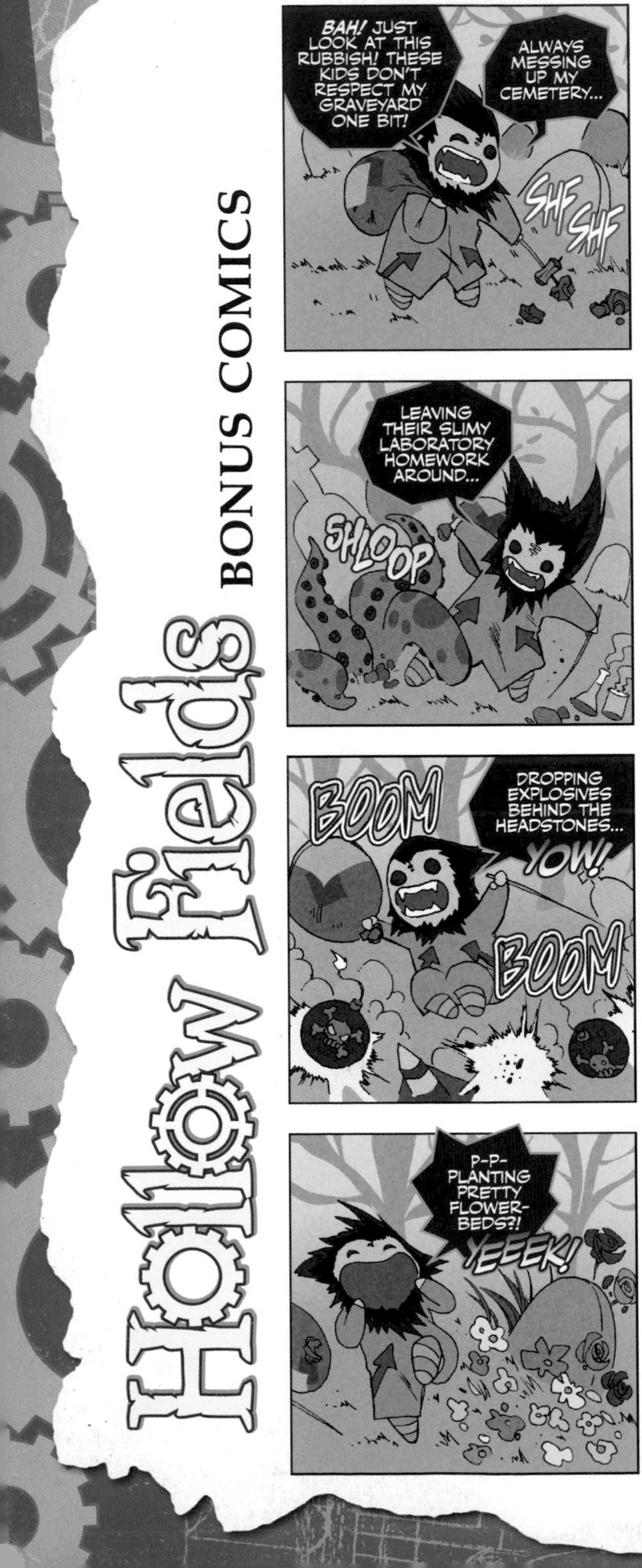
BAH! JUST LOOK AT THIS RUBBISH! THESE KIDS DON'T RESPECT MY GRAVEYARD ONE BIT!
ALWAYS MESSING UP MY CEMETERY...
SHF SHF
LEAVING THEIR SLIMY LABORATORY HOMEWORK AROUND...
SHLOOP
BOOM
DROPPING EXPLOSIVES BEHIND THE HEADSTONES...
YOW!
BOOM
P-P-PLANTING PRETTY FLOWER-BEDS?!
YEEEK!

Gone to Pieces

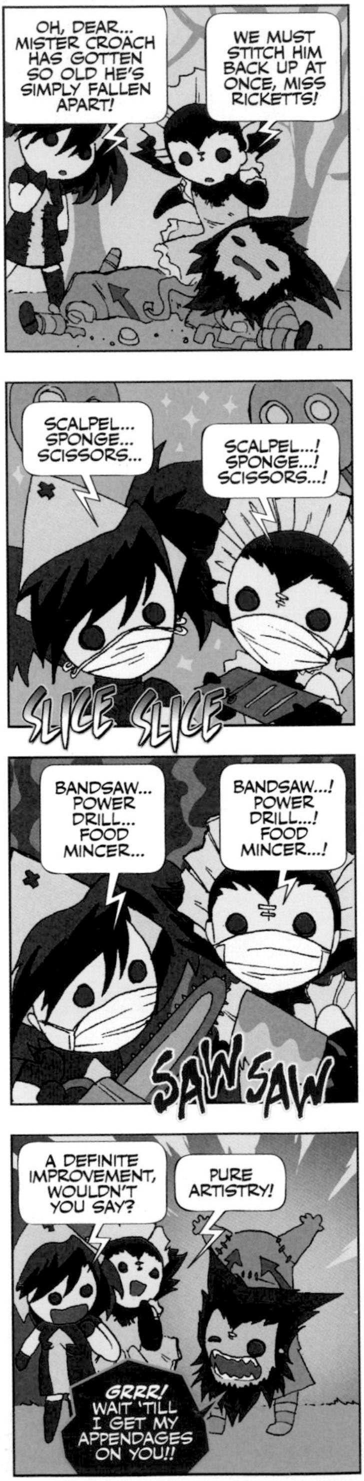
OH, DEAR... MISTER CROACH HAS GOTTEN SO OLD HE'S SIMPLY FALLEN APART!
WE MUST STITCH HIM BACK UP AT ONCE, MISS RICKETTS!
SCALPEL... SPONGE... SCISSORS...
SCALPEL...! SPONGE...! SCISSORS...!
SLICE SLICE
BANDSAW... POWER DRILL... FOOD MINCER...
BANDSAW...! POWER DRILL...! FOOD MINCER...!
SAW SAW
A DEFINITE IMPROVEMENT, WOULDN'T YOU SAY?
PURE ARTISTRY!
GRRR! WAIT 'TILL I GET MY APPENDAGES ON YOU!!

All Together

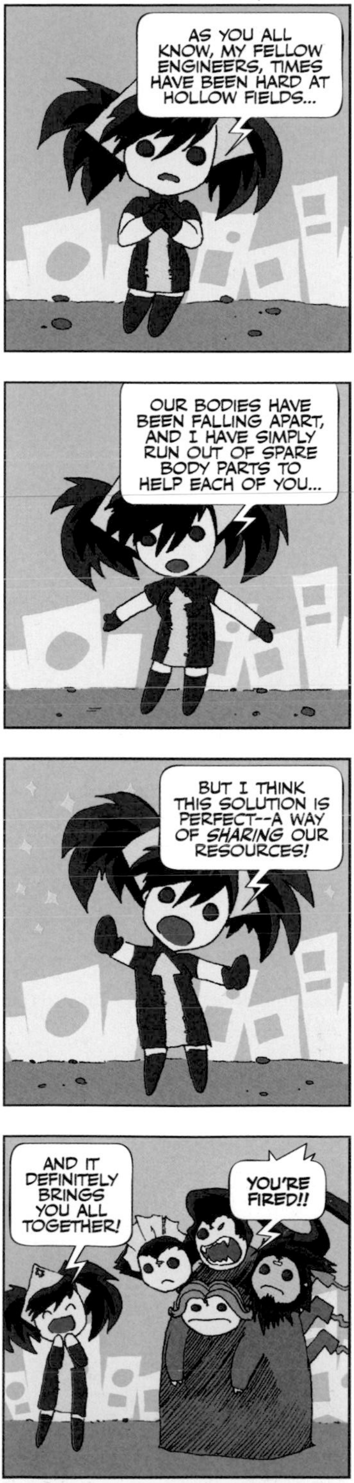
AS YOU ALL KNOW, MY FELLOW ENGINEERS, TIMES HAVE BEEN HARD AT HOLLOW FIELDS...
OUR BODIES HAVE BEEN FALLING APART, AND I HAVE SIMPLY RUN OUT OF SPARE BODY PARTS TO HELP EACH OF YOU...
BUT I THINK THIS SOLUTION IS PERFECT--A WAY OF *SHARING* OUR RESOURCES!
AND IT DEFINITELY BRINGS YOU ALL TOGETHER!
YOU'RE FIRED!!

We Can Rebuild Him

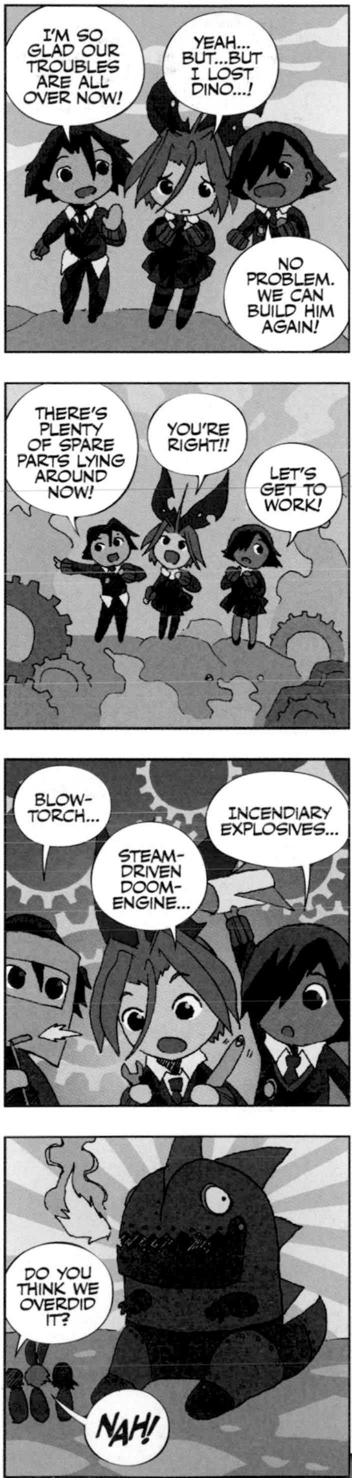
I'M SO GLAD OUR TROUBLES ARE ALL OVER NOW!
YEAH... BUT...BUT I LOST DINO...!
NO PROBLEM. WE CAN BUILD HIM AGAIN!
THERE'S PLENTY OF SPARE PARTS LYING AROUND NOW!
YOU'RE RIGHT!!
LET'S GET TO WORK!
BLOW-TORCH...
STEAM-DRIVEN DOOM-ENGINE...
INCENDIARY EXPLOSIVES...
DO YOU THINK WE OVERDID IT?
NAH!

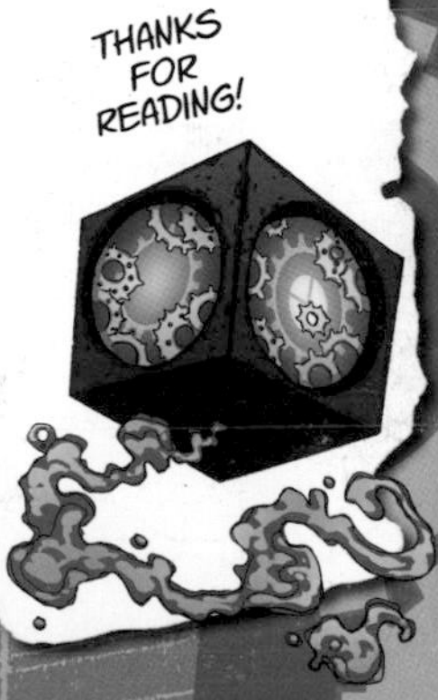
THANKS FOR READING!

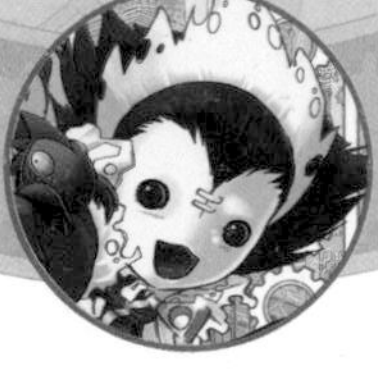

MADELEINE ROSCA

Born and raised in Gippsland, Australia, Madeleine Rosca earned her Bachelor of Fine Arts from Monash University before traveling to Melbourne to study multimedia and animation. After being employed as a graphic designer for a number of years, she moved to Tasmania to concentrate on her own creative work. Disappointingly, she has not yet seen a Tasmanian devil in the wild. Madeleine's creative influences include Lemony Snicket, Eoin Colfer, Shaun Tan, Daisuke Moriyama, and Graeme Base. *Hollow Fields* was her first published work and went on to make her a runner-up for Japan's first ever "International Manga Award." Currently, she works as a freelance illustrator for print media, games, and television, while self-publishing her webcomic series, *Rise From Ashes.* She can be found online at: **clockworkhands.com**

HONOEL A. IBARDOLAZA

Honoel A. Ibardolaza is an award-winning children's book author and illustrator. He is also a manga and comic book artist whose published works include *Blade for Barter* and *Laddertop.* Recently, he's published the bestselling coloring book *Mystical Cats in Secret Places: A Cat Lover's Coloring Book,* and is providing the vibrant colors in the new full-color editions of *Hollow Fields.*